Misers, Shrews, and

Polygamists

Misers, Shrews, and

Polygamists

SEXUALITY AND MALE-FEMALE

RELATIONS IN EIGHTEENTH-CENTURY

CHINESE FICTION

KEITH MCMAHON

DUKE UNIVERSITY PRESS

Durham & London

1995

© 1995 Duke University Press   All rights reserved   Printed in the United States of America on acid-free paper ∞   Designed by Cherie Holma Westmoreland   Typeset in Dante by Keystone Typesetting, Inc.   Library of Congress Cataloging-in-Publication Data appear on the last printed page of this book.

CONTENTS

CONTENTS

CONTENTS

PREFACE

The majority of people investigating gender and sexuality over the past dozen or so years have worked in American and European cultures and have rarely been able to find in-depth studies about these topics in non-European fields. This book is one of several recent attempts to alleviate that problem.

More translation and exposition of sources will be necessary in this study than in those on Western culture. Too many of the texts I rely on are utterly unknown to contemporary readers and scholars; most have never been and probably never will be translated. The linguistic and bibliographic demands of these works have required extensive explication, cross-referencing, and comparison of editions. Readers in fields in which such aspects are no longer at issue must understand the need for this approach, although they may skim over parts they deem too specialized, including some lengthy translations which I nevertheless feel will have little or no other chance to be seen in print.

As involved as I have become in the effort of gaining access to rare texts, however, I am still primarily interested in using them to map a broad range of sexual and gender-related behavior. My main goal will be to treat novels as if they were debating the issue of polygamy, a prominent material manifestation of male sexual privilege, even though polygamy was of course taken for granted in eighteenth-century China and by and large not openly questioned. In other words, although authors were in no way united in seeing polygamy as a problem, their works are full of signs that such male sexual privilege was ambiguous and problematic.

Numerous sources besides vernacular fiction provide information on polygamy and sexuality in general in China: e.g., the classical tale, biography and autobiography, court cases, collections of miscellaneous jottings, medical literature, genealogies, prescriptive texts on such things as feminine virtue, the art of sex, and household management. I limit myself to vernacular fiction because of what I have mentioned above: the rareness of and difficulty of gaining access to Chinese erotic novels, which make up over half of what this book covers. In fact, peculiar conditions surround research on erotic novels. Although the study of erotica is still highly restricted in China, over the last ten years I as a foreigner have been able to read and research books that relatively few mainland Chinese can ever see or discuss as openly. Some of these works exist only in China; most are in Beijing or are otherwise located in libraries here and there in Asia, Europe, and the United States. Without the sponsorship of the Committee on Scholarly Communications with the People's Republic of China (now called the Committee on Scholarly Communications with China, a unit of the National Academy of Sciences), I would never have gained the cooperation of educational authorities and the librarians of rare book rooms in China, which severely restrict access to many of the works discussed in this book. Nor could I have met with Chinese scholars and friends who have helped interpret many points of language and material life in both the rare and nonrare works. I have also spent many hours in the United States reading microfiche and microfilm copies of numerous other rare and obscure works not yet republished. Fortunately, scholars in the past two decades have produced numerous reference works providing plot summaries and other information about rare novels; the *Zhongguo tongsu xiaoshuo zongmu tiyao* (1990) and Ōtsuka Hidetaka's *Zōho Chūgoku tsūzoku shosetsu shomoku* (1987) are two of the most useful of these works. Because of the time and special effort it has taken to do such research, I am greatly interested in establishing a foundation of knowledge about these novels and their composite whole as erotic literature. Such knowledge should provide a point of reference for future studies in numerous fields.

I have written this book over many years and am indebted to numerous people for helping me in various aspects of my work. Chen Yupi, Li Ling, Pan Suiming, Shen Tianyou, Sun Xun, Yu Songqing, and Francois Wildt have provided the greatest assistance and inspiration. Others have read and/or critiqued parts of this work and will be noted at the appropriate places. Three anonymous readers criticized weaknesses, corrected errors, and gave supplemental information. The administrators of the affairs of foreign scholars (*waiban*) at Beijing University have for three lengthy periods provided me with a comfortable and economical setting for my studies. Other foreign students and scholars from Africa, Europe, and North America made those times the best of my life. Fellowships from the Committee on Scholarly Communication with the People's Republic of China and the liberality of the University of Kansas in granting me nonfinanced leaves have been of vital importance as well. The Chinese University Press, *Late Imperial China* (published by The Johns Hopkins University Press), and The University of Chicago Press have kindly permitted me to include previously published material in chapters 3, 5, and 7, respectively.

I am deeply sorry that Helen McMahon, my mother, passed away before she could see my work finished.

Notes on Romanization

This book uses the pinyin system of romanization. Titles of books will be kept in pinyin and only translated the first time they appear and whenever they are the subject of lengthy discussion (for example, a whole chapter or section of a chapter).

For readers unfamiliar with the pinyin system, its three most troublesome consonants are as follows:

C is pronounced *ts* as in "its," but functions as an initial (as in *cai*, rhyming with "eye").

Q is pronounced *ch* (*qing* sounds like *ching*, rhyming with "sing").

X is pronounced *sy*, a palatalized version of *sh* (*xi* sounds like *syee* or *shee*).

In addition, the reader may want to remember these other troublesome sounds:

Z is like the *ds* in "heads."

Zh is like the *j* in "Jim."

Zhi, chi, and *shi* sound like *jer, cher,* and *sher,* all rhyming with "her."

The *i* in *zi, ci,* and *si* is something like a shwa sound with the lips more closed.

1

POTENT POLYGAMISTS AND

CHASTE MONOGAMISTS

Sexuality and Male-Female Subjectivity in Qing Fiction

Having multiple wives was one of the main badges of male privilege in Ming and Qing China (1368–1644 and 1644–1911). This book is about how such male sexual privilege plays itself out in vernacular novels from about the mid-seventeenth to the mid-nineteenth centuries. I will read fiction for its representations of sexuality and male-female subjectivity, at the same time investigating the gender roles of the patriarchal polygamous family. I will use the terms miser and shrew as metaphors to caricaturize male and female extremes implied in the construction of these roles and often illustrated in these works. The two poles define a sexual economy in which man and woman occupy mutually alien positions from which each can theoretically take vital essence from or lose it to the other. In order to protect himself from such loss, the polygamous man must distance himself from any one woman and instead master and have healthy intercourse with many women. Miser is the caricature of this retentive self-containment at its extreme. *Pofu,* "shrew," is the caricature of the overflowing, male-enervating woman. She metaphorically "scatters" (*po*) her polluting fluids on the man, who is fragile unless he builds his defenses and masters her. With the miser and shrew in the periphery, the potent polygamist and his alter ego the wastrel are the central characters of these novels, positive and negative versions of the filial progenitor upon whom everyone's future is supposed to depend.

From the study of these and other characters, the main issues that will emerge are these: How does the man with many wives manage and

justify his sexual authority? What factors condition the wastrel's ruination? Why and how does the socially privileged man often escape or limit
his presumed authority, sometimes to the point of portraying himself as
abject before the shrewish woman? How do women accommodate or
coddle the man, or else oppose, undermine, and sometimes remold him?
Finally, with what logic and what limits does the man place himself lower
than spiritually and morally superior women—as in the case of the feminized scholar-poet—and to what extent does he thereby repair his own or
other men's bad image?

The reasons for my focus on polygamy have to do with the realities of
both Qing society and the contents of Qing fiction, and with the fact that
scholars have tended to discuss this topic only briefly or in passing. Few
so far have examined its constructedness according to the aspects of
sexuality, gender, and subjectivity.[1] Perhaps they have considered it as a
mere aspect of patriarchy and the rule of the male elite and therefore too
narrow a topic of study. In terms of the social-symbolic order, however,
polygamy was a model of success, a kind of perfected form of marriage
aspired to by lower-class men and even women (who would rise by
becoming concubines or chambermaids in wealthy households, for instance). The access to multiple sexual partners, whether marital or not,
was legalized, glorified, and widely enjoyed by Ming and Qing men, a
great number of whom were the most powerful and competitive members of their local and national elites. To be sure, polygamy was not the
model or ideal for every man and woman; and in fact monogamy was the
usual form of marriage, while polygamy was a matter of privilege and
means. Furthermore, many variations of marriage existed, including the
uxorilocal (called *ru zhui*), in which a man married into a woman's family,
and which plays a significant role both within and in place of polygamy in
many Qing novels discussed here. Nevertheless, to study sexuality and
gender in premodern China is also to study polygamy and its particular
assumption of the primacy of the male cycle of energy.

The fiction that most frequently illustrates the miser, shrew, polygamist, and other character types I discuss in this book often goes under the
rubric of *renqing xiaoshuo*, a term used by numerous scholars in modern
China meaning, literally, "fiction about human situations," with a strong
emphasis upon *qing*, "feelings, sentiment."[2] This loosely termed group of
works includes stories about love affairs, sexual encounters, marriage,
family life, and upbringing (not included are works primarily about such

things as dynastic history, battles against real and demonic enemies, or court cases, which nevertheless contain material relevant to the study of sexuality and which often make their way into works otherwise focused on *renqing*). The issue of desire and how to regulate it runs through all these situations. These domestic topics and the accompanying array of male and female character types are most fully charted in a number of lengthy novels of the Ming and Qing, including *Honglou meng* (Dream of the Red Chamber, also known as Story of the Stone) and several lesser-known literati novels, as well as numerous shorter works both erotic and nonerotic.

The organizing principle of my discussion is in fact to treat works according to whether or not they contain sexual detail and according to relative length and complexity of portrayal. The shorter works (twenty chapters or so) provide idealistic and rather formulaic portraits of monogamy and polygamy. These are the scholar-beauty romances (*caizi jiaren xiaoshuo*) of chapters 5 and 6 and *Shenlou zhi* (The Mirage of Love) of chapter 12. The lengthy novels (of one hundred or so chapters) contain highly detailed and problematizing representations of gender and sexuality. These are the works examined in chapters 7 to 11 and 13—that is, *Yesou puyan* (A Country Codger's Words of Exposure), *Honglou meng*, *Lin Lan Xiang* (The Six Wives of the Wastrel Geng), *Qilu deng* (Lantern at the Fork in the Road), *Lüye xianzong* (Trails of Immortals in the Green Wilds), and *Ernü yingxiong zhuan* (Tales of Boy and Girl Heroes). The shrew and the miser appear in many of these works but are often the subjects of individual novels and stories—especially in the case of the shrew—and as such form their own subgenres. They will be treated in chapters 3 and 4.

The period during which most of this fiction was written is between the early Qing around the 1650s and the end of the mid-Qing in the early 1800s. Exact dates are often hard to establish: some works may very well have been written as early as the late Ming, others as late as the 1860s. *Ernü yingxiong zhuan* is from the third quarter of the nineteenth century, but I include it because of the example it offers as a novel in critical revision of *Honglou meng*, which—along with other lengthy works like *Rulin waishi* (Scholars), *Yesou puyan*, *Lin Lan Xiang*, *Qilu deng*, and *Lüye xianzong*—is from the core years of this period, the mid-eighteenth century and the middle of the Qianlong emperor's reign, from 1736 to 1796. In their survey of Chinese society in this period, Susan Naquin and

Evelyn Rawski define the "eighteenth century" that they cover as extending from about 1680 to 1820, roughly corresponding to the time covered here.[3] This segmentation of time has to do with the stability and prosperity that obtained then, and the fact that China had not yet begun to suffer the massive invasion of Western power and influence. These works of fiction are the last to give a rendition of Chinese social life in an as yet relatively undisturbed state, though of course influence did not occur overnight after the Opium Wars in the 1830s and 1840s, nor was contact and economic or social influence absent before decline began. Prosperity is evident in the growth of agricultural output and the amount of internal and external trade.[4] Decline is apparent from the tripling of population to reach approximately 300 million by 1800, and the overtaxing of China's economic capacity, which seems to have reached its limit given the technical levels of production and transportation. The late eighteenth century saw the beginning of widespread opium addiction, though this was not very evident in fiction of the time, which instead occasionally portrays the vogue of tobacco smoking.[5] If *Rulin waishi* and other works are any sign, then the eighteenth century saw a high degree of cynicism about success in the examination system (the government-supervised method of selecting candidates to serve in the local, provincial, and national administrations), which was accessible by legitimate means to an ever smaller percentage of men. Instead, the practice of buying lower degrees increased toward the end of the dynasty and made it easy for wealthy but otherwise ineligible men to gain the attendant prestige and serve in office, as numerous novels illustrate.

The method of this research will be to examine the constructedness of fictional character types such as miser, shrew, henpecked husband, doting mother, wastrel, and benevolent polygynist. That is, I will investigate them according to the ways they are informed by both the ideology of political and economic orders, and by the collective fantasy of the symbolic order.[6] In what follows, I will explain my application of the concepts of ideology and symbolic order, which I keep separate in order to delineate my greater focus on the symbolic. Although densely related and perhaps in the long run distinguishable only for heuristic reasons, ideological and symbolic orders name the political and economic field on the one hand, which is not necessarily or always commensurate with the personal and collective field of fantasy and sexual unconscious on the other.[7] This distinction is especially useful in illustrating the ways in which various texts or character types enact conformity or subversion within the patriarchal system without necessarily representing the interests of groups or classes in a politically and economically defined hierarchy.

Gender derives central meaning from the kinship structure. The laws of kinship define the symbolic order, which is primarily structured by the paternal family—its rules of descent, incest prohibitions, and the binaries of male and female, senior and junior, and inner and outer.[8] The symbolic function of this order is in effect to assign each subject a place and a role in the kin group even before he or she is born. A basic premise of my study is that the rules or laws of kinship—including gender definition and hierarchy—are such because of historical and social construction, not innate or natural necessity. With this in mind, I will be particularly interested in subjectivities that appear to escape the normative symbolic order defined by patriarchal polygamy.[9]

One of the most important aspects of gender that I will examine is the representation of male and female sexual capacities, especially as found in the ars erotica. Inherent in that portrayal is the assumption of the primacy of the male cycle of energy (what I will sometimes call the miserly-ascetic paradigm, defined in chapter 4). In the ars erotica, that cycle of fullness and depletion and the economization of *yang* essence centrally define and justify the polygynist's role and, by association, those of the other gendered subjects surrounding him. The order of the patriarchal-polygamous family; the representation of sexuality in sexual intercourse; and the playing out of hierarchical binaries such as man and woman, masculine and feminine, husband and wife, mother and son, and so forth (up to and including what might be called subsidiary binaries such as polygynist and concubine, main wife and concubine, mother-in-law and daughter-in-law, or son and father's sister's daughter)—I will survey all these as they function in their particular symbolic order in the context of the economic mode of production of Qing China, which I will briefly define as follows.

For my purposes in this study, the miser and his practice of usury metaphorically define the economic mode of production in the society of Qing fiction. In other words, he and his miserly-ascetic paradigm encapsulate the imaginary version of real conditions as allegorized in these works. According to that allegory (which I discuss more fully below), the miser is in the business of collecting night soil from everyone and then selling the product to farmers. The night soil fertilizes crops, which when they fail lead farmers to go into debt to the miser, who exacts higher and higher rates of interest from the farmers and hoards more and more of their debt-paying rice. Soon famine occurs because the price of rice is too high. Some benevolent officials and members of the local elite may provide relief to some folk who are left and perhaps punish a few misers.

According to Confucian state values, the one who deals in money and trade is a grade lower than the one who plows the earth. Nevertheless, in spite of this traditional denigration of mercantilism, in fact the miser and the hedonist merchant have wealth and/or life-styles that far outstrip their supposed superiors, that is, the peasants and even the officials. Of course, the miser is an allegorical reduction of the mercantilist landlord or businessman, who is an acquisitive materialist and lover of luxury— not a filthy, self-denying, shit- and gold-collecting miser. But from the perspective of the lowest and poorest in the social hierarchy, who are supposed to be satisfied with little to feed their minds and bodies, the mercantilist's wealth is usury by another name.

In nonallegorical terms, the social and economic order in the works I discuss is roughly as follows: The emperor reigns in the guise of a benevolent polygamist-patriarch called the Son of Heaven. He rules with the help of an underpaid but powerful officialdom ostensibly steeped in the Confucian canon and holding highly coveted positions. Parallel to the civil bureaucracy, a hereditary military class also exists with its own set of examinations for selecting leaders who are nevertheless held to be subordinate to civil officials. The military is useful in guarding border regions and quelling internal unrest due, for example, to popular religious uprisings, famine rioting, or rebellious non-Han minorities. The major portion of the population consists of peasants and urban commoners, who produce and market agricultural and other goods and engage in numerous menial occupations. Many hereditary and semihereditary classes exist (the latter being ones from which the individual could choose to depart), e.g., artisans, slaves, servants, actors, doctors, etc. Buddhist and Taoist religious personnel are numerous, many but not all government-registered, and including hermits, mendicants, and esoteric practitioners (e.g., the suppliers of aphrodisiacs and secret erotic arts in Qing fiction), as well as relatively wealthy and heavily patronized abbots and abbesses. Finally, there are merchants of all levels, the richest of whom, however, are still insecure if they rely only on money for their well-being. In other words, in Qing China the rich merchant still felt it necessary to, for example, place his son on the road to officialdom, buy himself or his son an official position (as I have said above, an increasingly viable option in the mid- to late Qing), or use his money to curry favor with (underpaid) officials. Otherwise he was too vulnerable to official harassment and intervention in his mercantile activities. In short, the hierarchy of power (*ming,* name, politically recognized fame) over money (*li,* profit) was always clearly in place.

How are the aspects of ideology and symbolic order projected onto and embodied by individual and collective subjects? Fiction can be seen as part of a broad representational system consisting of the repertoire of images and stories through which a society identifies itself and its subjects, or through which it "figures consensus" (in Kaja Silverman's words).[10] It is through these images and stories that subjects are enlisted in ideological and symbolic orders in light of such things as kinship rules, political ideology, economic conditions, and class rank. In other words, fiction can also be seen—like dreams, psychic symptoms, and types of patterned behavior—as registering the workings of conscious and unconscious fantasies, or of what can also be called the "fantasmatic." In Jean LaPlanche's and J.-B. Pontalis's terms, the primary function of the fantasmatic is the "mise-en-scène of desire"—that is, the staging of scenarios in which subjects play parts, defending and justifying themselves and acting out wishes, in all this basing themselves on the collective repertoire of social and symbolic roles.[11]

The major fantasy in this book is that of the polygynist utopia of the erotic romances, the world in which a benevolent and potent polygynist (who is also usually a landlord, merchant, exam candidate, or official) enjoys the assemblage of wife (usually of the same or higher class) and concubines who are beautiful, sexy, and not jealous (usually but not always from lower social classes). This fantasy consists of the playing out not only of the polygynist's desires, however, which will prove to be not so transparently unified to begin with, but of many subjects' desires, counterdesires, delayed desires, displaced ones, and so forth. The characters of Qing novels are as if part of a grand theatrical scene in which men and women, wives and husbands, paternal and maternal cousins all have assigned roles, but also in which they can exceed or bend their roles, or be reassigned parts.[12] Under certain temporary conditions, for instance, women can turn into men; likewise, men can turn into women, always retaining, however, certain male-privileging effects—thus the many sto-

ries in which cross-dressing or some form of it occurs. Some male characters in particular come close to embodying twentieth-century definitions
of masochism, which especially lends itself to reversals and changes of
position in which normative subjectivity is thrown into abeyance or
assaulted. Although I will not attempt a theorization of the term masochism in the context of eighteenth-century China, the mention of it here
(with Freud, Gilles Deleuze, and Kaja Silverman, inter alia, in mind)
is important because of the possibility it names of subversive, non-
normative male subjectivities.[13] Alongside the complaisant and self-
gratified man who the polygynist is presumed to be, there are other not-
so-centered male subjects, as we will find, who express deficiency (e.g.,
the initiate in the ars erotica), paranoia (the miser), or inferiority to
women and desire for abdication (e.g., Jia Baoyu in *Honglou meng*). There
are also examples of super-compensating potency (e.g., Wen Suchen in
Yesou puyan). Women, on the other hand, are normatively defined as
inferior and deficient. But again, as we will find, certain female characters
defy or modify the normative order: thus, for example, the shrew, the
talented beauty of the chaste romance, or the warrior woman.

Of all characters, the most central in these novels is also one who
unconsciously places himself on the road to self-destruction, the young
wastrel. He is central because he is the one who can most effectively
threaten everyone else's present and future. Although he could supposedly repair himself by changing his ways, as numerous novels assert,
other works demonstrate that due to inherent weakness, the wastrel will
never change except if the superior woman sets things straight again. In
short, (1) he is inherently weak, and (2) his supposed inferior is really his
superior. The situation is one in which male weakness depends for its
correction on the female other whom the man normally expels from the
ruling brotherhood. "Brothers are like hands and feet. A wife is like a
piece of clothing" (*xiongdi ru shouzu, qizi ru yifu*), the motto goes. The
Qing novel, with the exception of *Honglou meng* (which is problematic in
other ways, as I will show), only goes so far as to say, "Wear the virtuous
wife rightly and you will succeed," or "Wear the right wife and you will
succeed." The superior and right wife must nevertheless always agree to
be taken off, put away, and exchanged, even if she has saved her husband.
Only when the man occupies a feminine position vis-à-vis other men
does he have to obey the same order of expendability. In his hands,
feminine sacrifice then becomes something beautiful and redemptive, as

witnessed, for example, in Qu Yuan's female impersonation in the face of rejection by his ruler (in the pre-Han poem *Li sao*, Encountering Sorrow).

The final question of this preliminary introduction concerns the availability of the study of polygamy to other scholars interested in sexuality and gender subjectivity. In Chinese, Turkic, Arab, and other cultures, polygamy offers an example of an overt form of what by juxtaposition has for the most part been practiced illegally, surreptitiously, or metaphorically in Eurocentric cultures. In contrast to such things as keeping mistresses, visiting prostitutes, and having greater freedom in divorce, polygamy represents a particularly unabashed version of the fantasy of male sexual and reproductive freedom. Two questions can then be asked. Although polygamy has now been outlawed and almost entirely shamed out of existence in China, what still remains in its aftermath? This is a question that I believe must be asked in all studies of gender and sexuality in twentieth-century China (just as similar questions must be asked about what of the slave past remains in contemporary race relations in the United States, or what of opium-trading colonialism remains in current Euro-American interactions with China). But framed spatially rather than temporally, the question becomes: What do we recognize of polygamy in repressed or displaced forms elsewhere? How does polygamy clarify aspects of male centrality (including masochism) in other cultural orders—especially, for example, in light of the distinctions among types of wives and concubines, or the ars erotica's construct of the male cycle of energy? These questions help define what I now structure as the surreptitious counterparts to polygamy, its resistant alter-versions in monogamous cultures. Polygynists and wastrels, in short, are everywhere.

Finally, in one sense this study shows the impossibility of polygamy, the fact that it is a male fantasy in which real women have no place—something that Qing novels more or less already articulate. However, it is also true, as I have said above, that polygamy is not as transparent in its male privileging as it first appears. It can also be viewed as a form of disavowal of or compensation for male impotence and inadequacy. Moreover, as an institution and not a fantasy, it is something in which real women do in fact participate for the sake of social maneuvering and advancement, including the domination of men and their resources. One hardly sees a slave holding the senior position on a plantation, for example, but one can see a matriarch holding such a position in a patriarchal-polygamist family, although of course her power rarely extends outside the family.

The Various Character Types and the Theme

of Female Superiority

The threesome of miser, shrew, and polygamist is a crystallization of the dozen or so character types featured in this book. The miser and the shrew are the two most rancorously alienated of all—the miser because he is afraid of being consumed by the woman, her wastrel offspring, and other competing men; the shrew because she hates the way men and their female allies treat her as expendable. To repeat, the essential gesture of the miser is retention, that of the shrew is scattering. As for the polygamist, he despises the miser and ignores the shrew. He is the sexual boss who sits at the top of society and takes as many women and men as he wants. (The polyandrous woman also appears in Qing fiction but is rarer by far and is never legitimized in the same way as the polygynist; she is always a libertine, never, for example, a benevolent matriarch.) In all, the dozen or so character types include misers and ascetics, that is, nonpolygamous, self-contained men who flee the sexual battle altogether; shrews and lascivious women, who do their utmost to defeat or seduce the polygamist; impotent, henpecked husbands, whom shrews force into abjection; lecherous polygamists and wastrels, who incite and outflank the shrew and make nonsense of the miser and other representatives of containment; doting mothers, whom pedant fathers detest for letting their sons turn into wastrels; self-sacrificing women, who are victims of the polygamist and shrew; potent and benevolent polygamists, who are like reformed wastrels; and, finally, talented male-impersonating beauties and handsome effeminate scholars, who are models of monogamous union.

A recurrent theme of these fictional arrangements of male and female behavior is the woman's superiority over the man. The shrew is a belligerent manifestation of such superiority. Resorting to cutting words and clever strategy, she succeeds in defying the man and exposing his innate impotence. The self-sacrificing woman and the talented beauty, on the other hand, are virtuous manifestations of female excellence, chaste paragons who put base men to shame. The talented beauty is the most successful and self-determined of superior women in that she wins the right of monogamy and her own choice of marriage partner. She is a supremely capable woman who proves her excellence through wit and literary skill.

The theme of talented women, moreover, implies the inferiority of men, and produces effeminate and vaguely desexualized male personae like Jia Baoyu of *Honglou meng* (mid-eighteenth century) or the monogamist scholars of the chaste romances (mid-seventeenth to eighteenth centuries). To be sure, these types repair the image of the intemperate polygamist made prominent ever since the wastrel Ximen Qing in *Jin Ping Mei* (Golden Lotus, also known as The Plum in the Golden Vase, late sixteenth century). However, although refined and unlustful, the feminized man like Jia Baoyu also represents a male unraveling. To him, the superior woman is a sign of the failure of his own sex; he himself has reached a dead end beyond which he sees no way out. As for the monogamist scholar, in these works he is still a tentative model not very fully portrayed. The fullest model of a successful man in Qing fiction is still that of the potent polygamist, who in terms of Ming-Qing literary history amounts to an idealistic reparation of the dissipated Ximen Qing.

Increasing numbers of scholars have written about sexuality and gender in the Ming and Qing, addressing both fiction[14] and nonfiction.[15] Susan Naquin's and Evelyn Rawski's *Chinese Society in the Eighteenth Century* (1987) provides the most succinct account of marriage, family life, and gender roles in eighteenth-century China, and is the most convenient background reading for the social and economic conditions of that period. Erotic fiction has still been under-studied, however, as has the phenomenon of polygamy in both its fantasmatic and real-institutional forms, as I have already mentioned. With the increasing availability of erotic works through photographic reproduction and republication, a large body of materials awaits students of the history of sexuality in China. Putting polygamy at the center of the present study is to acknowledge its structuring importance in the social and symbolic hierarchy of Ming and Qing China.

Likewise, the theme of the superiority of women has until recently received little scholarly attention. In this book, it will be considered as part of the same scenario as polygamy and the constructions of male privilege in general. As this and other recent studies show, the elevation of women is capable of multiple functions: for example, the critique of and compensation for bad male behavior, the feminization and purification (or atonement) of the alienated male self, the projection of greater self-determination for the female self, or the idealization of companionate, monogamous love. Male veneration of the woman also has the effect of entrapping her in the binary of either chastity or lasciviousness.

At the pole of chastity, man and woman are suspended in an infantile state of innocence and androgyny. A series of oppositions takes shape: for example, sexualized polygamy contrasts with desexualized and cross-gendered monogamy, potent polygamists with apologists for male baseness, sexy and unjealous concubines with chaste and self-determining beauties, and so forth.

The most expedient way to elaborate such contrasts is to describe the characteristic tendencies of polygamists and their fellow characters first in a generalizing and composite fashion without much regard to specific sources. The following summary relates in somewhat archetypal fashion the essential male and female mentalities of Qing fiction. Once these essentials are set forth, I will follow with a discussion of fiction's place among the various sources of Qing history, then a further account of the social assumptions necessary to understand sexual life in these works.

Misers, Shrews, and Polygamists

The polygamous man portrayed in Qing erotic romances would like to have as many women as he can for free, in effect gratuitously to have sex without end. Although the hero of these romances always settles for a finite number of wives, this final containment of his amounts to an aesthetic closure and an after-the-fact bow to the ideology of temperance.

If the woman attempts to be as nomadic as the man, she is called unchaste, to keep on being which she must become shrewish—that is, good at defying those who accuse and despise her. To a promiscuous husband who won't agree to her request for male lovers, she counters: "Do you mean that only the governor is allowed to make a fire; the commoners can't even light a lamp?"[16] Few shrews choose to be so daring, and most instead mainly demand that the man be monogamous. Virtuous women have other alternatives if, like the shrew, they wish to be more than maidens who sew in the inner chambers and await becoming either wives or concubines: they may dress as men and go out to win public honor in the form of examination success; they may become warrior women (xianü) and battle for righteous causes; or, more humbly, they may stay at home but study the classics, learn to write poetry, and produce their own literary collections, as many women did in the Qing.

Shrew is also the name for the demonic woman, the one who attempts to subdue the man by means of the power of her sexuality, which includes both the force of female pollution and the capacity to steal male *yang* essence. She represents the woman's ability to attract and control the man. A sorceress in *Yesou puyan,* for example, evokes her special powers (*shu*) by baring her breasts, rubbing them with her hands, manipulating her navel, and taking three steps forward and three backward. If after reciting a spell she still fails to subdue the man, she then resorts to her most lethal weapon, her genitals, which she directs at her enemy and uses to shoot him with her *"yin* gas" (*yinqi,* ch. 80, 9b–10a). In this fantasy, she literally "scatters" her polluting effluvia on the man.

The shrew rages at the rule of chastity. In the Ming and Qing, a woman can win honor for herself and her community if she maintains lifelong celibacy after her husband dies; but the least suspicion that she is unchaste turns her into a "lascivious woman" (*yinfu*). As she reflects to herself in the novel *Zui chunfeng* (Drunken with the Spring Winds), the angry woman finds satisfaction in neither chastity nor lasciviousness.[17]

If a woman is skillful enough, she controls men by taking actions or using words that make him lose face, by plotting against female rivals for her husband's attention, or by using more long-term means such as the manipulation of her children prior to their passing under the control of the patriarch.[18] She does not even have to be clever to perform such manipulation. Simply by doting on and coddling her son or grandson, she can turn him into a wastrel who ignores his father's rule and wastes his father's wealth.

Two emblematic situations—those of the wastrel and the prostitute—describe sons and daughters in Qing fiction and define the conditions for a disastrous relationship between man and woman. An emblematic situation embodies an essential or stereotyped relationship such as that of the shrew and the henpecked husband, the indulgent mother and the spoiled son, or character types such as the wastrel or the female paragon. The first of the two emblematic situations is the family consisting of the miserly or the pedantic father, the indulgent mother, and their consequently spoiled, wastrel son (as in *Qilu deng,* discussed in chapter 10 below).

The spoiled son meets and falls in love with the woman who emblemizes the second situation, the prostitute who is managed by her own mother and father. All daughters in Qing China are in a sense "managed" by their mothers and fathers, who hope for the best marriage deal in the form of a son-in-law who brings them profit and good face. To make a literal prostitute of their daughter is to make her profitable in a more baldly utilitarian way than usual. She is the lure set out for the wastrel who falls for prostitutes he thinks truly love him. When the wastrel runs out of money and the prostitute-daughter's parents won't allow the youths to marry, the daughter becomes hysterical, swallows poison, and dies (Jin Zhonger in *Lüye xianzong,* discussed in chapter 11). Like the raging shrew, the daughter who commits suicide is a hysteric who acts in an unseemly or desperate way in order to defy her manipulators, whether husband or parents, who are motivated by unbending standards such as chastity, profit, and face.

Highly improved versions of the wastrel and the prostitute are the scholar and the beauty, a pair of talented and handsome monogamous lovers who find each other and marry without their parents' money or supervision. The scholar in this case is loyal to one woman alone, who wins him in freedom from parents and polygamists.

At their opposite extremes, men are either philandering wastrels or ascetic misers; women are either lascivious shrews or chaste self-sacrificers. In between are the beauties and scholars, who each contain the other in cross-gendered symmetry, each having the looks or taking on the attributes of the other. They also complement each other in the syntax and imagery of the poetry they exchange in lieu of engaging in premarital sex. Such complementarity makes them a perfect match, the only monogamous one in Qing fiction.

Miser is a name for various types of economizing and pleasure-deferring men. In a literal sense, the miser is the mean landlord and usurer who forces his tenants into virtual slavery and lets starving debtors freeze to death after refusing them another loan. In a metaphorical sense, he is the neo-Confucian pedant who lives by stored wisdom and rules by doctrine. He is the polygynist who collects and saves women. If he is a follower of the ars erotica, he also saves semen, which he ejaculates rarely in order to avoid wasting innate *yang* energy, of which he imagines he has a finite amount in his lifetime. The truly mean miser, on the other hand, finds women too troublesome and replaces them with money. In other words, he liberates himself from dependent attraction to women and escapes from marriage in all but name only, attempting utterly to disregard both of his torturers, the shrewish wife and the wastrel son.

Miserliness is also a name for the male reaction to the extreme difficulty of self-control, especially in regard to women. Instead of reforming into some version of a temperate man, the miser peevishly outflanks both wastrel and henpecked husband, two prime examples of men who lose control. As the "Sutra of Wife-fearing" states, unbridled "seeking of women" leads to helpless "fear" of them (see *Cu hulu*). The miser is the most successful creator of superego, which he uses to deny his former ego that was spellbound by women. With the superego he attempts to kill motherly love and wifely emotionality—in other words, what he perceives to be women's unlimited capacity to flood him with demands. His hatred of motherly love includes hatred of a product of that love: the spoiled, wastrel son, who robs the miser's wealth and disobeys his rules.

As representative of the superego, the miser is a keeper of boundaries, especially the one between the women's inner and the men's outer precincts of the house. The enforcement of chastity and the maintenance of the patriline are ostensibly the chief goals of dividing inner from outer, but another important goal is to keep women from interfering in men's— especially father's and married brother's—financial affairs, which women attempt to manipulate for their own sake and that of their natal and uterine families.[19]

The miser also hates altruism, although he is clever at mouthing altruistic phrases and quoting from classics about altruistic behavior. He enacts a parody of the legalist philosopher Han Fei's (third century B.C.) interpretations of the *Laozi* (i.e., *Lao tzu* or *Tao te ching,* the Taoist text of ca. fourth or third century B.C.), which single out such sayings as, "In ruling people . . . nothing is more important than frugality" (ch. 59).[20] As the *Laozi* states, when virtues such as benevolence and righteousness appeared, humanity had already begun to decline (ch. 18). For the miser, the reign of feces was the ideal age, the one in which the most valuable currency was the night soil used to fertilize crops for the next harvest, as mentioned above—crops that, according to his rule, barely kept the people's bellies full. In the *Laozi*'s words, "Empty their minds, fill their bellies" (ch. 3). The more there is to imagine, the more there is to desire. The more virtues there are, the more the miser must be considerate of others—that is, ancestors, women, children, and other competing men.

The shrew is subversive of male privilege. In dominating the man, she attempts to punish the superego and remake it in her own image. If the man is miserly enough—that is, if his superego is strong enough—then he can usually manage to stay beyond her reach. But in order to stay beyond, as it turns out, he must occupy a very small realm upon which he can keep a firm grasp—perhaps only a single room—together with all his money and the keys to all the locks of his house.

In the end, however, the world belongs to the polygamists, whose conduct of desire is considered the most authoritative and admirable. They hold society's highest positions, from emperor to local official, merchant, and landlord. They laugh at the pathetic miser, kick the shrew, or, if she is outrageous enough, stop visiting her or expel her from the home. The polygamist buys marvelous aphrodisiacs from itinerant Tibetan monks and meets one sexy woman after another, all of whom want to be kept by him, whether as prostitute, concubine, or adulterous paramour. Unfortunately, however, polygamists are also expected to spend ostentatiously. Having collected his bevy of women and built his empire of wealth, he and his wastrel descendants will continue to spend both money and energy of desire until, as the proverb states, "by the fifth generation they are finished" (wushi er zhan). This is more or less the situation illustrated in Honglou meng, whose Baoyu is of the fourth generation.

Moderation is the virtue that men use to stem that dissolution without becoming too miserly. For instance, the man is moderate when he stops at one or two concubines. In scholar-beauty fiction, the middle way tends to create monogamous or two-wife polygynous men who are soft enough not to become miserly and misogynous but who also have enough self-discipline to study. It is as if father and mother ally to raise a temperate son, who then marries only one or two wives. Moreover, the temperate son's wife is a "talented" woman who is equal or superior to the man in literary skills and moral or even martial courage. In Honglou meng, Ernü yingxiong zhuan, and other works, the male counterpart to the talented woman is a young man who is feminine in appearance and emotionality. He does not chase after women or associate with "wine and meat comrades" (jiurou pengyou), as does the wastrel. In Ernü yingxiong zhuan, he assumes the role of what I will call the "coddled polygynist," whose wives both coddle and control him in order to keep him from succumbing to his innate weaknesses. He in turn listens to their words and never exceeds the proper limits of being coddled. Qing fiction thus creates the perfect couple by (1) portraying women as superior to men and (2) the crossing of gender characteristics, both of which have the effect of desexualizing the normally philanderous man. The representatives of this ideal match appear in their most stylized and rationalized form in the chaste romances of the early to mid-Qing. In the context of the miserly and polygamous society of Qing fiction, the monogamous scholar and beauty embody the most symmetrically idealized form of moderation—the version, incidentally, that European readers saw starting in the eighteenth century in the first translated works of Chinese vernacular fiction, including *Haoqiu zhuan* (The Fortunate Union) and *Yu Jiao Li* (translated into French as Les Deux Cousines), both originally from the seventeenth century.[21] The Age of Enlightenment was thus exposed to the cleanest examples of a romantic genre that was otherwise full of eroticism and fully countenanced polygamy, as found in scores of works that have yet to be translated.

Marriage and Sexuality in Fiction and
Other Sources of Qing History

The reason for my focus on polygamy, as I have said, in part reflects the material covered, which repeatedly centers around either situations of polygamy or the avoidance of it, and in part reflects actual conditions in the society in which this fiction was written. The main characters of most of these works represent the elite ten or so percent of the Qing population, a group that tended to strive for extended families in which polygamy was commonly practiced. Such things as the actual percent of polygamous families or the average number of wives in them are difficult if not impossible to ascertain. What fiction represents is the aspiration to polygamy, and, at the very least, the caricature of what such situations were probably like. Since more conventional historical sources provide only glimpses into the polygamous family, historians have been limited in their discussion of this crucial aspect of traditional Chinese life. They have also limited themselves, perhaps, because of their caution vis-à-vis the evidence of fiction which, besides constituting largely uncharted territory, is supposedly more blatant than conventional historical sources in exaggerating, distorting, and, in short, doing whatever it wants to manipulate its contents. But regardless of the type of source, the stance of this book is that narrative and linguistic constructions are all that can be known of such things as male and female, penis and vagina, or "we" and "other"—thus my emphasis on the constructedness of gender and sexuality. This is not to deny so-called concrete evidence, but only to emphasize that "facts" do not occur in isolation but are determined by expectation and interpretation.

But neither is this to say that fiction is a supreme and self-sufficient source for Qing social history. Medical texts, for example, are crucial in defining the general image of health and what men, women, and children should do to maintain health and prevent or cure illness. The ars erotica prescribes an economy of sexual conduct and provides images of the ideal and, by implication, nonideal man and woman and their sexual behavior. Prescriptive works on governing the household treat common problems such as inheritance, selection of spouses, maintenance of chaste relations, conduct of sons, and so forth. Numerous historical works provide, for example, biographies and autobiographies, genealogies of great families, information on the application of family law and on marriage customs of various regions, cases of virtuous or other remarkable conduct such as widow suicide or suicide of loyal lovers, and anecdotes about sensational phenomena such as hermaphroditism, sexual vampirism, or possession by demons. Court cases contain detailed accounts of sexual and other related crimes and provide valuable information about everyday life. Fiction and drama do, however, illustrate many of the chief characters of Qing society, including the central and peripheral members of the polygamous household and their mainly urban neighbors of high and low rank.

This book will cite a number of these sources, but by far most of these will be vernacular fiction, many under discussion for the first time. Besides treatment of sexuality and gender, then, it will be necessary to engage in basic introduction and exposition of fictional sources and in so doing to concentrate on the literariness of these works. This means, for example, to distinguish between what is formulaic or hyperbolic and what can be taken as representative of real situations, between what frequently recurs and what is unique to one or two works, to identify recurring themes and their variations, to trace central and recurring plot lines and their permutations, to describe character types and their reduced or admixed forms, and to locate significant social issues that fiction dramatizes via plot manipulation, caricature, and setting.

Although it is difficult to describe what this fiction does not include, it is nevertheless an important exercise to imagine what those things are in order to have a better idea of the scope of these works. I will attempt to cite items mainly having to do with sexuality. The Qing fiction treated in this book barely describes the pain of footbinding and the close-up vicissitudes of life with crippled feet.[22] In their descriptions of sexual promiscuity, these works rarely portray the realities of unwanted pregnancy, abortion, sexual disease, or female infanticide.[23] Body functions such as urination, defecation, and sexual intercourse—heterosexual, homosexual, both simultaneously, vaginal, anal, oral, and oral-anal[24]—are all described in detail, but such functions as childbirth and nursing, rarely. The common folk belief in women as sources of pollution mainly appears in fantastic or figurative form, as in the above case of the sorceress or in the shrew's rage, but in the novels I examine the everyday belief and its manifestations are rare in extensive and particularistic form.[25] A few instances briefly portray men repelled at the supposed odor or ugliness of an exposed woman.[26] In one case a man avoids intercourse with his postpartum wife, although no direct mention is made of the one-hundred-day postpartum taboo.[27] The inconvenience or complications of menstruation are more common, however, especially in *Honglou meng,* which makes several mentions of women's illness due to menstrual irregularity.[28] Menstrual blood appears in its most explicit form in an erotic novel which makes it into a hyperbolic detail of closure to a long session of sex: a man and woman are vigorously making love, but while the man performs cunnilingus, the woman's period suddenly arrives and splashes forth like a fountain, wetting the man from head to toe. Two nearby maids laugh and congratulate the woman for giving first birth to a son, then get bath water for the man, who meanwhile spits out blood but otherwise shows no sign of fear or disgust.[29] In another work, a man and woman make love for a lengthy time during her period.[30] Elsewhere, menstruation is sometimes the excuse of a woman wishing to avoid intercourse.[31] Another type of female blood, the virgin's hymen blood, is a celebrated sign of chastity and, in erotic fiction at least, is both a mark of her initial pain at intercourse and a formulaic feature of the occasion of penetrating a virgin. Finally, as Bret Hinsch has already noted, although male homosexuality is extremely common in Chinese sources, lesbianism is rare, and in a form that excludes heterosexuality is even rarer.[32]

The above summary underscores the fact that, for the most part, Chinese vernacular fiction is not a context for playing out the everyday scenes of women's lives except as part of the dialogue with men and as viewed by men, who wrote most if not all of these works. It is always possible that some authors of the anonymous works of Qing fiction were women, but such a fact cannot yet be known. The list of what cannot be found in fiction obviously includes many more things: for example, extended interaction with foreigners, life among farmers and the "mean" classes,[33] and the lives of eunuchs other than as evil plotters. I will indicate other subjects in passing.

As for the question of who wrote and read these works, it is for the most part only possible to make suppositions, some of which are based on biographical fact. Prefaces and other biographical sources often stereotypically portray writers as frustrated literati who never succeeded in the life of official advancement; many writers perhaps did not care for such success. Since the eighteenth century reportedly saw an increase in nonofficial career opportunities for members of the lower elite, with or without examination degrees, it is possible that many unknown writers were also from this new group, which included editors of exam essays, painters and calligraphers, poets and writers of belles lettres, government and other clerks, and secretaries of merchants and officials.[34] All these occupations appear in Qing fiction, especially *Rulin waishi;* and some authors were in fact from this group. The social status of writers probably ranged from the lowest, perhaps including literate members of the "mean" class of actors, to the highest, including current or former but then impoverished members of the elite, such as Cao Xueqin, the author of *Honglou meng.* Although it is not known if women were among these writers, there were in those times female poets, dramatists, and storytellers. The readers of vernacular fiction were presumably officials, other literati, merchants, and the male and female members of the households of these and other mostly urban folk who had the means to learn how to read. The majority of writers probably lived in or around Jiangnan (the lower Yangtse River region) and also the territory between it and the capital; but writers and, of course, readers came from other regions as well. The *Qilu deng* author was from Henan; the setting of *Shenlou zhi* is in Canton, although the author may not have come from there. Some writers wrote for and probably earned a profit, such as the authors of the scholar-beauty romances, especially the erotic ones. Other authors wrote mainly for themselves and their circle of relatives and friends and were not in a hurry to finish their works, much less earn a profit; these include the authors of *Honglou meng, Lüye xianzong, Qilu deng,* and *Yesou puyan.*

It also has to be remembered that government censorship of erotic literature made the writing and publishing of such works potentially dangerous. Literati values, moreover, held the vernacular novel as a whole in low esteem compared to poetry and prose in the classical language. Records of those who wrote these novels are accordingly infrequent and often secondhand. Lists of censored erotic works, especially the one Ding Richang issued in 1868, can nevertheless be helpful in determining which works were common up to a certain time. Novels that were only slightly erotic were probably considered inoffensive, including ones that borrowed or else supplied the contents of operas that were popular during the Qing.[35] Operas with lewd innuendoes were in fact popular throughout the Ming and Qing (authorities banned an especially bawdy type in Beijing in 1785);[36] and female impersonation, with its inherent erotic possibilities, was common throughout the Qing and after. Nevertheless, fiction could and did include details that would be utterly impossible to stage in public.

It is easier to place these works in their historical context by discussing the customs that prevailed in Qing society and by outlining the general situation of marriage, the family, and sexual relations. One of the most important alliances in Chinese society was that between man and woman and their respective families through marriage. In Naquin and Rawski's words, the family was the "basic unit of production and consumption" (33). "Virtually universal" for women (108), marriage was centrally motivated by the imperative to have male descendants, for the sake of which unfortunate results sometimes occurred if the wife did not bear a son. Female infanticide was reportedly high, especially in certain regions. Adoption and concubinage were the morally and legally accepted methods for obtaining a son if the wife did not bear one. In some cases among commoners, however, if a couple failed to have a son, they would borrow a man or woman from outside the family to help produce one, as apparently happened in southern Shaanxi and other regions, according to Xu Ke's *Qingbai leichao* (1917, Classified Collection of Unofficial Sources of Qing History).[37]

The most common and accepted form of marriage was the virilocal monogamous one, in which the woman married into the man's home. But uxorilocal marriage, in which the man married into the woman's home, was also common, especially in certain regions[38] and under certain conditions—for example, when a family with an only daughter was in need of labor and / or if a prospective husband was too poor to marry virilocally.[39] Uxorilocal marriage in fiction is often into an elite family with an especially talented daughter whose parents can't bear to marry her away from home. In its satire of examination learning and the ladder of success, *Rulin waishi* portrays uxorilocal marriage as an easy way for poor or venal men of mediocre talent to advance themselves.[40] Another common form of marriage was the so-called minor one in which a young girl was adopted into a family whose son she would later marry. Such an arrangement, however, is rarely a focus of portrayal in early to mid-Qing fiction.[41]

As I have noted, polygyny was the most desired and respected form of marriage for men, even if it occurred in only about 10 percent or so of all marriages and regardless of the fact that in the Qing population of eligible partners, men outnumbered women.[42] As some moralists complained, wealthy men took more than their share of women. The average number of concubines per polygamist is difficult to determine since sources such as genealogies often report only the concubines who bore sons. Fictional cases generally go from one to four or five concubines, although a few works feature polygynists who take as many as twelve (*Xinghua tian*) or twenty wives (*Langshi qiguan*). The reverse situation of a woman having more than one husband or lover was considered an utmost abomination. But in poor regions of Gansu and elsewhere, the shortage of women reportedly led to two or more brothers marrying one woman, who, however, was not privileged in the way a male polygamist was.[43] Some works of fiction toy with the appearance of a woman almost marrying two husbands—always, however, as part of a comedy-of-errors-style confusion of identities. As for a woman who is not a prostitute but nevertheless has multiple male lovers, the erotic *Zhaoyang qushi* (The Lascivious History of Han Empress Feiyan), *Ruyi jun zhuan* (The Tale of Tang Empress Wu's Favorite, Master Pleasure), and especially *Zui chunfeng* (Drunken with the Spring Winds, about a woman from a rich urban family)—the former two from the Ming, the latter the Qing—provide the best examples.

As for choice of marriage partners, control was in the hands of parents and grandparents, as dictated by custom and law. In spite of this norm, more or less self-determined situations like those written about in scholar-beauty romances seem actually to have been possible, although they may have been rare.[44] A Qing poet of the Qianlong era, however, wrote that, "Following the dictates of one's parents is the tradition of the classic rites; setting one's own life's course is only found in novels and stories," of which he did not approve.[45]

The virtue of female chastity was something to be made public, espe-cially among commoners in the Qing, when the government awarded special praise to widow chastity, for the sake of which memorial arches were built and names listed in honor of outstanding cases. The honor to the woman in such instances inevitably brought honor to family and community as well.[46] Women were commemorated for going to the extremes of suicide or self-disfigurement to preserve their chastity in times of war and plunder or other violent situations.[47] Virginity was also commended, although not in such prominently documented ways. Some parts of Guangdong reportedly had the custom of taking the cloth stained with the bride's virgin blood, covering it with a red cloth, and placing this "cloth of marital happiness" (*xipa*) on a red tray to show to the families of husband and wife.[48] In one novel, the man takes the virgin's cloth and stores it forever in a small treasure box.[49] In general, erotic fiction reflects a fascination with virginal blood not only as a sign of purity but as an effect of pain at first intercourse and as cause for the man's tenderness for the delicate maiden.

Although high in social status, the extended family in which polyg-amy was most common ended up being a corporation whose prosperity was often difficult to maintain. In Hugh Baker's words, such families were "open to fission," whether because of conflicts between brothers and their individual families or because of the societywide custom of partible inheritance. Each son, whether a wife's or a concubine's, sup-posedly inherited an equal share of the patriarchal wealth.[50] Downward mobility was thus a risk even for those who managed to gain enough wealth to form a household to begin with and then own enough prop-erty or goods to pass on to sons. As for those at the bottom of the social hierarchy, it is estimated that 10 percent or so of the poorest men were forever without the prospect of marriage, because of both poverty and the unequal access of men to women.[51]

The majority of households were either two-generation "elemen-tary" or three-generation "stem" families, that is, ones in which the middle generation consisted of only one married couple, as opposed to the "extended" family in which the middle generation consisted of two or more couples.[52] According to Baker's study of prosperous extended families in southern China, a typical cycle was such that the members of the third generation would earn little and generally lead a life of leisure, while those of the fourth generation would sell more and more property and slowly sink into poverty (131). Again, the stereotyped impression was that "by the fifth generation, a family was finished." Nevertheless, a wealthy family could maintain local dominance for a century or more. Qing romances commonly end with a projection of prosperity into an indefinite future, but other novels concentrate on the inevitability of decline brought on by the gambling and philandering of males and by fission due to female jealousy and covetous bickering.

As shown in numerous novels, the upbringing of children, especially sons, was of critical importance in Chinese society because of both the need for care in old age and hopes for upward—and fear of downward—mobility. Among the poorest people, children might be sold to escape debt. In more stable homes, sons and daughters stayed carefree with the mother or other women of the family until age six or seven. At this time the son would come under paternal authority and learn some profitable skill. If the household could afford it, he would begin schooling for hopeful attainment of a civil service degree. Such advancement was legally open to all men except those of the "mean" class, which included musicians, actors, and lowly yamen employees (but the eighteenth century also saw a loosening of those restrictions in the form of a government decree allowing their descendants to sit for exams).[53] However, regardless of class, 90 percent of China's men are said to have found it impossible from the start to enter the chain of examination success.[54] Poverty, lack of influence, and the excess number of contenders made such a desirable option increasingly difficult to entertain. As for the daughter, she would undergo the painful process of footbinding and commence education in feminine arts such as sewing and weaving in preparation for marriage into her husband's household. Women's education in letters was common in elite families, as reflected in many Qing novels, including some which portray women achieving ideal monogamous matches. Talented and literate courtesans and nuns also continued to exist, as they had for centuries.

Concerning age of marriage, Qing law stated that women could marry once they reached fourteen, men when they reached sixteen. But in actual practice young people tended to marry in their late teens or around twenty.[55] Although men and women were supposedly rigidly separated before marriage—as were nonmarried, non-blood-related men and women after marriage—it is difficult to determine how strictly these rules were applied. Historical and fictional sources demonstrate that segregation was stricter among the upper classes, who could afford, for one thing, to have large enough homes to maintain separate quarters for women, especially unmarried daughters. But among the elite it was nevertheless possible for unmarried cousins, for example, to become familiar and even fall in love, whether or not they succeeded in getting married.[56] Novels make access between unmarried men and women, cousins or not, seem extraordinarily easy, although the same novels usually refer to the rules of segregation and portray at least the partial enforcement of those rules, as will be seen in the chapters below. Erotic works go to extremes to dramatize easy sexual access, but nonerotic works play with breaking the rules of segregation as well. In a famous scene of *Rulin waishi*, for example, Du Shaoqing promenades hand in hand with his wife in public in Nanjing. Doing such a thing is scandalous both because respectable women should not be so openly visible and because a man should not touch his wife except in the bedchamber (ch. 33, 454). In another episode, the poetess Shen Qiongzhi establishes herself in Nanjing as a dealer selling her own poetry, mountings of paintings and calligraphy, and embroidery. When she travels alone in public, young men trail after her gawking and catcalling, to which she responds with angry insults (ch. 41, 563–64). Such things as a literatus walking with his wife in public or an independent, educated woman setting herself up as something other than a courtesan were probably more likely seen in Nanjing and other cities of the lower Yangtze delta than elsewhere. But such individuals would in any case not be free from criticism or open harassment. Unmarried or upper-class women ordinarily went out of their homes only on holidays or other special occasions, and then most properly if accompanied by other women or male and female servants; otherwise they would go out only in a covered carriage or sedan chair. In fiction, most of the women seen walking the streets are middle-aged or older go-betweens, flower sellers, nuns, and fortune-tellers. In actual society there would have been more than these, including women and girls of the common class except those around marriageable age, who were probably kept out of sight.

The ages at which youths first knew of or had sex can be found in numerous novels, which, of course, can only be taken as supplying suggestive evidence. The narrator in *Xingshi yinyuan zhuan* (Marriage Fate to Arouse the World) laments that spoiled upper-class youths know sex by age eleven (ch. 44, 638). An urban common woman in *Yu Lou Chun* (The Cross-dressed Scholar's Three Wives) states that "most people" know about sex at around thirteen or fourteen (ch. 2, 11a). Erotic novels like *Shenlou zhi* portray men and women in wealthy merchant households first having sex at age fourteen (ch. 2). *Honglou meng* has Baoyu starting at age eleven or twelve, with his maid Xiren older by two years (ch. 5). These ages in part reflect the fact that men of the elite class began sexual activity and married earlier than most.[57] Their easy access to maids or prostitutes is one thing, however; that they would have had such early premarital relations with women of their own class, even if so often portrayed in fiction, is more difficult to assume.

The above has been a synchronic picture of marriage, gender roles, and sexuality in the early to mid-Qing period, or roughly the eighteenth century. The indeterminacy of dating and authorship of most of the fictional works I cover will prevent a more precise diachrony than "early to mid-Qing." Nevertheless, concentrating on that period, I will use fiction to describe a relatively recent and intense expression of male privilege, that of polygyny, which was legal and widespread until the early years of the twentieth century, and is still part of the memory and background of many contemporary Chinese. This fiction shows that, long before modern Chinese governments officially condemned polygamy and made monogamy the only legal form of marriage, numerous voices in the Qing either were feeling compelled to create careful justifications of polygamy, as if defending against some opposition, or were engaging in detailed accounts implying the impossibility of successful polygamy, especially from the woman's point of view. The later Western Christian influence of the nineteenth and twentieth centuries no doubt had a major moral and economic effect on the transition from polygamy to monogamy, although it is not yet clear how extensive such influence was and exactly how that transition occurred.[58] Explanations of present sexual relations must take into account the evolution from this recent past, which is full of its shrews, wastrels, misers, and ascetics—all of whom, especially the shrew and the wastrel, still inhabit the current imagination even if polygamy has been declared illegal and many other forms of male privilege have been dismantled.

Finally, the words I have chosen for the two extremes of male and female character types, "miser" and "shrew," are originally of narrow semantic range but are temporarily borrowed for broader though not totalizing use. That is, for instance, they do not mean that all male or female behavior in these novels should fit along a scale of miserliness or shrew-ishness. I originally used the words in an earlier study which already laid out the reductive formula of male retention and female scattering, for which miser and shrew are intended to stand.[59] Twentieth-century ste-reotypes continue to reflect the same or related ideas, although "miser" and "shrew" should probably be replaced by words more appropriate to current times. The question Did (or do) misers and shrews really exist? is answerable only in a narrow sense and is probably not even worth asking. The two terms indicate modes or moments of behavior, not permanent and integral mentalities that exist in mass numbers or fixed wholes. "Polygamist" is also a borrowed term and could easily have been replaced by "wastrel" or "libertine," which in fact resonate better with "miser" and "shrew" than does "polygamist." "Wastrel" and "libertine," however, do not convey the sense critical to this study of the legitimized and condoned access of one man to many women. A succinct way of describ-ing miser, shrew, and polygamist in one breath is this: in the end, the miser and the polygamist are alike in equating potency with number, which ultimately translates into gold / semen. Although weak in terms of political and economic strength, the shrew is someone who does what-ever she can to manipulate—whether to attack, evade, or coddle—the man's obsession with potency and numbers.

2

POLYGAMY ACCORDING TO FICTION

AND PRESCRIPTIVE MODELS

Starting with the late-sixteenth-century appearance of *Jin Ping Mei* and other erotic novels and stories, the sexual affairs and daily, intimate life of the polygamous family became common subjects of Chinese vernacular fiction. Read collectively, these works can be seen debating the viability of polygamy and, on a broader level, the compatibility of male and female sexualities and of the male-female relationship in general. Through this debate they attack the fundamental problem of the regulation of desire and, in their collective conclusion, propose two solutions: the abdication of the potent male or his heroic remolding according to a neo-traditional ideal.

Abdication or idealization, incompatibility and domination by one or the other gender, and harmonious symmetry—all appear in representations of gender and sexuality found in both fiction and other sources and models. After briefly outlining the types of novels treated in this book, the alleged reasons for polygamy, and some of the terminology of polygamous practice, this chapter will examine a few of the most important nonfictional sources for understanding the representation of gender, sexuality, and male-female relations in Qing China: prescriptive Confucian texts, precepts of household management, medical belief, and, at greatest length, the ars erotica. Then follows a discussion of polygamy in *Jin Ping Mei* and other late Ming fiction, which provides models and foils for the later novels discussed in the main part of this study.

The explicit portrayal of sexuality, whether within or outside marriage, manifests itself in two general ways in Ming and Qing novels: works like

Jin Ping Mei or the mid-Qing *Lüye xianzong* represent sexual desire as something uncontainable and intractable, and depict intercourse as illicit and madly driven by lust. In the early to mid-Qing, another type of erotic novel comes into existence which instead domesticates sexual desire by containing it within idealized polygamous households (e.g., the erotic scholar-beauty romances, *Yesou puyan,* and *Shenlou zhi*). These works repair the examples set by Ming characters such as *Jin Ping Mei*'s Ximen Qing and Pan Jinlian by emphasizing the benefits of polygamy and portraying polygamists who are like rectified Ximen Qings.

Nonerotic novels about love and marriage follow a similar double track. Some works expose the problems of the polygamous household, in many cases echoing or even imitating *Jin Ping Mei*'s portrayal of the wastrel (e.g., *Honglou meng, Lin Lan Xiang, Qilu deng,* and *Ernü yingxiong zhuan*). Paralleling fiction about idealized polygamous households, numerous works represent happy monogamy or at most two-wife polygyny, and in so doing portray chaste women and temperate men (e.g., the chaste scholar-beauty romances).

The novels discussed in this book will thus fall into the categories of erotic (that is, containing explicit sexual detail) or nonerotic, and within each of these divide into works which depict male-female relations as discordant or harmonious. In terms of organization of discussion, to repeat from the last chapter, I will separately treat (1) relatively short works, erotic and nonerotic, which tend to predictability of plot and flatness of character portrayal, and which feature either monogamous or polygamous harmony (that is, the chaste and erotic romances of chapters 5 and 6, and *Shenlou zhi* of chapter 12); and (2) lengthy literati novels, also erotic or nonerotic, which contain more idiosyncratic and detailed portrayals of marriage, family life, and sexual desire (the novels discussed in chapter 7 to 11 and 13, that is, *Yesou puyan, Honglou meng, Lin Lan Xiang, Qilu deng, Lüye xianzong,* and *Ernü yingxiong zhuan*). The shrew and the miser will be treated in their own chapters (3 and 4, respectively), which cover novels from each of the above categories of erotic and nonerotic, harmony and incompatibility, and relative length and degree of detail.

As a set of well-worked-out customs and practices that have evolved through many centuries, polygamy was quite beyond any threat to its existence until twentieth-century laws began to whittle it away and social opinion began to discourage it. The novels and stories I examine in this book reflect the fact that men of sufficient means and rank were expected to and wanted to have more than one wife. In the legal terminology of the time, polygamy was defined in such a way that a man was allowed only one main wife, with certain special exceptions.[1] He could have secondary wives or concubines, however, who were different in kind from and ranked below the main wife, and in theory served her as well as the husband; these lesser consorts were also legal members of his family.

As for terminology used in Qing fiction about polygamy, no word exists in Chinese (or English) that defines the man who has relations with both women and men both inside and outside the family, but I will sometimes assume that polygamy applies in this broader sense as well— that is, that it refers to a man who assumes the privilege of having multiple sexual partners, regardless of whether he takes them as wives, concubines, or lovers (in other words, that polygamy is an institution-alized form of male desire for unrestricted access to sexual partners). Chinese terms for monogamy, bigamy, polygamy, polygyny, and second-ary wives or concubines do not always correspond well to English terms. (Technically, polygamy refers to a man or woman with multiple spouses, while polygyny refers specifically to a man with multiple wives; the terms will be used interchangeably in this study, however, since polyandry—the case of a woman taking multiple husbands—is virtually nonexistent in these works.) In a number of Ming and Qing works monogamy is called *yifu yiqi*, "one-husband one-wife," and is used specifically to promote a man's having one wife and no other women at all. Numerous works have heroes who marry just two women, a situation that I will call "two-wife polygyny," in Chinese sometimes referred to as *yifu erqi*, "one-husband two-wives"; in these cases, the two wives are happily equal in rank or agreeably distinguished by only a slight difference in hierarchy. Terms for polygamy and polygyny, however, nowadays called *yifu duoqi*, "one-husband many-wives," do not appear in Ming and Qing fiction. Instead, Chinese merely designates the number of wives and concubines with a simple formula, e.g., *yiqi sanqie*, "one-wife three-concubines." This for-mula is more accurate than polygamy, polygyny, and *yifu duoqi*, which do not comprehend the strict hierarchical distinction between wife (*qi*) and concubine (*qie*). Words for concubines or chambermaids are numerous, with some relatively synonymous and some designating higher or lower levels of appellation and status. *Rufuren*, meaning "as if a (main) wife," is a euphemistic term of respect used to refer to someone else's concubine.

Fushi or *ceshi*, literally, "associate-chamber" or "side-chamber," are respectful terms for one's own concubines. These three contrast with the more colloquial and diminutive *xiaoqie*, "little concubine," and *xiaolaopo*, literally "little wife," which is slightly pejorative. Two other terms are *pianfang*, "side-room," colloquial for one's concubine, and *tongfang*, "intra-room," a term for a maid who is in sexual relationship with the man (*yi taitai*, a common later term, does not appear in the Qing works discussed here, although *yi niang*, "sister-mother"—i.e., "sister" of the primary mother-wife—occurs in *Honglou meng* and elsewhere and is another respectful name for concubine).

Whatever the number or category of women, why and how does a man become a polygamist? In general, the given reasons come down to filial duty, pleasure, and prestige, for which the man could take as many wives as he could afford and as was seemly for his social rank (he might also, of course, maintain nonlegal relationships, short or long term, with courtesans or male lovers, for example). If his wife failed to bear him a son, custom dictated that he should try to have one of a concubine in order to maintain the ancestral line. However, whether or not his wife bore him a son, he could at his pleasure—but best if not too rashly—acquire attractive women to create a harem. In addition, in both fiction and reality, women were often presented as gifts or rewards between men forming alliances. A man already betrothed to someone else might nevertheless welcome such an offer or find it unwise to refuse.[2]

As for why a woman would join a polygamous family (if she had a choice), her motives were mainly her own and her family's economic benefit. She should ideally find that marriage to such a man was a secure and prestigious alternative to the life she had been leading or might otherwise lead. Women of both high and low social ranks and educational levels joined polygamous households, and as wives allowed or even encouraged their husbands to take concubines. Of course, many were forced to join such households, and many opposed polygamy and either refused to participate in it or made it difficult for their husbands and his wife or concubine(s) to enjoy themselves.

What were these family situations like? How did man and women cooperate to form a harmonious or at least workable household? What kinds of things went wrong and why? The common theme of these novels is that success or failure in running the family depends most upon the regulation of desire and upon the man's choice and treatment of his women. He has to satisfy a number of women without destroying himself or allowing them to destroy each other. In the absence of firm control of himself and others, especially in the event of passionate favoritism, his household will decline or collapse.

The situations of polygamous life in fiction can be better understood by first elucidating the models of prescribed behavior for the man and his wives. Both erotic and nonerotic models exist from ancient times up to the Ming and Qing, each to some degree inscribing its own contained framework. That is, each prescriptive work—whether of the Confucian canon, the sexual arts, or medicine, for example—provides its own formula for family relations while often ignoring the contents or emphasis of a neighboring formula. Medical belief, for instance, justifies the dependent status of women by means of a detailed and pessimistic rationale for women's inherent sickliness and emotional instability. Female weakness is a given in other prescriptive works and in fiction, which do not necessarily explain it according to the medical rationale, however, and some works counterbalance it with the assertion of some aspect of female strength, in many cases superior to male strength. Thus, the following summation of traditional precepts and prescriptive models assumes the diversity of formulas, all of which, like fiction, manipulate their stories in their own ways and, of course, are only partially believed or adhered to in Qing society, real or fictional.

The Problems of Polygyny in History, Fiction, and Prescriptive Texts

Ancient history supplies plenty of examples of the disasters of polygyny. Records of tyrants such as the infamous last rulers of the Xia, Shang, and Western Zhou periods attest to the dangers of infatuation with female favorites other than the main wife.[3] The havoc wrought by these "kingdom-toppling" women culminates with the Tang Emperor Xuanzong and his favorite Yang Guifei, who was said by many in the Tang and later to be the cause of his ruin and the devastation brought by the An Lushan rebellion (in 755). Besides recording such events, canonic and official history contains numerous statements about the nefarious effects of female beauty: for example, the famous quotes from the ancient chronicle, the *Zuo zhuan* (The Commentary of Mr. Zuo, circa third-century B.C.), "Where there is extreme beauty, there is certain to be extreme evil"; and, "Women are sinister beings [*youwu*] capable of perverting men's virtue."[4]

The health of the man has always been an important issue. In 541 B.C., the physician He judges the Marquis of Jin's illness to be the result of sexual excess. "The illness cannot be cured. This is a case of being intimate with women; the illness makes one become as if insane." He says that a man should regulate intercourse with women just as one regulates music by means of the "five regular intervals." "Thus the superior man does not listen to music where the hands work on with licentious notes, pleasing the ears but injurious to the mind, where the rules of equable harmony are forgotten. So it is with all things."[5]

Presumably, if the Marquis regulated himself correctly, he could have healthy intercourse with many women. The ancient ars erotica, which in its earliest form is at least as old as the above passage from the *Zuo zhuan*, in fact encourages a man "to have intercourse with as many young women [i.e., virgins] as he can," *duo yu shao nü*; the more women he engages, the more vital his *qi*- energy will become. At the same time, in order to avoid "depletion" (*shuai*) he must "curtail his emission of semen," *mo shu xie jing*.[6] Such restraint is a fundamental notion of the ancient ars erotica and all medical knowledge and folk wisdom ever since. The man must avoid overindulgence; he must look upon women not as tools for satisfying his sexual desire but as partners in a healthful exercise. He should strictly economize seminal discharge. "If one has an insatiable desire for the beauties of women and exerts all one's energies to express that desire, then the hundred arteries will suffer harm and the hundred illnesses will break out."[7]

Taking the form of prescriptive manuals, the ars erotica provides the polygamist with models of ideal sexual behavior. Other prescriptive texts such as the *Li ji* (Book of Rites) or works on governing the home provide models for all kinds of behavior except sexual. The ideal of both erotic and nonerotic works is a cultivated and temperate gentleman, benevolent to women and consummate in his knowledge of sexual techniques. He leads women but does not force himself on them. Women, in turn, gladly serve him as ministers serve an emperor.

Such a happy situation obtains in few works of fiction outside of Qing erotic romances. Among characters in other novels and stories from *Jin*

Ping Mei on, the precepts of the ars erotica, the *Li ji,* and other prescriptive texts are as if forgotten or proven hugely inadequate. Although fiction itself contains prescriptive formulas, many taken directly from ancient and later texts, it is by generic nature mainly an account of divergences from prescription. The prescriptive works pretend that the polygamist can avoid problems if he conducts himself properly; the "realistic" books of history or fiction concentrate on the seriously problematic nature of male-female relations. In fiction, the man is all too prone to excess and the woman all too prone not to cooperate with him or other women. The man learns the right way, if he learns it at all, only after making disastrous mistakes, like the Marquis of Jin in the *Zuo zhuan.* What follows will elucidate these problems by first treating the nonerotic prescriptive models, then the erotic; both models must be assumed for the readings of fiction given later on.

Sexual Segregation in Nonerotic Prescriptive Works

As if addressing the disastrous situations of history like those alluded to above, the *Li ji* and other Confucian classics establish codes of conduct for family life. The precepts in these texts mainly take the form of ritual and custom, although they are often reinforced by law. When concerned with the relations of the sexes, ritual and law primarily deal with the establishment and preservation of boundaries and hierarchies. Adherence starts from the age at which boy and girl should no longer freely mingle and proceeds to the occasions of betrothal, marriage, and subsequent daily life, including conduct at the death of family members (as seen in the minute attention to the degrees of male and female mourning depending upon gender and degree of relation). Strictures against such things as adultery and incest also exist. But sexual behavior itself is not discussed; it is to occur only in the bedchamber, the only place, in fact, where touching is allowed.

The *Li ji* is fastidious about the separation of the sexes. The famous dictum concerning touching is, "Male and female, in giving and receiving, do not allow their hands to touch" (*nannü shoushou buqin*).[8] Other relevant sayings are: "Male and female should not sit together . . . , nor have the same stand or rack for their clothes, nor use the same towel or comb, [and once again] nor let their hands touch in giving and receiving."

Also, "Male and female, without the intervention of the matchmaker, do not know each other's name."[9] The most encompassing rule about boundaries between the sexes concerns the division between inner and outer precincts of the house. Women should reside within and should not freely emerge or even be seen by outsiders. Further, "The men should not speak of what belongs to the inside of the house, nor the women of what belongs to the outside."[10] In other words, "Outside affairs should not be talked of inside the threshold of the women's apartments, nor inside affairs outside it."[11]

All the above quotes are codicils of the first sentences of the *Li ji*: "Always and in everything let there be reverence"; "the desires should not be indulged; the will should not be gratified to the full; pleasure should not be carried to excess."[12] Since words are not enough in themselves, the practical measure is taken of dividing inner from outer in order to prevent unseemly contact. In addition, rules are established to deal with such things as which men and women can meet when and where. Certain relationships need more restraint than others—for example, that between grown sons and their father's young concubines. Qing law dictated death to the man who married his dead father's concubine.[13] Yuan Cai's *Shifan* (Precepts for Social Life), a Song dynasty book (1178) on family and property, addresses such problems numerous times; for example, as Patricia Ebrey translates, "If you keep maids and concubines, precautions and restrictions are needed both with regard to your sons and younger brothers within the family and with regard to servants outside it." One of the worst cases would be the suicide of a maid or concubine who became illicitly pregnant; her suicide could create severe legal consequences for the man. Also, "When men do not prohibit their maids and concubines from freely coming and going, sometimes a woman may have relations with an outsider and get pregnant. If the master simply drives the woman away without clearly establishing her guilt, often after he has died she claims that the child was his and tries to get the boy accepted into the family. This easily gives rise to lawsuits."[14]

The crux of many Ming and Qing stories is precisely the boundary that is not well kept. Illicit relationships occur because women are accidentally or negligently allowed too much access or exposure, often through actual doorways, windows, and gaps in walls surrounding compounds.[15] All boundaries can be reduced to the surface of the body itself, with its several "apertures," *qiao*, above and below. The rule for all such openings is that as long as they are properly contained, the family and the body will maintain a state of moral well-being. Good morality and good health are seen as parallel, since the prime causes of illness in traditional medical terms are excess invasions from without or discharges from within.[16]

Qing medical science has its own set of prescriptions about male and female health that overlap with the larger Confucian model of proper behavior. Women are considered inherently prone to sickliness and emotionality and thus more difficult to cure than men. Menstruation and childbearing are two of the most dissipating influences on the woman's health.[17] Although men may also suffer dissipation, they nevertheless have the choice to maintain or improve health by regulated sexual abstinence; women are imperiled whether abstinent or not.[18] As Charlotte Furth demonstrates, the woman's safest route is to accept her inherent weakness and sickliness, to recognize her dependency on the family, and then to bear children wisely. During pregnancy she must maintain "passionless calm," regulate lust and anger, and later assist in the careful watch over the child's health, which is seen as inherently precarious due to the mother's polluting influence.[19] In its view of childhood diseases, medical belief echoes folk superstition about female pollution, the harmful effects of which the child supposedly inherits from the womb and outgrows with difficulty. As Furth reports, however, medical theory rationalizes and softens the folk concept of pollution by viewing it as medically treatable and by taking an attitude of "pity and compassion" toward women rather than encouraging fear and taboo.[20] Between folk and medical belief, women face either pollution or sickliness, either "negative sexual power [or] socially acceptable weakness"[21]—that is, in parallel terms, either being shrewish and unchaste, or obeying the strictures about living wisely in the inner chambers.

Compared to the *Li ji* and other Confucian works prescribing rules of household behavior, medical belief deals more directly with the conduct of the body in sexual situations. Confucian canon ignores the topic of intercourse, although it acknowledges the harm of suppressing sexual desire. It is clearly admitted, even if not often openly, that "appetite for food and sex is nature" (*shise xing ye,* from *Mengzi*),[22] or that "the things which humans greatly desire are comprehended in meat and drink and sexual pleasure" (from the *Li ji*).[23] Chinese medicine makes the same assumptions and somewhat enters the bedchamber, but still with stern regard. It is left to the ars erotica to continue the prescriptive approach but nevertheless to be explicit and affirmative in discussing the subject of sexual intercourse.

Sexual Health and Virtue in the Ancient Ars Erotica

The precepts of ritual custom dovetail neatly with those of the sexual arts, which begin where works like the Li ji leave off just outside the bedchamber. The ars erotica presents sexual intercourse as an extension of ritual and ceremony, which are based upon values of reverence and equilibrium and are conducted in the manner of an artistic performance. As the ars erotica teaches, in the midst of sensual arousal, proper order and rhythm are always to be maintained. At the same time, the main focus is on the smooth and pleasurable flow of the act of intercourse itself. Sex in its procreative function appears in a separate section of the texts and has its own set of preparations, although reverence and equilibrium are equally if not more important.[24] Likewise, as will be discussed below and in the next chapter, the problems of unaccommodating women are also reduced and set aside from the main focus on successful intercourse. However considerate of women it teaches the man to be, the ars erotica nevertheless considers intercourse to be for his main benefit and geared to his cycle of interest and energy.

The ars erotica has existed from very early times in China and by the Qing appears in several genres, including ones oriented for either men or women.[25] Its earliest extant texts, ostensibly addressed to emperors or other male rulers, were unearthed at Mawangdui in Hunan Province in the 1970s and date at the latest to 168 B.C., the formation of their contents having of course occurred long before that. Titles of books on the "art of the bedchamber" (fangzhong shu) appear in bibliographies of dynastic histories from the Han to the Sui and Tang. In the Han, the works are classed under the rubric of fangzhong, "bedchamber"; by the Sui and Tang, they are classed under medical science. Thereafter, the old titles disappear, though much of their subject matter lives on in medical literature and the esoteric texts of Taoist alchemy and Buddhist meditation. Although future research may lead to revisions of our present understanding, in general, from the Song dynasty on, the ars erotica goes "underground." Some new works show up—most notably the Sunü

37

miaolun (The Subtle Discourse of the Essential Woman)[26] and numerous late Ming erotic picture albums—but never in official bibliographies. The most sensational literary manifestation of sexual culture is in stories, novels, plays, and love poetry, which themselves lead a somewhat underground existence because of the severe penalties imposed by Ming and Qing policies of censorship.

A major problem in studying the relevance of the ars erotica to fiction is the difficulty of knowing what form of the ars erotica, if any, might have been available to Ming and Qing authors. Just because the *Sunü miaolun* or *Xiu zhen yanyi* (Exposition of Cultivating the True Essence)[27] existed in the Ming does not mean authors definitely read or heard about them. Extant pre-Ming sources appear not to have survived in integral form in the Ming and Qing (although they did survive in Japan because of their introduction there in the tenth century). However, the art of the bedchamber was also traditionally (and probably primarily) taught via oral transmission, which though difficult to gauge is well attested in fiction and other sources. Moreover, enough of the teachings of the ars erotica appears in vernacular novels to confirm its transmission in at least fragmented form. In order to understand these fragments and how they inform the representation of sexuality in fiction, it is necessary to briefly summarize the contents of the ars erotica from its pre-Han origins to its form in the Ming. For my purposes, these contents are uniform enough throughout this long stretch of time to dispel worry about possibly drastic anachronism.[28] In what follows I will cover the major points of consistency in these works, mainly citing Tamba Yasuyori's tenth-century collection, *Ishimpō* (in Chinese, *Yixin fang,* The Essentials of Medical Prescriptions), the most concentrated and accessible group of texts available today.[29]

The ars erotica teaches that sexual intercourse can enhance health and promote longevity. As found in its tenth century form, but perhaps dating from the Han, the *Sunü jing* (The Classic of the Essential Woman) quotes the aged but ever vigorous Pengzu, a mythical sage-practitioner, as saying that humans began having shorter lives when they lost the ancient knowledge of the art of sexual intercourse.[30] Ge Hong's fourth-century *Baopuzi* (The Master Who Embraces Simplicity) warns: "Humans cannot be without sexual intercourse; without it they will suffer illness and disease."[31] Such affirmation is then balanced by caution against overindulgence. All texts of the ars erotica would agree with a fifteenth-century work on "nourishing life," *yang sheng* (the art of self-cultivation through ritual, exercise, and nutrition), that sums up both positive and negative aspects of sexual intercourse: "The affairs of the bedchamber can kill and they can give life."[32]

When being cautionary, the ars erotica in fact echoes the history books which warn of the dangers of beautiful women. The *Sunü jing* says that "the woman's superiority over the man is like water's ability to put out fire," the same words occurring later in Ming and Qing fiction. Having sex with a woman is like "riding a galloping horse with a rotten rein," or "nearing a precipice over a deep pit of sharp knives."[33] In issuing these warnings, however, the ars erotica means to sober the man before he approaches the woman, not to scare him away. Instead of condemning the woman's sexual arousal, the bedchamber texts tell men how to conduce and outlast it. In short, despite what is almost admitted as fatal male deficiency, the ars erotica builds intercourse into something completely within the man's control.

Self-control is in fact of prime importance in these texts, which state that both man and woman should "act with proper measure," *jie du*.[34] They should first settle themselves and harmonize their spirits. They should avoid excesses of heat or cold, hunger or fullness.[35] The man should begin by caressing and kissing the woman,[36] then first enter the vagina to a "shallow" (*qian*) point making slow and delicate moves.[37] Then he makes deeper thrusts, all along synchronizing his rhythm with both his breathing and her movements, and alternating between fast and slow, deep and shallow.[38] A similar but less detailed process appears in some works of Ming and Qing fiction. The woman must be the first to attain satisfaction (or "joy," *kuaiyi*).[39] The man should then "withdraw while still alive," *shenghuan,* that is, while still erect and without having ejaculated[40]—few men in Ming and Qing fiction curtail emission.[41] Throughout, the man should be aware of the woman's feelings and movements, that is, all her sexual indications.

Compared to erotic fiction, the works of the art of the bedchamber are decidedly lacking in vulgarity. Besides warning against excess, the texts use language that is itself refined and devoid of ribaldry. In effect, the ars erotica treats what is often regarded as the most obscene subject as if it were not obscene at all, but instead something through which one can cultivate virtue and good health—including the virtue and health of any children one might beget. The ars erotica explicitly models itself after works like the *Li ji* by expounding Confucian virtues such as the "five constants," *wuchang*. Now "benevolence, justice, propriety, trustworthiness, and wisdom" (*ren, yi, li, xin, zhi*) apply to the conduct of the penis. The following passage from the Tang *Yufang mijue* (Secret Formulas of the Jade Chamber), though obscure in some of its language, nevertheless illustrates how the ars erotica makes sex into virtuous behavior. In my translation, I have taken material that might normally be footnoted and have instead kept it bracketed in the text, thus preserving the sense of decipherment that must often attend the reading of such esoteric works. This will also be the first of a number of examples I give of the language of the high erotic (that is, high as in high culture):

> In its true embodiment of the Five Constants, the Jade Stalk resides deep within the hermetic place [when soft within the foreskin?]; it is disciplined and self-controlled; it contains within itself the utmost virtue; it bestows and moves without cease. The interpretation of this behavior of the Jade Stalk is thus: To bestow generously is its benevolence. To have an opening in the middle is its justice [to be "just right" (*yi*, justice) in controlling the flow of semen through the urinary tract?[42]] Having a ridge [*jie*] around its head [top or extremity, *duan*] is its propriety [to be self-disciplined and temperate?; the "ridge" is that of the glans]. To be able to rise when desirous and to stop when desire ceases is its trustworthiness. To lower or raise itself when about to engage in the act is its wisdom [to be able to be gentle or aggressive depending on the circumstances?].[43]

The five virtues named here are all implicitly based on a standard of equilibrium and self-containment. The jade stalk "resides deep within the hermetic place," from which it then "bestows generously," justly, courteously, reliably, and wisely when engaging in the act of sex. Regardless of the obscurity and possible humor of parts of this passage, it is clear that the ideal jade stalk leaves seclusion when it is right to do so and returns when desire ceases, without excess and without loss. The man knows the proper administration of sexual energy. There is no underestimation or overestimation of capacity.

Given the emphasis on self-control in the above passage and many others like it, what is the nature of pleasure in the ars erotica? For the man, the satisfaction of desire is ostensibly replaced by the cultivation of sexual virtue. The guided and at times meditative ("deep within the hermetic place") practice of such virtue supposedly counters the tendency to violent or hasty excitation. By encouraging the man to be conscious of himself and conscientious in his interaction with the woman, in other words, the ars erotica has him turn a blinding urge into an aesthetic act.

The man's pleasure is hardly mentioned; the woman's is minutely analyzed. "To be able to rise when desirous and to stop when desire ceases" implies that whatever occurs in between is assumed and unproblematic. Forestalling his most intense physical pleasure, the man indulges himself only during brief and rare moments of ejaculation, which the ars erotica ignores in favor of describing the woman before, during, and after her climax. Both ars erotica and fiction concentrate on the woman's pleasure by detailing such things as the sounds she makes, the numbness she feels, or the copious flow of her sexual waters. Fiction, however, also tends to add the male climax, which it often describes with the formulaic *yixie ruzhu,* "and he ejaculated in one great torrent."

The relative silence about male pleasure is a prime example of the ars erotica's way of muting male sexual inferiority while elevating sex into a self-contained and repeatable act for the man's benefit. Again, the woman's role and the function of reproduction are reduced and bracketed aside. Within the contained realm of well-engineered intercourse, the ars erotica does imply—although it does not state in so many words—that the woman is a potential threat and that the man is in fact her inferior in sexual capacity. What is the exhortation to curtail emission if not an indirect way of stating that the man's energy and pleasure decrease with frequency of ejaculation? The woman, on the other hand, is portrayed as suffering no such loss. Instead of speaking in terms of pleasure, however, the ars erotica rather construes this alleged variance between the sexes in terms of benefit or harm to the man's health and then teaches him to make up for his sexual vulnerability by applying discipline and skill, mastering knowledge of the woman's sexuality, and believing in the value of intercourse with numerous women. Staying with one woman is in effect viewed as harmful to the man's health and, by implication, as privileging her instead of the man. The assumption is that only by making himself transferable does the man avoid the powers of any one woman and approach his goal, which is not just pleasure anyway, but also increase of vitality and longevity.

The Woman in the Ars Erotica

It would be easy to think that, although the woman supposedly benefits from the man's expertise, her role in the ars erotica is mainly that of a passive recipient of the man's beneficence. In the short run, she enjoys the pleasure guaranteed by the man's skill and endurance; in the long run, she also finds that through regular intercourse her body becomes better tuned and "freed of illness," *chu bing*.[44] In all this she is profoundly other to the man. He must not succumb to her attractions, which he puts out of his mind by, for instance, looking upon the woman as an "enemy" (*dijia*) or as "tile and stone" (*washi*), meanwhile looking upon himself as precious "gold or jade," *jinyu*.[45] In some texts of Taoist sexual alchemy, the man actually tries to defeat the woman-enemy by causing her to have orgasm first and then "stealing" her essence; otherwise, following her own set of yogic practices, she "wins" by stealing essence from him. In the ars erotica, however, looking upon the woman as enemy is mainly a strategy to forestall lack of control or fear of such lack, especially on the part of the inexperienced man. It is still supposed to be the case that both partners benefit from an ultimately harmonious act.

Nevertheless, the woman clearly plays an active role both in controlling herself and affecting the man, even though we gain access to that role mainly by reading against the text. According to prescriptive works on feminine virtue, when outside of the bedchamber, the woman is above all required to be chaste and submissive. She may admonish her husband if she sees him acting unwisely, but she should do nothing more if he ignores her advice. In the bedchamber, on the other hand, she should conform to the same model turned inside out, as it were. That is, she is expected to unleash herself in such a way that she achieves complete satisfaction but without making excessive demands on the man.

How does a woman maneuver both within and beyond the prescribed models of either chaste or voluptuous behavior? In general, in or out of the bedchamber, her influence on the man lies in her ability not only to fulfill his expectations but also to define them and to exert her own. She may be with a man who himself feels constrained by prescriptive models and dislikes submissive women. With a less accommodating man, the woman may resort to strategies by which, for example, she satisfies him by allowing him to feel he is a good partner. She captivates him by engaging in perversions that play to his mastery or by convincing him that the intensity of her love and arousal exceeds that of other women. She may practice the women's ars erotica, which besides telling her how to please or subdue the man also teaches her to protect herself by doing such thing as "locking the 'gate of spring'" and thereby suppressing her loss of vital energy. A set of rites and exercises exists to help her re-strengthen her "original *qi*," which has declined since the commencement of menses,[46] and which declines even further if she is not careful during intercourse and childbirth (the female ars erotica, briefly appearing in some of the texts mentioned above, occurs in forms supposedly intended for the use of nuns and other solo women practitioners of sexual yoga; prostitutes also had arts of handling men).[47]

Moreover, in addition to the control she may exert over her flow of *qi*, she also enjoys the privileges extended to her by virtue of her reproductive capacity. Although she must rely on good luck, she may reward the man by becoming pregnant and bearing him a son—in the case of a concubine sometimes thereby becoming the most prestigious woman in the household. As mother the woman has the advantage of control over the early upbringing of her children, whom she influences in ways not necessarily in accord with patriarchal wishes. If as main wife she fails to have a son, she is nevertheless considered the chief mother in charge of the upbringing of an adopted son or one born of a concubine, who normally enters the family only after a ritual vow of submission to the primary wife. All the woman's capacities combine to make up her tools of social engagement, which include resistance to the man's and others' domination over her. The dynamics of such relations, though more apparent in later works, are already implicit in the ars erotica texts I discuss here and in the next chapter.

The ars erotica has the woman assuming an ostensibly active role in one situation, that in which she is personified as Sunü, "Essential Woman,"[48] the Yellow Emperor's teacher of sexual arts (in the second-century B.C. Mawangdui texts, the teachers of sexual arts are men; in the later *Ishimpō* and *Sunü miaolun* they are women). It is she who tells the emperor that the more intercourse he has with young women the better. Her main role is to bolster his sexual confidence and instruct him in being considerate of women and interpreting their various sexual indications.[49] The job of reassuring and advising the man is not as subordinate as it might appear. We may imagine a woman taking the opportunity to mold the man's interpretations of both herself and other women, and thereby imposing her will upon him. Being given the role of mysterious other, she has only to realize how far she can or wants to go in teaching the dependent man about the needs and desires of women. His less than total self-possession makes him both needful of the woman and vulnerable to her.

The threat of female influence is in fact thematic throughout Chinese history and is the subject of warnings in the ars erotica. But these warnings have the ultimate effect of superficially shunting the dangers aside. In a reductive categorization of harmful women, the sex treatises list the sexual-somatic indications of women who are to be shunned, the so-called malignant women, *enü*.[50] They have ugly and inauspicious features that cause men harm—for example, coarse skin, masculine voice, large mouth, coarse and long pubic hairs, malodorous underarms, inability to have orgasm, excess sexual waters, and coldness of the vagina—many of which appear as negative signs in later literature and folk wisdom as well.[51] Jealous women are also to be avoided, advice that historical and fictional polygamists are frequently unable to follow.[52] In general, as I will discuss in the next chapter, the ars erotica assumes that threatening and polluting women exist but that they are easily singled out and then excluded.

At the same time, both the numerous taboos against sexual intercourse and the long list of undesirable features in women make the possibility of perfect union seem rather remote (taboos—*jinji*—include those against intercourse when too hungry or full, drunk, worried, nervous, too cold or hot, during violent weather, and so forth).[53] In other words, the ars erotica limits its guarantee of perfect coition by providing a long list of restrictions which narrow the definition and perception of desirable relations. In short, few conditions and few women meet the man's ideal expectations. The more remote the ideal is made to appear, the more control the setters of definitions have over supposed passage to that ideal—thus the industries of producing erotic albums and manuals, supplying sexual paraphernalia (including aphrodisiacs), interpreting facial and bodily features, professing sexual wisdom, selecting and procuring women and men for polygamous customers, and so forth.

The Aesthetics of Technique

Once the right conditions prevail and intercourse finally begins, the ars erotica has a capacity for intricacy that recalls the regimes of etiquette of the *Li ji* and other texts of ancient ritual. The most notably intricate and stylized behavior is found in thrusting techniques and body positions. "To act in proper measure" (*jie du*) not only means to be temperate but also never to act irregularly or unconsciously. The man counts his thrusts and periodically alternates their depth and rhythm. He and the woman engage in positions which have names, choreographies, and health and pleasure functions. The adoption of formulaic positions in intercourse distantly recalls the "battle formations" (*zhen*) of ancient military strategy, or the stances in martial arts and *taijiquan*. Examples of the names of positions are: "low-branched pine tree" (*yan gai song,* intercourse with the woman on her back hugging the man with her arms and legs) or "dark cicada cleaving to a branch" (*xuanchan fu,* intercourse with the man entering from a superior position behind).[54] Few if any of these high erotic terms appear in fiction, which rarely refers to positions by name, but when it does, it echoes the above imagism with more explicitly kinetic euphemisms, such as "pushing the boat along with the current" (*shun shui tui zhou*), that is, intercourse with the man in the superior position; "putting out the prone candle" (*dao jiao la*), intercourse with the woman in the superior position; and "taking the fire from the other side of the mountain" (*ge shan qu huo*), vaginal intercourse from behind. These three correspond to three of the four basic positions of the ars erotica, which, however, lists as many as thirty elaborations; the fourth position, which occurs more rarely in fiction, has the couple lying side by side.[55]

The most commonly mentioned thrusting technique of the ars erotica is "nine shallow and one deep" (*jiuqian yishen*). According to the *Sunü miaolun,* the application of this method is based on a calculation of what is too deep or too shallow for the benefit of the man or woman.[56] Fiction uses the same term with moderate frequency but without the detail found in the ars erotica, which also gives variations rarely found in fiction such as "eight deep and six shallow" or "five shallow and six deep."[57] Erotic novels, moreover, tend to use their own (presumably vernacular) term for thrusting, *chousong,* literally, "pull out and send in."[58]

Applying the wisdom of the art of the bedchamber, the polygamist should preside over a family of happy women with whom he engages in artful and detailed sexual gymnastics. Enjoyment of good health and pleasure, not love or passion, is the main motivation. As said above, the raw pleasure of the senses is supplemented and even replaced by the stylized execution of positions and techniques of thrusting. The sexual act is interspersed with lyric moments such as when the "jade stalk," *yujing,* has not yet entered the "cinnabar cleft," *danxue.* The penis then is like a "humble pine tree opposite a deep cave"; the vagina, already aroused, gives forth waters that are "like a hidden spring issuing from a deep valley."[59] Despite the fact that fiction hardly quotes the ars erotica and only uses a few of its terms regularly, the general tone and style of such high erotic passages continues through the Qing, as will be seen in translations later on, even in works which are otherwise condemning of sexual pleasure.

The Ars Erotica in Ming, Qing Fiction

Although capable of occasional lyric moments himself, the first major fictional polygamist, Ximen Qing, consults the ars erotica only once and repeatedly acts contrary to its teachings.[60] Erotic albums and books on the arts of the bedchamber appear in relatively few Ming and Qing novels and stories, while none of the treatises discussed above show up at all;[61] the term for "art of the bedchamber," *fangzhong shu*, is likewise rare. The model polygamist of the ars erotica appears mainly in Qing erotic romances, in several of which he learns the secret arts orally from an adept monk. The contents of the arts appear in brief excerpts only, sometimes merely consisting of an aphrodisiac.[62] In episodes about wastrel polygamists, the teachings of the ars erotica are for the most part evident indirectly and negatively, such as in portrayals of the danger to the man of lascivious or jealous women or in descriptions of a man's death or illness because, as in Ximen Qing's case, of excess discharge of semen and/or overuse of aphrodisiacs.

The mid-seventeenth-century *Rou putuan* (Prayer Mat of Flesh, also known as the Carnal Prayer Mat) is one of the few Ming and Qing works to affirm the ars erotica. The narrator condones the health-giving properties of sexual intercourse, saying that sex is like a medicine which "can't be taken too rarely, nor too often; one should neither dislike it, nor like it too much."[63] *Rou putuan* also quotes from what may have been an erotic picture album of the time portraying the stages of intercourse in the same high-erotic style as the ars erotica discussed above. The album goes by a generic name, "album of spring in the palace" (*chungong cezi*, ch. 3, 19b–22a), and contains thirty-six illustrations.[64] To be sure, the hero of *Rou putuan* soon forgets the wisdom of temperance and takes woman after woman in a series of illicit conquests that end in his utter repudiation of sexual desire.

A manual with erotic pictures appears in a later Qing novel, *Nao huacong* (Ruckus in the Flowering Bushes), in which it goes by another generic name, "album of spring desire," *chunyi pu*. It is perhaps the kind intended to assist newlyweds and other initiates, like the one in *Rou putuan*, but in this case it is merely designated as "something to cure drowsiness."[65] The manual details the three positions listed above ("pushing the boat along with the current," etc.), thus using language which, along with words such as *chousong* ("thrusting") and various colloquialisms for the genitals, are characteristic of vernacular fiction but not the high erotic.

It should be noted that esoteric Taoism and Buddhism contain what can be roughly thought of as a third set of terms for sexual practice besides those of the high (or literary) erotic and vernacular fiction. This set uses words like "selecting the tripod," *ze ding*, that is, finding a suitable female partner; "stove," *lu*, the vagina; or "the battle of absorption," *caizhan*, the practice of stealing or absorbing the other's vital essence during intercourse. Another important concept is "returning semen," *hui jing*, to the *nihuan* point inside the head behind the eyes, that is, the practice of redirecting seminal energy up through the backbone to the head. Found in the ars erotica as well, this concept is also called "returning *jing* [seminal essence or energy] to supplement the brain," *huan jing bu nao*, an expression that occurs as early as the late Eastern Han.[66] These and other Taoist or Buddhist terms and ideas were current in the Ming and Qing and also appear in fiction but, like terms such as "nine shallow and one deep," not often and not in a meticulously applied way. Fiction tends instead to concentrate on descriptions of the woman's beautiful body, her sexual reactions, and such things as the sheer number of thrusts, which usually go into the hundreds and thousands (a poor performance is under a hundred[67] or only a few hundred).[68] Thrusting also includes intervals for changes of position, rhythm, and sometimes partners, thus vaguely reflecting the teaching of the ars erotica and, in the last instance in particular, repeating the recommendation to switch partners frequently, as in the motto "to have intercourse with as many young women as one can."

Regardless of the relatively inarticulate influence of the art of the bedchamber on erotic fiction, it is clear that oral and written discourses on intercourse and sexual alchemy were current throughout the Ming and Qing. Some works included illustrations, most notably the elaborate multicolor albums of the late Ming, the time of the first great surge of erotic fiction. For our purposes below, the significance of the ars erotica lies in (1) the way in which it captures the image of a successful sexual hero and in (2) how fiction takes roughly the same hero and either undoes or improves upon him. The ars erotica must be assumed as part of the main picture of sexuality in China, though certainly not as the prime or most influential source of erotic lore. It can be seen as crystallizing a polygynist utopia that is elsewhere displaced because of official censorship and social pressure, which includes female opposition to (or manipulation within) polygyny. The ars erotica in turn exercises its own censorship by ignoring the mutually related problems of jealousy and the impossibility of keeping the sexual arts secret among men.

Polygamy in *Jin Ping Mei* and Other Late Ming Fiction

The Wastrel Polygamist in Jin Ping Mei

In Chinese literary history, *Jin Ping Mei* (Golden Lotus, also known as The Plum in the Golden Vase) provides an unprecedented and never again equaled amount of detail on the sexual life of a polygamous household.[69] Later fiction is highly imitative of *Jin Ping Mei* in character portrayal, situation, and theme. In what follows I will summarize the depiction of polygamy in *Jin Ping Mei* and other late Ming works by addressing the following points: the defense of or attack upon the system of polygamy, how the man treats his women, they him, and the women each other.

Ximen Qing's death under the body of the lustful Pan Jinlian is due to his failure to listen to warnings. The ars erotica would tell him: "Woman's superiority over man is like water's ability to put out fire."[70] Wu the sorcerer tells Ximen Qing: "One must avoid excess of *yin*-waters."[71] The narrator addresses the reader in chapter 14: "From ancient times the man rules the outer precincts, the woman rules the inner. In most cases the reason a woman ruins a man's reputation is ignorance on the man's part of the right way to control women" (ch. 14, 7b). The word "control" (*yu*) in this quotation, occurs in both the ars erotica and fiction in the sense of "have intercourse with,"[72] the root meaning of *yu* being to "drive" a chariot, and hence to control.[73] In *Jin Ping Mei*, the promiscuous polygynist Ximen Qing is instead "ridden" by his concubine Pan Jinlian, who sits astride him as he dies of the fatal dose of aphrodisiac that she has accidentally given him (ch. 79, 9ab). *Qi*, "to ride (a horse)," is the word used in this scene and in an earlier one in which she sits astride her former husband Wu Da after poisoning him (ch. 5, 8ab). Ximen Qing's failure to understand the art of "driving" comprises his failure not only to control individual women in intercourse but also to manage them as a group. His greatest mistake in such management is in fact one of the worst a polygamist can commit: favoritism and thus failure to treat his wives equally.

Ximen Qing can be characterized as a handsome, rich, ill-educated upstart who acquires woman after woman not to enhance his and their health but to build a small empire in which he can reign as indulgently as possible. An orphan, he is outside the filial structure, responsible to no one, and thus, in the moralistic view, all the more likely to commit transgressions. However, miniature sexual emperor though he may be, he is not the worst of such types in Chinese fiction. In spite of the fact that he abuses women, he does not go so far as to kidnap and rape them or brutally injure them during intercourse. He is simply the *da jiba dada* (ch. 50, 5b), the sometimes benevolent but often bad-tempered and cruel "big daddy prick," as one of his paramours calls him. He takes care of his women as long as they don't cross him by sleeping with other men or making too many demands upon him.

Unlike the man in the ars erotica, who appears only in a sexual context, Ximen Qing is unable to rely on his penis alone. Money and material comfort are his chief means of control over women. The promise of reward leads married women to have affairs with him and, in one case, induces a husband to become a willing cuckold. To Ximen Qing, money buys moral compensation, as he indicates when boasting that he could buy pardon from heaven for whatever crimes he commits (ch. 57, 9b–10a).

The relations that money buys are conveniently ephemeral and nonbinding to the rich man. Pan Jinlian observes, "All of us in this family are love-mates of the dewdrop" (ch. 12, 12a), that is, *lushui fuqi*, an expression referring to illicit love matches, which are as ephemeral as the dew. *Jin Ping Mei* is a picture of the world without the *Li ji*, with no standards except the rule of the rich man and his nonstandard of "lovemates of the dewdrop." That the man is the buyer and never the one bought is something that Pan Jinlian also affirms when she says, "Even ten women couldn't buy for keeps one man's heart" (ch. 23, 10a).

As to his good qualities, Ximen Qing can be said to work hard to please his women in sex, though he must increasingly rely on aphrodisiacs and "sex tools" (*yinqi*) to achieve his goal. He is also capable of humbling himself before women, as when he tries to reconcile his differences with his main wife Yueniang: "He knelt down as low as a dwarf and, like a chicken held by the neck before being finished off, pleaded with her up and down" (ch. 21, 2b). He also knows sentiment and sorrow, as when he is grief-stricken over Song Huilian's or Li Pinger's deaths.

But in the end "he has a bad temper" (ch. 19, 12a). He sins in each of the Four Vices—Drink, Lust, Greed, and Anger. Because of his cruelty to women, he has the reputation of being "the chief of wife-beaters, the leader in treachery to women" (ch. 17, 9b). He is cruel to servants, as when he beats the boy Xiao Tieguner because of the loss of a woman's sleep slipper (ch. 28), or when he commits adultery with Song Huilian and has her husband Lai Wang put in jail and then exiled (ch. 26).

Shrew and lascivious woman in one, Pan Jinlian is the female version of the person of bad temper. She beats and scolds servants and assigns them unusual punishments, as when she has Qiuju "kneel in the courtyard with a stone balanced on her head" (ch. 28, 2b–4a). Pan Jinlian is an example of the dangerous jealous woman briefly warned about in the ars erotica. She allows Ximen Qing to sleep with other women but in the end must have the greatest share of his attention. As a woman she cannot abuse the man as he does her, but she has her own forms of abuse, such as throwing tantrums, speaking insolently, or plotting secretly to harm her rivals for his favor. Once when he shows up after a long hiatus, she accuses him of "liking the new and rejecting the old" and calls him a "cursed heart-breaker." She then "picks his hat off his head and throws it on the floor" (ch. 8, 7a). She also attempts to captivate him by using the sexual methods mentioned above: for example, by engaging in the perversion of allowing him to urinate in her mouth (the narrator intrudes at this point to assert that a main wife would never do such a thing—ch. 72, 11ab), by using to her own advantage the sexual paraphernalia and aphrodisiacs that he introduces,[74] and in general by making herself seem more devoted to him than any other woman.

Such portrayals of the polygamous family do not necessarily indicate the author's opposition to polygamy; his opinion is never so clear. Perhaps his premise is that if Ximen Qing knew the way of "controlling" or "driving" women and lived a moderate life, he would have a good household. But the author also delivers the message that desire is always greater than the capacity to fulfill it (as stated at Ximen Qing's death, ch. 79, 9b). Other novels and stories are more explicit in their affirmation of polygamy or monogamy.

Arguments for and against Polygamy

Jin Ping Mei alone could serve as a textbook about what can go wrong with polygamy. Other late Ming works contain actual statements about why polygamy is wrong and cannot work. For example, the theme of a late 1620s story by Ling Mengchu is that "sexual desire in man and woman is the same. A man relying on his energy alone to accommodate several women is already going too far, all the more so if he is a rich middle-aged man who must, as he inevitably will, have the most beautiful young women for concubines. . . . How can he possibly keep them satisfied?" The problem is not only one of a man's limited energy, about which Chinese medical science and the ars erotica already warn, but also the danger of sexually unfulfilled women. As Ling Mengchu says, the polygamist can "contain [the women's] bodies but not their hearts; as soon as there is the slightest chance, they will try to play with someone else."[75] Another of Ling's stories promotes the view that widowers should be as chaste as widows, who are honored in the Ming and Qing for not re-marrying after their husbands die (*Erke* story 11). Although it does not mention polygamy, the story implicitly condemns the betrayal of monogamous love, whether by man or woman, either in death or life.[76]

The late Ming author Fang Ruhao's three novels, *Chan Zhen yishi* (Lost Tales of the True Way), *Chan Zhen houshi* (Later Tales of the True Way), and *Dongdu ji* (also called *Dongyou ji,* Passage to the East), all contain critical and satirical portraits of polygamy. One of the clearest statements comes from *Dongdu ji:* "In the matching of *yin* and *yang* and in the marriage between man and woman, only one husband and one wife should live in the house. Who allowed the man to take more than his share? [lit., while enjoying one, be looking at another]. What if in taking more than his share he ends up causing another man to remain a widower?"[77] In this instance, polygamy is construed not as an injustice to women but as an unfair distribution among men of the male privilege of having a wife and therefore continuing one's line of descent.

Criticism of polygamy also appears in fiction about shrewish wives, although such works usually end with the shrew's defeat and the promotion of the benefits of polygamy (see chapter 3). A woman is called a shrew in these works mainly because of her hatred of polygamy. She rages at the man's promiscuity and at his irresponsibility in managing family wealth, especially when he spends money on women not of his home. She claims that monogamy is a set standard, asking, If men can have lovers, why can't women? She also complains that because of the risk of pregnancy, a woman suffers more than a man if she is promiscuous. Ming and Qing novels portray her using bizarre methods to prevail over the man and eliminate female rivals: she stamps the man's penis with a mark which, if smudged, proves he has had a secret liaison; she uses black magic to cause rivals to go mad. Her power is so great that men form "wife-fearers clubs" to commiserate over their subjection to shrewish wives.

When the shrew is finally defeated, she realizes the good points of polygamy, such as, with more than one wife, each woman's danger of childbirth is reduced; or, although often left alone by the working or traveling husband and cut off from family and friends outside, wives can form friendships among themselves and keep each other company; or, with a number of beautiful women at home, the man is less inclined to seek diversion with women outside. *Jin Ping Mei*'s Meng Yulou voices a similar view when she considers Ximen Qing's marriage proposal. When she learns that he is already married, she says: "Even if he has a main wife, I'd as soon have her be elder sister while I humbly be the younger. Though he may have many wives, still, in the end, the man will be happier" (ch. 7, 9a). She is an example of the smart nonshrew. When she learns of Ximen Qing's bad temper, she replies: "Although a man may be cruel, he won't strike a wife who is prudent and untroublesome. As long as I do my job well and keep inner affairs from going out and outer affairs from coming in, he won't dare touch me" (ch. 7, 9ab).

An Overview

I end this chapter with a brief summary of the works covered in this book, continuing as above to frame the representation of sexuality in terms of arguments for and against polygamy. In the early to mid-Qing, novels appear which portray ideal conjugality, both monogamous and polygamous. Many works avoid sexual description altogether, implying or actually articulating a condemnation of obscene fiction. Among these "chaste" novels are the numerous scholar-beauty romances that begin to appear in the mid-seventeenth century. They feature self-determined love matches, monogamy or else a limited two-wife polygyny, and superior women who are as good as or better than men in intelligence, courage, and moral fiber.

In contrast with the chaste romances, the erotic ones tell of benevolent polygamists and their beautiful, sexy wives. These novels retain vestiges of the independent and superior woman but deprive her of her mobility outside the home and of her exclusive right to one man. Moreover, hierarchy among wives is now firmly in place, with the chaster, higher-class women at the top, the sexier, lower-class ones below. Even so, once he establishes his family, the hero of the erotic romance ceases having extramarital affairs. He is generous to his women and has consummate sexual skills which allow him to give enough love to all. It is as if the man is a dispenser of sexual welfare and domestic security in a society of few good men. The characters of the Qing erotic romance, in short, are like late embodiments of the artful players of the ancient ars erotica.

Having laid out the contrast between chaste and erotic romances, I will then place two works at the center of this study, the mid-Qing *Yesou puyan* and *Honglou meng,* each representing lengthy and complex workings-out of the chaste-erotic polarity. *Yesou puyan* presents one of the strongest defenses of polygamy to be found in Chinese literature, yet it strictly limits its eroticism by condemning deviant, orgasmic sexuality and by virtually disavowing the ars erotica. *Yesou puyan* is about a polygamist superman, Wen Suchen, who rids China of heterodoxy and restores the empire to orthodox Confucianism. Under the supervision of his sagely widow-mother, he collects a bevy of wives, including specialists in mathematics, medicine, poetry, and military science. He is sexually powerful in that he has strong *yang* energy, by which he manages to beget many sons, but believes in procreation only and shuns sex for pleasure. He evenly regulates cohabitation with his wives and maintains close, congenial relations with them all. *Yesou puyan's* hero is a super-correction of the bad polygamist Ximen Qing.

In contrast to *Yesou puyan* and other works about successful polygamists, *Honglou meng* presents as problematic a male hero and potential polygamist as can be found in Chinese literature. Jia Baoyu might be a polygamist except that doing so would cause too much pain to the woman he loves most, Lin Daiyu. He becomes far more intimate with her than the customs of a proper household should allow. In the end, since he cannot bear to have caused the pain which leads to her death, he abdicates the throne of patriarchal, polygamist heir, becoming a monk and abandoning his pregnant wife Baochai and his chamber-wife Xiren.

The same theme of the superiority of women found in the chaste romances continues in *Honglou meng,* now accompanied by a naive critique of men. The boy Jia Baoyu finds male lust repulsive; he thinks women are pure, especially before marriage, after which most are doomed to marry filthy men and become polluted themselves. Such a critique of men is already implicit in the romances which glorify monogamy and portray superior women who choose their own husbands. In *Honglou meng,* however, such self-determined love is impossible since the choice of the elders prevails over that of the youths.

After the chapters on *Yesou puyan* and *Honglou meng,* the next three will continue the study of the wastrel, concentrating on the process of his self-ruination and on his relations with the women who are closest to him—for example, the self-sacrificing wife and lascivious concubine (*Lin Lan Xiang*), the doting mother (*Qilu deng*), and the prostitute (*Lüye xianzong*). Two more chapters then discuss novels that represent blithe corrections of characters like Ximen Qing and Jia Baoyu (*Shenlou zhi* and *Ernü yingxiong zhuan*). In their polygamous fantasies, these works reflect, in part by denying, the decline evident in the period in which they appear, the early to mid-nineteenth century, which ends with the fall of the empire and the eventual disappearance of polygamy.

The miser and especially the shrew appear in a large number of works, in some cases as the main or one of the main characters. To repeat, besides the hoarder of money and the usurer that he is in his most literal form, the miser is also the ascetic, the orthodox pedant, the keeper of semen, or the shunner of women. Likewise, the polygamist is more than a man married to several women; he is also a wastrel, a spoiled or coddled son, a lecher, or a charming philanderer. Finally, the shrew is not merely the jealous woman but also the angry and resentful woman, the dominant woman, the demonic and polluting woman, or the lustful and sexually powerful woman.

3

SHREWS AND JEALOUSY

IN SEVENTEENTH- AND EIGHTEENTH-CENTURY

VERNACULAR FICTION

The *pofu* or "shrew" is in literal translation a "scattering woman," one who "spills" and "splashes," *po,* and in general acts in ways that make men lose face. In Qing fiction she frightens the man into submission by making him live in fear of her volatile temper. She refuses to serve the normative family order. Wishing to control the man and overpower all female rivals (co-wives, mothers-in-law, or sisters-in-law), she opposes polygamy even if the family becomes extinct because she bears no son.

In the portrayals of her attacks upon her husband, she can be seen symbolically as both a polluting force and a castrating one, the two of which sometimes overlap. The symbolism of pollution derives from the *po* ("to scatter") of *pofu,* in which what is scattered is left unnamed. Depending on the context, that which is scattered is either literal (or figurative) body fluids or else pollution metaphorically expressed as rage and jealousy. Her power also derives from an alleged sexual insatiability, which is often designated by the word *yin* of *yinfu,* "flooding" or "lascivious woman" (*yin* like *po* also carries the water radical).[1] In the novels examined in this book, "scattering" generally takes the form of jealous rage, authors for the most part repressing or displacing the image of female effluvia in its aspect as something vile and polluting.[2] Similarly, castration mainly takes the displaced forms of, for example, beating, slapping, and hair pulling, although in several instances it manifests itself in actual policing or attempted amputation of the penis. Regardless of specific manifestations, the power of the shrew is held to count for a wide variety of consequences, the most basic of which is the weakening of the man and male privilege in general.

The shrew can be looked at in two ways. First, she is simply a woman who roars at men and other family members who threaten her. Second, however, she is also a product of male imagination, which considers the woman's energy—especially her anger and desire—to be inexhaustible; the man, feeling suddenly passive and inept, is afraid of her and submits—thus the henpecked husband or the impotent man, both unaware of any reason except nature that might have caused the woman to be the way she is. In other words, in one sense the woman becomes shrewish because she is forced into more constrained positions than the man; in another sense she is shrewish by virtue of the man's alienation from her, which is manifested in his ineptness and fear of her. In either case, he "produces" the shrew, even if he thinks she appears on her own through no fault of his. Of course, men try to avoid the shrew by pretending she is not there. The polygamist finds new and submissive or opportunistic women; the miser retreats to bitter solitude and replaces women and children with money; the ascetic practices monasticism or retreats to carefree eremitism and reportedly enjoys the here and now. Both miser and ascetic share a dedication to frugality of desire; both cease giving to women and conserve male essence for their personal programs of "nourishing life," *yang sheng.*

As divergent as they may be, the miser and the shrew are both cast-offs of the central system of "nourishing life," that is, the ancestor-worshipping, kin-oriented family. They act on their own and are unable or refuse to participate in that family. "Nourishing life," usually a term for regimes devoted to personal health and longevity, is stretched here to apply to the regime of the normative family described in chapter 1. In that regime, one "nourishes" the "life" of one's dead ancestors. That is, in all activities, one ultimately strives to please not the self, not the spouse, not even merely the father and mother, but the dead ancestors. The correct polygamist has more than one wife not to satisfy his or their sexual desires but to ensure the birth of a son who will continue performing rituals for the father and his dead ancestors.

As castoffs from the normative order, the miser and shrew also represent desperate attempts to survive. The lecherous polygamist hardly worries about survival. The temperate polygamist, on the other hand, is the exemplary model in between miser and libertine. The moderate, temperate man, whether or not polygamous, loves virtue as much as or more than he loves women (as Confucius would have it);[3] he keeps aloof from wife and children, especially sons;[4] he retains semen and controls passions. The temperate man can be viewed as a moderate and reasonable miser. The actual miser, in contrast, is the full-blown male conserver of energy, interested in personal survival only, negligent of family and ancestors. The shrew, threatened badly enough with being passed over by the temperate man, is yet more threatened by the miser, the ascetic, and the promiscuous polygamist, all of whom cast her utterly aside. She is the loudest of all these characters, desperate yet vigorous in life energy since she refuses to take the honored path of thwarted and mistreated women, virtuous self-sacrifice and ultimately suicide.

Finally, the miser and shrew exemplify a reversal of the normal order of gender. As will be elaborated in chapters 4 and 5 below, in both aberrant and super-ideal societies as construed in Qing fiction, men become womenlike and women become menlike. The shrew is a *yang*-woman, the miser a *yin*-man. They defy the orthodox division between inner woman and outer man by attempting to take over each other's territory. The shrew "scatters" and "splashes," trying to control the man's outer activities and replace him as tyrant. The miser contracts and appropriates the woman's inner territory, from which he controls the world through debt-collecting usury.

The definitions of miser and shrew that I use cast this pair into abstract extremes that never appear as such in Ming and Qing fiction; the miser and shrew rarely even appear as a couple in these works. Novels instead focus on concrete characteristics, that is, the indomitable jealousy of the shrew and the incorrigible avarice of the miser. These characteristics are the subject of numerous literary works, a sampling of which I will examine below. The shrew will be discussed first since she receives a greater amount of attention in fiction than the miser—less only, in fact, than the wastrel polygamist. After a reexamination of the ars erotica in light of the shrew story, my focus will be on the arguments presented in seventeenth- and eighteenth-century fiction justifying or condemning the shrewish woman and upholding or criticizing polygamy and male sexual privilege. The works covered include *Liaodu yuan* (The Cure for Jealousy), *Chan Zhen yishi* (Lost Tales of the True Way), *Xingshi yinyuan zhuan* (Marriage Fate to Arouse the World), and *Cu hulu* (Gourd of Vinegar). Although the focus will be on the shrew in the context of polygamy, other contexts also exist, such as those of shrewish mothers-in-law who refuse to countenance their daughters-in-law or shrewish daughters-in-law who defy their mothers-in-law, in neither case of which is the husband necessarily a polygamist.[5] But all cases feature both the shrew vying with other women and the man abjectly submitting to the shrew.

Jealous Wives and Henpecked Husbands

Women's jealousy and the lengths to which it goes have been the subjects of story and commentary for many centuries in China. The seventh-century Tang encyclopedia *Yiwen leiju* (Classified Sourcebook for Literary Composition) has a lengthy entry for *du*,[6] including quotes from numerous earlier sources about famous jealous women and the nature of jealousy; for example, "If there is no jealousy, then descendants will be plentiful."[7] In the Ming and Qing dynasties, numerous plays, at least three novels, and a number of classical and vernacular stories are devoted to the shrew, called *pofu* (also *hanfu*, the "fierce" woman), and her attempts to avenge herself on men. As Yenna Wu has written, it is in the seventeenth century that the shrew turns from being a subject of joke and anecdote to being that of "full-blown comedy and satire" in the form of fiction and drama.[8]

A late Ming story in the *Xihu erji* (Stories of West Lake) collection begins with this generalization: "No one in the world can be more jealous than a woman. Her type of jealousy truly defies the imagination; there is nothing she will not do, no lengths to which she will not go."[9] The story tells about a Tang dynasty judge, Pei Xuan, who had a secret liaison with a maid; his wife had the maid killed, the maid's genitals cut off, and forced Pei Xuan to wear the piece of flesh on his face when he went to court. People joked about the incident, wondering whether he wore the piece of flesh horizontally, in which case his mouth would show through, or vertically, in which case his nose would show through.

The drift of this and other anecdotes about shrewish jealousy is to aver the ubiquity of the problem and, despite macabre outcomes, to record the amazement or laughter aroused in readers and spectators. But amazement or laughter trivialize what other works portray as a far-reaching problem. As the prologue to the novel *Xingshi yinyuan zhuan* (Marriage Fate to Arouse the World, circa mid- to late seventeenth century) states, there is no love or hate greater than that between man and woman.[10] The man who abuses his sexual privilege and mistreats a woman will be sure to suffer her revenge in this or the next life. Most works vindicate the man and show the woman to be afflicted by an aberrant humor of which she is eventually cured. But despite the fact that the blame falls more heavily on the woman, the man is never portrayed as entirely innocent and may, in fact, be the cause of her ill humor.[11]

The woman's complaints about the man's behavior and her inferior social status take the form of stinging diatribes and lists of grievances. Sequestered in the home, manipulated and exchanged by a kinship system based on exogamy, explicitly defined as inferior to men, the *pofu* gives vent to an anger that defies Confucian hypocrisy and expresses itself in actions and harangues that render men utterly submissive. Hers is the kind of chaos-making behavior that fiction writers and dramatists are most fond of portraying; they thrive especially on the portrayal of the abject and submissive man, even though they vindicate him in the end.

One of the woman's main complaints is that she is restricted to a single sexual partner, while a man may have many. At one extreme, her husband is promiscuous and has secret liaisons with maids or women outside the home, regardless of whether or not the wife bears him a son. At another extreme, he is faithfully monogamous, but she fails to bear him a son—in fiction, barrenness is often the fate of the shrew. Since the patrilineal family must have sons to carry on the family line, the man may humbly ask his wife to allow him to take a concubine. If she is a virtuous wife, he will not need to ask, although he might do so out of deference. The *pofu,* on the other hand, may indeed procure a concubine for her husband but will find him a *shinü,* as in *Cu hulu* (ch. 6), that is, a woman with an impenetrable vagina; or she may plot to murder the concubine her husband arranges for himself.[12] In any case, the *pofu*'s fury causes the husband to live in daily fear of her, although he still tends to deceive her whenever he can.

These novels propose three general solutions. The first is for the man to realize responsibility for his fate and to understand that enmity between husband and wife is predestined. In *Xingshi yinyuan zhuan,* didactic asides reiterate that every detail of life is predetermined; every action, every mouthful of food, and every drop of water is a calculated quantity. In drawing water from the well, take no more than is allotted; spillage causes a lessening of good fortune. In this miserly logic of predetermination, the individual is responsible for himself, and that self may stretch from one life to the next. The man thus suffers from a shrewish wife because in a previous life he mistreated her or other women. In the logic of the conservation of essences, he spilled semen recklessly and allowed too many women to have too much claim over him.

A second solution to the problem of the shrew draws upon legends about the cure of jealousy by means of medicine or food—a thick soup, for example, called *geng*, as seen in the popular late Ming play by Wu Bing (died ca. 1647), *Liaodu geng* (The Jealousy-curing Soup).[13] Other cures include the leaves of a tree, the *zhimu*, and the flesh of a bird, the *canggeng*, a type of oriole.[14] In the oriole prescription, it is said that a "jealousy stone," *dushi*, grows inside the woman and increases in size until she can be cured only by eating the flesh of this bird. By the logic of the cure, the jealous woman is merely ill, will soon see the wrongfulness of her behavior, and will accept the virtuous, fertile concubine. Such is the outcome for the shrews who fail to bear sons in both *Cu hulu* and *Liaodu yuan*.

A third solution is transcendence, as proposed in a treatise entitled *Papo jing* (Sutra of Wife-fearing) appended at the end of *Cu hulu*. A man suffers from *ju nei*, "fear of the inner one," his wife, because "he has wallowed in the river of love" (1a). "Seeking women," *qiu po*, inevitably leads to "fearing women," *pa po* (2ab). There are degrees of liberation from this affliction. An average enlightened man sleeps in the same bed with the woman, but under "another blanket," *yibei;* a superior man sleeps in "another bed" altogether, *yichuang* (this idea and these words already occur in Tang and Song texts); the next higher man "forgets physicality," *wang xing;* and the most enlightened man acts as if "no woman were present at all," *shi wu you po* (3ab). In short, the man's only way of avoiding subjection to the woman is to become progressively less aware of her.[15]

Whatever the solution, the problem is presented in formulaic, conditional terms: if the woman is jealous or shrewish, then the man is fearful of her. A fuller definition of *pa po* or *ju nei*, the male affliction complementary to female jealousy, is as follows: he is intimidated by her, dreads upsetting her, seeks to keep her happy, and can in no way escape her clutches as long as he is in her territory, the home, to which he always returns. But despite his subjection to her, he still tries to escape and cheat on her. Once he is away from home, "it can't be helped—the chicken-stealing cat can never change its ways."[16] These stories imply that all men, even gods and immortals, are *ju nei*. If this is so, then we can read a well-known statement of Confucius as an indirect reference to the wife-fearing syndrome: "The Master said, 'In one's household, it is the women and the small men that are difficult to deal with. If you let them get too close, they become insolent. If you keep them at a distance, they complain.' "[17]

As for the wife's perspective on all this, she has fewer legal and customary rights than men, is often considered best left uneducated, and is subordinate to her husband and her mother-in-law. She is pressured by rivalry with other wives of her husband or his brothers. She is deprived of financial independence in that, for example, she cannot take her dowry with her if she becomes a widow and remarries, nor can she inherit any of her natal family's wealth or property. All these conditions fuel the fires of shrewish behavior. As the prologue to *Xingshi yinyuan zhuan* states, there is no escape from this fury, no law that can control it, and no one on earth who can intercede between an estranged husband and wife. "She takes a dull knife, unsharpened for centuries, and saws it back and forth across your neck, so that you feel each and every long, drawn-out stroke."[18]

As a Taoist counterpart to the above quotation from Confucius, an anecdote about the fourth-century, B.C., philosopher Zhuangzi tells of him meeting a woman fanning the grave of her just-dead husband, who had said she could remarry once the soil of his grave had dried.[19] A conventional, miserly reading of this anecdote would accuse the woman of infidelity to her husband. A shrew's reading would say that the woman who is not allowed financial independence before or during widowhood should be able to hurry on to a new husband once the old one is dead; or that the deceased husband may have been one she was forced to marry and that she can at least choose her next husband. Whatever the case may be, in the view of this and numerous other women in Ming and Qing fiction, adulteresses included, the man is just as replaceable as the woman whose husband freely takes other lovers and remarries after she dies. The difference is that in a primarily virilocal society that transmits inheritance to sons only, a woman needs a husband much more than a man needs a wife. Thus, the woman fanning the grave can also be seen as eminently practical, as were many women who ignored Ming and Qing propaganda against widow remarriage.

The Ars Erotica, the Shrew Story, and the Sexual Power of the Woman

How is it that the shrew is so powerful, and what is the nature of her power? The "Sutra of Wife-fearing" posits that the woman's ability to subdue the ostensibly stronger and more privileged man is due to the sexual attraction which makes him "seek" her. The ars erotica and other sources of sexual wisdom give this reason: the supposedly innate sexual capability of women versus the innate weakness of men. The descriptions of the woman in the ars erotica at times make her arousal seem overwhelming and uncanny, something the man can never possibly encompass. Medical and folk traditions attach sinister power to women by imputing the harmful, sometimes demonic, influences of the pollutions of childbirth and menstruation, in addition to the effects of female beauty and sexuality. Given such power and attraction, the woman is in effect shrewish by default, simply because of her supposed innately superior capacity. The man is in turn naturally henpecked, his only alternative being to become miserly. Fiction and drama about the shrew assume but do not articulate in sexual terms the direness of this male-female imbalance. The ars erotica is more sexually explicit but solves the imbalance in a utopian fashion. Put together, the shrew story and the ars erotica tell a story that neither genre tells entirely by itself. The following is an attempt to construct a dialogue between the voices of the ars erotica and the shrew story and then join them from the point of view of a fictional man who responds to both.

The main issue of that dialogue is this: The ars erotica construes a polygamous household in which order and happiness seem possible if members follow certain rules of social and sexual behavior. When those prescriptions and their assumptions come under the light of the shrew story, however, it appears that the ars erotica ignores an inevitable problem—namely, the disruptions caused by jealousy. In short, what the ars erotica proposes—the polygamist utopia of promiscuous men and loving women—is precisely what the polygamist in his favoritism and the shrew in her jealousy will always finally undo.

The divergent focuses of the shrew story and the ars erotica are most apparent in their treatments of the woman's supposed insatiability. Fiction commonly implies that jealousy is the angry manifestation of insatiable sexual appetite.[20] A recurrent saying states that "the lust of a woman does not cease until she is buried beneath the earth" (furen yunian ru tu fang xiu). The ars erotica, on the other hand, avoids portraying the woman as insatiable, instead providing a version of sex in which man and woman are harmonious and commensurable. It teaches, for example, that they can attain the goal of happy coition if the man learns to keep his ejaculation from coming too quickly and too often. Otherwise, as the warning goes, sex with a woman is like "riding a galloping horse with a rotten rein," or "nearing a precipice over a deep pit of sharp knives." In making such statements, the ars erotica takes what the shrew story would label as insatiability and renders it manageable. The ars erotica then goes on to encourage the man to have intercourse with as many women as possible, as if to say: although one man cannot "outride" one woman (even if he practices ejaculation retention), he can outride many women by going from one to the next and thus, in a figurative sense, exhausting them one by one. In short, according to the logic of the ars erotica, the man will prolong youthfulness and attain longevity as long as he disciplines his jade stalk and consumes and expends many women.

Still hesitant, the male initiate may ask: Can women really be thus consumed and expended? What about the "shrew"? The ars erotica responds by pretending that the man can easily avoid women like her. In what amount to parenthetical warnings in an otherwise optimistic account, the sex manuals guarantee the man sexual success only if he avoids jealous and other "malignant" women, including "lascivious" ones (perhaps including women who practice their own ars erotica). Along the same lines, another caveat promises the man success only if he does not let women see the sex treatise. The woman's formidability thus still looms at the edges of the ars erotica, but in forms that through secrecy and special skill can supposedly be kept quiet and contained.[21]

As with other esoteric arts in China and elsewhere, the vowed secrecy of transmission of the art of sex is in fact a hallowed tradition that takes much for granted. Secrecy is above all essential in hiding the special techniques that will transform the man into a powerful and awe-inspiring polygamist from the sexually timid and inferior person he is innately. In other words, secrecy hides the fact that he must train or supplement himself in order to be adequate to the woman. Secrecy also hides the man's affairs with other women, and keeps women and other men from learning about the benefits of intercourse with multiple partners. In one story found in an ars erotica text, for example, the goddess Xiwangmu becomes an expert in "nourishing *yin*" (i.e., in the female ars erotica) and has frequent intercourse with young men, to the enhancement of her vitality and the detriment of theirs.[22] (As if countering this story, another ars erotica text asserts that too much intercourse is injurious to a woman's health; she should be rested while the man goes on to other women.)[23]

If we now bring in the shrew story, we find that it throws doubt on all such rationales for secrecy, demonstrating that deception is a prime cause of the woman's anger. Under the combined pressure to maintain secrecy, perform well sexually, and escape the shrew, then, how does the polygamous man respond? He has two general approaches: One, he does his best to follow secretly the recommendations of the ars erotica and get away with having as many women as he can. The happy polygamist of the erotic romances achieves success with this approach, whereas the henpecked husband of novels and stories about shrews tends to meet with failure. Two, he outwardly denies the value of sexual pleasure, in particular the woman's, and instead acts as if sex is for health and procreation only. This second alternative—especially the emphasis on procreation—applies under the ancestral order of values (*zongfa*), which sequesters women and has them serving the primary purpose of producing sons. The novel *Yesou puyan* provides an extended example of the second approach.

Further elaborated, these two ways of conquering inadequacy and escaping the shrew mean that inside the ars erotica, the man tacitly recognizes the woman's supposed sexual power. He adopts an artificial, imposed behavior in order to control himself since to lose control and be "natural" is to fail at intercourse. If he fails, he risks ill health, the woman's scorn, and the likelihood that she will seek other men. He thus takes aphrodisiacs or adopts the method of "nine shallow and one deep," for example, conserving heavily on "deep," and otherwise pretending the shrew will go away. Outside the ars erotica, under the orthodox, ancestral order, the woman is made subordinate to the man; she is subjected to an artificial, imposed behavior in the husband's favor. That is, for example, she must conform to standards of modesty which have her suppress behavior considered unbecoming to a woman; she is allowed one sexual partner for her whole life; she is sequestered inside the home and discouraged from participation in education and politics. Moreover, the orthodox order condemns the sex treatise for allowing too much room for female pleasure, not to mention pleasure in general.

In light of the messages of the ars erotica, orthodox morality, and the shrew story, the pleasure-seeking man is particularly bedeviled. Even if he escapes patriarchal surveillance and finds women with whom he succeeds in "conserving essence," he can enjoy himself only in fleeting moments, that is, during occasional failures in the shrew's vigilance.

Even in those rare moments he must still take into account the negative premises of the ars erotica: to have to make himself sexually adequate to the woman presumes that he is innately inept and can only approximate the woman's capacity. In other words, the woman is assumed to be able to enjoy true pleasure, the man to be unable to enjoy except by acts of deferring. Again, the woman is shrewish by default, simply because she is the man's antithesis in sexual performance, even in situations in which she might be an unjealous sexual partner.

The ars erotica, of course, is not pessimistic about its negative premises, nor does it extend the definition of shrew so far as to say that women are inherently shrewish or lascivious. Many fictional and historical texts, on the other hand, portray a sexual battle in which women are a menace and desire is intractable. In the shrew story, the woman's goal is to wrest power back from the man and make him monogamous. In a society controlled by women she would perhaps go further and become like the polyandrous Xiwangmu mentioned above. In such a polyandrous world the ars erotica, minus its encouragement to men to make love with as many women as possible, would perhaps become a text of indoctrination to make men better serve women in the act of love.

The shrew stories never portray quite such a reversed world of female supremacy, although near examples can be found in *Chan Zhen yishi* and *Cu hulu*, as discussed below. But however suppressed, the power of the woman's threat survives to the extent that men feel the need to maintain an air of propriety and keep secret their sexual interest in women, not to mention any hint of their own sexual inadequacy. As the logic of the shrew story implies, while the man may use the treatise or other means to increase the "quantity" of women with whom he has intercourse, the "qualitative" advantage belongs to the woman—just as the ars erotica implies in terms of the woman's advantage in pleasure.

The shrew story fills us in on what the ars erotica leaves out when it briefly warns about jealous and insatiable women. The ars erotica, in turn, allows us to see both the man's view of male-female sexual imbalance and strategies to remedy that imbalance. The rest of this chapter presents the pros and cons of polygamy as represented in selected seventeenth- and eighteenth-century novels about shrews. With this brief reconsideration of the ars erotica, the readings of the shrew and her henpecked husband can now take on a sexual dimension that is usually too implicit or abbreviated to come through otherwise.

The Repertoire of Stories about Shrews

The Cure for Jealousy

Arguments in favor of polygamy are most clearly expressed in the eight-chapter novel *Liaodu yuan* (The Cure for Jealousy), a work of unknown authorship and date of publication.[24] Since the writer of its preface[25] also wrote a preface bearing the date 1749 to the novel *Jin Shi yuan* (The Predestiny of Metal and Stone), *Liaodu yuan* may be from around that time, as Tan Zhengbi suggests.[26] The two novels share other significant features: in both, a spoiled, haughty daughter of a rich father contrasts with a virtuous commoner woman; in both, the decadent and haughty upper class benefits from the new blood of the honest lower class, the new blood coming from the lower-class second wife. A minor difference is that the woman in *Jin Shi yuan* is mainly lascivious (*yin*) rather than jealous, but *yin* and *du* (jealousy) are related traits of the *pofu* anyway.[27]

In *Liaodu yuan*, a man and woman of the upper class begin their marriage in love but grow apart as the wife finds it necessary to forbid her husband access to other women. Unfortunately, it turns out that she is barren because "when a woman suffers from jealousy [*cubing*, literally, the 'vinegar illness'], the Lord of Heaven will be sure to take her to task" (ch. 1, 5b). However, she still insists upon "monogamy," *yifu yiqi* (2b). The man must leave home and his wife's scrutiny to go to the capital and take the imperial examinations; she consents to his departure only because passing the exams is such a sure route to wealth and prestige. In the mountains on the way he is captured by bandits, then rescued by a husband and wife who are skilled in martial arts and who insist on giving him their daughter in marriage. Meanwhile, his upper-class first wife (as opposed to his "mountain wife," as she will now be called) is suspicious that he will dally with other women and pursues him to the capital. By coincidence the same bandits capture both her and the mountain wife, whom the now bigamist husband has left behind to continue his journey to the capital. The upper-class wife is weak and crippled by her bound feet, but the mountain wife, although already pregnant, is strong and agile (ch. 3, 3b). She manages to escape the bandit lair, carrying the upper-class wife on her back. Because of the mountain wife's kindness, the upper-class wife begins to soften but first falls ill of what the doctor diagnoses as the sickness of jealousy (ch. 3, 9b). The mountain wife prays for a cure, and divine intercession causes the upper-class wife to have a dream which enlightens her about the wrongness of her jealousy (ch. 4). The upper-class wife not only accepts the new wife, whom she even wants to promote to "main" (*zheng*) wife, but also purchases a troupe of actresses as a present for her husband. In the end the two wives and husband unite in the same bed for "a wonderful night, of which we need not give the details" (ch. 7, 9b). The story ends with the statement that nine-tenths of all women are jealous and the wish that they all imitate a woman like the mountain wife (ch. 8, 18b, 19ab).

Liaodu yuan is a narrative argument in favor of polygamy. In the first chapter two women discuss the issue of concubines: one states that the addition of concubines to her family benefits her, the main wife, by lessening her chance of "the pain of child bearing," *shengchan zhi ku* (ch. 1, 4a).[28] She also observes that the presence of pretty maids in the house keeps the husband happy at home and ultimately solidifies his affections for his wife (3b–4a). The second woman, who is the story's eventual upper-class wife, argues in favor of monogamy. She must suffer an ordeal before she can agree with the first woman and learn the truth of the proverb: "The peony may be beautiful, but it cannot do without the support of surrounding foliage" (ch. 4, 22a). This truth is illustrated when wanton youths (*fulang zidi*, ch. 4, 21a) later harass the hero's two wives on an outing in a park. Afterwards the upper-class wife decides that in order to be a true woman of her class, she must have a troupe of young women and servants to accompany her on such outings and make her less vulnerable to *fulang zidi* (who turn up in many stories in similar circumstances). She thereupon purchases the actresses and has them trained in martial arts; they form a "troupe of female generals" (ch. 6, 18a), which helps make the family look like that of an important official, whom villains will be too afraid to harass. (The troupe formerly belonged to a man and his jealous wife who argued over the use of the troupe but who then both died, leaving no offspring.) In sum, as proven by the events of the story, polygamy has the benefits of lending a family status and protection, ensuring the loyalty of the husband to his home and lessening the woman's risk in childbirth.

However, as partial to polygamy as this story might seem, it also delivers a message in favor of monogamy and the practice of uxorilocal marriage, in which the man marries into the woman's family. In *Liaodu yuan* the mountain wife's father has married into his wife's sonless family (ch. 2). Quite common but never much praised in Chinese society, uxorilocal marriage is the subject of a warning: "It has always been said: the man who marries into the wife's family brings nothing but a set of testicles" (from Ling Mengchu).[29] The uxorilocal family in this view gains no profit from such a marriage other than the sexual function of the husband, who may bring no resources with him and may be disloyal if he finds a better situation. Such marriage signifies weakness on the part of the male, who is typically too poor to afford a virilocal marriage (in which the woman marries into the man's family). The woman's family is also seen as appropriating the man either to provide labor or to perpetuate the family name by being adopted as son in a family with only female offspring.[30] The portrayal of the uxorilocal family in *Liaodu yuan*, however, foregrounds none of these negative messages, instead featuring a healthy marriage in which the mountain wife's parents enjoy a harmonious, monogamous attachment and share an interest in martial arts. They in turn insist on giving their daughter to the hero, who is thus somewhat like an uxorilocal son-in-law in receiving benefits from the wife's household. Moreover, his complicity in his own bigamy is camouflaged because of the fact that he does not initiate the relationship.

The marriage of these two families can be expressed as a matching of contraries. The strong mountain family marries into the weak upper-class family (in which weakness is both physical and affective in the timid upper-class husband—see, e.g., ch. 2, 15b—but is mainly physical in the bound-footed, upper-class wife). The virilocal, polygamous, elite family trades with the uxorilocal, monogamous, commoner family. Although the upwardly mobile uxorilocal element is absorbed or recontained by the established virilocal, the implication remains that the virilocal and polygamous need re-energization from the uxorilocal and monogamous. The physically and spiritually weak upper class relies on its dominant social position to perform its absorption of the socially weak lower class. The disparity between the low moral quality and high social position of the upper class undergoes repair in the process of absorption, disappearing altogether at the end of the story when the Empress ceremonially recognizes the two women as equal co-wives (ch. 8). Polygyny typically consists of one wife ranked above all other women, whether they are concubines or maidservants. In contrast, like the chaste romances to be discussed in chapter 5, *Liaodu yuan* features a male hero who is married to unjealous, equal co-wives.

In sum, although polygamy prevails in *Liaodu yuan*, the class which enjoys the privilege and luxury of polygamy admits a measure of weakness in itself and acknowledges that the lower-class monogamists are healthier. The polygamist then makes this contradiction vanish and feels justified and strengthened. In addition, in a reversal of roles that will be even more prominent in the scholar-beauty romances, the women do most of the acting, while the man receives the benefit of their willing participation in and arrangement of his polygamy.

Protests against Polygamy

The arguments against polygamy take the form of complaints about the unfair advantages men have over women. In the three late Ming works cited below, these arguments appear in lists of items, in some cases duplicated from one work to another.[31]

In a story from *Xihu erji* (Stories of West Lake, Second Collection) of the 1640s, a woman has "six hates" or "detestable things," *liu kehen*, paraphrased as follows:

> First, "one husband, one wife," *yifu yiqi*, is "a set number," *dingshu*. How is it that men can have "little wives," *xiao laopo*, when we women cannot have "little husbands," *xiao laogong*?
>
> Second, when a woman has an illicit affair, it is called "a failure to keep to the inner chambers," *bushou guimen*, a crime punishable by death or divorce. But a man who has an illicit affair is never executed or divorced. If we women were like the wife who made her husband wear his lover's genitals on his face, we would be accused of unforgivable wrongdoing.
>
> Third, for a man to have concubines or commit adultery is abominable enough, so "how does he suddenly come up with his 'male-to-male affections' [*nanfeng*] and deprive us of our pleasure [*leshi*]?" "For that matter, we have that organ too; if you are so in need of it, I'm willing to take you in there as well."
>
> Fourth, "If a woman steals love with another man, but ends up being with child and giving birth to a bastard [*sihaizi*], she is the one saddled with the evidence . . . , so that even a bad woman doesn't dare let herself go entirely and is always a little apprehensive." But whether they "steal" women or "little officials," *xiao guan* (i.e., boys), men are left with no evidence, so they "do whatever wild things they please."

Fifth, a man's "thing," *dongxi*, should only act when it sees his wife. But "it is precisely when it sees a new possibility that it becomes extraordinarily bold." With another woman it performs well, but with his wife it is "like a rain-soaked chicken."[32]

Sixth, even if he is cut off from concubines or catamites and is kept from going where he pleases, "he still has his five fingers." He also has "the night pot [*yehu*], with its shape just like a woman's thing which he can thrust himself into and out of—and so another way for him to indulge himself."[33]

In a story from *Erke pai'an jingqi* (Sequel to Tales That Amaze, 1630s), the woman has "three hates," *sanhen*: "Heaven and Earth, her father and mother, and artisans who make fancy porcelain wares" (story 10, 156). She hates Heaven and Earth because they gave "this thing," *ciwu*, to other women besides her. She hates her parents because they married her late and to an older man who had long since lost his virginity. "She had missed the chance to see the old fellow lose his virginity and was forever ill at ease because of it."[34] Finally, she hates the porcelain makers for producing fancy "urinary receptacles," *niaoqi*. "When a woman urinates, she sits on the pot and that's it." But the porcelain artisans create receptacles which allow a man "to move his penis in and out, the mere sight of which infuriates her."[35]

Finally, in *Chan Zhen yishi* (Lost Tales of the True Way, 1620s?), the community of "Henville," *Ciji shi*, is governed by a female tyrant who has a list of ten rules, most of which redress wrongs that men commonly commit against women.[36]

The tyrant forbids

insult and mistreatment of the mistress of the house. A woman's lot in life is exceedingly difficult and painful. She endures the dangers of childbirth and the hardships of household duties. She is like a bird locked in a cage, a fish swimming in an urn. Men should be sympathetic and understanding. They should love and protect her to their utmost, be yielding and submissive, and accept her control.

She forbids the "willful taking of concubines and mistresses. . . . To have no offspring is better than inconsiderately taking additional wives." She forbids "intimacy with maids and manservants" and allows as servants "only slovenly old men and dull-witted maids." She forbids widowers to remarry.

She also forbids men

unexcused entry and exit. The male disposition is extremely base. Since he is inhibited at home, when a man goes out, he will inevitably filch like a rat, pilfer like a dog, and slyly commit deceitful and adulterous acts. Women, being situated in the inner chambers, have no way to learn of their husbands' crimes. Henceforth, whenever a man goes out, he must seek permission from the mistress of the house concerning his destinations, activities, and companions. Upon his return, he must make a clear report before he may enter and take his meal.[37]

The "tyrant" herself, Youshi (the *you* of *youwu*, "dangerous woman"), also called the "Wife of Yang Wei," *Yang Wei zhi fu,* has large breasts and feet, a fierce mien, and dark skin, all features contrary to the ideal image of the woman in the Ming and Qing.[38] Her husband's name puns with *yangwei,* a term for male impotence; in this case, being henpecked and impotent explicitly coincide in the same man.

These three seventeenth-century characters—the one with "six hates," the one with "three hates," and the female tyrant—protest against both the unfair advantages men have over women biologically and the irresponsible way men dominate women by virtue of social privilege. The most radical of the women's reforms is the demand for monogamy, which not only denies men polygamous freedom but also undercuts traditional values of filiality by ultimately maintaining that it is better to have no sons than to take a concubine in order to bear one (the common alternative of adoption does not appear in these examples but does in *Cu hulu* below). The satirical tone of these stories filters and ventriloquizes the female voice that these lists can nevertheless be imagined as representing.[39] Complaints about male adultery or female rules of chastity, for example, can be imagined as real. Complaints about "male affections," "five fingers," or "night pots" sound like possible jokes that men passed around in satire of the shrew and their supposed victimization by her.

A modern reader may wonder why, in spite of their radical and explicit nature, none of these three lists expresses protest against what now seem some of the most obvious marks of a woman's repression, such as the customs of bound feet and confinement to the inner chambers. Occasional critics of footbinding have existed ever since it began to be widespread in the Song.[40] The Kangxi emperor, a Manchu, even banned this Han custom in a 1662 edict that he later rescinded, however, because of its failure to take hold. Wu Jingzi's *Rulin waishi,* of the mid-eighteenth century, portrays Du Shaoqing and his wife walking outdoors hand in

71

hand and thus defying the customs of female sequestration and public noncontact between husband and wife. Sometime later, around 1800, *Jinghua yuan* (Flowers in the Mirror) portrays the pain of footbinding.[41] Only hints of "liberated" feet appear in the works examined here, for example, in the negative reference to the big feet of the shrewish wife of Yang Wei and in the positive portrayal of the agility of the mountain wife in *Liaodu yuan*, although whether or not she has natural feet is unclear.[42] In the end, the protests of women in these seventeenth-century works stay within the framework by virtue of which men govern the outside world and bound-footed women govern the home.

Nevertheless, the shrew adamantly asserts her jurisdiction by insisting that sexual activity be confined solely to the home and to the one wife. She insists that the man curb his lust, whether heterosexual, homosexual, or masturbatory, and otherwise does what she can, from her restricted position, to manipulate or punish the man who takes free rein. And that is what the story of the shrew is about: how a wife uses subtle or overt means to detect her husband's misbehavior and then punish him for it. In one story the shrew knows of her husband's philandering because of his lapse in sexual energy. "If only a man's penis were detachable," she wishes, and could be removed when he left home.[43] In a late Ming play by Wang Tingna, *Shi hou ji* (Roar of the Lion), the shrew puts a leash on her husband. In other cases, she victimizes his lovers. The Han Empress Lü hated Emperor Gaozu's concubine Lady Qi and ordered her head shaved and her feet, hands, ears, and eyes removed. With the Empress and others like her as precedent, women in later history and fiction have had the tongues, eyes, ears, noses, and genitals of concubines or maids mutilated or amputated. Women like Wang Xifeng in *Honglou meng* use subtler, more artful means to eliminate their rivals. Regardless of the woman's methods of discovery, the man never succeeds in keeping his secrets.

The Shrew's Hatred and Torture of her Husband in *Xingshi yinyuan zhuan*

Of all the shrew stories in Chinese literature, *Xingshi yinyuan zhuan* (Marriage Fate to Arouse the World) is by far the most extensive in its treatment of a wife's hatred of her husband. It also stands out in that the husband is clearly blamed for his wife's rage, which almost causes his death in the last chapter, when she shoots him with an arrow as he emerges from the privy.[44] But he survives, she dies, and he makes a new beginning with his second wife. With the shrew and her scandalous behavior comprising the core of the book, the main theme is the return to original purity and simplicity. The novel uncovers what ultimately causes this terrible marriage and all other social aberrations: wantonness and waste, which are the roots, and fate or karmic retribution (ming, yinguo baoying), which is the infallible mechanism behind all human events.

Xingshi yinyuan zhuan begins with the story of a family whose wastrel and philanderous son, Chao Yuan, incurs the wrath of a fox demoness. The novel then follows with the story of two families whose children are reincarnations of the wastrel and the fox. When the two unwitting karmic enemies are married, the reincarnated wastrel, Di Xichen, becomes a wife-fearer, while the reincarnated fox, Sujie, becomes his shrewish victimizer.

In portraying human beings at their worst, *Xingshi yinyuan zhuan* is like the sixteenth-century *Jin Ping Mei*, to which it makes occasional allusion. Virtuous characters are few but, with the obvious exception of the shrew, tend to be female and to be restricted to minor roles, with the exception of the noble widow Mme. Chao (see ch. 32). She exemplifies the chaste widow honored by Ming and Qing government decree. She exceeds everyone in purity and thereby uplifts the family and community in a way men no longer can. Her alleged incorruptibility makes her superior to the men of her class, of whom the better examples tend to be ineffective and only modestly good, like Di Xichen's father or Mme. Chao's coddled grandson, Chao Liang, who still wants to sleep in his grandmother's room after his marriage (ch. 49). Other instances of good women used as foils to put men to shame include another upper-class widow, Tong Nainai, and a hired cook-cum-concubine, Tiao Geng, whose name means "stir" or "mix the soup," as in the soup that the shrewish wife must eat to be cured of jealousy.[45]

As for "bad" characters, the *pofu* Sujie is the most prominent. She behaves as if she were possessed by an unknown force, about which she wonders in a rare moment of lucidity (ch. 59). In the causal scheme of the book, she is only reacting to wrongs suffered in a previous life at the hands of a man. In metaphysical terms, cause and effect are respectively characterized as male and female, so that husbands and fathers are the prime moral movers, and the woman is the expression or concrete manifestation of the man—a scheme that reflects traditional *yin-yang* theory.[46]

The main theme of *Xingshi yinyuan zhuan*, the return to original purity and simplicity, is enacted in a scene of social paradise that appears about a quarter of the way through the book (ch. 23). A new set of characters emerges, some of whom are reincarnations of characters from earlier chapters. The paradise is devoid of illiteracy, thievery, women who appear improperly in public, and shrews and henpecked husbands. Its economy is that of self-sufficient agriculture; people do not yet know how to earn money or run businesses (ch. 25). It is like a benevolent version of the miser's utopia that I have mentioned previously, in which everyone's belly is full and mind is empty—except that now everyone can read. Somehow, however, exploitation and greed for money and property emerge, and social decline commences. At the top of the list of fallen people are members of the local elite, literati-landlords who do not till their own land but cheat poorer folk into working for them (ch. 26, 385). Next down are the elite's sons, spoiled and ill-educated wastrels who consume their fathers' wealth; they know sex at age eleven or twelve (ch. 44, 638); they marry too early; they attract sycophants for friends. Under them are the hired help, male and female, permanent and temporary, who steal from the landlord and ruin his tools and work animals. At the bottom are the basest people who, as the author describes, "without regard for high or low, rich or poor, old or young, male or female, all make themselves a short tiny stool, pad it with a little four-inch-square double-layered straw mat, leave a hole in the middle, and then engage in that profitable business that I leave the reader to surmise for himself" (ch. 26, 388). This metaphor portrays women and men as indiscriminate sex machines, one of which later appears in the guise of the pedant Wang Weilu, who likes listening secretly to others making love at night (*ting renjia bangsheng*, ch. 35, 518). In the end he falls ill and must hire women to take turns sitting on him as he lies in bed with an unquenchable erection.[47]

One of the prime targets of shrewish rage is in fact the man's body, especially his sex. Sujie's father-in-law hires the female cook Tiao Geng, whom he also intends to have as concubine. Sujie plots against both the cook and the father-in-law, whom she repeatedly attempts to castrate (ch. 56, 812). Likewise, Di Xichen's second shrewish wife, Jijie, puts marks on her husband's penis which she checks everyday to see if he has had sex with a certain housemaid (ch. 79).[48] The title of the chapter in which this occurs, "Jijie Makes a Ruckus in the Grape Arbor," is seemingly a satirical allusion to chapter 27 of *Jin Ping Mei,* in which Ximen Qing creates a "ruckus" (*nao*) in a "grape arbor" (*putaojia*) and abuses the genitals of Pan Jinlian. Although there is no actual "grape arbor" in the scene in *Xingshi yinyuan zhuan,* the words appear in the title, thus making Jijie's abuse of her husband's penis into a type of intertextual revenge across a century or so of narrative history. Jijie's ruckus also resonates intratextually with an earlier scene in *Xingshi yinyuan zhuan* in which Sujie "scatters" (*po*) the contents of a chamber pot on her husband and his friend in an actual grape arbor (as the two men are telling stories about a "Wife-fearers Club," ch. 58, 839). As with the attempted castration above, the polluting function of the shrew's "scattering" assumes a more literal form than usual, with the author actually playing on the word *po.* As for the grape arbor, it has a long history of significance in connection with the rampaging shrew; in a well-known joke, a man hides the fact that his wife scratched his face by saying that "a grape arbor collapsed" on him (*daole putaojia*).[49]

The Gourd of Vinegar

The last novel to be considered here, *Cu hulu* (Gourd of Vinegar), is about turning a jealous, "vinegar" wife back into someone more "palatable" ("vinegar" is from the saying "to 'eat' vinegar," *chicu,* which means to be jealous).[50] The book begins by reflecting that a man is free to develop himself until he marries, when he suddenly suffers the constrictions of wife and home. Does this mean that all men fear their wives, the narrator asks; he is afraid so. For "during the sexual act [the wife] is indeed on the bottom, but outside of that she is always climbing on top of her husband's head and taking a dump" (ch. 1, 2a). This image supplies another brief instance of shrewish "scattering" taking the form of bodily pollution.

The story tells of the marriage between a "haughty and spoiled" daughter of a wealthy family and a decent, frugal orphan of modest means. The husband immediately becomes henpecked and lives in daily fear of his wife; he is gray-haired earlier than usual; he stutters from fear when addressing her (ch. 1, 8b). She limits his errands out of the house to the time it takes for an incense stick to burn down. She deliberately frightens him to make him submissive, and when angry beats him black

且笑广評演小說

醋葫蘆

天下之惡皆可懲惟妒婦之惡寂不易懲何則彼挾柔黠之資陰狠之才因以行此專制斷制不稔於恩勢必不止況行乾者剛陽用德繞指是什且隨成哉卓吾秉翁嘆種茶者之如彼悲受虐者之若此發等提智譯怕婆經柰何向竟沉淪糜布登如衣妙音冰為姊媚歎欺則伏雌教主安得不更演傳閱宜讚胡也今兹怕婆寶匯尖是集也人寶一快厥幾其有鞷

且笑广主人識

Title page to Yannan tang edition of *Cu hulu* (Gourd of Vinegar).

The shrew and her henpecked husband, *Cu hulu*.

The shrew at the court of the Judge of Hell, *Cu hulu*.

The shrew being punished by demons, *Cu hulu*.

and blue so that he is ashamed to be seen in public. The commentator remarks that the wife must be the man's reincarnated mother getting back at her unfilial son (ch. 1, 14a; the shrew as the man's mother will be discussed in the chapter on *Yesou puyan*).

After forty years of marriage the wife is still childless and wishes to adopt a son, but the husband, though overtly abject, secretly desires a concubine. To keep him loyal, she stamps a mark on his penis each day, which she checks at night to determine the extent of punishment according to how much of the mark is rubbed off; he worries about its being rubbed off from the friction of his clothing (ch. 4). After awhile she agrees to his taking a concubine, but gets him a *shinü*, that is, a woman with an impenetrable vagina.[51] He cannot find a way inside; the concubine wonders why he "urinates" on her stomach (ch. 6, 13ab); later she dies. When he then gets the concubine's maid pregnant, his wife tries unsuccessfully to have the maid murdered. Side plots take up most of the rest of the novel and include the disastrous adoption of a wastrel nephew from the wife's side of the family. Finally, as in other stories, divine intervention reforms the shrew. In remorse for having "killed" the maid, the wife's soul journeys to the netherworld where she has a bone of jealousy removed from her back.[52] When she returns to the *yang*-world, the maid and her son, who is a reincarnation of the recently dead concubine, emerge from hiding and join the family; the "bottle of vinegar" is finally emptied (ch. 20, 18b).

To justify her ways, the wife in *Cu hulu* appeals to the examples of powerful women in history and fiction such as the Tang Empress Wu Zetian (who ruled China from 684 to 704) and the wife of Yang Wei in *Chan Zhen yishi*. She revives special rites of husbandly submission that held sway when these women were in power.[53] The existence of such allusions, along with the stories reviewed above and other material on jealousy from Ming, Qing, and earlier sources, suffices to indicate the coherence and magnitude of the repertoire of references that was available to those who wrote about shrews.[54] Literature from the Tang to the Qing presents the problem of the shrew as eternal and universal. The recording of her behavior, which constitutes a reaction against male freedom and privilege, amounts to a confession that male rule always meets with female obstacles that cannot be readily eliminated. Although the shrew is treated as a joke or comic epiphenomenon and is eventually defeated in these stories, her ability to bring about the man's utter abjection is the subject of intense and detailed portrayal. The man can do nothing to prevent the shrew's "imperious" temperament, as it is called in *Xingshi yinyuan zhuan—huangdi xing*, literally, "emperor's nature" (ch. 95, 1351). As many of the works suggest, if she had the chance, she would confront and subdue even the emperor, if not also the gods in heaven.[55]

As I have said previously, there are two directions the solution of this sexual problem takes in Chinese fiction. One is the reclamation and restoration of male potency, especially as expressed in polygamy and the imperative to bear good sons. The other is the admission of failure and the softening or withering away of the values that support such male privilege. *Liaodu yuan* defends polygamy and suggests means to revitalize the polygamous family. The eighteenth-century *Yesou puyan*, in which the shrew takes the form of wise mother instead of jealous wife, makes an even stronger case for the revival of male energy and virtue. On the other hand, the words and deeds of the women in *Xihu erji, Erke pai'an jingqi, Chan Zhen yishi, Xingshi yinyuan zhuan,* and *Cu hulu* represent attacks on polygamy. An indirect version of that attack continues in *Honglou meng*, though through not the voice of a shrew but that of an effeminate young man, Jia Baoyu, who refuses to follow the path of patriarch and polygamist.

First, however, I will discuss one of the man's chief ways of escaping the shrew: the self-containing avarice of the miser, who takes sexual desire—which according to the "Sutra of Wife-fearing" is the prime cause of henpecked behavior—and replaces it with accumulation of money.

4

THE SELF-CONTAINING MAN: THE MISER

AND THE ASCETIC

If the man is determined to pursue the difficult task of escaping the shrew, he must emulate one of three types of men who are not fascinated by women: the temperate polygamist, the miser, and the ascetic. All three practice the art of self-containment, which centers on guarding the flow of semen. The temperate polygamist either limits sexual pleasure or, if he follows the ars erotica, regulates and stylizes his sex and avoids passionate fascination. The miser reduces everything in life to the quantitative proportions of money and in so doing pretends to be able to control all containers and contain all things. The ascetic practices a less rigid, more carefree kind of self-containment characterized by nonattachment. In the form of recluse or eremite, he is a traditionally favorite model for the literatus poet or painter who, as the mood suits him, fancies himself detached from the world. Whether realized or imagined, the ascetic represents someone who is supposedly free of material desire and social and marital-sexual ties.

Self-containment is a relative term as it applies to each of the above three types and is especially fluid in the ascetic. He does not necessarily punish his body, as might be thought from the common English definition of the word. In fiction, the ascetic is often a trickster or knave who wanders his way through life with no home, no family, and no possessions. He seems to practice a straightforward containment when he withdraws from the normative family world and contains himself sexually. But he also seeks to undo the definition of containment by utterly relativizing it; he states, for example, that all measurements and boundaries are relative to the perspective of the perceiver. In another moment, however, the ascetic is caught thinking that he contains within himself all that he needs to be alive in the most "nourished" way; he may even practice esoteric disciplines to make himself immortal, thus behaving with miserly literalism again. The pseudo-ascetic "flower-monk" (*hua heshang*), however, is a sex adept who takes such relativizing detachment to a hedonist rather than ascetic extreme. He practices an unabashed nomadism of the penis, getting whatever he can where he can and then escaping to parts unknown or else withdrawing into the disguise of a true, that is, celibate, ascetic. The monk who loves wine and meat (*jiurou heshang*) is a similar type of trickster who nevertheless draws a strict line at the level of sexual indulgence. For example, he will act as if he means to have sex with a woman, then deliberately stop and laughingly run away. Of the three men—temperate polygamist, miser, and ascetic—the ascetic is the most suspicious or subversive of containers, caught in them but constantly trying to dissolve or relativize them.[1]

In contrast, the temperate polygamist believes in self-containment as a practicable, self-regulating method by which he can govern self, women, family, and state. He believes in a state of social equilibrium which all members of society can and should attain cooperatively according to ethical values decorously based on obedience. The miser, on the other hand, does not share the temperate polygamist's faith in ethical values; he sees too clearly the impracticality of virtue. But he is not inclined to the ascetic's nonattachment either. A strict materialist, he takes acquisitive and usurious self-containment as the only way to survive. No human can be trusted as much as himself, and he can't be trusted as much as his money. His simple formula of being tight and unscrupulous allows him to out-contain all others.

In this study, the miser is the central character-metaphor of the self-containing man and master of the world who rules by never leaving his own home. There he sits in his "Alone-Ruler-of-all-Chair" (from *Changyan dao* below), emulating the nonaction of the Taoist ruler idealized in the *Laozi* (or *Tao Te Ching*). In what follows, I will explain this allegory both by citing it as it appears in texts and by exaggerating and extrapolating it into a caricature of male ideology in general. Self-containment will be the main descriptive term for this ideology, which is powerful in its social and symbolic effects because of its rationalization into something that is innately male and unavailable to females due to their inherent deficiency. In a further distinction, self-containment has the aspects of both an economic and sexual paradigm, thus the term "miserly-ascetic paradigm" which I have occasionally used previously. The miserly part of the paradigm applies to the political and economic order of society as a whole, including the local scene of the family. The ascetic paradigm represents the aspect of sexuality in which the key binary is male semen retention versus female scattering and flooding. In allegorical terms, the miser can be compared to a money jar which can never be emptied except at usurious rates of interest. The ascetic is a retractable penis which either forswears sex and engages in seminal retention for the sake of health and immortality, or else engages in sex for the tricksterish purpose of stealing essence from women but never marrying them or staying with them for long. The ascetic, like Ji Dian, who will be discussed toward the end of this chapter, rejects the miserly half of the paradigm—that is, the economic rule of profit and loss—but still follows the sexual paradigm. The male who comes closest to rejecting the paradigm in both aspects is the feminized scholar-poet of the chaste romances and *Honglou meng,* which will be discussed in the following chapters.

The Miser in Ming and Qing Fiction

As the characters *po* and *yin* indicate, the shrew "sprays," "scatters," and "floods." She is especially effective with her mouth, which she uses to vent rage upon her husband or other adversaries, whom she "curses in the open street" (*ma jie*). The miser, on the other hand, called *linse gui,* is retentive, against expenditure, afraid of leakage; he doesn't even like to go outside: "He coops himself up all day in his house, always has his eyebrows in a frown, takes his tea weak and his rice plain, and keeps a key ever so securely dangling from his side."[2]

In sexual terms, as I have said, a man is miserly when he practices the retention of *yang*-essence or semen. The semantic relation between semen retention and miserliness is apparent in both early and later texts that use the two terms, *se* and *benqian.* The *Hou Hanshu* (History of the Later Han) contains a reference to the importance of conserving essence that uses the key word *se* of *linse,* where *se* means "to be frugal." A late Ming work echoes this idea in stating that "the main point of the art of the mysterious female is to treasure the spirit [*bao shen*] and be frugal with essence [*se jing*]."[3] Ming and Qing fiction often refer to the penis as "capital," *benqian,* which must be spent wisely if spent at all. When a woman captivates a man, she drains him of his capital—unless he is skilled at retaining and replenishing *yang*-energy.

Traditional gender ideals have it that the man should be active and disseminating, the woman passive and receptive. But, as will be elaborated further below, in their warlike extremes the miser and shrew each attempt to appropriate and outdo the other and in so doing switch poles: in the miser's version of being a woman, the nurturing receptivity of the woman becomes his avaricious retention; nurture becomes avarice, receptivity retention. He turns the rectum into a womb that produces children in the form of feces, which he then exchanges for money. In the shrew's case, the warming dissemination of the man becomes her cold scattering or even dismembering; warmth turns to cold, dissemination to scattering. Her appropriation of the penis and its functions of pleasure and reproduction takes such forms as her leashing and stamp marking of the penis, her installation of an infertile woman as concubine, and her destruction of female rivals.

Like the shrew, the miser appears from early times on. The Song dynasty compendium of stories and anecdotes from the Han to the Song, *Taiping guangji* (Encyclopedic Anthology of the Reign of Great Peace), has a special section entitled "Avarice," *Linse,* devoted to noteworthy misers.[4] Misers also appear in a section of Feng Menglong's late Ming joke collection, *Gujin xiaoshi* (History of Jokes, Ancient to Modern).[5] By general definition misers share the traits of hoarding and stubbornness, refusing to part with even the smallest amount of money or property.[6] As with Molière's *avare,* the only way to get anything out of misers is to outwit them. They have no friends; they expect their wives, children, servants, and dogs to share their miserly values. They dress poorly, eat cheaply, and live in filth.

Although the miser often shows up as a stock character in vernacular fiction, not as many works are devoted to him as to the shrew. The closest in length to *Cu hulu* or *Liaodu yuan* is the early nineteenth-century *Changyan dao* (As the Old Saying Has It), an allegorical satire about money and its rule of everyone's life in the "Country of Petty People" (*Xiaoren guo*).[7] This short novel, written with an intense hatred of money, focuses on a miserly *caizhu,* "wealthy baron," who is obsessed with money and possessions. His name is Qian Yu, "Money-stupid," and his style-name (*hao*) is Qian Shiming, a pun on "Money-is-life" (or "money-is-like-life").[8]

Another piece about the miser appears in the early Qing story collection *Zhaoshi bei* (The Cup That Reflects the World). There, a man runs a public toilet to earn money by selling the waste as night soil to farmers.[9] This work portrays the association of filth and money in as neat a form as I have seen in Chinese fiction, and has been the inspiring example for both my image of the miser and my allegorization of the Qing economic mode of production as outlined in chapter 1.

The Miser's Reign

A powerful figure in his local society, the miser is the landlord who lends money, land, and goods at such outrageous rates of interest that indebted peasants and laborers are forced to sell their wives and children. In the early Qing romance *Qingmeng tuo* (Awakened from the Love Dream), he is called a "local despot." During a drought, if other landlords want 50 percent of the tenants' harvest, he wants 80 percent;[10] during famine, he hoards rice which he sells at many times the normal rate. The common people hate him to the core, but no one can touch him except for the plundering bandits portrayed in works like *Shuihu zhuan* (Water Margin, from the sixteenth century) and its many imitators, which portray bandits as righteous heroes who punish exploitative members of the official and landed elite.

In the allegorical terms of *Changyan dao,* the miser views himself and the realm he controls as a sealed vessel which can be opened only to be filled, never to pour out. Qian Shiming lives in the "City of No Escape," in the "Village of [i.e., dominated by] One Single Family." He stays in a "room to himself," in which he hangs a plaque with the words "Here Am I." The room is sealed and dark: "From above leaks no water; from the four sides penetrates no light." There "he sits in his Alone-Ruler-of-all-Chair, benighted and unenlightened, with no idea of the meaning of Heaven and Earth" (129–32). In this allegory, he is the malignant, microcosmic version of the supposedly benign emperor who rules from his throne in Beijing.

Qian Shiming has two sycophantic servants who provide him with special services. He has a very large scrotum, *da luanfu,* which occasionally needs to be blown up with air. The two servants stand on either side of him "slowly and laboriously inflating his scrotum" until Qian feels comfortable again (131). Qian eats more than the usual miser but still sticks to the cheap and the filthy; some of his favorite dishes are "salted dried stinky fish," "fried salted garlic-stalk with dung bagasse," "salted eggs with maggots," and "stomach full of pork grease" (147). After his meals, "if he happens to have to fart, since his bottom is quite large and his legs gross and fat, here too he must have his boys stand at either side, lift up his ample buttocks, and then wait for him to slowly let out his fart" (131). The service to an important man's testicles or buttocks is a recurrent motif in literature and vulgar parlance. *Xingshi yinyuan zhuan* describes how the flatterers of a rich man can't wait to "lift up his buttocks and lick his anus"; they can't wait to "pull out his scrotum [*luanfu*] and carry him on their shoulders."[11] In another Qing novel, flatterers of an important official "hold his buttocks and cup his farts."[12] The man in these images is the wealthy leader of the dog pack, who gets licked by but never licks the dogs in his service.

The Miser and Filth

The miser is dirty and unkempt. The one who runs the public outhouse is so busy that "he doesn't even wash his face or rinse his mouth" (*Zhaoshi bei*, 75). In *Qingmeng tuo* the miser never washes his clothes because they are so full of patches that he is afraid they will fall to pieces from scrubbing (ch. 7, 13a).

The mid-Qing *Yesou puyan* provides the most minutely detailed description of a miser that I have found in Chinese vernacular fiction:

> [His] face was black with filth as he stood hot and sweating in the blazing sun. His hands held bamboo counting chips. His eyes, like a hawk's always searching for prey, held guard over the man in charge of accounts and other housemembers who were taking care of a grain sale. When he saw [his visitors] enter, . . . he sent a boy to conduct them to the study. They entered and looked around: there was a square table piled with rent-account books, an abacus resting across the top. . . . Chairs and stools were scattered all over, both upright and overturned. Signs on the wall said: "I swear never to enter the Silver Guild," and "Never lend out pawned items." The floor was carpeted with chicken and duck shit. . . . The little servant poured tea for [the two visitors, one of whom] was about to take his cup when he saw the boy's

head: it was bald with sores, oozing puss all sticky with dust and dirt, and draining down his temples. . . . Two tracks of thick yellow snot came out of the boy's nose and explored around the edges of his mouth; they were like the well buckets of Huqiu Mountain: one went down while the other came up. His hands were like ash rakes and they too were covered with suppurating sores, oozing puss in a frightful sight.[13]

The saying "he values shit as if it were gold," *xi fen ru jin,* is a common epithet used to describe the miser. The opposite of this saying "to spend money as if it were dirt," *hui jin ru tu,* is the epithet for the miser's wastrel son, also a stock character. The father's resistance to throwing things away is opposed by the son's unbridled waste, especially when it comes to sex and gambling. In general, the miser shows little interest in sex, only wanting to make money. In the early Qing novel *Shi wu pi* (Peerless Through the World), he cares only for "profit," *lixi,* having no concern for "romance," *fengyue;* for him, spring is important because night soil then sells for a higher price.[14] When the virtuous but sonless wife in *Qingmeng tuo* urges her miserly husband to take a concubine, he refuses because he reckons that after he dies, the concubine will abscond with his money and marry someone else. However, when the miser in *Changyan dao* does show sexual interest in another woman, his shrewish wife flies into a rage lasting for hours—illustrating one of the few cases of a miser actually married to a shrew (ch. 9).[15]

"The Miser Gets Rich from His New Pits" in *Zhaoshi bei* portrays the miser earning money through the sale of night soil. To him, "his night soil is even more valuable than gold" (70). He builds an outhouse, paints the walls, and decorates the inside with hangings of poems and paintings. He has a friend compose an inscription for the building, the "Hall of High Rank," *Chijue tang,* which puns with "Hall of Chewing Shit" (71).[16] He attracts customers by announcing that he will distribute free toilet paper. The customer first "obtains a B.M. chit" (84), then gets his paper, which is better than the usual "rice-stalks or broken tile" that most peasants use for such purposes (71). "The old man sits there in front of his new pits, with the people crowding around him for toilet paper"; "those by the door take their paper inside, while others come out fastening up their belts" (88).

The extent of the miser's scatophilic frugality is apparent in the episode in which he buys salt. He is happy to be given a free lotus leaf in addition to the one used to wrap the salt. As he walks home, however, he suddenly feels a rumbling in his bowels: "It was more painful than the sensations of a woman in labor whose baby is about to come out or those of a sick drunkard whose vomit has just hit his throat" (83). Finally, he can't hold back any longer:

He thereupon lifted high his worthy bum and grandly proclaimed his precious buttocks. It was like the breaking of a terrace around a rice paddy or the bursting of a dike by a river—it all flowed out in one vigorous stream. He then picked up a piece of broken tile and corked up the opening. Feeling much better, he fastened up his pants, took the extra lotus leaf and, folding it up from four sides, placed the matter in the middle. He took a rice stalk and neatly tied up the ends, then proceeded on his way. (83)

Afraid that a friend he meets on the road will detect the bad smell, he hastily throws the packet away. But after he arrives home, he discovers that he threw away the salt not the waste and in anger hurls the packet onto the ground before he can think twice to save it too. "In an instant a yellow-brown cur ran up, its tail wagging as if it hadn't seen the sight of food in a thousand years, and noisily lapped up the rich morsel" (86). Versions of this story are still told as jokes today.

The Miser's Downfall and Death

The miser is so mean that his own dog bites him. In *Qingmeng tuo* he scuffles with a desperate man to whom he refuses a loan, falls on top of his watchdog, which then swipes at him, blinds him in one eye, and bites off an ear (ch. 7, 16ab).

In general, despite such disasters, the miser fails to reform, carrying his avarice to the grave. Not long after the incident with his dog, the *Qingmeng tuo* miser tries to rescue his account books from a fire; he is forced to take shelter in the pit of an outhouse, which catches fire, collapses, and kills him (17a).

Another miser who remains stingy to the end appears in *Rulin waishi*. On his deathbed he holds up two fingers, which family members think indicate two people he misses or perhaps two places where he has buried gold. But he means to signal to someone to cut one of the two wicks in the lamp in order to save oil (ch. 5, 82, and ch. 6, 85); he dies directly after communicating this order.

The Miser and Taoist Nonaction

To the miser, numbers are more important than things. Hell is to be in debt; heaven is to have everyone in debt to him. The skillful keeping of numbers will get him to "heaven" only if he avoids the attractions of material things, that is, the dissipating pleasures his wealth could buy. He places his wealth in suspension and, like the ascetic man or chaste widow, lives as if he were already dead, as if he were a piece of waste. "He takes his own flesh and blood and treats it like 'dead ashes and dried wood [*sihui gaomu*]'" (*Zhaoshi bei*, 75), the classic words used to refer to a chaste widow or severe scholar.

As a caricature of the usurious ruling class and its canonic tradition, the miser is like a half-educated misreader of ancient texts about rulership and the preservation of the self. He overadheres to medical advice to men about continence and extends the saving of sperm to the saving of money, property, material goods, and waste. He is a literalist adherent of the male ideology of self-containment and equilibrium.

Culling randomly from ancient sayings about self-preservation and strategies of rulership, the miser can easily locate words and strategies that suit his tendencies. For example, he is like a Yangist practitioner of preserving one's nature, *xing* (Yangism refers to the school of thought connected with the fourth-century B.C. philosopher Yangzi or Yang Zhu). As A. C. Graham translates, one ideally "'keep[s] one's nature intact,'" "'protect[s] one genuineness,'" and does "'not let . . . the body be tied by other things.'" Yangzi is of course famous for his statement: "'If by plucking out one hair [I] could benefit the world [I] would not do it.'"[17]

The project of guaranteeing one's intactness begins at the very boundary of the lips and teeth, images that the miser finds in numerous sources. The Legalist philosopher Han Fei's "Wielding Power," a third-century B.C. text of advice to rulers, says (echoing the *Laozi*): "Whatever comes from the lips, from the teeth, it is not I who says the first words."[18] Like the Taoist practitioner of nonaction (*wuwei*), the miser gains power by guarding the issuance of words and gestures; being silent, he maintains an emptiness that allows him to concentrate on his numbers and wait for others to make mistakes and fall into his debt.[19]

The miser is a Han Fei–like practitioner of "frugality," *se*. In Han Fei's "Explaining *Laozi*," the miser finds praise of frugality plus a singling out of his favorite machines of production, the stomach and bowels: "In ruling people and serving heaven, nothing is more important than frugality" (*Laozi*).[20] "Take the bowels and stomach as foundation," but satisfy them with the minimum because "nothing causes more disaster than desire."[21]

The miser knows that his welfare depends on the guarding of apertures and the maintenance of boundaries. In "Interpreting *Laozi*," Han Fei says, "The openings and apertures of the body are the windows and doors of the spirit."[22] Since the senses are exhausted by too much contact with the outside, it is best to stay inside, as the miser does in his "room to himself" in *Changyan dao*. Anyway, as Han Fei says (quoting the *Laozi*), "Even without going out the door one can know the cosmos; even without looking out the window one can know the way of heaven."[23]

Like Molière's *avare* the miser suffers from paranoia,[24] which causes him to forget other parts of the philosophy of Laozi and Han Fei, such as the statements "Excessive meanness is sure to lead to great expense; too much store is sure to end in immense loss,"[25] or, "There is no misfortune greater than being covetous."[26] But such caveats are mere decorations and conscience soothers compared to the main emphasis on frugality and retention.

The Miser as Alchemist, Mother, and Maiden

Another model for the miser besides the Legalist-Taoist one is that of the alchemist. The miser is an alchemist of waste, which he turns into gold. Waste represents a crucial link in the great process of transformation from vegetation to food, waste-fertilizer, and then back to vegetation and food. If the alchemist-miser can capitalize on the key links in this process—like the miser at the door of his public toilet in *Zhaoshi bei*—then he can be the richest man in the world. As the *Laozi* says, by being frugal one can "accumulate virtue"—the miser reads money as virtue; and by accumulating virtue-money one can "possess the state."[27]

Waste also represents entropy; it is something that has leaked out from the fullness of the body. Going out isn't as good as coming in. The miser is fearful of loss, for which he compensates by being frugal, that is, staying at the baseline, being like waste or living in it. For him, offal is the Way. He buys into entropy and death, which are also the Way. As the

Laozi says, "The Way is to the world as the River and the Sea are to rivulets and streams."[28] That is, the flow of food into waste is like the flow of the "rivulets and streams," the "world," into the "River and the Sea," the "Way."

The cyclic production of waste gets us back to the miser's form of reversed sexuality. The miser emulates the ideal of "keep[ing] to the role of the female" that he reads in the *Laozi*.[29] To begin with, he is only nominally a man since he barely fulfills the normal male roles of husband and father. He renounces both the depleting male desire to "drive" women and the moral imperative to nourish sons. Along with these renunciations, he appropriates the role of women by becoming mother of money, replacing children with money and waste, and thereby ensuring himself an ever-increasing number of obedient and profit-earning descendants. This reproductive imagery is exemplified in the allegory of *Changyan dao*, in which the miser is originally a peddler of "firewood," *chai*, punning with *cai*, "wealth," when suddenly one day a piece of "mother money," *muqian*, falls out of the sky onto his scales (132). It is then that he begins to acquire wealth, for "mother money" guarantees the birth of "child money," *ziqian* (126, 135–36). In short, as alchemist and mother, the miser uses his and others' precious rectums as factories through which he converts consumed substance into accumulations of money; he converts pleasure into number, life into death.

As for his attitude toward his real children, the miser in the *Zhaoshi bei* story is more devoted to the business of his public toilets than to the welfare of his only son, who runs away from home, learns to gamble, and begins to squander his father's money. In *Qingmeng tuo* the miser will spend only a small sum to purchase a homely wife for his handsome son. After she dies of neglect, the son takes a second wife at a bride-price of one hundred taels, only thirty of which the miser is willing to pay; the miser's wife pawns jewelry to make up the rest (15a). Whether his efforts to contain himself are successful or not, the miser at least pretends that money and waste allow him to be independent of women and children, especially the shrew and the wastrel, his two worst enemies.

Besides keeping to the role of the female by becoming the mother of waste, he also copies the ways of both the chaste maiden and the prostitute. His retention of money and control of desire allow him to accumulate virtue, like the chaste but alluring maiden waiting for the right suitor. As prostitute, he uses his wealth to attract client-debtors, or, like the owner of the night-soil pits, he uses toilet paper to lure customer-suitors to his pleasure-filled outhouse. All along he never leaves home, his outhouse, but simply waits for people to succumb to nature, that is, to the inevitability that all food must end up as waste, all pleasure must end up as spent energy.

The Ascetic Ji Dian

The ascetic half of the miserly-ascetic paradigm is embodied in a type who likewise features in numerous stories and novels from early times to the Ming and Qing. He will also appear in the chapters below on erotic romances, *Lüye xianzong,* and *Shenlou zhi.* He is often a peripheral or helper character who guides needy people or serves as an example of wise detachment, but in erotic works he typically appears in his sexually active form, providing men with advice for the enhancement of sexual performance. The sex-adept ascetic is commonly an evil character but, in cases when he is not, offers the wisdom of *yang*-preservation and, in the end, self-willed temperance or even abstinence. It should also be noted that the ascetic—particularly in the guise of the eremite—is often primarily defined as someone who withdraws because of frustration with public service, especially in times of bad government; his interaction with women is not necessarily an issue. In some cases he merely half retires, that is, withdraws from the public arena but continues family life as before. Like the miser, the ascetic may not be primarily or most obviously defined by his relation with women, but that relation—or, more precisely, denial of that relation—is an inherent part of his life path and his practice of self-containment. The following discussion will focus mainly on the celibate Ji Gong, Master Ji, also known as Ji Dian or Crazy Ji, a Hangzhou-area Buddhist of the Song dynasty about whom stories and legends exist in several versions through the Ming and Qing, both short and long, and with numerous variations.

The ascetic escapes women through a more deliberate denial than the miser, who is typically too busy and mistrustful of others to have time for women and family; the ascetic takes a vow not to indulge in sex. He forbids himself liquor and meat, and forswears wealth and property, depending on alms to keep alive. Vow-breaking ascetics can be said to consist of two types, one of which is exemplified by "wine-and-meat monks," *jiurou heshang,* like the famous Lu Zhishen in *Shuihu zhuan* or the crazy Ji Dian. Even the worst drunkards and meat lovers, however, are still known to stop short of indulgence in sex. The other type is exemplified by the many "flower" monks (*hua heshang*), mysterious Tibetan lamas, and Taoist sex adepts, who do just what they are not supposed to do and become notorious sex fiends. Some practice the art of retracting the penis, thereby pretending to be female and thus infiltrating homes and harems to seduce women.[30] Ostensibly ascetic, the sex-adept monk is in the end a more illicit, tricksterish variation of the polygynist philanderer; in fiction, their ending is either destruction or enlightened renunciation of sexual desire.

The ascetic may be like Master Xiyi (the *hao* or style-name of the Song dynasty eremite Chen Tuan), who roams obliviously in congested urban areas, "as if there were no one around."[31] In contrast to the more socially engaged Ji Dian, Xiyi and ones like him are the least sociable of the ascetics. The Buddhist Ji Dian loves wine and meat, which he enjoys with friends as they chat and write poetry. He at least loosely attaches himself to his monastery (Xiyi is completely independent), to which he occasionally brings benefit in the form of protection or alms.[32] Ji Dian is a laughing enjoyer of life and a trickster whose favorite trick is the disappearing act: he somersaults, sometimes exposing his penis as his robe falls open, then runs off wherever he pleases until he feels like showing up again.

The ascetic in Chinese fiction and folklore commonly acts in a way that parodies sex and mocks women. An example is Ji Dian's exposure of his penis, a parodic reversal of the sexual trickster's retraction. In one of Ji Dian's most famous episodes, the Empress gives alms to his temple, having dreamt of a *lohan* (that is, *arhat,* a kind of Buddhist saint) who told her that the temple was in need of repair. Upon delivering the money, she asks to see the *lohan* in person. Neither the other monks nor Ji Dian, who made himself appear as the *lohan* in her dream, will admit he is the one, but she recognizes him anyway. When she asks him what he can do in return for her alms, he replies that all he knows is turning a somersault, which he then performs and "to be sure, exposed that thing in front [*qianmiande wushi*] for all to see."[33] In another episode, a monk elder poses a Zen riddle which Ji Dian explains by likewise turning a somersault and exposing his penis.[34] The elder is overjoyed by the "correctness" of the answer; the Empress, far from being insulted, believes such action is Ji Dian's way of ensuring that she will be reborn as a man in her next life. In light of the Empress's reaction, the ascetic's avoidance of sex can be construed as a sign of advancement along the ladder of birth and rebirth. In other words, to have relations with women, who are lower forms of beings than men, is to regress on one's way to enlightenment. Even the highest woman acknowledges her lowly position.

Avoidance and parody of sex also occur in episodes in which the ascetic is far more intimate with women than Ji Dian is with the Empress. The ascetic may almost or actually climb in bed with a woman but stop short of sex or else play a trick on her. In one episode, Ji Dian is presented with a courtesan who pulls him into her room for a night of pleasure; he exclaims that such acts are sinful and quickly departs.[35] In another episode, he tiptoes into the room of his friend's sleeping courtesan and lifts her blanket, only to lay one of her embroidered shoes over her vagina and then leave.[36] In the eighteenth-century *Lüye xianzong*, the ascetic hero Leng Yubing ("Colder Than Ice") asks to sleep with his friend's prostitute-girlfriend. She happily gets in bed with him but finds his body to be ice cold; he then begins to emit cold water from his mouth, causing her to flee in horror.[37]

The common thread of episodes such as these is the man's deliberate demonstration that he has no need for women and suffers from no distraction by them, no matter how close he comes. The same demonstration of containment is a subject of intense portrayal in *Yesou puyan*, discussed in a later chapter, in which chaste exposure of the body—like Ji Dian's chaste exhibitionism—is again the vehicle by which the man proves his resistance to both sexual desire and attraction to women.

It is possible to include as an example of the ascetic a type of character who, strictly speaking, is neither a monk-ascetic nor eremite: the *xia* hero or warrior stalwart. As found in *Shuihu zhuan*, *Chan Zhen yishi*, or *Shi wu pi*, for instance, such characters either openly eschew women or simply show no special interest in them (*bu tan nüse*).[38] Like Ji Dian, some *xia* heroes love to drink, such as Li Kui in *Shuihu zhuan* and Gan Baihong in *Shi wu pi*; some are monks as well, for example, Lu Zhishen or Wu Song in *Shuihu zhuan*. In addition, like Ji Dian, the *xia* heroes disdain wealth and above all despise misers. Again, like the ascetic, they reject and even battle against the order of miserly economics but still adhere to the hierarchy of gender. "All men are brothers" is the motto of *Shuihu zhuan*'s all-male assembly of rebel-bandits who battle corrupt officials, rob bad rich people, and kill lascivious women.

Whatever the combination of characteristics, the ascetic and his variants represent viable and honored alternatives in Chinese society for men who meet with frustration in public or private life. Sometimes it is not a matter of frustration but of supposed enlightenment about the trueness of one's being or the futility of pursuing a normal life. The laughing, unkempt, in some cases scrofulous monk is the antithesis of the traditional patriarch, the economic and moral pillar of society. But although antithetical in other respects, the ascetic and the polygamist are still very alike in that ascetic withdrawal is hardly more available to women than is polygamy, which is of course not available at all. The gendered construction of ascetic withdrawal is thus the topic I will treat in concluding this chapter.

Self-Containment, Male and Female

Ascetic withdrawal is a gendered concept in that it is a mode primarily advised for the man. Fictional male ascetics draw themselves in, they absorb essences, they replenish themselves; they are wary or mocking of sexual expenditure. They may accidentally or uncontrollably succumb to women, but they recontain themselves and swear never to indulge again. They know that if they do indulge, they will suffer fatal loss of energy and become "fearers of the inner one" (*ju nei*).

In female form, ascetics appear as sexually active nuns or as women either driven by misfortune or led by enlightenment into renouncing life as marriageable or otherwise sexually available persons. Most play minor roles; and it is often the case that their renunciation arouses suspicion: in other words, nuns are suspected of being sexually active because women are known to be inherently lascivious and undisciplined. The nun Miaoyu in *Honglou meng* is a rare example of a celibate woman who plays a substantial role, but she has also traditionally been suspected by readers and commentators of being unchaste.

Female warriors (*xianü*), counterparts to male chivalric figures, also appear as both central and peripheral characters in numerous Qing novels—for example, Thirteenth Sister in *Ernü yingxiong zhuan* or Tang Sai'er in *Nüxian waishi* (History of the Female Immortal), both celibate and both central to their stories (although Thirteenth Sister eventually marries). A common female character type who is not, strictly speaking, an ascetic is the go-between, an often tricksterish woman who travels between households matching couples, sometimes facilitating illicit affairs, and assisting with sexual and medical advice and such things as herbal abortion drugs; she is wise to the desires of her paying clients. The go-between is in effect celibate and independent since she is typically beyond childbearing years and is widowed or else not explicitly part of a husband-led household. Except for highly active characters like Thirteenth Sister, however, celibacy is usually the end of the woman's story.

The rationale for this silence about ascetic women has to do with the fact that the values of filiality discourage celibacy in anyone, but in women more than men. Moreover, both the ars erotica and traditional medical science assert that celibacy is an unhealthy choice for humans, but again more so for women than men. As Charlotte Furth has shown, while medical belief affirms that men can preserve and even gain strength through continence, women who want to remain normal and healthy are advised to remain sexually active, although even that activity cannot prevent the ill effects of childbirth or menstruation.[39] In short, no matter how they behave, women are destined to be uncontainable, just as the shrew and the lascivious woman affirm to the aggressive extreme.

Fiction adheres to social and medical-erotic values by generally failing to portray women as vigorous celibates. The usual mode of hermetic behavior for women is one of involuntary asceticism. For example, to be or seem a virtuous woman, she is obliged to follow classic models of modesty and self-sacrifice, as *Lin Lan Xiang*'s Yan Mengqing goes too far in doing. The virtuous woman is supposed to confine her activities to the home and avoid casual contact with men and even women who are not of the household (e.g., go-betweens and nuns). In short, few women enjoy the tricksterish forms of self-containment of men like Ji Dian. The range of choice between happy polygamous indulgence and carefree ascetic withdrawal belongs mainly to men. Women can actively resist this situation only by realizing their "true" potential and putting to good use their supposed shrewish propensity to "overflow" and enervate the man. Otherwise, they have to learn to master the sane and self-prevailing ways of characters like the nonweeping, nonrepressed Meng Yulou in *Jin Ping Mei*, Xuan Ainiang in *Lin Lan Xiang*, and Xue Baochai in *Honglou meng*.

The next two chapters go in the opposite direction from the scowling miser and rampaging shrew by treating the talented, good-looking, and refined couple of the beauty and the scholar. The chaste romances of chapter 5 present a world in which the woman accomplishes her goal of monogamy without resort to shrewishness. As the shrew prevails over her henpecked husband, so also the beauty prevails over the scholar. But in the beauty's case, she stands out because of superior wits and literary talent, not power of temper. The erotic romances of chapter 6, on the other hand, portray a world in which one man, the polygamist adept, wisely and benevolently presides over a bevy of smart and sexy women, none of whom are jealous or conniving. Such a man knows how to achieve an equilibrium that avoids both excess indulgence and excess meanness; he is the latter-day protagonist of the story told in the ancient ars erotica.

5

THE CHASTE "BEAUTY-SCHOLAR"

ROMANCE AND THE SUPERIORITY OF

THE TALENTED WOMAN[1]

The Romantic Marriage of
Talented Beauty and Handsome Scholar

In the mid-seventeenth century a type of vernacular romance appeared that literary studies and colloquial parlance refer to as the story of the "scholar and the beauty" (*caizi jiaren*). One of the most prominent features of these works is their portrayal of smart, capable, and chaste young women who are equal to or better than their male counterparts in terms of literary talent, moral fiber, and wit. Along with the excellence and chastity of the woman, these works also feature monogamous or at most two-wife polygynous marriage. The male partner in this marriage conforms to none of the types dealt with so far in this book: potent polygynist, wastrel, miser, ascetic, or henpecked husband. He is instead an effeminate scholar-poet who in effect yields his right to polygyny (except in limited form), and allows the woman to take the superior and active role. Instead of being a shrew, the woman is in turn metamorphized into a talented female scholar who wins monogamy and her own choice of husband. As my examples will demonstrate, however, to a great extent the woman achieves her superiority only by becoming like a man, that is, by cross-dressing and literally acting and writing like him. The relationship of the beauty and scholar thus takes on the characteristics of the friendship between two literati men. An asymmetry emerges in their exchange of gender characteristics in that while she chastely engages in cross-dressing and male-impersonation, a man cannot perform the complementary opposite without, as we will see, erotic complicity.

In referring to these works, I use the term "chaste romances" in order to distinguish them from contemporaneous erotic romances in which scholars and beauties are unchaste and scholars marry three or more beauties. There is an almost rule-bound distinction between the variables of "chaste" and "one or two" wives on the one hand, and "erotic" and "three or more" wives on the other—almost rule-bound because borderline cases exist, as I will show. The illusion of symmetrical parity that can be maintained between one man and one or even two women breaks down once the man has more than two wives. Because of the singularity of the woman in the chaste works, I will make a further differentiation and sometimes refer to these stories as "beauty-scholar" romances instead of using the usual word order of "scholar-beauty" (Chinese allows both word orders, but not to my knowledge with a difference in connotation). In what follows, I will first discuss the historical and literary context of the beauty-scholar romance and then its definition as a genre of vernacular fiction. The main body of this chapter will consist of examining individual works, with special focus on the portrayal of female superiority, symmetry and asymmetry between man and woman, and the peculiar recurrence of two-wife polygyny.

Not an isolated phenomenon, the prominence in chaste romances of talented women and their romantic marriage to handsome scholars is part of a remolding among high-literate circles of prescribed male and female roles. The beauty-scholar romance is a playing ground for positions expressed since the late sixteenth century by noted literati critical of norms governing women and marriage, especially such things as the oversequestration of women or the dictum that it is virtuous for a woman to be uneducated.[2] The sixteenth-century thinker Li Zhi's and others' statements that women are as intelligent as men or that women should be allowed their own choice in marriage have a definite connection with the way such statements are played out as themes in these romances.[3] Many examples from literature corroborate the elevation of women. Liao Zhongan and Aiyama Kiwamu cite numerous late Ming and early Qing works, including beauty-scholar romances and prefaces to women's poetry collections, that all make use of the same literary allusion to assert the superior essence of women and, by implication, the baseness of men.[4] Paul Ropp discusses the early Qing author Pu Songling (1640–1715), who uses classical language to create many of the same portraits met in the vernacular romances; for example, women more "strong-willed, . . . intelligent, and . . . courageous" than men, or lovers who choose their own partners and marry monogamously.[5] Patrick Hanan writes of Li Yu (1611–79 or 80), whose drama and fiction are full of clever women with brilliant schemes, women who are more active than men in pursuing goals of self-interest, which they put ahead of the traditional goals of self-sacrifice.[6] Similar views on women continue in the mid-Qing among prominent male literati such as Wu Jingzi (1701–54), Cao Xueqin (1715?–63?), Yuan Mei (1716–98), Dai Zhen (1724–77), Ji Yun (1724–1805), Li Ruzhen (ca. 1763–1830), and Yu Zhengxie (1775–1840), who variously take up the praise of women and the criticism of such things as footbinding, widow chastity, or concubinage.[7]

By the time these romances appear, Chinese literature has already had a long tradition of featuring the companionship between literatus and talented courtesan. The late Ming in particular sees a celebration of the romantic and intellectual relationship between these two.[8] Ming drama and both classical and vernacular fiction contain numerous stories about the love affairs of scholars and, instead of courtesans, chaste beauties. In continuation of these traditions, the beauty-scholar romance portrays chaste women who, like a small but significant number of real counterparts in the mid-seventeenth century, are active in male social and literary spheres normally off-limits to them.[9] The romance can also be seen as expanding the traditional equation between chastity and female excellence that Susan Mann has discussed in terms of Qing propaganda on widow chastity. The public honoring of chaste widows in China functioned to suggest that "female chastity was a metaphor for community honor." The worth and honor of a family could be enhanced by the chastity of its widows.[10] Going beyond the image of woman as passive sufferer, the beauty-scholar romance provides the chaste female with powers of self-determination and self-invention that exceed not only normal female roles but male ones as well. In other words, although self-sacrificing chastity is still the main model for female excellence, the scope of chastity also expands to allow for active female self-direction, at least in the imaginary realm of the romances and other Qing works of fiction and drama.[11]

The chaste Qing romance must also be seen against the tendencies of previous fiction, in particular, the late Ming erotic story and its portrayals of men and women easily given to illicit sexual passion. The romances covered in this chapter—especially the "classics" of the early period such as *Haoqiu zhuan* (The Fortunate Union), *Ping Shan Leng Yan* (Les deux jeunes filles lettrés, or "The Two Talented Beauties"), and *Yu Jiao Li* (Les deux cousines, or "The Two Cousins")[12]—react against the "decadence" of late Ming fiction but at the same time continue the liberationist trend of the late Ming works on a more rational and self-controlled level.[13] The liberation I refer to in the chaste romances is the lovers' freedom to choose their own marriage partners rather than acquiesce to parental arrangement; the woman in particular gains a greater privilege of choice, often winning a monogamous marriage. The price of this freedom, however, is the rationalization and de-eroticization of love. The lovers must promise, as it were, not to indulge themselves before marriage; above all, the woman must remain chaste. In addition, superior man and woman must wend their way through a complex series of obstacles before they attain union in the end.

Viewed in the political context of the Ming Qing transition, the sense of reform and decorum in these works suggests the early Qing atmosphere of governmental stability and of confidence in the new dynasty. The chastity of the woman perhaps also implies the chastity of the Han-Chinese literatus or the Han in general, including those hoping that the Qing Manchus will appreciate their talents. In another light, however, chaste loyalty also evokes the image of those Han still loyal to the fallen Ming. As a model for supra-conformist female behavior, then, the beauty can be seen as a vehicle not only for the instancing of freer access between man and woman but also for the declaration of Han purity vis-à-vis the disreputable Ming or the usurping Qing.[14]

Another important factor in the production of these works is the possibility of female readership and even authorship. Since a prominent motif in the romances, talented women dressing as men, also occurs in Qing plays and chantefables written by and for women, it is tempting to think that some romances were written by women.[15] But since known male authors also wrote such works, this and similar motifs are not alone decisive in determining an author's gender. Nevertheless, considering both the prominence of female literary activities in the seventeenth and eighteenth centuries and the ambiguities of the motif of cross-dressing, female readership should be assumed. The question of authorship, however, is one of ongoing speculation.[16]

With these brief historical considerations as background, my interest below will be to describe the characteristic way the beauty-scholar romance balances woman and man. As formulaic and predictable as these novels may be, they always construct a tension between (1) the normal way marriages are arranged, with partners chosen by the parents and with talented women possibly married to boorish or profligate men, and (2) the ideal, nonconformist way played out in the story. Idealism is grounded in a formulaic symmetry or equivalence that patterns the lovers' approach to marriage: man and woman are both single children missing at least one parent; or the lovers cross with each other in that woman impersonates man and man resembles woman. Such similarity and mirror opposition imply a perfect dovetailing of male and female, sometimes neutralizing sexual differences and at other times creating an outright exchange of masculine and feminine characteristics. As a genre, the beauty-scholar romances work toward a vision of man and woman who are not really male and female and who do everything they can to avoid having sex. The couple replaces sex with words: poems, letters, and engaging conversation. Resembling two literati friends, they become *zhiji*, "intimate companions" or "knowers-of-each-other's-innermost," not *yuanjia*, "enemies enamoured," the term for the infatuated lovers of late Ming fiction, whose capsule of passion explodes in the end because of excess indulgence. In the late Ming erotic story, passion exceeds the capacity to fulfill it; in the chaste Qing romance, the lovers contain their passion and achieve everlasting harmony.

Definition of the Chaste *Caizi Jiaren* Romance

The chaste, or what I will also call classic, beauty-scholar romance can be defined as a novel of around ten to twenty chapters about a young man and woman (sometimes a man and two women) who represent the best in intelligence, looks, and moral character that civilization has to offer.[17] They meet by chance and get to know each other, often through the exchange of literary messages, especially love poetry. It is spontaneously apparent that they are meant for each other. Mean people try to steal the woman away or otherwise prevent the two from uniting but fail because the youths are so much cleverer and more virtuous. Their love exists just outside—but not too far from—the traditional system of marriage according to "ritual," *li*, that is, following the arrangement of the parents

and matching the wealth and rank of the two families. The match of the
beauty and scholar is for their own benefit rather than their parents',
although they ultimately obtain their parents' blessings and conform to
the standards that their parents would apply anyway. The classic romances are devoid of descriptions of sex, although they vary in whether
or not they allow the unmarried lovers to embrace or hold hands. Realistic detail is extremely sparse. For example, in one work the lovers elope,
but the precise steps they take to do so are completely omitted (*Zhuchun
yuan*, chs. 16 and 17). The language is correspondingly polite and elegant,
rarely obscene or colorfully colloquial as in other fiction of the period.

Both the chaste and erotic romances share the generic features of
length and plot just outlined but differ in two main respects: the number
of the man's partners and the presence or not of explicit sexual detail.
More precisely, the chaste romances at most allow the man two main
wives and an additional maid as concubine; the erotic romances give the
man two or more wives, concubines, and / or paramours, male or female.
These latter works continue the erotic trend begun in the sixteenth
century, but differ in that they center on ultimately conjugal, not adulterous or otherwise illicit, sex. The contrast between chaste and erotic is
essential in defining the theme of the superiority of women, which is
attenuated in the erotic romances because of the recentering of the sexual
interests of the man. The erotic romance sometimes harks back to the
chaste romance by having the man save sex with his premier one or two
wives until marriage. The erotic romance can even describe in great detail
sex among characters other than the hero and heroine, or allow the hero a
premarital liaison with someone other than his heroine, but finally have
him and his heroine remain premaritally chaste and monogamous (as in
Taohua yanshi). Nevertheless, the women of the erotic romance, whether
or not premaritally chaste, have fewer superior qualities than the heroines
of the classic beauty-scholar novels. Sometimes the polygamist's women
split among themselves the superior features of the monogamist's one
chaste wife; that is, one wife might be intelligent, another beautiful, and a
third valiant.[18] At the same time, despite the lesser stature of the women,
the hero of the erotic romance is still a talented and benevolent husband
whom the women gladly and unjealously serve. In the end, the chaste and
erotic romances are alike in instancing fulfilled love in a civilized marriage
of scholar and beauty or beauties.

How and why is *caizi jiaren* fiction (chaste or erotic) defined as a genre of vernacular fiction? The origin of the *caizi jiaren*–type story can be taken back to the famous Han dynasty love affair between Zhuo Wenjun and Sima Xiangru, or Tang tales such as "Yingying zhuan" (The Tale of Yingying) or "Liwa zhuan" (The Tale of Liwa), or Yuan and Ming operas such as *Xixiang ji* (Romance of the Western Chamber, in which the term *caizi jiaren* itself appears)[19] or *Mudan ting* (Peony Pavilion). The lovers in these stories elope, meet secretly, or simply are a "true" match in spite of parental opposition.[20] Such stories are extremely common in the Ming and Qing in both operatic and fictional forms, one often being an adaptation from the other.[21] As comic romances (although some of the above antecedents are not comic), *caizi jiaren* stories differ little from those in any culture about a young man and woman who are destined to be together, encounter obstacles to their union, but finally overcome them and unite in marriage. As a group of like books, not simply stories with universal features, however, the *caizi jiaren* romances constitute a genre that attains a specific historical identity because of its appearance in ten- or twenty-chapter (or so) form around the early Qing. This identity has been noted in studies of literary history like Lu Xun's *A Brief History of Chinese Fiction* (1930) since the 1930s.[22]

The mainland scholar Lin Chen has written one of the most comprehensive studies of the genre in recent years. He and others have noted the obvious prominence of remarkable women in these novels.[23] Many scholars observe the formulaic quality of character portrayal and plot. In his seminal study of 1934, Guo Changhe dismissed the genre for its lack of imagination; the topic of *caizi jiaren* fiction was hardly touched for the next fifty years.[24] Recent scholarship has redeemed these works mainly by celebrating their promotion of self-determination in marriage, an idea that the novels themselves do not openly promote. As Lin Chen notes, although the term *caizi jiaren* was common by the early Qing, it already bore what was then the notorious connotation of self-determined marriage between two talented and good-looking youths (56). Some of the works even eschew the appearance of free choice, such as *Haoqiu zhuan* and *Xing fengliu* (Love Awakening), so that this feature, or any other for that matter, is not universal for this genre.[25]

Identification of the existence of the "scholar-beauty book," or *caizi jiaren shu* (also *caizi jiaren xiaoshuo*), must have come about shortly after the fiction started being written and its formulas became set. The term *caizi jiaren*—or *jiaren caizi*—appears in the romances themselves in both positive and negative senses, but in neither sense very often. Although authors write about *caizi* and *jiaren*, they perhaps avoid the words themselves because of their notorious connotations.[26] One of the earliest cases of the recognition of this group of books is Liu Tingji's derogatory reference in about 1715. For him these "recent" books are a nuisance but are not as bad as the obscene novels and stories that the late Ming and early Qing produced in great number, although he has high praise for *Jin Ping Mei*.[27] Another famous reference is the one in *Honglou meng* about "beauty-scholar and other such books," *jiaren caizi deng shu* (perhaps significantly putting "beauty" before "scholar"), which are well-established by *Honglou meng*'s time in the early and mid-eighteenth century. The romances are said to be all alike, of inferior literary quality, and obscene.[28] A passage in one of the later romances, *Zhuchun yuan xiaoshi* (The Garden of Spring Residence), reflects awareness of such criticism and declares its attempt to be different.[29]

In his description of the evolution of *caizi jiaren* fiction, Lin Chen says that the most active phase of production is from the late Shunzhi reign period (ends 1661) to the late Kangxi (ends 1722). In the early period, from circa the 1640s to circa the 1670s, the love story is intertwined with episodes about national events, is complex in plot, and is little occupied with the realistic concerns of everyday life. From the 1670s on, the *caizi jiaren* story appears both in works that continue as before but with minor variations and in those which have a greater variety of contents.[30]

In what follows in this and the next chapters, I will examine the *caizi jiaren* romance along a continuum from the chaste to the erotic. This continuum is not historical since chaste and erotic romances existed at the same time from the start. But there does seem to be a gradual attenuation of the superior woman's role the further one gets from the chaste romances of the early Qing—for example, *Yu Jiao Li, Ping Shan Leng Yan,* and *Haoqiu zhuan*. In general, the more erotic the story, the less central the woman and the more polygamous the man. The remarkable woman of the classic ten- to twenty-chapter romance appears in later works of the same length and in longer ones like *Honglou meng* and *Lin Lan Xiang* but tends not to be as boldly heroic as before. This tempering of heroism, incidentally, seems to parallel a shift among female literati after the early Qing to more cloistered literary and artistic activity. As Ellen Widmer and others have described, and as depicted in *Honglou meng* and actually found, for instance, in Yuan Mei's circle of women writers and painters, eighteenth-century women were more cloistered than their seventeenth-century predecessors, who tended to travel more and associated more with non-kin women.[31]

The Remarkable Woman and Her Relationship with the Man

As I have mentioned above, the talented and independent woman is not new in Chinese literature, nor is her attachment to a handsome scholar. Her appearance in such a number of romances of the early- to mid-Qing, however, is a strong identifying feature of these works.[32] A woman who can do as well as or better than men, she often dresses as a man in order to move about more freely than custom ordinarily allows; she goes out to get what she wants rather than wait for things to come to her in her inner chambers.[33] A motto of hers in one instance is "Though in body I am a woman, in ambition I surpass men" (*Baigui zhi,* ch. 1, 6). Dressed as a man she can say what she wishes, even set up her own marriage. She is typically an only child cherished by her parents, especially her father, who educates her as if she were a boy.[34] She helps her father and her lover out of predicaments (*Yuzhi ji, Yu Jiao Li,* and others). Her poetic skill startles even the emperor (*Ping Shan Leng Yan, Fenghuang chi*). She is worth ten sons or ten men. But in the end all she wants is the man she has chosen for herself, the one worthy of her; she doesn't even mind if, as often happens, he takes a second wife.

Her equality to or superiority over her husband is part of a symmetry of mutual correspondence which extends to numerous areas beyond talent and willpower.[35] For example, if she is an only daughter with a father and deceased mother, then he is an only son with a mother and deceased father (*Yu Jiao Li*). Even if not as neatly symmetrical as this, the lovers are both typically only children with one or both parents deceased.[36] They are monogamous and sexually balanced, for "man and woman are the same as concerns the great desire" (*Dingqing ren,* ch. 3, 23). All she wants is for them "to be equal husband and wife" (*Dingqing ren,* ch. 12, 112). In one work, symmetry of plot development also helps establish their complementarity; that is, they run into parallel sequences of difficulties, thus showing that their fates are intertwined (*Feihua yong*).

When they are together, they conduct discussions in which the woman has as much input as or more than the man. The man does not condescend to the woman. Certain deprecating expressions that other male characters use, such as derogatory references to the "woman's way of thinking" (*furen jianshi*), are not part of the handsome scholar's vocabulary (*Lin er bao*, ch. 1, 5). We may even imagine that the couple will die in old age at the same moment, seated peacefully with smiles on their faces, as do an elderly well-matched husband and wife in *Baigui zhi* (The Tale of the White Jade Tablet) whose corpses never rot (ch. 16, 118).

The crossing of gender characteristics is a major aspect of the lovers' complementarity. The young man and woman look alike or at least easily pass as members of each other's gender.[37] In *Haoqiu zhuan* and *Xing fengliu* the young man is "just like a beautiful woman" (*Haoqiu zhuan*, ch. 1, 2; and *Xing fengliu*, ch. 1, 2). In *Feihua yong* (The Song of Fluttering Flowers) it is said that the young hero would be beautiful if he were to dress as a woman (ch. 5, 45), although he does not actually do so. Usually only the woman cross-dresses. The other half of the cross-dress story occurs only in Ming and Qing erotic works, in which a man disguises as a woman either to seduce unsuspecting women[38] or to have homosexual liaisons with men who like female impersonators.[39] The classic beauty-scholar romance is the story of the upward mobility of the woman, so that a man dressing and acting like a woman would be not only illogical but perverse. In short, gender hierarchy dictates (1) that men do not willingly go "down" except to undermine or pervert the supposedly natural social order[40] and, moreover, (2) that women going "up" must act like men in order to prove their superiority.

Besides the lack of symmetry in cross-dressing, there is often a similar imbalance in the ratio of men to women. Although famous early works such as *Haoqiu zhuan* and *Ping Shan Leng Yan* feature monogamous relationships, in many other romances the author allows the man a second wife and perhaps a maid as concubine. But the story is always carefully worked out so that the two wives, often good friends, are equal in rank and are not jealous of each other or of the maid.[41] The maid herself is the close companion of one of the wives (also often a go-between for the man and woman) and therefore mercifully kept in the family rather than married off and never seen again. However, as indicated above, if there are any more than these two wives, then the novel is usually erotic, and the plot is a series of sexual adventures in which the man collects one woman after another, to become the successful and benevolent polygamist found in Qing works like *Shenlou zhi, Wushan yanshi* (The Fantasy of Mt. Wu), or *Xinghua tian* (The Paradise of Apricot Blossoms).

We must now flesh out the above characteristics—(1) the talents of the woman, especially her brilliance at impersonating men, (2) the symmetry between man and woman, and (3) the asymmetry of one scholar married to two beauties—by looking more closely at individual novels. My selection of works is in part based on availability in either modern published form or rare library edition.[42] In addition, since Richard Hessney has treated some of the most prominent romances elsewhere, I have chosen works that appear not to have been well known in Qing times and that to date have never or rarely been introduced in English. In order to give a sense of a probable model for other romances, I include one that is well known, *Yu Jiao Li,* one of the so-called classics of the genre. None of the works have determinable authors or precise dates of composition. Finally, in this and the next chapters I will devote more than the usual space to describing story contents, for the sake both of introducing new material and of providing information that I will use to make comparisons between works and to draw conclusions about them.

Women Impersonating Men in Baigui zhi and Fenghuang chi

In *Baigui zhi* (The Tale of the White Jade Tablet), a sixteen-chapter novel of the late eighteenth or early nineteenth century, altogether five women disguise themselves as men in order to take the imperial exams or meet face to face with the men they hope to marry.[43] Dressed as a man, a heroine avoids openly breaking the rule of noncontact between unmarried men and women. As in numerous other works, one of the heroines even impersonates the man she eventually marries (chs. 7, 8). At the end, the emperor is about to marry two of the highest imperial examinees to his daughter and the daughter of a prince but then learns that the two examinees are women. He forgives them, saying that it is too bad such talented women can't be put to use serving the state: "Alas, what can be done about it?" (ch. 16, 117).

Although disguising oneself as a man is a breach of propriety—and deception of the emperor is the greatest crime of all—the women are ultimately forgiven because they are seen to have no alternative and to mean no harm. At first, when the father of one of the women discovers she has secretly arranged her own betrothal, he tries to have her buried alive. Later another man orders the arrest of his daughter and her secret lover. In both cases, the women are forced to fend for themselves and perceive that the best way of doing so is to disguise as men. The spectacularity of their success is what finally gains them their way.

In *Baigui zhi* there are no bad women, only bad men: the two fathers just mentioned, whose wives openly oppose their husbands' harshness, and a young scholar who has as much talent (*cai*) as the good youths but lacks virtue (*de*). He impersonates one of the heroes in order to marry one of the beauties; failing that, he tries to elope with another beauty, fails again, and dies in prison (chs. 5 and 6). The same two beauties eventually become co-wives of the hero whom the impostor tried to impersonate. In another part of the novel, the bad man is one who blithely promises his sister to another man without consulting her or other family members; his wife upbraids him and has him undo his promise (ch. 12, 84).

Fenghuang chi (The Phoenix Pool), in sixteen chapters and written before 1754,[44] uses the ploy of impersonation to create a many-layered and deliberately playful series of disguises whereby the two brilliant heroines become altogether six people—three men and three women. In one of her impersonations, the first heroine disguises as her future husband and marries the second heroine; in another strategy, the first heroine in effect marries herself (*zi jia zile*, ch. 15, 3b): having once disguised as a Mr. Shi, she leads others to believe that she is married to him. As usual in the chaste romance, the male-impersonating heroine is the mastermind of strategies and the most talented of the main characters. Also as in other romances, symmetrical matching in *Fenghuang chi* extends to members of both the same and opposite sexes. For example, one of the main heroes, a scholar, befriends an expert in military arts. The scholar marries a beauty for a "civil" marriage, while the military talent marries a female military talent for a "martial" marriage. Before their marriages, the scholar and another hero—both orphans, one poor and one rich—befriend each other because they are two rare talents who can find no one else in the empire as worthy as each other.

In *Fenghuang chi* as in *Baigui zhi*, the exposure of the heroine's clever disguise is not a scandal but instead a joke contributing to a "good romantic tale" (*jiahua*, ch. 7, 9a). In the first step of exposure, the maid of the undisguised heroine seeks to have sex with the male servant of the supposed husband (i.e., the main heroine). Like the "husband," however, the "male" servant is also a woman in disguise. The maid creeps into the sleeping servant's room at night,

> felt around the lower part of "his" body, but found nothing there! It was plain and flat just like herself! . . . She thought she must have felt the wrong place, maybe the back, not the front. . . . So she felt "him" once more, inch by inch from the top down, first reaching two breasts, already rising up high, then felt down below. But, in fact, again all she found was that whatever she had, "he" had, whatever she hadn't, "he" hadn't. (ch. 7, 10ab)

This sole passage of semierotic detail is an example of how the chaste romance allows a measure of ribaldry but strictly at the level of a lower-class character like the maid. She later reports to her mistress (the undisguised heroine) not what actually happened but that she saw the supposed male servant picking lice from "his" clothing, under which she noticed "he" had breasts. The revelation of the servant's disguise leads to the unveiling of the supposed husband's. The undisguised heroine is finally relieved rather than outraged since she had wondered about her "husband's" failure to make love to her. The two heroines then swear sisterhood and begin plotting their marriages to the two heroes.

The stories about women impersonating men make little mention of the practical difficulties of such disguise, especially the concealment of the woman's bound feet. In his early nineteenth-century *Fusheng liuji* (Six Episodes of a Floating Life), Shen Fu provides a biographical account of his wife's disguising as a man in order to accompany him on a brief outing. Her feet are troublesome but not insurmountably so in the contained situation of the episode.[45] In the mildly erotic *Qingmeng tuo,* the disguised woman's feet begin to hurt during her escape on foot from the villain; she trips when someone unaware of her "little feet" (*xiao jiao,* ch. 12, 8b) has her turn around too abruptly. Another erotic polygamous romance, *Wufeng yin* (Song of the Five Phoenixes), provides a description of how the cross-dressed woman successfully hides her bound feet: she stuffs the front of her shoes with foot-wrapping material, then sews her shoes to her socks to keep her feet from slipping out (ch. 12, 7a).[46] The chaste beauty-scholar romances are rarely so realistic, but it is not surprising to find such detail in the polygamous romance, which treats the woman's body and feet with erotic interest.

An important aspect of the ploy of impersonation in *Fenghuang chi* and other works is the comedy of errors produced by multiple disguises and by the consequent potential for confusion of bed partners. A play with numbers is also at work, generating duplication, triplication, and so forth, and creating such statements as "Two beauties turn into six people; six beauties combine into two people" (ch. 13, 14b). Such ability at transformation gives the woman something like supernatural power over forces that would normally control her fate.

Symmetry of Experience in Feihua yong

The early Qing *Feihua yong* (The Song of Fluttering Flowers), in sixteen chapters, takes symmetry to another height of artificiality by making the experiences of the two lovers precisely parallel.[47] Two seven-year-olds, a boy and a girl, spontaneously exchange couplets as they and their parents watch a festival; the two are matched then and there. Misfortune causes each of their families to split apart and both children to end up with adopted parents. The boy and girl meet again, though without recognizing each other, secretly exchange poetry, and make a marriage pact. Circumstances force them to separate once more and eventually each is adopted by the other's father, again without recognition. The play of symmetry is such that the man and woman exchange not only poetic couplets but also family units in order to show that they are equal and meant for each other. This notion is restated toward the end of the novel when their trading of surnames is compared to "*yin* changing into *yang*, *yang* changing into *yin*" (ch. 15, 141). Since it is impossible for them actually to exchange genders, they merely exchange parents. They approximate switching genders in two places where such switches are imagined: First, as a youngster, she is said to be so bright that "if she were a boy" she could certainly gain fame in the literary world (ch. 3, 25). Later, when they meet for the second time, she remarks to herself how beautiful he would be if dressed as a woman (ch. 5, 45).

The ancient theory of interplay between *yin* and *yang* suggests a continuous interrelatedness of the two poles both within and between individuals. As it applies in these novels, such symmetry suggests both formal equivalence (or even distribution) and complementarity. The lovers are "equal" in that they have like abilities and are evenly balanced in status and power within their marriage. They are complementary in that they mirror each other (e.g., the girl's mother is dead and so is the boy's father), or they alternate attributes and situations (e.g., she impersonates a man, even her future husband, while he is like a woman; they exchange families). Sometimes they are equal in the sense of being identical but only temporarily or ephemerally, such as when the woman duplicates a man and the man looks like a woman.

The combination of identity and complementarity is most apparent in the lovers' quintessential form of interaction, the exchange of matched poetry. The nature of Chinese poetry allows for extensive symmetry. Let us say that you and I exchange a poem. We use the same tonal pattern, rhyme, and syntax; the classes of empty and full words in my couplet match those in yours. We mirror each other perfectly. At the same time, you are my complementary, not identical, image; we use words and imagery that are sometimes antithetic, sometimes analogous, but not exactly the same. Of course, regardless of gender, it is safe to assume that numerous external, asymmetrical factors—for example, poetic skill and social hierarchy—will influence the ostensible harmony of the poetic exchange.

In sum, symmetry as I use it here is an abstract term that includes such functions as equivalence, identity, and complementarity. It refers to a mirroring (i.e., the reflection of you in me and me in you) and connotes parallelism, the idea of similarity and analogy across an intermediate distance. As applied to the beauty-scholar story, symmetry implies that the lovers are equal in capacity, sometimes to the extent that they can duplicate or be mistaken for each other, although such plays on gender identity are mainly left to the imagination or are part of a temporary ruse. At the same time, it should be added, symmetry can be viewed as a mechanism through which one person, the man, projects in the other, the woman, a perfect (or "more perfect") image of himself. The mirror effect, in short, also functions to control or mold the reflection rather than simply to embody equivalence and complementarity. The idea of controlling the reflection has to do with idealizing the woman, a topic that I will further treat in concluding this chapter.

The Chaste Polygamous Romance *Yu Jiao Li*

Numerous chaste romances feature what I will call two-wife polygyny, in which neither wife assumes the subordinate rank of concubine. Symmetry still takes effect, in this case applying between the man and one or both of the women or between the women themselves. In these stories, the scholar wins two talented beauties instead of one; the two women are close friends and glad to stay together in a bigamous marriage. The illusion of symmetry in this case creates what is almost a marriage of three people to each other rather than one man to two women.

The twenty-four chapter *Yu Jiao Li* (The Two Cousins) of the early Qing provides one of the best-known examples of the kind of two-wife polygyny I am describing.[48] As in other romances featuring such a marriage, it is made clear very early that the man never intended to have more than one wife. As if to enhance the sense of monogamous singularity, the author constructs a system of equivalences in which both the scholar and the first beauty are only-children, she motherless and raised by her father, he fatherless and raised by his mother. When her parents fail to have a son, her father takes a series of concubines, all of whom fail to have children, although when he remarries them to other men they bear sons. The heroine is then born; her mother dies soon after. Having only a daughter changes from a misfortune into a blessing because it is a situation so singly intended by fate. She is so special that she is said to be more talented than "ten sons" (ch. 6, 68).[49]

As in other romances, her excellence allows her the superior position when it comes to selecting a husband, who must win her in a poetry competition with other suitors (chs. 6, 7). When the hero's poetry proves the best, his and her match is established. But villainous plots separate the couple, leaving him to meet another woman who eventually becomes his second betrothed. The second woman (cousin of the first) and he meet when she dresses as a man, having gone out to find a husband of her own choice. To achieve her goal, she stages a clever deception by inventing a sister, i.e., herself, and promising this sister to the man, withholding the truth from him until a later time.

In arranging the second match, the author makes sure that the hero does not appear to agree easily to marry another woman. When the disguised woman realizes that he is already betrothed, she tests him by asking what he would do if a second woman were available to him. He replies that he could not be of "two hearts" (ch. 14, 155). However, after becoming bosom friends with this "man," the hero is delighted to accept an offer of betrothal to the man's "sister." He reasons that since he has lost contact with his first love, the second offer is something within reach. When the "man" asks him what he would do if his first love reappeared, he says that he would marry both women and make them equal in status (ch. 14, 158). Later, the double marriage is legitimized by reference to the precedent of the ancient emperor Shun who married two sisters. In addition, having themselves become friends, the two women feel that by being married to the same man they will always have each other and thus will not have to worry about "boredom" in the "inner chambers" (ch. 16, 181). In the end the hero also takes as concubine one of his wives' maids who helped to arrange their marriage.

In *Yu Jiao Li* symmetry is at work to some degree between the man and each of the women. The man and the first woman mirror each other in being only children raised by one parent of the opposite sex to the child. The man and the second woman match in both having widowed mothers; they are both a same-sex and opposite-sex pair because of the woman's switching of gender roles. The two women correspond by being cousins, each of whom has a widowed parent, one male, the other female; like other same-sex and opposite-sex pairs, they become special friends when they display their talent through an exchange of matched poetry (ch. 15).

The cross-dressing in this case includes an element found in other romances, the ploy of the woman dividing herself in two—disguising herself as a man and inventing a "sister" self whom "she" betroths to the scholar-hero.[50] In some romances, the man also splits himself up in order to assume a disguise allowing him better access to the woman. In these cases, however, he enacts a form of self-degradation by turning to humbler social versions of his own gender—becoming, for example, the gardener or scholar's servant (*shutong*) in the woman's house (I will return to the man's self-lowering in the conclusion below and in later chapters where it is more obvious). In such disguises he is unlike the cross-dressed woman because he is too low in status to be able to arrange a betrothal between the heroine and a fictitious "brother" self. In works like *Fenghuang chi* and the erotic romance *Qingmeng tuo,* both beauty and scholar disguise themselves, thus acting out a symmetry of bisection, the woman going up the social ladder, the man going down.

Two-wife Polygyny in Wan Ru Yue, Zhuchun yuan, and Others

Other novels feature two-wife marriage with similar types of equivalences at work. The variations consist in the ways that the polygyny is justified and the women are ranked without causing ill will. In the early Qing *Lin er bao* (The Son of Good Fortune), of sixteen chapters (circa 1672),[51] the man and his first wife are only-children; he and his second wife have the same birth date. He is the son of a commoner; they are daughters of officials. After promising herself to the hero, the second woman disguises as a man in order to flee a forced marriage to another man, takes refuge in the first woman's family, and, as in *Fenghuang chi*, still in man's disguise marries the first woman. On the wedding night she briefly fondles the other woman before going to sleep (ch. 11, 118). Later she invents an excuse to delay consummation until she can get the hero to marry both women. She herself takes second rank in deference to the first wife, whose family took care of her during her hardship (ch. 16 works out the settlement of rank).

As in *Yu Jiao Li*, accident brings about the man's involvement with two women. But *Lin er bao* has one of the women playing a greater role in arranging the marriage, which the man and the other woman must accept as a fait accompli. *Lin er bao* also contrasts with *Yu Jiao Li* and other chaste romances in that it contains two scenes of light eroticism involving the main characters: the two women in bed, the one caressing the other, and the consummation between the man and the first woman. In the latter scene, slightly censored in the 1983 Shenyang edition, the male-impersonating woman reveals her disguise to the man but not the other woman; then in the dark she puts the man in her place in bed and lets him make love to the other woman, who does not discover the identity of her partner until the next morning. Although angry, the other woman soon acquiesces, and the male-impersonating woman finally removes her disguise (ch. 16, 166–69).

In *Wan Ru Yue* (The Two Wives Well-Met), sixteen chapters, also of the early Qing,[52] the symmetry works mainly between the two wives: they are born on the same date with only a two-hour difference, which thus determines their ranking; they have the same last name, Zhao, and first names with the same meaning, "Like a Son" and "As if a Son" (Ruzi and Wanzi); they are both talented only-children and, as in other such novels, are cherished "as if" they were sons. One is a poor southerner (though her ancestors were once illustrious office holders), the other a rich northerner.

In contrast to the heroes in *Yu Jiao Li* and *Lin er bao*, the man in *Wan Ru*

惜花主人批評

宛如約

醉月山居梓行

Title page from *Wan Ru Yue* (The Two Wives Well-Met).

Yue is more consciously involved in the process by which he ends up marrying two wives. Having already declared loyalty to the first woman, whom he met when she was disguised as a man, he is nevertheless irresistibly attracted to the second woman and allows himself to betroth her. Since the two women have the same surname, he concludes that marriage to both is "heaven's intent" (ch. 7, 65). As in other works, *Wan Ru Yue* has the women help him reach his conclusion. The poor woman, for instance, reckons that the man will be happier with two wives and that the women will have each other as "good friends" (ch. 10, 92, 95). The mutual consideration between the wives, who discuss the problem of their ranking at length (ch. 14), is based on a shared logic of reciprocity and deference: any jealousy one might feel can too easily incite jealousy in the other; since in the end the love one has for the man is the same as the other's, his rejection of one is just as bad as his rejection of the other (ch. 10, 91–92). In their decision to rank the poor woman first, the wives clearly choose as criterion of precedence their slight difference of age—not social status or beauty, which would be considered too crude for such chaste situations (ch. 14, 132–33).

Whether symmetry applies between man and woman, woman and woman, or man and man, whether it applies in the case of one-wife or two-wife marriage, it suggests that those of one gender can cross to the other gender. In one sense beauty and scholar are both men, as when she is disguised as a man and befriends the scholar. In another sense beauty and scholar are both women, as when she is disguised as a man married to the other beauty. In *Wan Ru Yue* it is even implied that all three are men since both women are "like sons." The symmetry is still skewed, of course, since a beauty never marries two scholars (although she almost does in a brief scene of *Qingmeng tuo* because of the confusion created by multiple disguises, ch. 17). The beauty-scholar romance camouflages such asymmetry, however, by portraying women as the main directors of action. Their excellence so overshadows the man's that his role as privileged mate is made to appear passive and harmless.

The mid-Qing novel *Zhuchun yuan xiaoshi* (The Garden of Spring Residence), in twenty-four chapters, was probably written about a century—mid- to late-eighteenth century—after the "classic" beauty-scholar romances, *Ping Shan Leng Yan, Haoqiu zhuan,* and *Yu Jiao Li,* which it praises in its prologue but from which it differs in portraying more traditionally feminine heroines.[53] Like *Yu Jiao Li,* it features a polygamous marriage with a maid added as a "side-chamber," *ceshi.* Again, the efforts and planning of the women bring about the man's union with two wives. He and the first woman are betrothed as children but then forced to separate. She never forgets the betrothal; but he goes on to meet another woman, whom he comes to know through an exchange of poetry. By chance the two women find themselves living in the same home and become good friends, neither knowing of the other's liaison with the hero. In pursuing the second woman, the man sends a message that accidentally reaches the first woman, whose existence is still unknown to him and who now learns of his other relationship. The same careful maneuvering occurs here as in *Yu Jiao Li* and other works to make it possible for the man to have two wives without his seeming to be an intentional, premeditated bigamist. The first woman uses hints and insinuations to pry open the second woman's secret love and include herself as well; she wishes to find a "way for both women to be satisfied" (ch. 10, 64). The first woman's cryptic remarks mystify and alarm the second woman, who is already moody and depressed from having failed to hear from her lover, whose latest message was intercepted by the first woman. When the truth finally emerges, the women become close allies and have as their next job to inform the man, who finally remembers his first betrothal and promises loyalty to both women (chs. 12, 13).

Compared to the women of the romances already discussed, the ones in *Zhuchun yuan* are more traditionally feminine in that they mainly confine themselves to the inner chambers and do not disguise as men. Their moodiness and use of subtle hinting and the man's "melancholy"— *chouchang* (ch. 11, 71)—suggest the convoluted emotional world of *Honglou meng* of the same period rather than the more straightforward and robust world of the classic romances in which women impersonate men and boldly compose poetry before the emperor.[54]

My last and brief example of two-wife polygamous marriage is from *Dingqing ren* (The Tale of Loyal Love), in sixteen chapters and probably of the mid- to late-seventeenth century.[55] In this case, when it seems the hero will never be able to marry the heroine, he marries her maid instead, as the heroine had instructed him, but he refuses to consummate the marriage (ch. 15, 135–36). Then, when the heroine shows up after all, he sleeps with her first and her maid second. Neither woman "is in the least bit jealous" (ch. 16, 152). In *Baigui zhi* the husband resolves the problem of priorities by sleeping with both women at once, for a scene of "many varieties of love" (ch. 16, 113). But in that case it is a matter of two women of the same class, not a woman and her maid. *Dingqing ren* thus features a more conventional type of polygamy, in which one woman is of the elite class and the other or others are from distinctly lower social ranks.

Three versions of the superior woman appear in *Dingqing ren*: (1) the heroine, (2) the talented and assertive maid who stands in for the heroine, and (3) a third woman who is forced to marry a villain. The third woman's superiority expresses itself as shrewish temper, which enables her to subdue the villain, whom she literally rides by trapping him beneath her and sitting astride him (ch. 9, 84, and ch. 10, 85). She eventually causes his death from *ju nei*, "fear of the inner one," that is, being henpecked (ch. 12, 106).[56] As shown above in chapter 3, of all women in Chinese literature, the shrew demands monogamy the most loudly. In *Dingqing ren*, however, she is posed against two "better" women who unjealously marry the same man.

The Recurrence of Marriage to Two Women

The recurrence of marriage to two women in so many of these stories suggests several possible interpretations. In literary history, the bigamous man typically marries his first wife while he is still poor and has not yet passed the imperial exams; he then travels to the capital, wins exam success, and is offered the beautiful daughter of a high official—thus the story of the famous Yuan opera *Pipa ji* (The Lute), for example. He may attempt to refuse the offer but risks the wrath of the high official, who may threaten to ruin the man's future (as in the Qing novel *Jin Lan fa*, chs. 12, 13). The hero may fail to reveal the existence of his "husk wife," *zaokang zhi qi*, the term used for the woman he leaves behind, and marry the official's daughter. In some stories, the "husk wife" dies of grief; in others, the second wife helps him reunite with his first wife by welcoming her into the marriage. The "bigamy" of the beauty-scholar romance may be looked at, then, as a kind of comic revision and resolution of the problem of the man's pre- and postexam success.

Along the same line, other explanations might say that bigamy bridges the gap between initial fate and subsequent revision, which can also be seen as paralleling the difference between arranged, procreative marriage versus self-determined, romantic marriage; the man marries a woman from each of these two categories. In other words, he marries both the socially correct woman his elders arrange for him and the talented beauty he meets on his own. Two-wife polygamy is also perhaps a compromise between monogamy, demanded by women, and polygamy, wished for by even superior men. Having two wives is as far as the decent man dares to go;[57] in other words, bigamy is like a chaste abbreviation of or metaphor for polygamy.

We may still wonder, however, Why, if the woman is so superior, does she allow her husband such advantage in marriage? Given the exchangeability of gender characteristics, one might say that the unit of two women and one man in fact does not instance an imbalance in favor of the man but rather a dynamic triangle in which all three are as if of the same sex; neither the man nor either of the two women is the stable pivot; each can mediate between the other two. The strong friendship between the women further dispels the seeming imbalance in favor of the man (in one Li Yu play, the two wives themselves are lovers).[58] Another implication in these works is that there are not enough good men in the world to match the number of good women. In the end, two superior women married to one superior man is better than one of the women married to a superior man but the other to a boor or no one at all. The paucity and thus preciousness of good men is also the message of *Honglou meng,* whose hero Jia Baoyu seems to wish he could have all the women of the garden to himself. He is miserable about the prospect of their marriage to far off and unknown men, most of whom he despises as inferior and "muddy" creatures (ch. 100). The outcome of the theory of male inferiority, however, is that, like the hero of the beauty-scholar romance, Baoyu presumes that he is better than the rest of mankind and thus more deserving of female company. Furthermore, while women are pitied, it is hardly suggested that, in order to understand a woman's lot, a man might exchange places with his female counterparts on a long term basis—although men do so in the late Ming homoerotic romances of *Bian er chai* (Hairpins beneath his Cap) and find that lot extremely difficult.[59]

Whatever the interpretation, it is significant that in these works two-wife polygamy marks the limit of maintainable chastity. To repeat, once the man goes beyond two wives or has sex with them or others before marriage, then the novel becomes erotic. The sexual interchangeability of the polygynous threesome breaks down once the marriage contains four or more, in which case the man returns to being the central figure and the women to being subordinate stations for his revolving visitation. The erotic romances sometimes have the man at first declare his three or more wives to be equal in rank but in the end grade the women according to both social class and personal quality, including sexual quality— that is, with the chaster ones at the top, the sexier below (as in *Xiuping yuan* and *Taohua ying,* discussed in the next chapter). The chaste romances scrupulously avoid ranking women according to quality. The characters carefully maintain a civility that marks a general attempt to avoid any more embarrassment than already exists because of the man's marriage to two women, who on their part aid in the avoidance of embarrassment by being so superior as to be above jealousy.

The Rational Optimism of the Beauty-Scholar Romance

Regardless of single or multiple marriage, the beauty and the scholar are absolutely pure and tower above all other couples. Their marriage is based on love between two individuals who want each other, not on the contract between two sets of parents who choose partners for their children. But although the couples of the Qing romances base their relationship on love, they still behave in rational fashion. They discipline lust; they eventually obtain the blessing of their parents and, for that matter, match themselves according to the same standards of class and merit that their parents would have used anyway. From the traditional perspective, they operate according to the ancient rule of "expediency," *quan,* to which these novels occasionally refer when young people, especially women, act more boldly than usual.[60] That is, within a habitually rigid framework, the young lovers "expediently" bend the rules of courtship because of the extraordinary circumstances of their absolutely perfect match. The woman's cleverness allows her to bend the rules to the extent that she climbs to the top of the social order and fools even the emperor, who is so impressed that he forgives her and lets her marry the man of her choice.

Many recent Chinese scholars have labeled these works as "progressive" (*jinbude*) for promoting freedom of choice in marriage and granting women a greater sphere of self-determination than normally allowed. The portrayal of such women delivers several didactic messages to men: consult with women before marrying them off, do not be so blatant in your polygamy, be more loyal to women, do not underestimate women, and so forth. Furthermore, love is to be the premise for marriage. Love, or *qing*, refers not to consuming passion but to the self-evident, meant-for-each-other quality that the young man and woman have from both (1) the traditional perspectives of fate (as in "match made in heaven") and parental blessing and (2) the subjective perspective of the two youths, now also emphasized. This subjective perspective gains validity because of the extraordinary capabilities of the youths, especially the woman, who is bolder than both her father and husband. But the word "subjective" connotes neither anarchic or indomitable will nor absolute egalitarianism; the *caizi* and especially *jiaren* are only tactically or *expediently* rebellious. The privilege of superior class combined with superior virtue and innate capability are still central factors in the lovers' match; those who possess such privileges and capacities have their way.

Another label besides progressive would be "rational optimism": that is, the world is full of opportunists and schemers who measure others according to benefit to themselves; but villainy can be outwitted and good marriages can be had as long as one is talented, good-looking, and virtuous in oneself, and so capable of steadfast devotion to another. The rationalism of these works comprises civility, meaning the proper channeling of passions, and symmetry, that is, the complementary balance of *yin* and *yang*. The play of alternating polar effects breaks down the normally overdetermined patterns of male and female behavior and allows sexual identities to cross over and contain each other. Instead of being sexual, the intercourse of the lovers is verbal, modeled on the polite medium of the written word, through which the youths pass the test of marriage by that time-honored means of establishing one's worth, poetic expression.

In short, the beauty-scholar romance is dedicated to the notion that one man and one woman (or two) can achieve perfect symmetry in a destiny of love that is actually consummated on earth. No one is punished for his or her brazenness, as in the late Ming story, or left unrequited, as in *Honglou meng*. The woman and man live to old age and die in short succession, without illness, proving that theirs is the best way to live.[61]

The Idealization of Women

Rational optimism, however, covers only the straightforward and positive messages of the beauty-scholar romances. In concluding we must further examine the ways that the crossing of gender characteristics, the superiority of the woman, and the subterfuge of polygamy call into question the comfort of symmetrical balance. Most significantly, no stories of monogamous love contain explicit descriptions of sex between either pre- or postmarital lovers. In short, where there is the superior woman, there is no sex.

The crux of the absence or presence of sexual description lies in the polarity of female superiority and male baseness. I will address this polarity in greater detail in the chapter on *Honglou meng* but for now will briefly examine some implications of the portrayal of male inferiority. Three key points come to mind. First, the inferior or what can also be called the self-deprecating man is such because he denies himself his normal customary privileges, especially those of polygyny. Second, the portrayal of symmetry involves not equivalence so much as a reversal of roles by which the woman uses (or is "allowed" to use) the man's words and clothing to attain a position superior to him. Third, the man in these works is demasculinized and, in effect, desexualized.

The self-deprecating man does not directly state his inferiority or submission, nor does he act it out through sexual perversion (as might the Freudian masochist, for example, to whom the scholar nevertheless bears significant resemblance).[62] It is instead through the portrayal of monogamy and female superiority that the inferiority of the man manifests itself; his self-deprecation is implied, not self-consciously expressed. He is a man who does not take advantage of his patriarchal, polygamous privileges or express his condescension to or lack of need for women. The henpecked husband of the shrew story is another version of the self-deprecator, as is the male author who portrays the man being hilariously abject before the shrewish woman.

As for the phenomenon of symmetry, the woman and man exchange positions, duplicate themselves, and simultaneously act in several roles— all as part of a transposition that removes them from their normal subject / object positions in the hierarchical family. The woman learns to act and write exactly like the man, thereby outdoing all men and utterly confusing husband, father, and emperor. In using men's learning to assert her superiority, the woman is as if educated by self-deprecating men and allowed by them to be dominant.[63] The dictim "It is a virtue for a woman to be untalented" no longer applies.

Finally, in the "real" world of phallic dominance, men relate to women only for sexual and reproductive purposes and only by viewing women as inferior and unclean. The chaste romance, however, portrays a fantastic world in which the woman is elevated beyond her normal roles. Such idealization allows both man and woman to escape the baseness and degradation of phallically defined sex. The man becomes demasculinized and sexless, no longer seeking woman after woman in a crescendo of promiscuous liaisons.[64] This idealization affects the style of writing as well, since the chaste romances, as previously indicated, are minimally obscene and particularistic, and tend to refinement of language and flatness of character.[65]

To return to the contrast between the chaste and erotic romances: When these narratives are chaste, the woman is superior to the man. Where sex is explicitly described, there is polygamy and the expendability of women. In other words, sex between monogamous man and woman, with the woman as superior being, is not imagined; when sex is imagined, it is illicit, promiscuous, and polygamous, whether legitimately polygynous or scandalously polyandrous. The two-wife polygynous romance already instances the disintegration of both chastity and female superiority, as exemplified in the episode of *Fenghuang chi* in which the lustful maid caresses the body of the supposed male servant. A similar example is the scene of *Lin er bao* in which the heroine in male disguise fondles the body of her pretended wife. These two and other romances already begin to deliver one of the central messages of the erotic, polygamous romances discussed in the next chapter, a message that is critical for the man's control over women—namely, that women must not be jealous of each other when married to the same man. This lesson is carried out in the greatest detail in a chaste work like *Wan Ru Yue,* in which co-wives still openly work out their relationship. In the erotic romances, not much trace is left of this conscious attempt among women to forestall jealousy; instead, the heroines are naturally unjealous.

6

THE EROTIC SCHOLAR-BEAUTY

ROMANCE

"Crossing the Wall"

That the romances discussed so far admit little if any eroticism has to do with the fact that female heroes traditionally cannot be shown having sex. True heroines must be chaste; even their male counterparts must know self-control. However, other romances of about the same length— ten to twenty chapters—instead tell of sexual scholars and beauties. In the erotic romance, the man becomes the central character in the form of a polygynist hero who attracts one woman after another. The woman's talents remain in vestiges only, having receded in face of the erotic interests of the author, male readers, and the characters in the story.

While the effeminate scholar-poet yields his superiority to the cross-dressed beauty, the potent polygynist of the erotic romances retrieves it, as it were, although he does so in a way that makes him appear deserving and justified. The image is that of a benevolent polygynist around whom women willingly gather. The erotic romance models itself on its chaste counterparts in order to engineer a polygyny in which there is neither female jealousy nor male degeneration. The construction of this benign polygyny involves the rational and deliberate addition of one wife after another, each agreeably ranked according to such criteria as social class, relative chastity and beauty, and degree of need for a handsome and caretaking man. Numerous devices assist in the construction and justification of this family: for example, the portrayal of women actively arranging their own or another woman's concubinage, the man's serving a wife's or concubine's sonless family by letting that family adopt one of his own sons, or the maintenance of orderly distinction between a more proper, chaste main wife versus sexier and more playful concubines. How sex is portrayed—adumbratively or explicitly, for example—is also a factor in a given novel's arrangement of the relationship between the man and a particular wife, concubine, or paramour.

The chaste romances already vary in how much they admit of the sexual. In the most famous works like *Haoqiu zhuan* or *Yu Jiao Li,* there is no question of the lovers touching before marriage, or even thinking of touching.[1] In *Dingqing ren,* however, the man communicates through the maid that he would like to have a tryst with the heroine; the latter refuses, not wishing to associate with a man who "steals fragrance and robs jade" (ch. 4, 32). In *Zhuchun yuan* the man and woman meet undisguised, face to face—that is, in classic emblematic terms, they "cross over the wall," *yu qiang* (ch. 7, 43)—but do not touch. In *Feihua yong* they hold hands, but when he wants to go further she gives him a "stern countenance," *zhengse* (ch. 5, 48)—an expression used in similar situations in numerous other works—and warns him to restrain himself. Later, when he tries to get closer again (they are already "nestling against each other"), she retorts, "Haven't you heard the prohibition against indulgence before the blood and *qi* have become settled?!" (ch. 6, 50–51; quoting from Confucius, the *Lunyu,* book 16, no. 7). These and all other examples I have seen confirm that no romances portray premarital sex between monogamous lovers, although it is possible that exceptions are still to be found.

In what follows I will discuss, novel by novel, situations which depart yet further from the example of the chaste romance. The standards of chaste versus erotic and the type or degree of eroticism in a work will, for my purposes, rest on factors such as the presence or absence of premarital chastity; the relative superiority of the woman, especially as expressed in her deeds of male impersonation; the numbers of wives; and the nature of sexual description. In the case of sexual description, terms like "sparse," "adumbrative," or "euphemistic" will be opposed to "extensive" and "explicit." "High erotic" will be opposed to "vernacular" or "vulgar." For example, the "jade door" (*yumen*) is a high erotic euphemism for the vulgar "cunt" (*bi*). "They did the clouds and rain" (*yunyu*) contrasts with a page long description of intercourse going into thousands of thrusts. The man squeezing the woman's bound foot, or the face-to-face meeting of an unmarried man and woman, the latter in man's clothing, are examples of fetishistic or censoring displacements of naked, genital contact.

I chose the works included in this chapter largely by chance. I was led to *Qingmeng tuo* (Awakened from the Love Dream) and *Yu Lou Chun* (The Cross-dressed Scholar's Three Wives) because of their mention in Liu Tingji's 1715 *Zaiyuan zazhi* (Miscellany from a Leisure Garden) and in the preface to the mid-Qing novel *Jin Shi yuan* (The Predestiny of Metal and Stone).[2] The preface and prologue to *Zhuchun yuan* refer to *Qingmeng tuo* and *Xiuping yuan* (Omen of the Illustrated Screen). References like these tend to indicate the popularity or notoriety of these works. Other works that I discuss simply happened to be accessible at various times and places, such as *Taohua yanshi* (The Peach Blossom Fantasy), *Hudie mei* (The Butterfly Go-between), or *Xinghua tian* (The Paradise of Apricot Blossoms). Numerous erotic romances not included are of comparable length and are similar in content, such as *Nao huacong* (Ruckus among the Flowering Bushes), *Wushan yanshi* (The Fantasy of Mt. Wu), and *Chundeng nao* (Ruckus by the Spring Lamp), to name a few;[3] to date, few scholars inside or outside China have ever discussed these three and many others.

Between Chaste and Erotic in *Jinxiang ting* and *Qingmeng tuo*

According to the standards of the chaste romance established above, if the hero and/or heroine engage in premarital sex, if the hero has more than two wives, or if the narrative contains sexual detail, then the work leaves the realm of the so-called chaste romance. However, many works exist which are just outside this realm in that the hero, for example, has a minor affair with a woman other than his future wife or wives, or the novel contains descriptions of sexual acts but among characters other than the main heroes and heroines. Ultimately, even a highly explicit work can maintain some of the basic standards of what I label the chaste romance. *Taohua yanshi*, for instance, in twelve chapters, contains descriptions of oral and anal, homo- and heterosexual intercourse among nonheroic characters who largely disappear after the obscene first half of the book. The second half is devoid of sexual encounter except for the hero's adumbratively described lovemaking with a beautiful fairy,[4] who then helps the heroine and her father out of predicament; the fairy later dies of sudden old age. To the end, the work preserves premarital chastity between the monogamous hero and heroine.

Less strenuous bending of the standards of the chaste romance occurs in a borderline erotic work like the early Qing *Jinxiang ting* (Pavilion of Embroidered Fragrance), in sixteen chapters. This novel contains a description in several dozen characters of sex between the hero and an imperial concubine, but is otherwise devoid of such promiscuity and soon drops the concubine from the narrative.[5] She is notoriously lustful and fond of young men, but, like other such women in Chinese fiction, eventually renounces the world to become a nun.

Jinxiang ting further stretches the limits of the classic romance by having the hero marry three women, the main wife being of the upper class, the other two of the lower. The ranking of wives now becomes an issue. In the chaste two-wife romance, the wives are equal; in *Jinxiang ting,* they are ranked based on class background and precedence of encounter, criteria which would be considered crude or irrelevant in the chaste romance. In this as in other works, the implicit rule is that the more wives there are, the less compunction the man has in taking one woman after another and the less punctilious the women are (or the author or husband is) in working out their ranking.

However, *Jinxiang ting* still defers to chastity and propriety in its emphasis upon the health and correctness of the hero's family. First, the hero and his wives do not consummate until marriage. In addition, each wife has a virtue that defines an identity no other can duplicate: the first is "wise and pure"; the second, "brave and valiant"; the third, "clever and perspicacious" (ch. 16, 169). These identities provide each woman with a comfortable niche that eliminates resentment due to ranking. As a final affirmation of the health of the marriage, the three wives produce four sons, thus continuing the family line of each house involved, the man's and the three women's (169). A sense of righteousness emerges (somewhat as in *Liaodu yuan* and as will be seen in *Chundeng mishi* below) in that the polygynous husband serves his wives uxorilocally by offering his extra sons to their patrilines—that is, naming them after the women's fathers, not himself.[6]

Mentioned in 1749 as one of several works popular since the early Qing, *Qingmeng tuo* (Awakened from the Love Dream), in twenty chapters, is also on a border between chaste and erotic.[7] Written sometime before 1715, it contains descriptions of sex, but only among peripheral and villainous characters in a side plot about a miser and his lascivious daughter-in-law (ch. 7). The confusion of identities arising from the various disguises that the young lovers assume in *Qingmeng tuo* is more sexually suggestive than in the classic romance. For example, one of the heroines purposely impersonates a man in order to get in bed with the other heroine (ch. 19); the main male character tries to sleep with a "man" whom he knows is his future wife in disguise (ch. 16)—both situations too risqué for *Yu Jiao Li* or *Fenghuang chi*. But despite its eroticism, *Qingmeng tuo* still has the hero swear he will have only one wife (ch. 6, 12a); and like the heroines of the chaste romances, the two women he eventually marries boldly disguise as men—the one to help save her calumnied father, the other to go out and seek a man of her choice.[8]

The level of the confusion of identities in *Qingmeng tuo* matches that in *Fenghuang chi* and in this case includes the ploy of the hero's disguise as a servant in the heroine's home.[9] The confusion of identities also produces a near case of the heroine's bigamy when two heroes seem to appear together at her door expecting to carry out formal marriage arrangements (ch. 17); the double appearance is illusory, and the potential bigamy of the heroine disappears.

The unchaste aspects of *Qingmeng tuo* take the form of either sexual innuendo or outright portrayal of sex. The hero is attracted to the heroine because of the smallness of her feet (ch. 1, 5b); he refuses an earlier woman after he accidently hears about the bigness of hers (2b). (The chaste romance would not allow size of feet to be a standard of judgment.) The hero uses poetry to flirt with the heroine, who tells him not to be so "cheeky," *qingbo* (ch. 4, 25b). The lascivious woman of the side plot invites sex with a beggar who has a large penis, which she notices when she spies him urinating one day. His seduction of her as she sleeps is explicitly described (ch. 7, 19b–20a); later, a jeering mob marches her along in the street and strips her (22a). In other examples of unchaste detail, the maid uses the excuse of menstruation in order to avoid sex with a man she is forced to marry in her mistress's stead (ch. 12, 2a).[10] And, in bed with the second heroine, the main heroine, disguised as the hero, finds the other woman's body so delightful that she wishes she herself had "that thing," *nahua*, a euphemism for the penis (ch. 19, 9a).

The inclusion of sexual, obscene, or otherwise mean detail—which in

Qingmeng tuo includes the filth and meanness of the miser—in fact draws the narrative closer to the norm of Chinese fiction established since the famous novels and stories of the late Ming. With its nonparticularized and nonvulgarized action, the chaste romance marks a departure from the norm and a break with the style of the "decadent" fiction of the Ming. *Qingmeng tuo* shows a relaxation from or perhaps parody of the high standards promoted by other beauty-scholar novelists, and illustrates an incipient indulgence in the polygynist erotic interests that are more fully realized in the works discussed below.

Further Departures from the Chaste Romance

High Erotic in Hudie mei and Xiuping yuan

The early Qing *Hudie mei* (The Butterfly Go-between), in sixteen chapters, relaxes the standards yet more.[11] The hero starts with one woman as his goal and does not consummate with her until marriage, but meanwhile he collects three other wives and one paramour. In this novel women no longer disguise as men—although for a moment one of the women imagines what it would be like "if she were a man" (ch. 4, 31b). The man has now turned into an attractive sexual hero to whom numerous women strive to attach themselves; it is as if he were a savior of women in a world of few good men. As in *Jinxiang ting*, the principle of symmetry tends no longer to apply as monogamy and bigamy give way to hierarchical polygamy. At the consummation of their marriage, when the main wife tries politely to let the slightly less beautiful second wife take first turn, the husband insists on the proper order of precedence: "High and low have their given sequence of lots" (ch. 14, 14b); the remaining two wives occupy yet lower positions due to their relative lack of chastity.

As usual, the man establishes contact with his main wife-to-be early in the novel but unlike the chaste scholar attempts seduction by secretly entering her room. She responds with a "stern countenance" and forbids him even to sit down (ch. 4, 27ab). Not one to agree to "secret and illicit meetings," she restricts their exchanges to poetry (30b). She thinks of herself on a par with the hero and imagines that if they went hunting together, she would be as good a shot as he (31b). She thus retains a vestige of the parity with men that women in the chaste romances more nearly gain; in this case, the vestige takes the form of a gesture of the imagination.

The hero cannot restrain himself, however, and has sex with the heroine's maid, whom he "temporarily takes instead of her mistress" (ch. 9, 5ab). The heroine later notices their appearance of intimacy and thinks to herself that the maid "has already taken first claim from my lot" (ch. 9, 6a). She is amused, not jealous, however, and lets them know that she knows.

When a powerful aging official, described as the famous Yang Su (d. 606) of the Sui dynasty, suddenly decides that he will have the heroine as his concubine, the hero sets out to search for a beauty to send to the aging official in the heroine's stead. It is during this separation, as in numerous such stories, that the hero encounters other women, the first of whom is a concubine dissatisfied with her husband. The hero thinks that she "is not a decent person" but has an affair with her anyway (ch. 10, 11b); she later dies of longing for him (ch. 15, 25a). Then, in a sequence that appears in various forms in many stories, a high-ranking man makes the hero drunk and tricks him into getting in bed with the man's unmarried daughter, thus sealing the hero's betrothal to her. The upright hero angrily refuses the match but gives in when he learns of the woman's talent in poetry; he still delays consummation, however (ch. 11, 19b–20a).

The hero finally finds a beautiful woman to present to the old official in place of the heroine, hoping some day to have this woman for himself. He refrains from touching her—in this case, as put in a narrative aside, because he is no "second rate person" (erliu renwu, ch. 11, 26b). Later, the old official gives her back without having consummated, after which she moves to the main heroine's home, where the two women become like sisters. Here it is a case of two women befriending each other and thus removing cause for later jealousy. The two then wed the hero, who marries uxorilocally into the main heroine's family (ch. 14). He makes love first with the heroine, then the returned woman, whom he finds to his surprise is still a virgin; then all three sleep in the same bed (15a).

The story ends when the heroine—glad that her husband has already slept with her maid and thus ensured the maid's inclusion in the family— in further cooperation urges him to fetch the woman he was tricked into marrying. At first he blushes to find that she knows of this woman but then retrieves her once he sees the heroine is not jealous. The final ranking of wives places his main love first, the woman he was tricked into marrying second, and the old official's returned concubine third. The third wife had originally been the concubine of a man with an ugly, jealous wife who never let her sleep with the husband (ch. 11). Having passed through a first husband and then the old official before joining the hero's family, she thus descends to a lower rank, even though she is a virgin. The maid, however, is yet lower, as dictated by her servant's status and the fact that she has already slept with the hero.

Despite *Hudie mei*'s allowance of polygamy, it makes the hero's acquisition of women appear relatively unintentional and refrains from the extended descriptions of sex found in other Qing novels such as *Rou putuan, Xinghua tian,* and *Wushan yanshi.* "Extended" here refers to details of sexual organs, thrusting, and sexual positions, as well as to the length of description—in one instance in *Xinghua tian* nearly six hundred characters (ch. 13, 184–87). *Hudie mei*'s portrayals are brief and adumbrative—as in, for example, "and they took themselves off to the *yang* terrace" (*tong fu yangtai,* ch. 14, 15a), a centuries-old euphemism for intercourse. When the hero takes the maid, the narrator makes note of her hymen blood and the shoe that falls off her tiny foot, which the man then feels and lightly squeezes (ch. 9, 15b). Virginal blood and bound feet are favored images in Qing erotic fiction and are here synecdochal for the fuller scene not described. Moreover, *Hudie mei* uses the language of the high erotic, as in the scenes of consummation between the hero and two of his wives (ch. 14, 14b–15a; ch. 15, 23b, 24a). A representative example of high erotic adumbration follows in this description of the interaction between the hero and his third wife:

> The door to the bridal chamber having been bolted, he used tender dexterity and the connoisseurship of a lover of perfumes and treasurer of jades, and thus carried Miss Qiuchan through the gauze curtains. There he lightly picked the flower bud and delicately tested the virginal rouge. The two of them became male and female phoenix companions, and how happy they were! (ch. 15, 23b)

Adumbration in this case as in others also means gentle treatment of the woman and sympathetic consideration for the virgin's pain. Examples of extended and explicit portrayals often describe robust, rough, or violent sex, as will be seen in *Yesou puyan, Lüye xianzong,* and *Shenlou zhi.*

Another high-erotic novel with some pretensions to being a "classic" beauty-scholar romance is *Xiuping yuan* (Omen of the Illustrated Screen) of the early Qing, in twenty chapters, with a preface supposedly of 1670.[12] Its hero likewise attracts one woman after another until he establishes himself and them in one harmonious household. He sleeps with only two of his five wives before marriage, saving chastity for the two premier wives and one other. *Xiuping yuan's* pretensions to being a classic romance lie in its direct utterance of *caizi jiaren* manifestos, some of which actually use the words *caizi* and *jiaren* (ch. 2, 3ab, 4b).[13] *Xiuping yuan* makes explicit the point usually implied in the chaste romance that scholars and beauties are special cases towering above everyone else. Now their privileges apply in sexual terms as well: "secret love" (*siqing*) is permissible for "scholars and beauties," although only for them, for whom things will always work out (ch. 20, 8a). Others may as well "pack up their pissing sticks and child-planting furrows and concern themselves with other things" (ch. 18, 6a, and ch. 20, 8a). For ideal lovers, who are masters of the art of sex and possess great "sexual capacity" (*seliang*, ch. 18, 5b), the "intercourse of *yin* and *yang*" (*yinyang jiaogou*) is the world's number one "legitimate activity" (*zhengjing shi,* ch. 18, 7ab).

It is common in works such as this that the polygamist's secondary wives come from various social ranks and walks of life and that, besides being sexual companions, they relate to him in the capacity of helpers.[14] *Xiuping yuan* begins when the hero falls in love with the daughter and only child of an official in whose house he finds a position as servant. She is the main heroine and the hero's eventual main wife. But while waiting to be taken in as servant in her home, he rents a room in a wineshop where he falls in love with the owner's daughter. He temporarily puts aside the high-class heroine in order to take advantage of "an immediate cash deal" with a member of the urban common class (ch. 3, 6a). A comment at the end of the chapter affirms that attractive women can be found in humble places. He hugs her on their first meeting, but like a clever girl, as the narrator says, she delays sex because women good at "stealing love" (*tou qing*) always put the man off in the beginning (ch. 3, 8a). Their eventual consummation is described using only a high erotic idiom, *dianluan daofeng* (lit., "upside down phoenixes," ch. 4, 8b).[15] She later becomes one of his helpers.

His next wife-to-be is the heroine's cousin, who acts as go-between for the hero and the heroine. This is the first in a series of alliances between women who assist in the establishment of the eventual polygynous marriage. The cousin arranges a secret meeting between herself and the hero, to whom she relinquishes her virginity (in another adumbrative description, ch. 6, 9b). Her brother discovers them, and her father has the hero put in jail—this being the main disaster of the story.

One of the jail officials—a member of the yet lower, so-called mean (*jianmin*) classes—takes pity on the hero and allows him to stay in his, the jailer's, home, where the jailer's daughter becomes the hero's next lover.[16] She helps him because of her "chivalrous" (*haoxia*) spirit, being a "man among women" (*nüzhong nanzi*, ch. 7, 7b) and the closest in the novel to a woman who disguises as a man. They swear loyalty to each other, but the text is not clear about whether or not they consummate. Also helping him at this time, the daughter of the wineshop owner tries to obtain for him news of the main heroine. Through such unjealous assistance, as the narrator says, she "secures herself some standing" in his future family (*zhan xie dibu*, ch. 8, 6b). Later the jailer's daughter meets the heroine's fallen cousin when the latter, dressed as a lower-class woman, flees home in order to avoid a forced marriage (ch. 11). Again, as in many of these novels, some or all of the hero's future wives befriend or ally with each other before marriage and in this way in effect eliminate cause for later jealousy.

The hero in *Xiuping yuan* first marries (1) the jailer's daughter, who out of "loyalty" to her "sister" makes sure he takes (2) the heroine's cousin next (ch. 13, 5a). Then he places first in the imperial examinations and marries (3) the heroine, (4) yet a new woman, presented to him by a high official, and (5) the wineshop owner's daughter, who has already moved into the heroine's home. The embarrassing problem remains of how to rank the women. He does not want to offend the jailer, for example, whose daughter cannot rank as highly as the heroine or the high official's daughter. He decides they will all be equal (ch. 16, 7a). However, social etiquette still requires an order for the five women, who therefore cast lots to decide their "seating positions" (*zuowei*, ch. 16, 8a). As chance has it, the wineshop owner's daughter and the heroine's upper-class but fallen cousin are the two lowest; the daughter of the jailer is next; the high official's daughter is second; and the heroine first. Regardless of rank, all feel privileged to serve such a man; they are like loyal and unjealous ministers to a sage emperor (ch. 12, 2b–3a).

The ranking also parallels the sexual quality of the five wives. When he finally takes the heroine to bed, he finds that she has an especially wonderful vagina, which makes it more difficult than usual for him to control his ejaculation (ch. 17, 5b–6b). Later he and his wives have a "glorious meeting" (*shenghui,* ch. 18, 2a) in one bed, in which he observes the order cast in the lots: he begins with the wineshop owner's daughter, moves to the heroine's cousin, and then to the jailer's daughter. The division between them and the two primary wives is marked by the official's daughter's (number two wife's) request that the hero wipe off his penis before he begins with her, for she "doesn't need other people's profit added to her own" (ch. 18, 3b). Like the main wife, she has an especially wonderful vagina that can "suck on" his penis (*hanza,* 3b). Then the hero makes love with the heroine, with whom he performs several "topics" (*timu*), or love positions, until she tires, after which he continues with the others until dawn (5a). As in other erotic novels and stories, the main wife is of the highest quality and must be conserved.[17]

In a type of ending common to other erotic romances, a Taoist wanderer leads the hero and his family to a land called Pure Valley, *Sugu,* which since ancient times has been apart from China. *Su* perhaps recalls the *su* of *Sunü,* "Essential Woman," who taught the art of love to the Yellow Emperor; *gu* recalls the maternal "valley" of the *Laozi* (ch. 6), or "dark valley," *yougu,* a euphemism in the ars erotica for the vagina. As the narrator says, for real lovers there will always be a Pure Valley.

Xiuping yuan's preface is dated 1670, which if reliable would establish the book as being from the same period as many of the earliest chaste romances. As an erotic romance, it fits the Qing mold of erotic fiction which describes sex mainly between a polygamist and his future wives, not between adulterous lovers who must separate in the end. For the hero and three of his wives, *Xiuping yuan* still follows the requirement of the chaste romance that the lovers not have sex until marriage. In addition, as in *Hudie mei,* its descriptions of sex follow the tradition of the high erotic, thus contrasting with more explicit Ming and Qing works which describe violent and / or extremely energetic sex—although an exception occurs in its ribald description of sex between a man and a prostitute (ch. 4, 3b–4a).

The model of polygyny illustrated in *Xiuping yuan* allows us to elaborate upon the high-erotic construction of polygyny that I have discussed in earlier chapters. Of chief importance is that the man avoid intimate attachment to any of his wives; romantic sentiment is secondary to self-control, pleasure, and concentration of energy. The exquisite quality of the two premier wives, especially the one who makes it difficult for the hero to suppress ejaculation, should remind him of the ars erotica's injunction to maintain coolness and distance. In other words, by this theory the woman weakens the man if he is unable to detach himself from her. Having multiple wives instead of just one or two is precisely for this reason then: to keep the man distanced by keeping the women diffused. He accomplishes such diffusion by means of a ranking and positioning by which he variously rewards (and in other novels punishes) women of upper and lower classes and varying sexual qualities. Diffusion works by first reducing the stature of each woman by making her one of many wives, but then also by re-elevating the women by giving each a reason of her own to feel privileged and thus supposedly less prone to be jealous or uncooperative. *Xiuping yuan* also portrays alliances by which the women of their own accord, as it were, form subgroups of friendship or common interest and thus derive a modicum of security and self-determination. The polygynist elevates and rewards the women of lower rank by letting them help create and then advance into his upper-class family. He rewards the two premier wives by granting them power over the other women and by treating the two in a way that is both privileging (of them) and effacing (of himself). For example, by not overusing them, he conserves and elevates them as if they were precious beings. At the same time, because he has less control over himself with them, he is less sexual with them—whether being less sexual also means being more politic and egalitarian is left out of the story but is perhaps implied. In short, compared to women of the lower class, women of his own class are more formidable and deserving of circumspection. Other strategies of privileging the woman include, as already mentioned, marrying her uxorilocally and / or letting her son take her father's surname rather than her husband's (see, e.g., *Jinxiang ting, Chundeng mishi,* and *Yu Lou Chun*). On the other hand, when polygyny suffers dysfunction, such questions of hierarchy and alliance have their destructive side, as will be seen in the chapter on *Lin Lan Xiang.* There hierarchy is the cause of jealousy, and female alliances are for the sake of either monopolizing the man or seeking refuge from his misbehavior.

The Heterosexual Male Cross-dresser in Yu Lou Chun

Referred to by Liu Tingji in 1715 and mentioned along with *Qingmeng tuo* in 1749 as having been popular for many years, *Yu Lou Chun* (The Cross-dressed Scholar's Three Wives) takes the exceptional route of having the hero disguise as a woman in order to escape calamity (ch. 3).[18] Although his feet "are a little big" (ch. 4, 25a), his impersonation succeeds and, as with the cross-dressed beauty, allows him to meet his future spouses face to face. However, unlike the chaste beauty, he takes advantage of his disguise to force sex with the heroine and her maid, who are portrayed as soon no longer needing to be forced. *Yu Lou Chun* then has the two unmarried women not only become pregnant but also meet with the approval of the heroine's parents, who are happy to have such a famous literatus as their son-in-law. The hero's sexual relation with the third wife, another talented woman and author of her own poetry collection, comes about legitimately and thus preserves a measure of the chaste romance's decency. In addition, although it goes further than *Hudie mei* or *Xiuping yuan*, *Yu Lou Chun* refrains from the extensive and explicit descriptions of sex found in works that Liu Tingji places in the most offensive class of erotic fiction.

The novel begins with a spring outing during which the hero's father, his friends, and three famous courtesans inadvertently insult an ugly, dark-complexioned exam candidate who cannot write good poetry and who soon avenges himself by bringing calamity on the hero's family. Ugliness and ineptness at poetry are quintessential qualities of the villain in both chaste and erotic romances. The hero's family is forced to scatter and the hero to disguise as a woman in order to escape capture. He passes through two stages of separation first from his parents and then from his wives. During the first stage, he lives as a woman in the heroine's home, where he seduces the maid as she sleeps (a passage of several hundred characters, ch. 4, 27b–28a). On another night he lies in bed with the heroine, who still thinks he is a woman, and says to her, "I have always been afraid of sleeping at my own head of the bed" (referring to the common practice by which two people sleep side by side but with one's head opposite the other's feet). She replies, "Well then, we'll sleep head by head in separate blankets" (ch. 5, 33a). He begins to reveal his secret, first making sure that she would be receptive to marriage with his supposed paternal cousin. In other words, like the cross-dressed beauty, he pretends to have a relative whom he promises to his future spouse. He has also previously written her a poem containing hints about his disguise, thus paving the way for the revelation of his manhood, which he soon presses upon her. The ten-character, euphemistic description of their sex ends with, "then the clouds dispersed and the rains ceased"

(34a)—again, as in *Hudie mei,* conforming to the unwritten rule that portrayal of sex between lovers from the elite class be adumbrative and in the high erotic.

He next meets his third wife, whose father also suffers the vengeance of the hero's ugly enemy. Still in woman's disguise, he accompanies the family in their exile, during which he reveals his real self and, with her father's blessing, uxorilocally marries the heroine, who will be his premier wife. After this, all three women bear sons, of whom the one belonging to the premier wife takes his mother's last name, thus serving her father's ancestral line.

During the second stage of the hero's long flight, polygyny is in effect forced upon him when he is kidnapped by nuns who require him to serve them sexually. The hero wanders into a temple housing several dozen nuns of all ages, who have been driven there, they say, because of early widowhood or jealousy between wife and concubine (ch. 8, 55a). Later they are all said to be adulterous wives or unchaste daughters from elite families which could not bear to force worse fates on the women but still had to drive them out of the home (59a). The nuns hold the hero for nine years, a period predicted by a Taoist who earlier provided him with secrets of the erotic arts, which now become necessary in order to preserve his "innate energy" (ch. 8, 55b).

Like the hero's disguising as a woman, the nuns' kidnapping of the man is a reversal of the usual situation. That is, the usual expectation is that women disguise as men and that lecherous monks kidnap women whom they force into sexual service.[19] In both of these reversals, the man suffers a seeming dishonor and entrapment but also gains an advantage. In the case of female impersonation, though forced to go down the social ladder, he gains easy intimacy with his future wives; in the case of being kidnapped, although he is forced to serve outcast women, the polygyny is one which he cannot refuse and for which he need not excuse himself— although he must carefully guard his "innate energy."

Toward the end of the novel, before the hero and his now grown-up sons reunite and participate in a victory over Japanese pirates, one of the sons involves himself in a homosexual love intrigue. An official falls in love with him and becomes ill from lack of consummation. When the hero's son learns why the official is ill, he agrees to consummate at some future time but in the end finds a handsome actor to take his place with the official. Meanwhile, he enjoys anally penetrating the official's catamite. In other words, although he likes intercourse with men, he does not allow himself the loss of face of being the one penetrated.[20]

Face-saving is another way of describing *Yu Lou Chun*'s and other novels' occasional attempts to hark back, so to speak, to the chaste romance. The legitimate union of the hero and the third heroine is one example of such attempts. The initially nonsexual intent of the cross-dressed hero and his passivity in being kidnapped by lascivious nuns are two more instances of the semblance of chastity in an otherwise unchaste work. Male cross-dressers elsewhere in Chinese fiction are intent from the start either on using their disguise to seduce unsuspecting women or on serving the homosexual interests of their male patrons. Another mark of chastity is the fact that female impersonation and homoeroticism occur in two separate characters and in separate parts of *Yu Lou Chun*. Other works of Ming and Qing fiction portray female impersonation and homoeroticism in a single character who is the one penetrated. The *Yu Lou Chun* author portrays the heterosexual cross-dresser and his homoerotic son both as penetrators and in this way preserves the chastity of their anuses.

Contagious Promiscuity in *Chundeng Mishi, Taohua Ying,* and *Xinghua Tian*

In the next three romances, erotic description is the main focus as the attractive and sexually potent hero meets one beauty after another, almost all of whom he marries after first having sexual affairs with them. No time is wasted getting into the description of sexual promiscuity, but despite such indulgence from the very start, all three novels end in conventional stability, that is, marriage and the deliberate end of the man's promiscuity.

Chundeng mishi (Dream Story under the Spring Lamp), in ten chapters, of uncertain date in the Qing but pre-1868, uses a number of ploys in order to legitimize the illicit behavior that the novel portrays.[21] For example, the illegitimate pregnancies of the two unmarried heroines, which would normally be considered "monstrously heinous" (ch. 9, 7a), in this case go uncondemned because the parents of the hero and two heroines have dreams affirming the correctness of the youths' match. The book begins with the statement that if a match is truly fated, then illicit promiscuity is permitted, an idea found in *Xiuping yuan* as well. Further, before the youths meet, the parents of the first woman have already planned to ask the hero to marry their daughter uxorilocally. A final legitimization occurs at the end of the book when the two women, who are cousins and only children, manage to have three sons, including a set of twins, thereby supplying a male descendant for each of the three families involved, the man's and the two women's. As in *Jinxiang ting* and *Yu Lou Chun*, the marriage is polygamous, but the man performs an uxorilocal service for his in-laws.

Much of the narration consists of moving from one sexual session to the next; the forward impetus takes the form of contagion. For example, when the hero has sex with Heroine One, her maid secretly observes them. As often happens in the Chinese erotic story, in order to avoid being exposed, the lovers compromise others by having them join in the illicit pleasures. The heroine invites the maid to participate, first arousing the maid's interest by describing how great the pleasure is: "Your spirit floats and flutters, your soul wanders dreamily; it's as if you are about to become immortal" (ch. 4, 6ab). Next, at the suggestion of Heroine One, Heroine Two becomes involved. Heroine One first applies saliva to Heroine Two's vagina to help with the virginal entry, exemplifying a type of gesture found in other works as well; the hero compliments Heroine One for such "expert" (*zaihang*) cooperation (ch. 6, 4b).[22] In their sharing of the man, the women are confident that he will be faithful to them since he is an "educated gentleman" (*dushu junzi*, ch. 5, 3a), as they affirm to each other when they plot their marriage to him.

The discovery of their pregnancy comes about when one of the women suddenly notices the largeness of her stomach, as if one stomach has grown on top of another (ch. 8, 6a). When Heroine One's father discovers his daughter's condition, he blames his wife for not keeping guard over her but scurries away when the enraged wife rams him with her head (ch. 9, 6a). Parental upset thus turns to slapstick, soon ending in acquiescence. A penultimate scene shows the cooperative marriage in action: one heroine guides the man's penis into the other, or one wipes him and herself off in preparation for the other's turn. In a final development following the birth of the three sons, Heroine One's maid is married to the hero's manservant, who earlier slept with the maid as a result of the sexual contagion. In such novels, for the hero to marry off the maid in this way is a sign of his lack of polygynous greed.

The next two novels say goodbye forever to monogamy and two-wife polygyny. The early Qing *Taohua ying* (In the Peach Blossom Shadow), in twelve chapters, is about an orphaned young man named Yuqing (a pun with *yujing*, "jade stalk"), who ends up with one wife and an additional five concubines whom he meets through sexual affairs on the way to winning his wife.[23] A notable feature of this book is that almost every sexual success is accompanied by examination success or career advancement. The other novel is *Xinghua tian* (The Paradise of Apricot Blossoms), in fourteen chapters (possibly late eighteenth to mid-nineteenth century), whose hero is of low birth and has no interest in advancement through learning and holding office; instead he uses "fun and pleasure as his ladder" (ch. 1, 2, 1a).[24] He ends up with a happy family of twelve wives and one hundred sons. The reason he stops at twelve is that his house would become unmanageable if, as his main wife fears, for a hundred "beddings" (*xiu*) a hundred more women would move in (ch. 13, 180–81, 8b).

Starting at seventeen, the hero of *Taohua ying* has one affair after another, little caring about the suitability of the women for marriage. He begins with the wife of a family servant and through her meets a lusty widow of thirty-six, who in turn has a beautiful daughter who in the end becomes the hero's main wife. The daughter spies him making love to her mother and finds herself aroused too. She refuses to have an illicit liaison with him, however, but agrees to be engaged. He succeeds only in peeking at her taking a bath and in having sex with a maid who helps him communicate with the daughter and later becomes one of his concubines.

The next woman Yuqing meets is the lustful concubine of another man. She eventually dies of pining for him, although her maid later joins his family. Sixth and seventh are two nuns, the younger of whom eventually becomes his concubine, the elder of whom is involved with a sex-adept monk, who himself plays a helping role in the story. Such monks are stock characters in erotic romances who present aphrodisiacs to the hero and teach him sexual techniques.[25] Already familiar with the "method of nine shallow and one deep" (ch. 4, 6a), the hero now receives from the monk a marvelous aphrodisiac as well as the wisdom of "the mutual nourishment of *yin* and *yang*" (*yinyang xiangzi*, ch. 5, 17b). As the monk explains, "Thus, when having intercourse, although you might wish to pluck nourishment from the woman's deepest *yin* [*caibu zhiyin*], it is not right to seek benefit only for yourself and cause the woman to suffer illness"[26] (ch. 5, 17b). The monk later urges upon the hero the proverbial wisdom of "boldly withdrawing at the height of one's success" (*jiliu yongtui*, ch. 7, 4a).

Taohua ying's celebration of sexual pleasure includes both hetero- and homosexuality; its hero is bisexual, although more heterosexual, and in anal intercourse is both active and passive. His first homosexual contact recalls the scene in the late Ming collection of male homoerotic romances, *Bian er chai,* in which the drunken hero is anally seduced while he sleeps (story 2). The seducer in each case is a helper character like the adept monk in *Taohua ying,* who rescues Yuqing's main wife-to-be from villains. As for the practice of "loving the south" (*mu nan,* a pun for "loving the male"), the beginning of chapter 6 states that this "obsession" (*pi'ai*) has existed since ancient times and that even emperors enjoy it, so why should anyone wonder that it is so popular "in these times" (*jinshi*).[27] Although Yuqing is angry when he discovers that he has been penetrated (ch. 6, 23a–24a), he is later mollified when he is allowed to sleep with the seducer's sexually deprived wife.[28] She eventually becomes one of Yuqing's concubines, a gift from her husband who then turns exclusively homosexual.[29] Later, when the hero is on his way to take the capital exams, he buys a handsome youth and enjoys sex with him. A skilled catamite who knows how to please his master, the boy "purposely moans and pretends to be in great pain." The narrator explains that the hero is not as attracted to men as to women, but on this occasion finds sex with the boy "even more pleasurable than with a woman" (ch. 9, 20a).

In the final episodes, the hero establishes his family and finally has sex with his main wife. He discovers how perfect her body is, gleaming white and without the slightest blemish (ch. 10, 8a). She has no pubic hair, a detail he had noticed when he first spied on her bathing and one that features in other Chinese erotica as well (ch. 3, 25a). Moreover, she is too delicate to endure much of his lovemaking and is in general "indifferent" about sex (*danran,* ch. 11, 16a). She is one to be orderly in "governing the home" (ch. 10, 9a), "to emphasize propriety" (ch. 11, 16a), and to be "serious"—in contrast to the others, who are all "playful" and sexy (*yan* vs. *qu,* ch. 11, 16a). She is absent during the penultimate scene of orgy common in these novels (here called "the glorious meeting of collective joy," *hehuan shenghui*, ch. 12, 19b–21a), and is disapproving when she later learns of its occurrence. The observation of such a sexual division of labor is sharper in *Taohua ying* than in *Xiuping yuan, Xinghua tian,* and other novels, in which the main wife calls for restraint or is of loftier sexual quality but nevertheless actively joins with everyone else.

In general, women are of three types in this and other novels: at one extreme are the overly lustful, like the widow or the adulterous concubine, both of whom the hero abandons. They exemplify the dark proverb which says that "a woman's lust will stop only when she is buried beneath the earth" (ch. 2, 10ab). The widow despairs and becomes a nun; the concubine dies. In the middle are the playful and sexy women ready at all times for sex. At the far end is the prudent and delicate wife who in sexual terms represents quality over quantity. As usual, women are at greater risk if they indulge; none achieves as much as the chaste woman in the classic romance.

As for the main male characters, *Taohua ying* also has three types, who are all promiscuous (that is, they have multiple male or female partners whether marriage is a factor or not) and who, like the women, take up positions either closer to or farther from normative gender roles. The first and most legitimate is the procreative, mainly heterosexual polygamist husband. Second is the initially procreative, mainly homosexual husband (although reported to have no children), who is promiscuous but primarily with male partners. The third is the adept monk, who disavows procreation (though he may have illegitimate children) and is promiscuous without being married. Unlike the women, all the men in *Taohua ying* succeed by the end of the story. At the end, the homosexual joins the adept in beckoning the hero to renounce "success and fame" and to retire with his wives from the public world. Instead of portraying the monk as an evil adept who steals female essence, for example, or having the homosexual die or disappear from the story, as do some erotic novels of the period,[30] *Taohua ying* incorporates them both into the final scene of hermetic utopia, where everyone builds longevity through his or her uninterrupted enjoyment of sexual and other self-cultivating activities.

In its almost exclusive focus on sex, *Xinghua tian* recalls *Rou putuan* but without the "tragic" ending in which the hero realizes the fatality of sex and cuts off his penis. In general, the Qing erotic romance ends with the man renouncing promiscuity, not sex. The most obvious resemblance to *Rou putuan* lies in the play of combinations by which the hero meets one woman through another or makes love to some or all of them at once, with each woman, for example, trying to outdo the last.[31]

Like the heroes in *Rou putuan, Taohua ying,* and other erotic novels, the one in *Xinghua tian* gains his powerful sexual skills by means of supernatural and esoteric techniques. A Taoist monk gives him aphrodisiacs, one of which, when flicked upon a woman, induces her to come to the man the same night. Another monk teaches him a method called *bijia gongfu,* "the practice of *bijia,*"[32] a *qigong* exercise by which the hero learns to strengthen his penis and make it "move by itself" (*zidong,* ch. 3, 36–37, 8b)—that is, extend and contract on its own (the aphrodisiac in *Taohua ying* has the same effect; ch. 5, 17b). The hero begins his sexual career immediately after receiving these aids, first with a prostitute and then with a married neighbor woman upon whom he flicks the aphrodisiac.

Like the hero in *Taohua ying,* he has no regard for whether or not a woman is married. As it turns out anyway, the husbands of the women he "steals" all conveniently die, and the women then ask to enter his family, none of them caring how many wives he already has. The main wife tolerates the addition of other wives since she herself is abandoned by her homosexual husband, who runs off with his young lover; she is happy to have such a potent new husband. In the context of these stories, husbands who die or abandon their wives are metaphors for sexually inadequate men. The homosexual is the most fully portrayed example of inadequacy vis-à-vis his wife; he does not like women and has to be forced into marriage. For him the "rear hall" (*houting*) is better because it is tight, in contrast to the vagina, which is "sticky, slippery, and slack; the more you thrust, the looser it gets"; "what's more it takes a great deal of energy" (ch. 1, 8, 2b).

Entering upon a quick succession of affairs, the hero first makes love with an innkeeper's wife and concubine, the former of whom then serves as go-between for the hero and his main wife-to-be, that is, the forlorn wife of the homosexual. Exclaiming that the hero's penis must be one of the "greatest treasures on earth" (*renjian zhibao,* ch. 6, 67, 4a), the innkeeper's wife gets in bed with the now aroused main wife-to-be and makes love with her; not long after, the hero has a tryst with the soon-to-be main wife. Scenes of women having sex together are relatively rare in Chinese fiction but typically follow this example in that the relationship is not portrayed as sufficient in itself but instead as a temporary replacement for or prelude to sex with a man.

The sexual chain of involvement lengthens when the two younger sisters of the homosexual's wife spy on her and the hero making love. They have already heard that his penis is "big, hard, hot, and long, and it doesn't leak!" (ch. 8, 93, 10a). The two sisters then make love with each other until they exhaust themselves and fall asleep; later they become two more of the hero's wives.[33]

The death of the homosexual husband marks the turning point after which the hero begins to build his family by marrying first his main wife, then her two sisters, and after that the wife and concubine of the innkeeper (who also dies); he then marries a recently orphaned neighbor woman, three prostitutes who present themselves to him, another recently widowed woman (the one upon whom he had flicked the aphrodisiac), her sister (also a widow), and finally another prostitute (like the others, in need of a secure home); he also takes in the maid of his first great love, a prostitute who died of unsated lust. The portrayal of helpless women in need of a capable husband marks *Xinghua tian*'s naturalization of the marriage of one man to so many women. The novelist creates not an undeserving sexual tyrant but a benevolent polygamist who is like someone dispensing sexual welfare in a society with too few potent and trustworthy males.

In the finale, the man constructs a "bed for the pleasure of all" (*hehuan chuang*), intended for great lovemaking sessions.[34] At this point the main wife begins to enforce an "order of the house" (*jiafa*), which includes rules against jealous infighting and secret promiscuity within the home. Later the hero dreams of an old Taoist who leads him to an "Apricot Blossom Cave" and enlightens him about the harm of "illicit sexual relations" (*jianyin*) and the heterodoxy of sexual techniques and aphrodisiacs.[35] Thereafter, the hero forswears sexual relations with women other than his twelve wives, who presently begin to bear sons to the number of one hundred—all with the propitious features of "square face, long earlobes, broad mouth, and strong body" (ch. 14, 192, 11b).

The Idealism of the Erotic Romance

Because they are highly sex oriented and allow a fantastic degree of promiscuity, *Chundeng mishi*, *Taohua ying*, and *Xinghua tian* hardly resemble the classic beauty-scholar romance. On the conservative end of these three works, *Chundeng mishi* stays within the bounds of the chaste romance by giving the hero no more than two wives, with whom he pointedly says he is satisfied (ch. 8, 4b), and by having him be filial by supplying a son for each patriline. However, the young lovers utterly flout the rule of chastity and go unpunished for their promiscuity and its consequences. At the other extreme, *Xinghua tian* takes the polygamous adventure about as far as possible for a narrative of such length. It features a hero who makes no pretense of being public-spirited or filial but who instead lives a life of pure pleasure and gets away with it.

But as love stories with comic endings, the three works still observe some of the guidelines of the early Qing model. They end with the happy marriage of a handsome scholar to beautiful women. That all of the characters are sexually active as well as handsome or beautiful shows that unabashed sex has become part of stories about lovers who meet on their own and marry. In late Ming erotic fiction, lovers also met without a go-between or parents' permission but could not marry and thus redeem their illicit involvement; they mostly encountered disastrous endings. In the Qing romance, sex is domesticated by being brought into the sphere of marriage. The enjoyment of sex no longer subverts social order but instead belongs to that order.

The late Ming illicit love story still appears in the Qing romance, but as a side plot taking place among nonheroic characters, as exemplified in *Qingmeng tuo*.[36] The heroic characters of the Qing romance may be punished for sexual transgression, but they will eventually prevail and make their bond last. Permanence is the end of sexual love in the romance, whereas ephemerality is the end in the story of illicit love. The Qing romance retains the theme of ephemerality only in reduced form at the very end when the man forswears promiscuity and, together with his wives, withdraws from the bustling world.

Ending with the curtailment of pleasure is conventional in both the Ming and Qing love story. In part a traditional form of aesthetic closure, such an ending is like an authorial gesture to guarantee or bless the success of indulgence by balancing it with caution; an author does not want to "incur the jealousy of heaven." In the Qing erotic romance, such endings parallel the chaste romance's corrective reaction to late Ming decadence. The erotic romance, in short, portrays a sexually harmonious, reformed household—in contrast, for example, to Ximen Qing's chaotic one in *Jin Ping Mei*.

Both the chaste and erotic romances have as their core the story of the monogamous, well-matched pair of the scholar and the beauty. In both types of romance one beauty (sometimes two) is outstanding in chastity and / or refinement, if not also wit and courage. The erotic romance then bluffs itself into letting the scholar be more deserving than the beauty by having him politely take a few more women, usually sexier and less refined than the main beauty. But politeness is crucial; it is the common denominator of all the romances and is another of the main defining features of the genre. These features can be summed up in a three-part definition: politeness and civility, which means that everyone treats each other with respect; moderation and rationalism, which means that no one overindulges in lust or passion; and romantic idealism, which means that superior people achieve outstanding love matches. Civility, moderation, and romantic idealism combine to eliminate the subversiveness and danger of passionate desire. The erotic romances, then, are like fictionalized offshoots of the ancient ars erotica, which was likewise polite, moderate, and idealistic.

A final comment must be made in order to link more firmly the chaste and erotic romances with the ideas of the shrew and the miser, and with the ways these ideas are played out in the much lengthier works of Qing fiction to be discussed below. As mentioned previously, both types of romance display an impoverishment of realistic detail, which the other works treated in this book more than make up for. Such an impoverishment is a form of disavowal, a refusal to admit conditions of social reality. The chaste romances fantastically elevate the woman; the erotic romances fantastically privilege the man. As demonstrated in the last chapter, the symmetry of the chaste romance represents an idealism that blurs the distinction between the sexes and desexualizes man and woman. The idealism of such symmetry projects a relationship in which there is fluid transposition and reversal of roles. In the context of traditional norms, the result of such a dialectic is that the man in effect demasculinizes himself and denies himself his customary sexual privileges. This blurring of the sexes thus does more to desexualize the man than the woman since the man is typically more sexually active to begin with; the already restricted woman merely cultivates a yet finer grade of chastity. In contrast, the erotic romance rebounds and sexualizes the man to the point that the semblance of balanced interchange and dialogue is erased. Everyone accepts that the polygynist hero is the most potent and desirable of men. If he wants a woman, then she unquestioningly gives herself to him. Just as in the chaste romance the man cooperates with the woman to demasculinize the man, so in the erotic romance the women in effect ally themselves with the man to deny women their power over themselves and the man. The erotic romances, like the ars erotica, refuse to admit the existence of the shrew, that is, the woman's capacity to reject or subdue the man.

Another way to put it is that the heroines of the chaste romances are benevolent shrews. They do not need to be malevolently shrewish since their men are already well-behaved. The beauties take the shrew's skill at haranguing and turn it into supreme aptitude in poetry and other literary arts. In contrast, the heroes of the erotic romances are benevolent misers who do not need to go so far as to retreat into filth and meanness. Their women never throw tantrums or make excessive demands of them. These happy polygamists accumulate banks of women and economize their semen, but turn such miserliness into an everlasting ability to satisfy their numerous wives.[37] The novels discussed in the next two chapters, *Yesou puyan* and *Honglou meng,* display the same chaste versus erotic dichotomy, with *Yesou puyan* resembling the polygamous romance and *Honglou meng* the monogamous. The "miserly," male-superior *Yesou puyan* contrasts with the "shrewish," male-self-deprecating *Honglou meng.* As will be seen, however, the two novels admit far more social reality and particularistic detail than do either type of romance, and do not reduce as neatly into the above categories of erotic and chaste.

7

A CASE FOR CONFUCIAN SEXUALITY:

CHASTE POLYGAMY IN *YESOU PUYAN*[1]

The Confucian Superman

Yesou puyan (A Country Codger's Words of Exposure) is a 154-chapter novel written by an eccentric polymath little known to either his mid-eighteenth century contemporaries or anyone afterwards. A miser's novel par excellence, it comes down firmly on the side of the economization of semen and the consolidation of a capital base of fertile women, in this case, two wives and four concubines. The hero is a potent Confucian superman who, though eschewing the ars erotica, nevertheless achieves the polygynous harmony idealized in the erotic romances. Each of his wives is outstanding in her own right and all produce children according to accurately gauged rhythms of fertility. The hero is one of the most ardently portrayed exemplars of manhood that Qing fiction has to offer, amounting to an unsung correction of failed polygamists like Ximen Qing or Jia Baoyu.

The harmonious whole of this Confucian household is predicated upon both an ascetic doctrine of sex for procreation only and a parental presence that oversees the hero's practice of polygyny, his sage widow mother. In terms of the symbolic order of miser, shrew, and polygamist, she is like a shrewish main wife raised to the level of stern matriarch, thus resolving two problems endemic to the polygynous family: that of the doting mother who produces the wastrel son, and that of jealousy between main wife and concubines. In other words, as stern matriarch she is neither doting mother nor jealous main wife. The hero's wives, in turn, although ostensibly ranked as two wives and four concubines, are in effect all concubines subordinate to the shrewish wife now metamorphosed into chaste widow mother. The polygamist hero, although endowed with supreme potency, at the same time reveres his mother and, under her direction, expends his energy only for the sake of procreation.

Conceived on a much broader scale than most of the works discussed so far, *Yesou puyan* follows but recombines the categories of chaste and erotic: it is a chaste polygamous romance that nevertheless contains many passages of explicit sexual or bodily description. By "chaste polygamy" is meant the fact that the hero has many talented wives, none of whom are jealous or shrewish, some of whom he chastely sleeps with before marriage but none of whom he has actual intercourse with until marriage and approval by his beloved sage mother. The rule still follows that once the man goes beyond two wives, the novel becomes erotic; but *Yesou puyan* is chastely erotic. When in a sane state of mind, the hero and heroines are always correct, losing control only during temporary madness brought on by external causes. Exposure of the body, often including its sexual functions, occurs repeatedly as the hero finds himself in situations of accidental, inescapable intimacy with women or when some acute illness ravages one of the characters. But all such scenes exist because of what the author makes appear a realistic need to admit them. In other words, the vicissitudes of life realistically do not admit of complete chastity.

The purpose of this chapter will be to untangle such concepts as chaste polygamy, chaste eroticism, or shrewish wife metamorphosed into sage widow mother. Since *Yesou puyan* is such a unique and rarely studied novel, what follows will first provide a general overview of the book and its author before examining its portrayal of sexuality. Despite its obscurity and relative lack of acceptance by popular and scholarly readers, I will view it to be as important as *Honglou meng* in presenting one of the major images of male character found in Qing fiction.

Yesou puyan is a panoramic novel about a China that is disturbed by eunuchs, demons, barbarians, and forces of Buddhist and Taoist perversion, which only a thorough Confucian revival can eradicate. The hero is a latter-day Confucian superman who never passes the official exams but who manages to rise to the position of advisor to the emperor, conquer all forces of evil, and eradicate Buddhism and Taoism from China. The novel combines a strictly orthodox vision with extensive descriptions of bizarre, unorthodox behavior which typically takes sexual form. The author portrays scenes of chaste kissing and caressing, therapeutic sexual massage, farcical lovemaking, *Jin Ping Mei*–like sexual abandon, and lewd genital acrobatics, as well as gruesome bestiality and sexual vampirism. Throughout pages of erotic danger and adventure, the hero displays supreme self control, even when offered or forced to accept the most desirous and desirable of women. Despite his own superhuman sexual power, he unswervingly preaches that sex is for procreation only: "The two ways of *yin* and *yang* are only meant to proliferate Heaven and Earth and to continue the descent of the ancestors. They are in no way meant for lustful enjoyment." The genitals should be looked upon as "ordinary, tiring things—only then are they like treasures" (ch. 68, 8b).[2]

With 154 chapters, *Yesou puyan* is one of the longest novels ever written in China.[3] Some twentieth-century scholars have placed it in a group of Qing works called novels of erudition or scholar-novels. The author is Xia Jingqu (1705–87), a native of Jiangyin in Jiangsu Province who, like other scholar-novelists, has chosen vernacular narrative as a form into which to pour his vast erudition: besides the usual core of Confucian learning in history, poetry, and moral thought, he is fluent in mathematics, astronomy, military science, and medicine. But he is unlike other erudite novelists in that he has a penchant for describing peculiarities and aberrations of sexual and other bodily functions.[4] At the same time, the author observes a clean-cut division between licentiousness outside in the world and correctness inside the mind. He is an orthodox moralist who for once chooses not to repress the consideration, in unsparing terms, of the problems and fantasies of sexuality. Moreover, he makes the reading of his book part of the solution. Challenging readers to find one instance in which he is actually indulging in his own lurid descriptions, he wants his "pornography" taken not as a vehicle of titillation, but as a test of virtuous self-control.

In calling for the restoration of a pure Confucianism, *Yesou puyan* makes its case by showing the decadence of society and the chaos of government, and then creating a hero who uses both vast learning and great martial and moral strength to correct all social wrongs. Xia's case for restoration centers on the victory of virtuous male energy, which takes the form of both supreme sexual potency and disciplined self-control. The intricacy of detail and strangeness of erotic description, unparalleled in any premodern Chinese fiction I know of, are part of a "scholarly" project: to present a complete and objective view of the world, of which sexuality is portrayed as one of many important parts, and to assert that integrity and control are possible even in the most provocative and compromising situations, which the hero frequently encounters. *Yesou puyan*'s message is of special interest in contrast to that of the far more famous *Honglou meng*, in which it is a question of the decline of a household and the resignation or abdication of male energy. The two novels, among the last major literary representations of male centrality in imperial China—neither of which is written under the influence of the other—evoke two extremes, one the super-valuation of masculinity, the other its debasement and devaluation.

The Author and his Work

The "novel of erudition" or "scholar-novel" is a term used by scholars from Lu Xun to C. T. Hsia to refer to a small group of Qing dynasty works in which the narrative is interspersed with learned discourse or is written in high literary language.[5] These works, mostly written before the Opium War, are lengthy and elaborate celebrations of traditional art and knowledge. Dense even for most native readers, few if any are likely to be translated in entirety into any foreign language. As C. T. Hsia suggests, after the Opium War scholar-novelists largely disappeared, apparently no longer able to engage in such purely self-contained pastimes. Novels from the rest of the nineteenth century are less ambitious in scope; many are devoted to satirical exposé of dynastic corruption and social decay. From the perspective of the mid-Qing, Xia Jingqu also observes decay but still has a vision—albeit a fantastic one—of China's grand-scale, self-contained renewal.

His novel was not published until about a hundred years after he finished it. He was perhaps restrained by poverty, to which he often refers in his poetry; such a long novel would be costly to print and would probably be unsellable. The presentation of a messianic Confucianist who has numerous sexual encounters would make such a book dangerous to print. Lu Xun thought that the author wished to write it only for himself and friends.[6] Its earliest extant edition is of 1881, in 152 chapters, which has a detailed interlineal commentary and critical comments at the end of each chapter but contains many lacunae. A version in 154 chapters by another publisher followed in 1882, this time without the interlineal commentary but containing identical critical comments at the end of each chapter, and with the lacunae filled.[7] After these editions, the novel gradually became known, going through several reprints and revisions up to the 1930s. Later editions are usually abridged, the shortest occurring in one hundred chapters.[8]

The novel attracted the attention of a number of Republican-period scholars such as Qian Jingfang, Jiang Ruicao, and Lu Xun in the teens and twenties, and Sun Kaidi, Tan Zhengbi, and Zhao Jingshen in the thirties. Zhao finally compiled the most authoritative biography of the author by traveling to Jiangyin and consulting the Xia family genealogy.[9] The book was a favorite of the historian Wu Han in prewar times.[10] Of lesser known figures of the Republican period, Wu Jinzhuang, an editor at Shangwu Press, reportedly thought the book was the best of China's vernacular novels; Zhou Yueran, however, a collector of Chinese and Western erotic books and writer of English textbooks, thought it completely without merit ("reactionarily orthodox, vulgar, and filthy").[11] As C. T. Hsia reports, in the early 1940s in Shanghai it was popular fare in operatic form, in which the famous actor Zhou Xinfang played the hero Wen Suchen.[12] But since the 1940s, as far as I can see, few Chinese scholars have touted the novel or made a study of it.

The author, Xia Jingqu, traveled widely in China, often with the officials to whom he served as secretary, his main form of employment. Despite his vast learning, he did not even pass the test to become a *xiucai*, the lowest level in the examination hierarchy, although he was known and respected by men of repute. Xia also left works on history, poetry, and medicine—portions of which find their way into the novel. His father died when Xia was a boy, as does the father of the novel's hero Wen Suchen. His mother, surnamed Tang, perhaps appears in Wen's venerated mother, Shui Furen (the water radical of Tang, lit. "soup," perhaps corresponding to Shui, "water"). After his first wife died, Xia married a second, by whom he had a son and a daughter. In his book, the author extravagantly gives his hero dozens of children by six women.[13]

We know a few scattered events in Xia's life. For example, in 1736 in Beijing he met Yang Mingshi (1661–1736), also of Jiangyin, who was a Confucian scholar, official (once the governor-general of Yunnan-Guizhou), and, his last position before death, tutor to an imperial prince. Yang's death figures briefly in the novel (ch. 11).[14] In 1747 Xia suffered a serious illness and was cared for by his younger sister, who from the evidence of his poetry appears to have been a close sibling. Similarly, in chapters 16 and 17 of the novel, Wen suffers from a major illness for many months and is intimately cared for by a woman—not his sister, however.[15] In 1750 Gao Bin (1683–1755), a prominent official and specialist in river control invited Xia to lecture on "nature and principle" (*xingli*). Some of Xia's poems refer to his relationship with Gao Bin.[16]

Based on the novel's portrayal of a special celebration for Wen's seventy-sixth birthday, Zhao Jingshen suggests that *Yesou puyan* was finished in the 1770s when Xia was in his seventies.[17] Reports by people who knew Xia directly or indirectly have it that in 1786, when he was eighty-one, he tried to present one of his works to the emperor, who was then traveling in the south. One source says the work was a commentary on history, but others say it was *Yesou puyan* and claim that either his wife or daughter coaxed or tricked him out of fulfilling his wish, to his great frustration.[18] Xia died in 1787 at age eighty-two.

Another of the many connections between the novel and Xia's own life is the reputed correspondence between the names of the hero's concubines and some of the author's personal possessions. In the novel Wen's ambition is to have a bevy of concubines who are his *zhiji*, "intimate friends," each of whom specializes in one of four areas—mathematics, poetry, medicine, and military science (ch. 8, 57–58). The names of these women were also supposedly ones Xia gave to favorite objects of daily use. Xuangu, Wen's mathematics specialist, was the name of Xia's abacus; Xiangling, Wen's poetry connoisseur, was the name of Xia's sleep mat; and Su'e, the medical consort, was the name of Xia's armrest for taking pulses. Two others are less clear: Naner, Wen's fourth concubine (chs. 118–19), was supposedly the name of the bar of the door to Xia's study, and Hongdou, Wen's second wife—equal co-consort to his first wife, Tian Shi (chs. 121–22)—was the name of Xia's seal.[19]

The title of the book comes from a proverb originating in the *Liezi* (circa 300 A.D.), *yeren xian pu*, which means "The rustic recommends sitting in the sun to get warm." A poor farmer who had never seen palaces or rich clothing found pleasure in warming himself in the spring sun. He thought to recommend this activity to the ruler and thereby gain reward.[20] Since *pu* by itself means to "sun" or "expose to the sun," *puyan* means "to expose words" or "words that expose." But without the sun radical, *pu* becomes the character *bao*, which means "violent" or "hot-tempered" (the character for *bao* can also be pronounced *pu*, also meaning to "expose"). Xia's book is thus his humble but genuine gift to the emperor that may also contain a more "scorching" intent. Whatever the intensity, the key gesture of *Yesou puyan* is exposure, especially of the body and its functions.

A brief summary of the plot of *A Country Codger's Words of Exposure* is as follows:

Yesou puyan takes place in the Ming dynasty between 1465 and 1519.[21] Its hero is Wen Suchen, whose name, Suchen or "Unappointed Minister," is an allusion to one of the titles given to Confucius, Suwang, "uncrowned king." Born under an auspicious omen, Suchen has the genius of a prodigy. His father dies, leaving a wife who is "a great female Confucian" (*nüzhong daru*). When little, Suchen, asked if he wants to become wealthy, replies that he wants to study; asked if he wants to test first in the official examinations, he replies that he wants to become a sage (ch. 1, 3). As a young man he sets out on a journey to expand his horizons; his ambitious goal is to eradicate heterodoxy—especially Buddhism—from the empire. His first encounter with evil is at West Lake in Hangzhou, where a water monster, upset by the geomantically harmful activities of a powerful eunuch, overturns Wen's boat. More evil emerges in the form of monks and their patrons, including the powerful eunuch, all of whom are engaged in a complex scheme to depose the emperor. Suchen begins the lengthy quest of opposing the plotters and on the way gathers concubines and starts a family, all along never failing to show devotion to his mother. He eventually becomes a confidant of the emperor (ch. 113); begins his eradication of Buddhism and Taoism (ch. 135); and, as a side product, effects the submission of Europe (*Ouluobazhou*) and its conversion to Confucianism (ch. 147, 559).[22] When Wen dies there is a spirit seat for him among the sages of the Confucian tradition.

Confucian Superman in a Lascivious World

Healthy Sexuality

Wen Suchen is an upright (*zhong*) man in a lascivious (*yin*) world. With one angry stare he causes the image worshiped at a festival of catamites (*longyang hui*) to fall to pieces and the revelers then to disperse (ch. 67,

493–94). He has extraordinary physical strength yet appears gentle and slight. He is broadly learned but does not take the accepted path of seeking office through the examination system. He is extremely potent sexually but, except for once when he goes mad (ch. 130), has sex only for the sake of begetting children, who are born in waves once he starts his family. Still, he is passionate and tender with his wives and shares himself among them fairly. As the narrator says: "Suchen is no philanderer, yet he is as full of sentiment as the love poet Song Yu" (ch. 1, 2).

A philosophy of proper, healthy sex informs what one might call *Yesou puyan*'s case for a Confucian sexuality, which can be assembled from numerous passages in the book. The sex organs should not be viewed as "living treasures," otherwise the vagina inevitably becomes like a "fire pit" to the man, the penis like a "sharp blade" to the woman (ch. 68, 9a). Suchen advises the imperial prince: "Curb desire, and sons will be plentiful. Accord with the menstrual period of the wife and concubines, and sleep with [*tong fang*] each only once a month" (ch. 88, 88).[23] But despite such limitations, Suchen still allows for the pleasure of the kissing and caressing before intercourse, as will be shown in a scene below.[24] In a discourse to his first concubine-to-be, Suchen says, "To begin with, the joy between man and woman resides only in the moments before coitus [*jiaohe*]. Then, passionate thoughts are deepest and pleasure [*xingqu*] is endless. But as soon as we experience coitus, then all wanes and dissipates." She is made to see that "the clouds and rain and the dream of Mt. Wu are actually nothing in the end but feet added to the snake: superfluous" (ch. 6, 11ab). Later, he explains to another woman that "the flash of ecstasy is all over in a second" (ch. 68, 8b). Suchen's ideas about sex distantly resemble those of a Qing medical treatise which recommends that "whenever husband and wife go to bed, neither should allow the slightest thoughts of desire but should simply sleep in each others' arms. In this way the correct *qi* of *yin* and *yang* will mutually react and inter-regulate, thereby bringing the utmost benefit." As soon as desire emerges and sex organs join, then "loss" (*bai*) commences.[25]

Like numerous Chinese novels and stories, *Yesou puyan* presents sexual themes in didactic fashion, dramatizing a broad range of sexual behavior in order to draw distinctions between healthy and aberrant. Wen Suchen is the healthy model, as shown early in the novel when he resists sexual opportunities three successive times, each more challenging than the last. In Xia Jingqu's picture, heroism resides not only in deeds of martial valor but also in the ability to "resist sexual pleasure," *que se,* as termed by *Yesou puyan's* commentator.[26]

Of the three women Wen resists, two later become his concubines; all are decent, not "lascivious" women. He becomes intimate with them by force of circumstance, not by intention, and although he likes them, he resists indulgence because it would be unfilial to have intercourse with someone unless his mother first gave her blessing. The nature of his "resistance" or "refusal of sex," *que se,* can be seen in the second of his accidental brushes with naked intimacy.

Some friends want to present their sister Xuangu as concubine to Suchen, but are afraid he will decline. Without telling him of their wish, they put him to sleep by making him drunk, then have her get into bed with him. In his drunken slumber he slips into intimate embrace with her but when he wakes delicately refuses to go any further. He separates her from himself by wrapping her in a blanket, then going to sleep, leaving her in confusion. The next day he at first rejects the offer of Xuangu but then accepts since it is clear that the affair has gone too far: the establishment of the intention to marry her to him and the occurrence of physical proximity made her in effect lose her virginity. Besides, he is already fond of her.

The second night, after spending the day warmly talking mathematics, he consents to go to bed with her.

After they washed their hands and feet, Xuangu helped him get ready for bed. She took off her hair ornaments, then her outer clothes, and hid a silk kerchief under the mat. When she climbed into bed, Suchen raised the embroidered quilt and let her snuggle underneath. He stretched out his arm to pillow her powdery neck. With the other hand he undid the buttons of her chemise and took it off, then loosened her belt and slipped off her lower garment. Xuangu didn't dare resist, letting Suchen have his way. At this moment he was absorbed in his pleasure and could give her nothing but affection. He gently cradled her powdery neck, cuddled against her fragrant cheek, and began to caress and fondle her. Xuangu was at the point of delirium, her fragrant soul as if drunk. But suddenly something seemed to startle him, and his hand abruptly shrank back. Then he put his arm around her slender waist and nestled his leg between her thighs. Resting thus entwined, he moved no more. Xuangu was like a bird afraid of being shot by an arrow [*jinggong zhi niao*].[27] (ch. 5, 11ab)

Full of shame and confusion, not knowing what his second rejection means, she begins to cry. The chapter ends at this dramatic point.

At the beginning of the next chapter he wipes her tears and consoles her by explaining that they can consummate only after receiving his mother's permission. Xuangu now understands model Confucian behavior, and they go to sleep. The next morning he wakes to find her slender jade finger drawing circles on his back—she had been dreaming of arcs and circles from their previous day's discussions. He is delighted by her desire to learn and proceeds to

> draw a great circle on Xuangu's stomach, saying, "Let this be the circle of the sky, 360 degrees all around." Pointing to her fragrant navel, he said, "Let this be the earth. The area around the navel is the surface of the earth, and the center of the navel is the center of the earth. Now if we measure from the surrounding area of the earth to the surrounding area of the sky, and if we measure from the earth's center to the surrounding area of the sky, aren't the measurements going to be different? Thus in computation there is what's called the 'difference between the earth's center and [points in] its surface.' This is as far as we got yesterday at dark [i.e., measuring areas of triangles, circles, etc.]."
>
> Xuangu laughed, "The sky and the earth are called the Two Greats, but in fact the Earth fitting into the Sky is but a small thing. Obviously the wife is by far smaller than the husband."
>
> Suchen laughed, "And the concubine is even smaller."
>
> Xuangu replied, "That goes without saying,"

and continued to ask further technical questions (ch. 8, 54–55).

Later he tells her of one of his life ambitions, to have concubines with whom he can discuss and transmit (*chuan*) four of his specialties—mathematics, poetry, medicine, and military strategy. He uses the same word *qiecuo* found in another novel of this period, *Lin Lan Xiang*, to refer to learned discussion between husband, wife, and concubines.[28] "Exchanging views on learned topics" would traditionally occur between men, but *Yesou puyan* and *Lin Lan Xiang* apply the term to intellectual companionship in marriage. The same type of relationship already occurs in the early Qing beauty-scholar romances, which, however, stay within or close to the bounds of monogamy. As I have said previously, the theme of intellectual companionship between man and woman, especially literatus and courtesan, has a long history in China, but as idealized in conjugal situations in *Yesou puyan, Lin Lan Xiang,* and the chaste romances, it possibly evokes a trend of the seventeenth and eighteenth centuries, the literary education of women, which was instituted in many elite households and was debated by numerous scholars, most famously Yuan Mei and Zhang Xuecheng.[29]

Besides the above scenes of chaste eroticism, *Yesou puyan* portrays situations of nonsexual intimacy in which proximity is therapeutic. Suchen can cure people, mainly women, by physically manipulating them, as with two of his future concubines. The first is Su'e, his medical specialist, who suffers ill effects after accidentally swallowing a powerful aphrodisiac. Suchen's cure includes pressing his leg tightly against her "jade door," *yuhu,* sucking firmly on her tongue, and thus stemming the loss of her vital energies and nourishing them with his own (ch. 18, 9ab). The second woman is Xiangling, his future poetry specialist, whose clothing he suddenly begins to pull off the first time he sees her. It turns out that she is on the verge of an illness the deadliness of which can be averted only by causing her a sudden cathartic fright. He perceives the illness in her unhealthy color and takes the only expedient course of action (ch. 19).

Suchen also offers therapy to women he does not marry. He rids them of demonic possession by writing characters, including his name, between their breasts, in one case writing on the women of the emperor's harem.[30] He cures a woman of sterility by transmitting to her the fertility-enhancing energy of his body. A *shinü,* literally, "stone-woman," she is unable to menstruate, her breasts are smaller than his, and her skin is pale white. By lying next to him, she begins to be "steamed" (*zheng*) by the *yang* energy he emanates. "As he slept . . . she gently took his hand and first massaged her breasts, then her abdomen, and then her vagina. She felt even more stimulated and excited, all over her body. She was numb in every spot and couldn't stop moaning and cooing" (ch. 94, 9a). Eventually, her menses begin to flow.[31] The reverse situation also occurs when Suchen receives intimate care from women. He is delirious from an illness and has no one to nurse him but Su'e, who must undress him, sleep with him to keep him warm, and clean him after a violent siege of diarrhea (ch. 16). In another case, the woman he massages into fertility later returns his favor by licking and curing wounds that he has suffered (ch. 97, 154, 156).

Most of the cures described above probably derive from esoteric practices or folk medicine and ritual. Evidence that what we see in *Yesou puyan* is not unique to this novel can be found in the early Qing *Ji Dian dashi zuiputi quanzhuan* (The Complete Story of the Drunken Buddhist Master Ji Dian), in which the drunkard monk Ji Dian likewise cures a young woman by means of naked proximity.[32] They both remove their upper clothes, then he sits with her all night back-to-back and arm tucked in arm until the parasite that infests her finally rushes out through her nose (ch. 16, 4ab). On another occasion, Ji Dian sees a pretty woman in an antique shop and suddenly starts biting her neck. By premonition he sees on her skin the marks of a rope she is about to use to hang herself; biting at her neck, he succeeds in snapping two strands of the imaginary rope, but she escapes before he can snap the third. Later that day she hangs herself after arguing with her husband and dies because the third strand of the rope fails to break (ch. 19, 1a–2a).

Like the ascetic Ji Dian, who tiptoes up to the bed of the sleeping courtesan, places her shoe on her vagina, and then leaves,[33] Xia Jingqu and Wen Suchen approach the female body as closely as possible in order to demonstrate their absolute imperviousness to the power of female attraction. In its nonribald version of Ji Dian's chaste exhibitionism, *Yesou puyan* spies on, pries into, and exposes as many bodies as it can through the eyes of moral or therapeutic correctness. In sexual situations, as long as it is the other person being lewd—not Suchen—then observation or exposure of anything is fair. The female sex organs are particularly singled out for examination and portrayal, in one case four times in close succession.[34] In the examples below, all consistent with the method of distancing that is the trademark of *Yesou puyan*, the intimacy and exposure that were innocent above now become dangerous and demonic.

The Lascivious World

It is belief in the virtue of family-oriented procreation that motivates Suchen's attacks on Buddhism and all other heterodox thought and behavior. He rejects anal intercourse, as he explains in a discourse on the principles of sex, because the fertilizing *yang* energy has nowhere to go inside the anus (ch. 71, 9ab). He opposes the use of aphrodisiacs and never brings up the topic of the ars erotica or any of its methods.[35] He hates the Buddhist monk or nun because they are unattached persons, outside the network of the filial family. To one young nun who falls sick from attraction to a man, Suchen prescribes the cure of "sexual desire," *seyu* (ch. 11, 79); she should return to normal life and take a husband.[36]

While the nun exemplifies the harms of celibacy, other deviants in the lascivious world possess monstrous sexual appetites which they nourish by theft from other human bodies. The novel's most grotesque scenes of sexual activity feature the theme of "stealing essence," where for the individual to fall prey is to experience depletion and death at the hands of the sexual predator. Like Tripitaka in the sixteenth-century novel *Xiyou ji* (Journey to the West, also called Monkey), who is a victim of male and female demons desiring his flesh as an aphrodisiac to gain immortality, Suchen and others become victims of humans searching for aphrodisiacs in the form of semen, aborted fetuses (ch. 14, 111), or human brains (ch. 113, 274). In what follows, the therapeutic virtues of Suchen's body make him the target of a harem master who attempts to appropriate Suchen's semen as a tonic for sexual strengthening.[37]

Suchen urinates in the snow one day, little knowing that he is about to be trapped. A man and his harem have urine buckets set by the side of the house, spy on passing men who urinate, and kidnap whoever has the largest penis:

> Suchen's *qi*-energy was rich and full and his *yang* circuits mighty and powerful. He was no ordinary man. So when he took a piss it needed a good bit of time. This session of pissing made a bucket of snow melt to the last crystal. The steam billowed up like smoke, like mist. And it was all seen from a window . . . by a beauty who watched to her heart's content. (ch. 65, 4b–5a)

In the ensuing scenes the author takes to the extreme his project of chaste exhibitionism—that is, writing about nudity or sex without having his hero intentionally indulge himself. After Suchen is seen from the window, he is invited inside and then drugged so that he is mentally aware but unable to control his limbs. The harem master's goal is to drink as much of Suchen's semen as possible. In one of the most notorious scenes in the novel, the women arouse Suchen to the point of ejaculation and then position his body so that his penis fits through a hole in the wall, on the other side of which awaits the master's mouth. The culmination of many such ordeals by involuntary arousal is a great orgy (*jiaogou hui*) in which the harem women strip and perform gymnastic tricks. Suchen knows that he will die if he emits too much semen; so before the orgy he steels himself by looking closely at the naked body of a woman of the harem who is his ally.

> He looked attentively at her tender and creamy white breasts, her fragrant navel and soft belly. He was trying to temper himself. Mme Sui was surprised to find him paying such attention to her body, since usually he wouldn't allow himself so much as a glance. So she deliberately kneeled in front of him, pretending she was setting her hair, and faced her vagina right before his eyes. He looked closely at this, and there he saw a mound of tender flesh, loose and white like snow; a fine seamlike opening, pink and gleaming like pearl. He thought to himself, "Though I have a wife and concubines, I've never once looked directly at its shape. If I hadn't collected myself during the night, I wouldn't have been able to endure the sight of it now." (ch. 67, 4b)

She thinks he wants to make love with her and offers herself, but he explains that he is conditioning himself in order to avoid harm later. In this case in which he is a victim, Suchen permits himself a closer than usual look at the naked woman; likewise, the author permits himself a tenderer than usual, though brief, description of the female genitals. He uses the tone of the high erotic while maintaining the perspective of the steeled observer. He then goes on to describe more of what he doesn't allow his hero to enjoy in what is one of the most virtuoso episodes of Chinese erotic literature.

When the day for the orgy arrives, the women enter his room, disrobe, and perform highly skilled somatic and genital acrobatics. They are capable of making parts of the abdomen bulge up and down, causing the navel to jump in and out (ch. 67, 7ab), inserting the big toe into the vagina (8b), or bringing the vagina into the mouth (9a). The final exhibition is by the ninth concubine, the most lustful of the women:

> The ninth concubine lay on the bed face up, spread her thighs and exposed her vagina. With an effort she pushed it out and surely as that made the "flower room"[38] protrude. She curled her body and brought her vagina up to her mouth. Sucking and mouthing it, she was all of an ugly sight. This she followed by extending the two petals of her "flower heart,"[39] which she fanned with air from her mouth to produce a swishing sound. They all bent their ears and listened carefully: there was the sound of spring silkworms eating leaves, then autumn insects fluttering their wings, now fragrant dew dripping onto flowers, a hidden spring flowing through rocks, frozen dew scattered over a window, a gentle breeze stroking bow strings, a baby sucking at its mother's breast. They were exquisite sounds, gurgling and rustling, that had everyone in the room looking with amazement, listening with surprise. They oohed and ahed, utterly stupefied, and bravoed to no end. (ch. 67, 9b)

Again, as in much of *Yesou puyan,* a cold eye, here paralyzed and invol-untary, regards hot things; disapproving judgment accompanies exotic de-scription. At the same time, what is ostensibly obscene and lascivious still carries notes of a sweet and dreamlike paradise. The vagina, which the hero has only just now found the presence of mind to regard, makes mu-sic evoking bucolic images and ending with the sound of a nursing baby. Such images conflate the Sirenlike quality of the dangerous woman with the notion of the nurturing home which Suchen otherwise idealizes. The tension is also something like that between woman as spectacle, divided into discrete and thus controllable mechanical parts (as also portrayed in the ars erotica), and woman as womblike paradise for the mothering of the man. While the many scenes of chaste exposure, including Suchen's observation of Mme Sui's vagina, may hint that the woman is the man's counterpart, no stranger than himself, the author's final construct is of the woman thus divided into lascivious spectacle versus paradise of retreat.

The above episode continues when the ninth concubine wins the prize for the best performance and gains the privilege of engaging in sexual combat with the hero, still prone and paralyzed except for his penis. After a long time during which they engage in intercourse and just as he is on the verge of ejaculation, he suddenly looks at her and realizes she is a fox demon. Somehow regaining strength, he flips over and wres-tles her down until she cries out, expels a putrid gas, as fox demons do, and dies. The episode concludes when Suchen escapes and brings about the execution of the harem master and the dispersal of his enormous household, which includes sixteen concubines and dozens of singing girls, maids, and servant boys (ch. 86, 77).

The events just recounted belong to *Yesou puyan's* inventory of deviant sexual practices, which consist of grotesque and demonic extremes that diverge from the center held by Suchen. The sexual acrobats are exam-ples of what might be called lyric grotesque, especially as dramatized in the scene of playing music with the vagina. Other episodes portray macabre types of deviation, from the monks who prey on fetuses or steal essence from kidnapped women to the tribe of snake-monsters in the southwest who rape and kill their human victims. The monsters repre-sent the most frenzied divergence from the civilized norm as they rip their human victims apart.[40]

In creating his inventory of deviants, the author could have drawn from his imagination and/or from written and oral sources, to which he could have added his own flourishes. The snake-monsters living on the periphery of China recall the similarly located subhumans in the pre-Han *Shanhai jing* (Classic of Mountains and Seas) and other repositories of myth and folklore; semihuman creatures kidnapping and/or copulating with humans are also within the range of fictive possibilities in China, as exemplified in the legends of the "White Ape," for instance.[41] Xia Jingqu would have heard or read about the practices of sexual alchemy and sexual vampirism, which existed in his day. Whether vaginal music was something he witnessed or heard about or was completely a product of his imagination is not yet clear. Nevertheless, the condemnation of deviant beings goes hand in hand with the vivid portrayal of, if not belief in, the effectiveness of such things as eating human brains and drinking other men's semen. In other words, Xia's fictional conclusion is that although evil practices such as these may be bad, they exist and work very well. How much he or others like him believed in what he portrayed may be difficult to ascertain, but we can at least ask how he might justify such portrayals as part of his panorama; this is a question that will be dealt with next.

The Rule of Expediency

In answer to how Xia Jingqu justifies his use of obscene and lurid imagery and how orthodox he is in light of his steadfast claim to propriety, I would say that he ignores conventional standards of literary decency in order to be more precise about the extension of orthodox correctness into the real world. Justifications for his portrayals can be found in editorial statements meant to forestall accusations of obscenity, such as the third of the "general premises" (*fanli*) at the beginning of the uncensored edition, which I paraphrase: *Yesou puyan* will cover a multitude of topics, namely, cosmic principle (*li*), the classics, history, filial piety, loyalty, military science, medicine, poetry, mathematics, emotions, moral learning (*daoxue*), sexual love (*chuntai*), and the comic and ribald (*xiexue*, la). In this list, sexual love appears as one legitimate topic among others. The fourth item of the general premises addresses the issue directly by stating that although the "obscene" (*huixie*) parts of the book seem improper, they are there for the purpose of didactic "admonition" (*quanjie*)—words that writers and publishers of obscene fiction in China often use to defend themselves.

The main defense, I think, can be found by consulting a well-known passage from *Mengzi:*

> Ch'un-yu K'un said, "Is it prescribed by the rites that, in giving and receiving, man and woman should not touch each other?" [*nannü shoushou buqin*]
>
> "It is," said Mencius.
>
> "When one's sister-in-law is drowning, does one stretch out a hand to help her?"
>
> "Not to help a sister-in-law who is drowning is to be a brute. It is prescribed by the rites that, in giving and receiving, man and woman should not touch each other, but in stretching out a helping hand to the drowning sister-in-law one uses one's discretion" [*quan*].[42]

Quan, "discretion," which may also be translated as "expediency," is a word already found to be of importance in the beauty-scholar romances. In *Yesou puyan* the term applies, for example, when Suchen rips the clothes off a woman in order to save her from a deadly illness. The word itself is used to excuse Suchen when he writes on the otherwise absolutely untouchable bare chests of the possessed women of the emperor's harem (ch. 108, 237). Although it is improper to touch a woman who is not your wife, if she is in danger, it is right to do whatever is necessary to save her. Xia Jingqu takes "discretion" or "expediency" to the limits of decency in order to portray a hero performing correctly in extreme situations; the extremes prove the integrity of the hero.

Yesou puyan alludes directly to this and other parts of the *Mengzi* when Suchen travels among the non-Chinese Miao people of the southwest. There he encounters customs which allow touching and kissing between a wife and a male visitor to the house, sex without the consent of the parents, and one's own choice of marriage partner (chs. 92–94). A "local wise man" (*tu shengren*) defends these practices and criticizes the Chinese for "taking so many precautions against sexual contact that the desires and longings men and women have for each other have no way to be let out" (ch. 94, 135). "According to the customs of China, man and woman cannot touch each other when exchanging objects [*nannü shoushou bu-qin*]. When the woman goes out she must cover her face. All this isolates *yin* from *yang,* completely blocks them up from each other," and eventually leads to "boring peek-holes and climbing over walls" (*zuan xue yu qiang*), this last a standard phrase for sexual transgression also found in

Mengzi.[43] Suchen expresses curt disagreement with this critique; another character says the wise man's words are nonsense (138), as does the commentary at the end of the chapter (ch. 92, 14a); otherwise, however, there is no debate.

The Mencian words cited by the wise man are the key to the novel's case for Confucian sexuality: how to conform to the centuries-old rule of sexual segregation. To ignore that rule is to be uncivilized, un-Chinese, and unfilial. For Xia Jingqu, one way of proving unswerving loyalty to the rule, as well as testing its precision, is to make every attempt to portray the most intimate contact between man and woman without admitting them as sexual partners and, in particular, without admitting the man, Suchen, son of the beloved mother, as willing or intentional participant. "Expediency," which is invoked when there is an accident or something beyond the subject's control, is the excuse that absolves Xia or Wen from accusations of unsegregated, unfilial behavior.

Another sign of the relevance of expediency and its relation to filiality is that none of the novel's explicit scenes of sexual intercourse is of the orthodox, procreative, and mother-approved relationship; all explicit scenes are of deviant sex. When Suchen finally consummates with each of three of his concubines, poems describe the occasions in highly adumbrative and elliptical fashion (ch. 58, 6a–7a). In other words, description of sex between Suchen and his consorts is not explicit because they are healthy and in no need of an expedient hand. To be sure, by portraying Suchen urinating or defeating the fox demon, Xia manages to skirt this rule and hint at what Suchen's sexual performance must be like. But in general only the unhealthy or the aberrant call for explicit treatment, which is necessary for the exposure and then cure of illness or correction of evil.

Expediency, Procreation, and Motherhood

The explicit sexual details that *Yesou puyan* begs expediency to observe are tools of the larger project of curing the social body as a whole; the core of that task is to rehabilitate the production of sons, that is, to stem the production of wastrels. Suchen's Confucian mission has him traversing the huge empire to attend to all that must be included for the repair of the giant household. He establishes a profusely procreative and intelligent community of women and descendants at home, and helps establish a healthy ruler at the capital who will maintain order in the nation and exert influence abroad. The key to the stability of the whole is the correct management of the home, which is where sex takes place; the household's main inhabitants are women, who, in Suchen's case, take his mother as model; she is the "symbolic center of the novel," as Stephen Roddy has suggested.[44]

In his study of the representation of literati in Qing fiction, Roddy observes how *Rulin waishi*, *Yesou puyan*, and other works of the eighteenth century focus attention upon the corruption that hinders worthy talent from participation in government. While *Rulin waishi* satirizes literati activity itself, *Yesou puyan*, as Roddy says, "remake[s] the literati into a more socially relevant vocation," with relevance "expediently" redefined, we might add (13). Roddy sees Wen Suchen as a "model of new possibilities for the failed or unenfranchised literatus unrecognized by his contemporaries" (258–59). Along with remaking the literati, *Yesou puyan* also focuses on other "previously marginalized social groups," as Roddy notes, especially women and male members of society outside the traditional ruling class. Suchen associates with righteous bandits and strongmen, warrior women, scholars, beggars, monks, nuns, urban commoners, seamen, farmers, Miao tribes-people, ape-humans, tiger-humans, and many others—including, last but not least, his wives, who themselves are of varied social levels. In short, the services of the Confucian superman bring him into vigorous and sometimes naked contact with a large range of people and meanwhile leave him no time to take what now seem to be irrelevant government exams.

In all this, however, expediency is mainly a generous detour to the narrower end of forming the healthy, procreative households that are to make up the new China. Suchen employs the services of a celibate warrior woman, for example, who tells him that her sword is her husband and that she swears never to marry (ch. 71, 515). Suchen does not permit such a notion as a sword standing for a husband and eventually arranges a marriage for her. In general, unlike other novels studied in this book, *Yesou puyan* refrains from fantasizing about extraordinary heroines. While Suchen is absent from home, his wife once disguises as him in order to stem suspicion that no man is around the house (ch. 42, 320). Otherwise, however, his wives never assume male disguise or leave home on personal missions, as do the chaste beauties of the romances.

Suchen's revered mother nevertheless fits into the category of the superior woman as found in Qing fiction. But as widow-mother, not wife of the hero, she is not in a relationship of symmetry or equivalence—and, in effect, competition—with him, as the chaste beauty would be. The beauty-scholar romance features self-determined love matches, monogamy, and superior young women. In contrast, *Yesou puyan* merely half permits self-determination by having the initially self-determined match finalized only with the mother's permission; the novel cancels monogamy and reduces the stature of superior young women, allowing them to be astute in a given specialty but having them stay at home and yield to a still more astute husband and mother-in-law. As a superior woman, in turn, Suchen's homebound mother is not up to the adventurous chaste beauty, although in terms of moral force she is the nearest to a shrew of any of *Yesou puyan*'s good women. She is furious and Suchen is abject when she finds out about his first concubine (ch. 9, 66). In contrast, since her health is poor and her period irregular, Suchen's main wife is happy to have the help of a concubine in bearing children and performing household duties. Although his mother finally relents and eventually permits him four more concubines, she continues to be a stern and revered presence throughout the book.

The cross-messages of such things as furious mother but gladdened wife, superior women but still more superior man, and half-permitted self-determination all reflect the cross-message I referred to above to define *Yesou puyan*: its label as a novel of "chaste polygamy," a contradictory combination according to the standards of chaste and erotic romances. *Yesou puyan* defuses this contradiction by allying a Confucian superman with his sage widow-mother in a rare union of miser and shrew, both of whom, however, assume attenuated, normative forms. In the erotic romance, the benevolent polygamist, who is a moderate and sanitized miser, gains the cooperation of his wives in fulfilling his wish for polygamy. In the chaste romance, the talented heroine, who is a benign shrew, gains the cooperation of her husband in meeting her demand for monogamy. In *Yesou puyan*, the widow-mother unites with the chaste polygamous son to deny monogamy, one of the woman's main goals, and unlimited sex for pleasure, one of the man's. The union is between the temperate miser and shrew, neither of whom would be so temperate, however, unless they were in the relationship of filial polygamist and his powerful, sage widow-mother.

The same cross-message of chaste polygamy has other versions: correctness inside the self and licentiousness outside in the world, or the combination of expediency within orthodoxy. The second part of this chapter will throw further light on *Yesou puyan's* cross-messages through comparison with *Honglou meng* and other Ming and Qing novels and stories. Both *Yesou puyan* and *Honglou meng* have prominent matriarchs and, in line with the scholar-beauty tradition, relatively contained and unintentional polygamists, but otherwise they greatly diverge in their representations of the centrality of men, marriage, and procreation.

Yesou Puyan in Light of *Honglou Meng* and Other Fiction of the Ming and Qing

Yesou puyan and *Honglou meng* draw each other into dialogue because of their comparably extended but divergent portrayals of masculinity. *Yesou puyan* affirms the supremacy of male potency; *Honglou meng* takes its critique of men to the point of rejecting male sexuality as polygynous men would have it. At the same time, although the two novels diverge in their portraits of men, they do share two conclusions about sex and women: one, that sexual pleasure is superfluous, not to mention potentially detrimental to health and moral well-being; and two, that the hero's ideal female partner is both a scholarly (or literary) and romantic companion.

The differing treatments of the family in these two novels, as well as the similar conclusions about lust and ideal male-female relations, can be illuminated in terms of the portrayal of sexual behavior in Ming and Qing fiction up to the eighteenth century. The sixteenth-century *Jin Ping Mei* is the starting point of this history since later works can be seen as reacting to and attempting to address the wrongs committed by *Jin Ping Mei's* polygamist-tyrant, Ximen Qing. For him, sexual pleasure is not superfluous, and women provide an endless opportunity for sexual play.

Jin Ping Mei is similar to *Yesou puyan* in that its explicit descriptions are mainly of what is portrayed as immoderate sexual behavior. Its theme is the insatiability of desire, a condition that its main male character is unable to escape. Ximen Qing uses aphrodisiacs and sex tools to maintain his strength with an ever-increasing number of women and frequency of bouts; in the end he dies of priapism. Two harem masters like Ximen Qing appear in *Yesou puyan,* the first and less harmful of whom eventually repents (chs. 26–32), the second of whom sexually vampirizes Suchen but finally meets his doom. In the second case, *Yesou puyan* seems to overturn *Jin Ping Mei* in the scene in which Suchen, like Ximen Qing, lies drugged and prone while the most lustful woman of the harem rides him to the point of ejaculation. Ximen Qing is a lecherous polygamist whose energy finally gives way; Suchen is a chaste polygamist who conquers the lascivious woman by means of innate *yang* strength. Where *Jin Ping Mei* only admits a negative sexual hero, *Yesou puyan* compensates and, like the erotic romances, proves a positive one can exist.

As I have said previously, erotic scenes in other works of Ming and Qing fiction fall into two broad categories. The first portrays sex between premarital or adulterous partners who are punished or separated in the end. Examples occur mainly in the late Ming, especially in the story anthologies *San Yan* (The Three Collections), *Er Pai* (The Two Collections), and *Huanxi yuanjia* (Enemies Enamoured). Ximen Qing–like characters and illicit lovers continue in the Qing but tend to appear as secondary characters in works such as the shrew novels, the erotic romances, *Honglou meng, Yesou puyan,* and *Lüye xianzong.* The second category of erotic scenes mainly occurs in the erotic scholar-beauty romances, which portray preconjugal and conjugal rather than adulterous relations. The focus is on sex enjoyed by a man and his eventual wife and concubines, many of whom find refuge in him from danger or loneliness and some of whom are his helpers. These works end with their polygamist heroes finding lasting contentment in the domesticity of drinking wine and composing poetry with their wives and concubines.

Yesou puyan and *Honglou meng* share elements of both these categories. In both novels, immoderate and illicit sex takes place among people who are peripheral to or less refined than the main characters. In both works, the woman is viewed as a lasting scholarly and romantic companion, like the lasting though also sexy companions in the erotic romances. But the novels differ when it comes to conjugal sexuality. *Yesou puyan* uses high erotic style to describe sex between Suchen and his wives, who have happy relationships. In *Honglou meng,* which is closer in this respect to *Jin Ping Mei,* examples of ideal conjugal sexuality are not to be found. Baoyu's world in the garden is for the most part clean of sex and adult sexual roles. *Yesou puyan* is about the vigor of the procreative system, in which polygamy is a central feature. *Honglou meng* is about the decay of that system, whose adult male members, except for Baoyu's father, are mainly interested in philandering and other socially unconstructive pursuits such as alchemy and gambling. *Yesou puyan* extols male energy through its hero Wen Suchen; *Honglou meng* portrays a hero who rejects most of the male sex, which he perceives as base and made of "mud," in contrast to the female, which is clean and made of "water." Suchen is a confirmed polygamist; Baoyu, although also a lover of more than one woman, could never vigorously commit himself to polygamy.

The two novels are as if in critical or revisionist opposition to each other. Wen Suchen is like a cured Baoyu, rarely beset with frustration or indecision, and never *chouchang*, a word used to express Baoyu's melancholy. Baoyu's awareness of the suffering of women is a form of male apology for the sorrowful lot of women; such an awareness would deprive Suchen of his life's ambition to be a polygamist. Baoyu is a sensitive and therefore immobilized version of Suchen; Baoyu takes the depraved state of men to heart and is unable to reassume command. The two are alike in that they surround themselves with women, who receive from them respect and good care; both treat women as *zhiji*, "intimate companions." But Baoyu's life in a garden otherwise inhabited only by women suggests an attempt to sever himself from the society of men and through women cleanse himself of base male reality. Suchen treats his home, which consists of a great garden inhabited by his mother, wives, concubines, and children, as a place to which he returns or retires after constructive excursions into the world. Baoyu has few male friends, and those he has tend to be compassionate and feminine like himself; Suchen has a number of close male friends, none of whom are effeminate or dandy. Baoyu has a homoerotic liaison with a young friend; Suchen would revile such an act.

In terms of mothers or mother figures, the novels diverge in that although the presiding elder in each family is a matriarch, the one in *Yesou puyan* is there to uphold and revive the patriarchal order, while the one in *Honglou meng* reigns in spite of that order and for lack of any man who could take on the presiding role as well as she. Suchen is abject before his mother; Baoyu is only abject before his father. Baoyu finds refuge in women, in particular his grandmother, the family matriarch, who indulges him, protects him from his angry father, and allows Baoyu to have a chamber-wife at age eleven. Moreover, as will be discussed in the next chapter, instead of being displaced into the position of chaste widow mother, the shrew in *Honglou meng* (e.g., Wang Xifeng) remains at the level of wife and thus retains her power as defined in the shrew story, including the power to eliminate female rivals.

Another contrast between the two novels lies in the nature of grotesque and explicit detail. Grotesque, naturalistic detail is rare in *Honglou meng* in general, but Jia Baoyu's having diarrhea, urinating, or ejaculating—all three of which Suchen does in florid detail—are described adumbratively if at all.[45] However, although *Yesou puyan* is more explicit in the sense I have shown, all that is *yin*—having to do with licentiousness or unorthodox forms of desire—is strictly external to Suchen. Baoyu is not so clear-cut: he loves to lick the rouge off young women's lips and to read forbidden books about love.

Aside from the kind of detail they use and the character of their heroes, *Yesou puyan* and *Honglou meng* differ most in their treatments of love. *Yesou puyan* is absent of the love found in the monogamous affairs of such works as the Yuan and Ming operas *Xixiang ji* and *Mudan ting,* and the Qing beauty-scholar romances. The Ming and Qing monogamous love story elevates sentiment (*qing*) and loyalty; the lovers secretly fall in love and then endure great travail before they publicly unite in the end. *Honglou meng* projects a mythical framework in which two spirits fall in love in heaven but can live out their love only by being reincarnated on earth, called the land of "red dust" (*hongchen*). In other words, they must be mortal in order to experience love; they cannot love in heaven because love cannot be that good. Words that apply to this monogamous love, but not to the more rational version of polygamous love in *Yesou puyan,* are *qianquan* and *chanmian,* to be "intertwined and inseparable" in a fashion that would be impossible between two people in a polygamous situation. In the end in *Honglou meng,* the "entanglements" cause signals to be crossed and the lovers to miss their chance; they cannot even unite on earth, and Baoyu can only marry the socially acceptable woman, not the one with whom he is "intertwined."

Yesou puyan insists upon rationalizing and desentimentalizing love, as the temperate polygamist knows to do. The goal is hygienic in the sense that one is to maintain the health of the ancestral *qi* in both the family and oneself. The rule for controlling desire is that a man should not cohabit with women unless he has parental blessing and intends to have offspring, especially sons. At the same time, of course, he can have as many sons as he wants: Wen Suchen has two dozen and lives to see a great-great-grandson. In real life, such procreative success was mainly the privilege of royalty, like the Kangxi emperor (reigned 1662–1722), under whom the author lived part of his life and who himself had thirty-six sons, twenty of whom lived to maturity.[46] Outside of reproduction, the woman is a subordinate *zhiji* to the man, a term usually reserved for friendship between men. *Yesou puyan*'s position, then, is that men and women should renounce genital pleasure and discipline orgasm; they should condemn lust but celibacy as well. In short, *Yesou puyan* presents another Confucian attempt at the middle way of moderation and equilibrium, this time with important qualifications about "expediency" broadened and made more explicit.

The Marriage of Confucian Orthodoxy and Erotic Literature

Viewed alongside other fiction of the Ming and Qing, *Yesou puyan* repeats numerous contents of the chaste and especially of the erotic romances in such things as creating situations of easy intimacy between the hero and women, making the polygamous hero seem unintentionally polygamous (and doing so by such tricks as having someone make him drunk to get him in bed with a woman), having the hero gain intimacy with women through rescuing or helping them or being helped by them, having the wife disguise as her husband, having her welcome the addition of a concubine, and so forth. *Yesou puyan*'s desentimentalization of love places it apart from the most famous Ming and Qing stories about love, but somewhat echoes the rationalization of love found in the chaste and erotic romances. Xia's refusal to portray explicit conjugal sex aligns him with writers of chaste and high-erotic romances, but his cold excursions into grotesque and explicit bodily and sexual detail otherwise place him in a category of his own. He thus diverges from the other authors of Ming and Qing erotic fiction, who write more hotly and straightforwardly of robust, lustful sex, whether illicit or conjugal.

Seen in the context of scholarly and philosophical trends, *Yesou puyan* advocates an enthusiastic return to China's reputed original Confucianism, shorn of Buddhist and Taoist influence, but also explores heretofore taboo territory by offering a highly detailed and precise cataloguing of orthodox and unorthodox forms of sexuality. *Yesou puyan* is a narrative embodiment of the exhaustive and precise scholarship of Qing evidential research of the same period.[47] However, instead of using precision to turn up evidence undermining accepted belief, Xia Jingqu uses minute detail to assert the extent of his controlling vision of the world. His cold observation of hot detail represents a marriage of the traditions of Confucian orthodoxy and those of erotic literature that is unprecedented in scope.

8

POLYGYNY, CROSSING OF GENDER, AND

THE SUPERIORITY OF WOMEN IN

HONGLOU MENG

Honglou meng and the Chaste and Erotic Romances

Cherished, read, and reread for over two centuries now, *Honglou meng* (Dream of the Red Chamber, also called Story of the Stone or Dream of Red Mansions) assumes the role of the giant among all novels in China. Only a handful of other works are said to be of comparable excellence. In this chapter, however, I place it alongside humbler novels and submit it to survey according to the concepts of shrew, miser, and the beauty-scholar principle of symmetry, all of which continue to revolve around the issue of polygamy. Like *Yesou puyan*, *Honglou meng* resists labels that were easily applied to "chaste monogamous" versus "erotic polygamous" romances. Nevertheless, what was clear-cut before can be experimentally applied to *Honglou meng* in order to determine what it ambiguously implies, resists, or as if it were a living being, would never think of. As I view it, *Honglou meng* is a story of semierotic polygamy overlaid with a dream of semi-chaste monogamy. Semierotic polygamy means such things as Baoyu's premarital sex with the maid Xiren (Aroma) and his free intimacy, often including physical contact, with Qingwen (Skybright), Daiyu, Baochai, and other women of the garden.[1] The dream of semichaste monogamy refers to Baoyu's and Daiyu's mythically predestined but unsuccessful love affair, and to their avoidance of sexual contact but nevertheless repeated indulgence in postinnocent, premarital association of the sort that societal rules forbid or strictly limit—it is only the fact that they are cousins that allows them to meet each other to begin with.

The symmetry of the chaste romances also figures in *Honglou meng* and performs the same functions of marking destiny and balance between lovers, of blurring or crossing gender distinctions, and of tending to monogamize the man. However, *Honglou meng* allows more of the man crossing into woman but a less spectacular form of the woman crossing into man. For example, no woman dresses as a man to go out of the house and achieve supreme public success. In addition, along with allowing a greater crossing of male to female, *Honglou meng* goes further with the polarity of female purity and male baseness than any novel in the Qing. The character type of the effeminate scholar-poet and venerator of women also manifests itself more self-consciously than any such types discussed so far.

The "semierotic" or "semichaste" ambiguity of *Honglou meng* is summed up in one of the main ideas of the book, itself a vaguely defined term: *yiyin*, "lust of the mind" (or "lust of intention," as Lu Tonglin translates, 1991), which is applied to Baoyu to indicate the special kind of refined wastrel that he is. But wastrel is too harsh a word for him, as spoiled and coddled as he nevertheless is. Not upright enough to qualify as a talented and chaste scholar, neither is he degenerate like the wastrel and libertine who consorts with only the most unrefined and / or manipulative of women (as stereotyped in *Lin Lan Xiang*, for example, discussed in the next chapter). In terms of the contrast between chaste and erotic romances, if Baoyu were unambiguously unlustful according to the standards of the chaste romance, then he would be able unhesitatingly to choose Daiyu as his one love. However, although he loves Daiyu the most, he loves many other women as well and besides is too weak to escape the control of family politics. On the other hand, if he and the women were healthily lustful according to erotic scholar-beauty standards, he would be able to marry not only Daiyu but also Baochai (who as a woman of the same class as Daiyu would normally not be available as equal co-wife or concubine), Xiren, Qingwen, and numbers of others, as he in fact does in wishful eighteenth- and nineteenth-century sequels to *Honglou meng*.[2] However, *Honglou meng* goes in both directions and neither at the same time, ending with the impossibility of both happy monogamy and happy polygamy.

According to the concepts of miser and shrew, *Honglou meng* contrasts with *Yesou puyan* is being a "shrew's" novel in which, as might be expected, women are superior while men are weak and venal. The best men tend to feminization and, in Baoyu's case, relative desexualization.

The shrew's debate of monogamy versus polygamy continues in *Honglou meng,* and polygynists are as irrepressible as usual in their desire for new sexual partners. Although monogamous love generally fails, it is dreamt of as a beautiful and heroic ideal, just as enacted in the classic beauty-scholar romances. In general, even the finest men in *Honglou meng,* such as Liu Xianglian or Baoyu, fail to live up to the more loyal and heroically self-sacrificing women such as You Sanjie, Daiyu, or Siqi (Chess), all of whom die for the sake of their one love.

Not a novel with a comic ending like *Yesou puyan* or the romances, *Honglou meng* ends with the death of many of its women and with monk-hood for its main hero. It features not the "benevolent" but the full-blown shrew, Wang Xifeng, who, for instance, allows her husband only a concubine whom she can control and plots the destruction of other women he tries to keep. The talented women in *Honglou meng* recall the chaste beauties of the romances but are weaker in that they weep, fall ill, and succumb in the face of overwhelming obstacles. Female talent and purity, instead of benefiting or liberating women, in fact make them more isolated from and dependent upon the politics of the male world. Comic endings tend to be fleeting and partial, as in the short-lived happy marriage of Shi Xiangyun, an unfortunate in early life but one of the few women to find a fitting mate who then dies, or in the monogamous dedication of Feng Yuan, a lover of men who suddenly falls in love with the young Yinglian (Caltrop), forswears men, and commits himself to her alone but who is then murdered by the wastrel Xue Pan.

In chaste romances, the woman travels the route of talent, that is, classical education and exam success, in order to gain recognition as one who deserves monogamous marriage to a man of her choice. In *Honglou meng,* the women are talented but unable to express themselves outside of the small arena of the garden; only one man recognizes them, Baoyu, and he is powerless to help them. *Honglou meng* parts sharply with the romances by denying the merit of education for the sake of examination success. In expressing the superiority of women, *Honglou meng* focuses on essential female purity and male baseness rather than on women actively imitating men in order to prove their worth. The implication is that women are innately superior and in no need of the male ladder of success to prove it. *Honglou meng* is still like the romances, however, in staging a male "veneration of the feminine" which, as Louise Edwards has said, is still "a masculine privilege in which the feminine becomes the venerated 'other' for the masculine self."[3] In short, women are elevated, while men, although "base," derive a kind of masochistic atonement via their sorrow for the female lot.

An alternate but parallel reading of the theme of female superiority in *Honglou meng* would say that the feminization of men and the veneration of women are signs not so much of sorrow or sympathy for the female lot but of the frustration of the alienated male self who wishes to escape or criticize the corrupt world of other contending males. As I have indicated in my discussion of beauty-scholar romances, the theme of female talent can in part be read as a case of male appropriation of the feminine for the sake of foregrounding the man's, not the woman's, unrecognized talent. Such a male use of the female voice is a tradition going back to the pre-Han poem, the *Li sao* (Encountering Sorrow), in which the spurned statesman Qu Yuan pretends to be a spurned female lover. In echo of this tradition, some nineteenth- and early twentieth-century readings of *Honglou meng* have claimed that women in the novel stand for the pure Han patriot, while men represent the filthy, uncivilized Manchu. In a similar vein, Kang-i Sun Chang and Ellen Widmer note the correlation in the seventeenth century between the privileging of the talented woman artist or writer and the expression of Ming loyalism on the part of disenfranchised Han literati.[4] Martin Huang discusses gender fluidity and the feminization of men in *Honglou meng* in the context of an identity crisis as experienced by the politically "marginalized" male literatus.[5] My discussion will concentrate on the crossing of masculine and feminine in the context not of historical or literary trope but of gender ideology (i.e., the shaping or construction of normative gender roles) and, in particular, of the prescriptions and desires of polygyny. In regard to the above interpretations, I would not go so far as to say that the portrayals of women in *Honglou meng* are mere projections of male anxiety or self-privileging veneration. My premise throughout is that these portrayals are not purely male-centered and masculine-active but are heavily imprinted with and indebted to feminine activity, however imbalanced the political and gender hierarchies between men and women may be.

The Study of *Honglou meng* in China

Like many of the novels studied in this book, *Honglou meng* has traveled a circuitous route on its way into the hands of modern readers. Cao Xueqin is said to have started writing his work sometime in the 1740s and to have finished about the first eighty chapters by the mid-1750s.[6] When he died sometime between 1762 and 1764, he left his work incomplete; it is no longer clear, if it ever was, how many more chapters he planned or had finished. The novel then circulated in manuscript form for almost forty years until it was apparently revised and supplemented, supposedly by Gao E, to make a 120-chapter version in 1791.[7] This is the edition most people knew until the early twentieth century, when scholars like Hu Shih and Yu Pingbo began to examine the discrepancies between the "original" and the "revised" first eighty chapters and the inconsistencies between the first eighty and the supplemented forty.[8] Still, it was not until 1958 and then 1982 that scholarly 120-chapter editions were produced for mass publication with the first eighty chapters in their prerevised form.[9]

The author, Cao Xueqin, perhaps born around 1715–16 (some say 1724), was the grandson of a Chinese bannerman and high official, Cao Yin, whose mother was the court-appointed rearer of the Kangxi emperor (reigned 1662–1722) and who himself was an imperial tutor. The family had long been associated with the Manchus, having early on served in the Chinese corps of the Manchu army that conquered Ming China in 1644.[10] The family had attained high imperial favor by the time of Cao's grandfather's generation but, with the advance of the succeeding Yongzheng emperor (reigned 1723–35), suffered a sharp decline after 1727, when Cao Xueqin was perhaps ten years old.

The supposed author of the 120-chapter version, Gao E (ca. 1738–1805), was Chinese from Manchuria. He is said to have executed his revision and supplementation between about 1788 and 1791,[11] when he and Cheng Weiyuan (b. ca. 1747) produced a first printed edition of the novel, which was the most common until 1927. In 1792 Gao published a revised edition, which for various reasons became the most commonly circulated version from 1927 until 1982.[12] For many years, scholars have debated the degree of Gao E's authorship of the last forty chapters, some even stating that he for the most part only edited what Cao actually left behind.

The difference between the two Gao E versions is too slight to concern us here, but the difference between the reputed Cao Xueqin and Gao E versions deserves some attention. In general, Gao E tends to temper Cao Xueqin's satire and to improve somewhat the image of certain characters. For example, Cao's Baoyu burns books on "eight-legged" exam essays (that is, model essays in a prescribed eight-part format; ch. 36); Gao cuts this and other such passages possibly because they carry antistate or anti-neo-Confucian connotations.[13] Gao makes Baoyu's father somewhat stricter with Baoyu and deletes a mention of the father's youthful abandon; Gao also makes Wang Xifeng less wicked in her conniving.[14]

Many changes are for the sake of internal consistency of character, vocabulary, and objects of material culture. For example, Gao cuts out the use of the sedan chair and of charcoal braziers for indoor heating, two items common in the south, from which Cao Xueqin originally came, but rare or nonexistent in the north, in which the novel takes place.[15] In one case, however, Gao commits an anachronism when he suddenly has Baochai handing Wang Xifeng a tobacco pipe (ch. 101). Not only does no one smoke in the first eighty chapters, but smoking was probably not yet in vogue in Cao's time, fifty or so years before Gao, though among women it was supposedly common in Manchuria, Gao E's but not Cao Xueqin's home.[16]

Many of the above facts or suppositions have been painstakingly re-searched by scholars over many years; much of what I discuss here has been touched upon by scholars and commentators again and again. The study of *Honglou meng* in China, commonly called "Red Studies" or "Redology" (*Hongxue*) since the late Qing,[17] is a story of its own with a large field of interpretations. Several books have appeared in post-Mao China recounting highlights of this story up to the 1970s and early 1980s, providing useful information to scholars extending previous lines of in-quiry or delving into new ones.[18] I will survey the highlights that are most relevant to the consideration of male-female relations and the issues of gender ideology.

Nineteenth- and early to mid-twentieth-century commentators have often applied allegorical interpretations to *Honglou meng*, saying, for in-stance, that the novel is a roman-à-clef based on historical and political figures (an approach that tended to fall into disrepute after the 1930s). Others have said that the novel is entirely and precisely about Cao Xue-qin's own life. In 1917 Cai Yuanpei allegorized the contraposition of "dirty" men and "clean" women as an opposition between Manchu and Han. He read the novel as a vehicle of anti-Manchu, pro-Han patriotism, equating Baoyu with an imperial prince and the twelve beauties (*shi'er chai*) with famous Han literati of the time. He related Baoyu's love of lip rouge to the Manchu softness for Han culture.[19] Others have echoed Cai Yuanpei by asserting, for instance, that the women in *Honglou meng* are weak and cultured like the Han, while the men are strong and wild like the Manchus,[20] or that the "love of rouge" symbolizes "love of the Zhu royal house of the Ming," since the word Zhu also means "red."[21] Baoyu's relations with the women of *Honglou meng* have been equated with the Qing minister Heshen's (1750–99) relations with his concubines, one of whose sons was named Yubao,[22] or the Shunzhi emperor's (reigned 1644–61) relations with the famous Han courtesan Dong Xiaowan.[23] Baoyu has also been compared to the official examiner and the women to his student examinees, with Baochai said to be like an impostor who ends by testing number one and Daiyu like someone who tries to steal first place and gets expelled.[24]

Numerous scholars have touched on the phenomenon of the crossing of gender characteristics. Li Chendong commented in 1942 that the "feminization" (*nüxinghua*) of Baoyu and other male characters was an expression of cultured refinement deliberately fostered in traditional upper-class households.[25] In 1953 Zhou Ruchang, one of the most prolific modern students of *Honglou meng*, asserted that the commentator Zhiyan zhai (Red Inkstone Studio, pen name of the otherwise unknown individual) was a woman, namely, Shi Xiangyun in the novel and Cao Xueqin's real spouse.[26] In 1990 Liu Mengxi used the pronoun "she" to refer to *Honglou meng*.[27] One unsolved mystery that has occasionally received attention from the 1920s on is *Honglou meng*'s lack of explicit reference to bound feet. Scholars have gathered proof for both the presence and absence of bound feet, centering their arguments around passages, for example, in which women are nimbler than might be thought possible for having such tiny and crippled feet.[28] The custom was so deeply entrenched that it is difficult to imagine *Honglou meng*'s women as exceptions. The lack of clarity tends to indicate an avoidance of or aversion to one of the most intense forms of physical pain that women suffered, or else amounts to a case of nonindulgence in a traditional form of male lust, the love of bound feet, as exemplified in many erotic novels of the same mid-Qing period. Finally, *Honglou meng* has often been said by both supporters and detractors to be an "erotic" or "pornographic book," *yinshu*, or to be "conducive to lasciviousness," *daoyin*. Kan Duo, a 1920s *Honglou meng* enthusiast, viewed *Honglou meng* as a "transformation of" *Jin Ping Mei* and drew parallels between Baoyu and Ximen Qing, Daiyu and Pan Jinlian, Baochai and Li Pinger, and Baoyu's "interluminescent jade" and Ximen Qing's "jade stalk."[29]

Throughout the years of debate and interpretation, the intensity of interest in *Honglou meng* has led to monumental efforts of research, acrimonious disagreement, and even falsification of evidence, including reputed portraits of Cao Xueqin and excerpts of his poetry. *Honglou meng* has also been a focus of contention over whether or not China can produce great fiction, with many claiming the book's supreme value—for example, Hu Shih, Li Chendong, Zhou Ruchang, Liu Ts'un-yan, or Tang Degang[30]—and others variously deprecating but still admiring it—for example, Yu Pingbo, Liu Dajie, or Lu Xun.[31] After the 1970s, studies in China and elsewhere have continued to refine earlier interpretive and investigative work, while some have moved into new directions of literary and cultural criticism.[32] Such singling out of a work is all the more reason for putting it in the broader context of the less commonly observed fiction of the period, which participates in the same play with symmetry and crossing of gender, the same elevation of women, and the same debate about polygamy.

The following brief account of the novel's plot provides the final background for the discussion of these common themes of *Honglou meng* and other Qing fiction: According to the mythical revelation of the first chapter, Baoyu, whose name means "precious jade," is destined from previous existence in heaven to live out a love bond on earth with a woman, Daiyu (meaning "dark-lustrous jade"). However, his devotion to her in heaven outdoes that on earth, where he is frequently distracted by other women, especially the third main character, Baochai (meaning "precious clasp"), who is healthier and more socially adept than Daiyu. Baoyu loves Daiyu more, but his elders choose Baochai for him, and in Gao E's "sequel" (as the last forty chapters are often called) trick him into thinking he is marrying Daiyu but marry him to Baochai. Much of the novel preceding the marriage takes place in the Grand Prospect Garden, which the family had built for the special home visit of their elder daughter, an imperial concubine. There, Baoyu, Daiyu, Baochai, his younger sister, girl cousins, and everyone's maids live from the time of their carefree early adolescence until the women either marry off or die. The last dwellers move out of the garden when it is discovered to be haunted; not long after, the Jia family is accused of wrongdoing, and government authorities raid their home. In the end, Baoyu tests high in the state exams but then runs away to become a monk, leaving Baochai with an unborn son.

Symmetry and the Superiority of Women

Although the sequel ends with the birth of a son, a formulaic conclusion in Qing novels, the absence of sons, good sons, or of good men in general is one of the earliest themes in *Honglou meng*. Chapter 1 begins with Zhen Shiyin, who has an only daughter, Yinglian; chapter 2 introduces Lin Ruhai, who also has an only-child daughter, Daiyu, even after taking several concubines (like the father in *Yu Jiao Li*). Like the many fathers with only-born daughters in the beauty-scholar romances, Lin "loves her as if she were a jewel" (ch. 2, 24) and has her learn to read and write as if she were a son. Next, Leng Zixing narrates the history of the Jia family and how its men grow worse with each generation, the latest of which ends with the spoiled Baoyu who, when he takes the one-year-old's ritual test of ambition, shows a penchant for cosmetics and jewelry instead of properly masculine objects. He is the only hope left, however, since his elder brother is dead and his half-brother Huan, son of a concubine, is lowly in looks and talent. The grown men in the Jia household include wastrels like Xue Pan, lovers of amusement like Jia She and Jia Zhen, or abdicating figures like the Taoist practitioner Jia Jing. The people who run the great household and, when possible, control the bad or ineffective men, are women like Wang Xifeng, brought up "like a boy" (ch. 3, 42) and "more than a match for most men,"[33] or Grandmother Jia, the matriarch of the family.

Cao Xueqin channels the actual articulation of the inferiority of men and superiority of women through Baoyu, who already at seven or eight years old defines men as essentially base, like "mud," and women as pure, like clear "water." Women make him feel "clean and refreshed," *qingshuang;* men are "dirty and smelly to the utmost degree," *zhuochou biren* (ch. 2, 28–29). Since he later adds that women also become dirty after they marry (ch. 59, 833), his distinction is primarily between young, unmarried virgins and all other women plus all or most men.

One of the main statements by which Baoyu sums up his theory of the sexes contains an allusion originating in the Southern Song (1127–1279) and already well known by the time of the late Ming and Qing: "The energy [*qi*] of luminescent virtue that runs through the cosmos only takes hold and grows in women" (tiandijian lingshu zhi qi zhi zhongyu nüzi), that is, no longer in men (ch. 111, 1528). Baoyu also adds that "Men are nothing but the muddy left-over dregs" (ch. 20, 283).[34] As Liao Zhongan and Aiyama Kiwamu have shown independently, the idea of virtuous or luminescent *qi* "taking hold in" (*zhongyu*) women and no longer in men supposedly originates with the Southern Song literatus Xie Ximeng (fl. 1184). The story has it that Xie preferred the company of a prostitute named Lu to that of his teacher and philosopher, the famous Lu Jiuyuan and main philosophical opponent of Zhu Xi, the founder of so-called neo-Confucianism.[35] Xie mocked his teacher by saying that ever since the death in the Western Jin (265–316) of four valorous and brilliant men likewise named Lu, "the brilliant and luminous *qi* no longer took hold in men, but only in women" (yingling zhi qi buzhongyu shi zhi nanzi, er zhongyu furen), that is, in people like Miss Lu.[36] As Liao and Aiyama go on to demonstrate, a number of beauty-scholar romances and the prefaces to three late Ming, early Qing collections of women's poetry all quote Xie's statement or some variation of it, with the words *ling* and *zhongyu* recurring most frequently. Qing commentators to *Rulin waishi* also quote Xie's words in reference to a "female talent" (*cainü*) in the novel who is more skilled in eight-legged essays than her negligent husband, who prefers poetry and refuses to study for the state exams.[37] Liao and Aiyama believe that the original statement attributed to Xie Ximeng was not widely seized upon until the late Ming, when the theme of the talented and superior woman began to draw extra attention. Cao Xueqin extends this theme by using a broader system of characters than in the romances and at the same time deepening the problem of women's fate by refusing them the happy ending of the beauty and the scholar.

The superiority of women in *Honglou meng* reproduces the same play of symmetry found in the romances in which, for example, the man's father is dead, as is the woman's mother; or one wife is named Like a Son, the other As If a Son; or scholar and beauty look alike. In *Honglou meng,* which is ten or more times longer than the romances, the symmetry suggests a similar rebalancing of the male-female relationship in favor of the woman, but Cao Xueqin gives more attention to the less symmetrical, less equal actualities of daily relations between women and men. Likewise, Baoyu's tendency to be undriven by sex, even though he is among so many handsome women and men, coincides with the aforementioned association between symmetry and desexualization. Nevertheless, unlike the monogamous scholars, Baoyu does not quite succeed in removing himself from the polygamous role that society assigns him.

The manifestations of symmetry can be divided into three aspects: (1) the relationships between one or more male-female pairs, the symmetries of which represent destiny, balance, and ideal match; (2) the correspondences between the paired women of two-wife polygyny; and (3) the crossing of masculine and feminine characteristics, which creates the illusion of parity or interchangeability of male and female roles. Other manifestations of symmetry exist in Qing fiction: exchange of matched poetry, both the form and content of which embody mutual awareness and response; parallel action or experience, which have the man and woman living complementary lives (as in *Feihua yong*, for example, where the man and woman are each adopted into the other's family); and disguise and impersonation, which serve to split a character into two and allow her or him to form otherwise impossible relationships. Of these, poetry writing takes up a major part of *Honglou meng;* parallel action plays a minimal role; and impersonation occurs only for the purpose of amusement. In the cases of parallel action and impersonation, it is probably that *Honglou meng* puts itself above such comedy-of-error ploys of the so-called vulgar romances. Whatever manifestation symmetry takes, however, it should be clear that I apply the word to *Honglou meng* assuming the background of the beauty-scholar romances, in which symmetry is more obvious and formulaic. In *Honglou meng,* symmetry will often be apparent because of its absence or vestiges in situations where it would be more pronounced in the romances, especially, for example, in the cases of two-wife polygyny and male impersonation.

In the first of the three aspects of symmetry—the relationship between a man and a woman or between two or more pairs of man and woman— Baoyu and Daiyu share an "yu" in their names; Baoyu and Baochai share a "bao." The two couples are also each defined by a matching pair of substances. Baoyu and Daiyu are a match of "wood and stone," Baoyu and Baochai of "gold and jade." In terms of kinship, Baoyu and Daiyu are paternal cousins, while Baoyu and Baochai are maternal cousins. More precisely, Daiyu is the daughter of Baoyu's *father's younger* sister, while Baochai is the daughter of Baoyu's *mother's elder* sister (whether the author consciously created such a neatness of symmetry is unclear). As · usual in Chinese fiction, one or more subordinate pairs of characters mirror the main pair or pairs. The best examples are the maid Siqi and her lover Pan You'an, who are also paternal cousins who fail to unite in the end, although they go further in confirming their mutual devotion than Baoyu and Daiyu.[38]

In the symmetry of the paired women of the two-wife polygynist—the second of the three aspects—since Baoyu's marriage to two beauties fails, the prevailing note is of negative contrast, not neat likeness or complementarity. Baochai is healthily plump, Daiyu consumptively thin; Baochai is cool and self-controlled, Daiyu tearful and oversensitive; Baochai is orthodox, Daiyu antiorthodox. Baochai is proper and emotionally distant from Baoyu; Daiyu is intimate. In this latter contrast, other women resonate with Baochai and Daiyu: the maids Xiren and Sheyue (Musk) with Baochai, the maids Qingwen and, in some respects, Wu'er (Fivey) and Siqi with Daiyu.[39]

In Baoyu's own view of his two possible mates, Baochai's "heavenly beauty" contrasts with Daiyu's "divine intelligence" (*xianzi* and *lingqiao*).[40] In chapter 5, he actually dreams of a woman who is half Baochai and half Daiyu, the one time in *Honglou meng* where the bigamous ideal comes near to fruition. Other manifestations of bigamy or two-wife polygyny occur in more dispersed form in Baoyu's divided loyalty to the two women. A final shadow of bigamy appears when Daiyu and Baochai separately but simultaneously think they are promised in marriage to Baoyu (ch. 95), thus figuring a hypothetical bigamy or, in effect, double monogamy, one true and one false.

The third aspect of symmetry involves the crossing of gender characteristics, which in *Honglou meng* occurs among numerous characters, not only or primarily the central ones. The cross between Daiyu and Baoyu comes out most clearly when the country woman Liu Laolao mistakes Daiyu's room for a boy's and Baoyu's for a girl's (ch. 40, 547; ch. 41, 574). However, Baoyu's crossing as a woman appears numerous times, whereas Daiyu's crossing as a man is otherwise absent; instead, other women cross as men, such as Wang Xifeng and Shi Xiangyun. As for Baochai, she exhibits a vaguer form of gender crossing in that as a cherished daughter she is educated as a boy would be and is considered "ten times better than" her wastrel brother, Xue Pan (ch. 4, 64).

Honglou meng goes further than other works I have covered in portraying or suggesting the femininity of the man. In addition to Liu Laolao, for example, a visiting doctor thinks Baoyu's room is a girl's (ch. 51, 718). The poor-sighted Grandmother Jia once mistakes Baoyu for a girl (ch. 50, 700) and another time remarks upon how much he likes to be around "girls" (*yatou*), though for "frolic" not sex: "I figure that he must be a girl at heart, but was mistakenly reincarnated as a boy" (ch. 78, 1116).[41] In yet another instance, his servant Mingyan (Tealeaf) prays that Baoyu will have the fortune to be reborn as a woman, no more as a "filthy" man (ch. 43, 600).[42]

Other men in the novel possess feminine characteristics—for example, Zhen Baoyu, who is Jia Baoyu's southern cousin and double in looks and behavior. The mirror pair of Zhen ("true") and Jia ("false") is the nearest *Honglou meng* comes to character-splitting, although the double is neither a disguise nor part of a comedy-of-errors style impersonation. Zhen Baoyu later becomes more career-minded than Jia Baoyu, however, thus contradicting their initially shared refusal to climb the male ladder of success. Baoyu's young friend Qin Zhong is also "girlish in air" (*you nü'er zhi tai*, ch. 7, 115); as a couple he and Baoyu mirror two other pretty boys at their school (ch. 9 and ch. 15, 207). Another feminine man is Jiang Yuhan, an actor of female roles who impresses Baoyu with his "charm and tenderness"—in Chinese, *wumei*, which usually describes beautiful women or flowers,[43] and *wenrou*, commonly descriptive of the warmth and softness of women (e.g., ch. 28, 398).

The topic of men crossing into women occupies the Zhiyan zhai commentator as well, who notes how the author once compared him with Baochai and Daiyu.[44] Later he compares Baoyu with a delicate and bashful girl and Baoyu's servant Mingyan with a clever maid.[45] The author's reported comparison of Zhiyan zhai with Baochai and Daiyu eventually led the scholar Zhou Ruchang to identify Zhiyan zhai as a woman—that is, as Shi Xiangyun in the novel and Cao Xueqin's wife in reality.[46] Other scholars have disagreed, since on numerous occasions the Zhiyan zhai commentary speaks with what sounds like a male voice.[47]

The ideal of feminine beauty in men is not new with the appearance of *Honglou meng* or the Qing novel. Men described in terms of feminine beauty appear in historical and literary sources in the Wei and Jin periods and throughout the Six Dynasties (220–588). The practices of men applying women's face powder and rouge and perfuming their clothing are well attested in those times.[48] Terms like "jade one" (*yuren*) were used to refer to such men, who are among the most likely predecessors of the stereotyped image of the "refined and delicate student" (*wenruo shusheng*), an image which was firmly set by Ming and Qing times, especially as figured in the role of the "young male" (*xiaosheng*) in traditional opera. It is also important to note that the image of the beautiful or feminine man applies in both homosexual and heterosexual contexts.[49]

The crossing of women into men is mainly concentrated in two of

Baoyu's cousins, Shi Xiangyun and Wang Xifeng, the former of whom is one of several possible matches for marriage with him; she is a rival for his love in Daiyu's eyes. Shi's masculine bearing comes across when she puts on an outfit which Daiyu jokingly compares to that of a "saucy Tartar boy." Others laugh at how she likes to dress as a boy and looks handsomer then than as a girl (ch. 49, 679–80). The actress Fangguan (Parfumee) is another playful cross-dresser; she and Baoyu are said to look like brothers (ch. 63, 889). She dresses up as a "barbarian" boy, which delights Shi Xiangyun, Tanchun, and Li Wan, who dress two other girls in boy's clothing to accompany her.[50]

Wang Xifeng is the most shrewish example of the gender-crossed woman in *Honglou meng*. In her youth, she is said to have been brought up like a boy, which in her case means in behavior, not education. In other words, she is not a "talented woman" whose being treated as a boy means being taught to read the classics and write in high literary language. The gender-crossed nature of her name emerges when a storyteller refers to a man of former times with the same name as hers (ch. 54, 758). Wang Xifeng plays the role of tough, able-tongued, sometimes foul-mouthed manager of the Jia household.[51] She can be as mercenary and usurious as the miser but at the same time is capable of the classic shrewish plotting of a rival woman's destruction. She allows her husband concubines in order to appear the virtuous wife, but hardly lets Jia Lian get near Pinger (Patience) and humiliates You Erjie into committing suicide.

These examples illustrate some of the ways symmetry works in *Honglou meng*. In its most abstract form, symmetry suggests perfect balance and fluidity of exchange, but in concrete form centers around the masculine pole, as I have shown previously. However, *Honglou meng* makes the operations of symmetry appear slipperier than in the beauty-scholar romances. The beauty switches to a masculine role then back to her feminine role with what, in contrast to the process in *Honglou meng*, is mechanical precision. Baoyu, Shi Xiangyun, Fangguan, and others float between masculine and feminine, as if to signify that gender roles float to begin with and are not strictly prescribed or embodied. At the same time, however, *Honglou meng* provides no neat solution to the problems of arranged marriage and of polygyny versus monogamy. In Cao's portrayals, men are too polygynous and lustful to be capable of loyalty to one woman. "Lust of the mind" keeps Baoyu as distracted as he would be if he were carnally lustful. Against such odds, then, the shrewish Wang

Xifeng fights back; the oversensitive Daiyu weeps; others commit suicide or become nuns; the supposedly best tempered, like Baochai, live the rest of their lives alone or, if possible, with their male offspring, whom they may perhaps turn into "better" men.

The Prepolygamist's Mingling with Women

In the erotic romance, imperfection or lack of symmetry coincides with the presence of polygamy. The same coincidence occurs in *Honglou meng* but is less obvious since the novel is only mildly erotic and Baoyu is still in a state of prepolygamy. The assumption that he will be polygamous— whether he would follow through or not with this assumption is moot— is clear from the fact that his father has two concubines and that Baoyu already has Xiren as chambermaid and sexual partner. Moreover, Grandmother Jia actually anticipates that he will be polygamous like other men of his class when she says, "I know quite well that Baoyu will be one who won't take to the admonishments of his wife and concubines" (ch. 78, 1116).

In his prepolygamous adolescence, however, Baoyu wishes that he and the women of the garden would never marry and would instead remain in a state of innocent intimacy. As I have mentioned previously, he is possessed of a certain kind of lust, so-called lust of the mind, *yiyin*, by which he is supposedly able to enjoy the company of girls without brazenly desiring them, as Grandmother Jia observes. He is "the number one lustful man in the history of the world," says the Fairy Disillusionment in his dream; that is, he has the highest quality of lust, not the kind that centers on the "flesh" alone (*pilu*, ch. 5, 90). As the fairy tells him, he is not the type of man "whose driving desire is to have all the beautiful women in the world available for his casual moments of pleasure" (ch. 5, 90). With this distinction made, the fairy introduces him to sex by giving him a beautiful session of love with a woman who combines the looks of Baochai and Daiyu. Then the fairy lets the two lovers out into a terrifying wilderness—in short, she teaches him the impossibility of all-in-one love.[52]

Back in the waking world, Baoyu conforms to the fairy's characterization of his type of lust by mainly indulging in the bliss of daily life, not sex, among the women of the garden. To be sure, his maid Xiren is available to him, as sanctioned by his mother and grandmother. But after his first sex with Xiren, instead of fixing on her for awhile before moving on to the next woman, as the hero in the erotic romance would do, Baoyu in general practices the lust of intimacy without sex.[53] Instead of desiring women for sexual satisfaction, he merely wants them for play, with the additional requirement for the maids that they get him tea, prepare his bath, do his sewing, and so forth, since after all he is the young master. During much of this mingling, and in spite of being the young master and prepolygamist, Baoyu acts as if he wishes he were one of the women, that is, no longer distinguished from them by his male sex.

The contradiction between his male centrality and his attempts to act as if sexual difference could be erased intrudes upon numerous scenes of daily life in the garden. Baoyu enjoys watching women put on makeup or comb their hair; he is captivated by their image from a distance or by certain of their features up close; he wants to be able to touch them and participate in their activities. But these attempts to savor the quality of life in the women's quarters meet with signs of rupture and ephemerality due to the inevitable resurfacing of his sexual difference from women. They are suspicious of him, jealous of each other, and, most crucially, set apart from him because of the greater social restrictions placed upon them as women.

Baoyu's Daily Life Among Women

As summed up in the last chapter, descriptive detail in *Yesou puyan* is an expression of controlling presence in both the outer male and inner female worlds. The novelist's devotion to detail in *Honglou meng*, however, especially in the description of women's lives, instead evokes abdication of control, like Baoyu's refusal to accede to the male world of both work and play.[54] Within this intricately detailed life in the garden, itself an escapist world, Baoyu tries to escape further, as when one morning he eludes his maids and steals over to Daiyu's apartments, where she and Shi Xiangyun are still asleep. Baoyu's intimacy with his cousins is such that he can observe them sleeping and can pull the covers up over their bare arms, as he does for Xiangyun (ch. 21, 288); but after they awaken he must briefly depart while they dress. In a less restricted category, the maids may attend to him as he dresses; he may take baths with them and touch or caress them. In other words, with his cousins of the same class, he is more observant of the rule of no contact between unmarried members of the opposite sex.

Baoyu returns to accompany Xiangyun and Daiyu in their morning ablutions. Putting into practice his theory that women are purer than men, he washes his face with Xiangyun's used wash water, refusing fresh soap, despite the maid's sarcasm: "You and these bad habits of yours; when are you ever going to change?" (289). The term "bad habit," *mao-bing*, literally "fault" or "defect," is a reference to Baoyu's "bad habit of loving rouge" (*ai hongde maobing*)—that is, licking or eating women's lip rouge, which in this instance takes the form of Xiangyun's used wash water. These habits of his are like mock attempts to ingest women and thus purify himself through them.

The doing of hair follows as he watches Xiangyun comb (*shu*) hers, then pleads with her to comb his, which he wears in this special way:

> While at home, he wore no head-covering, nor did he knot his hair in the usual manner of an uncapped youth. Instead he had the short hair on all sides done into little braids, which were gathered on top to form one great queue, all of which was held together by red silk thread. There were four pearl clips along the length of the queue, the end of which was fastened by a gold clasp. (ch. 21, 289)

Baoyu is past the age at which the hair is worn in two central knots at the top left and right sides of the head, a style called *zongjiao*, but has not yet reached the age of the "capped" youth, twenty. Nor does he adopt the Manchu style of clipping all the hair from the sides of the head and leaving a long braid or queue from the top. His hairstyle is particular to the aristocracy, which favors feminine practices such as braiding and thread-ing the hair and attaching clasps of precious materials. In this scene, one of the four larger braids is missing its pearl clip, which Xiangyun thinks Baoyu lost, but which Daiyu sarcastically (*lengxiao*) suggests, to Baoyu's silent response, that he gave to some other favorite of his.

This scene ends just as Xiangyun slaps out of his hand some lip rouge that he is about to eat and just as his maid Xiren arrives to scold him for leaving his own apartments to wash in Daiyu's. One of Xiren's duties, as charged by Baoyu's mother, is to keep him from indulging in such irregu-lar behavior, which falls under the definition of "lust of the mind," as the Fairy Disillusionment would put it, or "the bad habit of loving rouge," as Xiren or Xiangyun would say.[55]

Hair combing is one of the daily activities that attracts Baoyu's attention, as once when he watches Baochai comb (*long*) Daiyu's hair. Briefly lost in thought, he wishes he had not just moments before signaled to Daiyu to reset (*min*) her hair, which had fallen out of place. He could have enjoyed watching Baochai both set and comb Daiyu's hair and could have viewed his two loves in close proximity for that much longer (ch. 42, 589). The fact that he can signal to Daiyu with the movement of his eyes (*shige yanse*, 585) is a mark of their special intimacy, a kind which Baoyu and Baochai do not share. But for Baochai to comb Daiyu's hair is a sign of a rapprochement that at first Baoyu does not notice. The two young women had been at odds during their early acquaintance but had recently reconciled, as Baoyu learns only later. He is "bewildered" that Baochai and Daiyu seem not only reconciled but "even friendlier by far than with any of the others" (ch. 49, 677). In short, he can never master the female rivalries and alliances that shift and revolve around him.

On another occasion, he combs (*shubi*) the maid Sheyue's hair, since she complains of an itchy scalp. But he only gets as far as three or four strokes when a jealous Qingwen charges in and "says sarcastically, 'I see you're already putting her hair up for marriage even before the nuptial glass of wine!'" Baoyu offers to do Qingwen's hair but she responds, "'I'm not so lucky,'" and storms out (ch. 20, 281).

In all these instances of hair combing or other intimacy, Baoyu never quite frees himself from the role of intruder into the society of women. As a man and young master, he cannot have intimacy with more than one woman without the complications of jealousy. His "lust of the mind" only supposedly exempts him from being an ordinary carnal man. In the end, none of the women can believe in the harmlessness of "lust of the mind," which is not articulated to them anyway and does not completely rule out lust of the body.

Another area of detail in *Honglou meng* is that of luxurious clothing and of outfits in general, descriptions of which, as Louise Edwards notes, are concentrated on female and feminine male characters.[56] The clothing speaks the person, as when Shi Xiangyun appears in sumptuous furs one day looking like a young man. For the talented woman in the beauty-scholar romance, dressing as a man is a concrete though fantastical way of solving problems that a woman normally can do little about. In *Honglou meng*, Xiangyun's dressing as a man is a vestige of what the beauty actually does; or, in reverse, what the beauty does is an exaggeration of what Xiangyun does in miniature, which is tentatively to act out a freer role than she can actually play. Xiangyun's fate is somewhat similar to Daiyu's. Both women are like the talented beauty in being orphaned only daughters who are "as talented as" men or more so. Xiangyun is brought up by uncaring relatives who allow her only short visits to the Jias', where her choice of dress lets her be as far from her real condition as possible in terms of both social status and gender.

As to her outfit, she appears before Daiyu, Baochai, Baoyu, and others wearing a sable coat lent her by Grandmother Jia, such fur being allowed by sumptuary law only to certain high ranks.[57] As David Hawkes translates, "Under the fur coat she had on a short, narrow-sleeved, ermine-lined tunic jacket of russet green, edge-fastened down the centre front, purfled at neck and cuffs with a triple band of braiding in contrasting colours, and patterned all over with dragon-roundels embroidered in gold thread and coloured silks."[58] The lushness of description in this passage is evident in the modifying phrase of twenty-one characters that precedes the main noun phrase of four characters standing for "short ermine-lined tunic jacket." At the end of the passage, the apparent masculinity of such dress is summed up in a descriptive epithet usually reserved for martial heroes: literally, "she had a wasp-waist, ape-shoulders, crane-stance, and mantis-shape," which are euphemistic for slender waist, strong back and arms, and an aura of grandeur and litheness. In a final touch, the others laughingly comment that Xiangyun always likes to dress as a boy and that she is even handsomer that way than as a girl.

The health and richness of Xiangyun's image is undercut by the fact that the fur coat is something she borrows and could never own, and that the "Princess Zhaojun hood" she wears alludes to the unfortunate fate of women, in this case the Han Princess who, as part of a bargain in a peace treaty, was married to a faraway "barbarian" ruler. Of course, the pervading message of doom in *Honglou meng* is that women have to be married out of the family to unknown, foreign "barbarians."

Women's Illnesses

The above scenes of life among women are exemplary of detail in *Honglou meng* but still lack the underside found in the novel's repeated reference to illness or infirmity in women. As Charlotte Furth has observed, Qing medical science viewed women as inherently prone to illness and harder to treat than men.[59] Women's sicknesses supposedly derived from two related causes: menstrual or gynecological irregularity and inability to control their emotions.[60] Furth continues, "The classical medical model taught women that menstrual function was central to their overall pattern of health or disease, and encouraged minute attention to its variations" (63). *Honglou meng* bears out these conclusions about female infirmity, although it retains in one minor instance the porno-erotic tradition's image of the sexually "inexhaustible female," to which Chinese medical science did not subscribe, as Furth reports.[61] That exception aside, *Honglou meng* exhibits the same minute attention to menstrual irregularity, the best examples being the discussion of Qin Keqing's illness and death in two early chapters (chs. 10, 11) and Wang Xifeng's constant infirmity throughout later chapters. Xifeng has abnormal periods, suffers a miscarriage, and later develops chronic menstrual bleeding.[62]

But besides essential disposition, which is not named as such in the novel, *Honglou meng* also suggests that female illness is caused by the fact that women generally lead more difficult lives than men. Because of his advantage in status, Baoyu is in fact partly the cause of illness and death in several women, including ones closest to him. His maid Qingwen is ill with a cold caught when Baoyu awakes and calls for hot water in the chilly hours of the night. The next day Baoyu tries to take responsibility for her cure and among other things gives her some European snuff to make her sneeze. This act gives the author a chance for a detailed description of the beautiful but infirm young woman:

> She took up a little of the snuff with her fingernail and sniffed it into her nose, but nothing happened. So she took up a good bunch more this time and suddenly felt a tingling gush penetrate straight into her head. She sneezed five or six times in a row, as tears began to flow from her eyes and mucus from her nose. Qingwen hurriedly closed the box and laughed, "My goodness, how fast it works! Give me some tissue." At once there was a young maid to hand her a wad of fine tissue. Qingwen then took one after another and blew her nose. (ch. 52, 725)

Since in *Honglou meng* women are better creatures than dirty men, Qingwen's sneezing and blowing her nose should be considered exquisite details. The weak, sickly, or forlorn woman in general is one of the most constant and conventional images in the Chinese literary tradition and is invested with high aesthetic value. The beauty "Xi Shi holding her stomach in pain and furling her brows" (*Xi Shi peng xin er pin mei*) is an ancient image from this tradition, echoed in later epithets for beautiful women such as "so slight that a gust of wind could blow her down" (*ruo bujing feng*), a phrase applied in *Honglou meng* to both Daiyu and Baochai.[63] In fact, Daiyu's nickname, Piner (Frowner), is an allusion to Xi Shi and her facial image of discomfort.

Qingwen's cold can be said to result from Baoyu's privilege of being able to order maids to assist him in the middle of the night, when he is easily frightened because of the dark and frequently wakes calling out (ch. 77, 1111). On a similar occasion, Xiren wakes with a fever the morning after she stays up late scolding Baoyu for his failings: bizarre imagination, licking lip rouge, and laxity in studies (ch. 19, 272).

One of the most finely observed scenes of such services by maids again centers on Qingwen. She is still sick but Baoyu needs her to repair a hole burnt in a precious Russian jacket that he does not want Grandmother Jia to know he has ruined. The description is like a sewing demonstration:

> First she opened up the lining and secured a bamboo darning mushroom about the size of the mouth of a teacup under the inside of the hole. Then she took a knife to scrape around the burnt opening and make the threads soft and loose again. This she followed by taking the needle and thread and sewing in one direction then another in order to create a criss-cross pattern. Using this special method, she first sewed the foundation, then began to thread back and forth in imitation of the surrounding pattern. After every few stitches she would check herself, then patch some more, and examine it again. The effort was exhausting and made her dizzy. Her eyes became blurry, she grew short of breath, her energy began to ebb. After every four or five stitches she had to lean back on the pillow and rest awhile. (ch. 52, 735)

Baoyu is sensitive to her hardship but exasperates her with his ministrations. She reprimands him: "Little ancestor, just get to sleep! If you stay up any longer, your eyes will show it tomorrow and be all sunken in. Then what will you do?!" She fears that his mother and grandmother will reprimand her for letting him stay up too late. He goes to bed; she stays up until the clock strikes four.

The most prominently ill woman is Daiyu, whose chronic infirmity couples with emotional wounds to lead to her death precisely when Baoyu marries Baochai. Both Daiyu and Qingwen suffer rejection by the

晴雯

Qingwen sewing Baoyu's Russian jacket.

Jia household, Daiyu when the family chooses the healthier Baochai as Baoyu's wife, Qingwen when Baoyu's mother banishes her from her indentured service for being too good-looking and likely to influence Baoyu. Both women allow Baoyu to indulge his "lust of the mind," unlike Baochai and Xiren, who repeatedly scold him for it. Baochai and Xiren always keep an eye to public approval, especially of the elders, and avoid the warm and personal intimacy of Daiyu and Qingwen.[64]

Such focus on women's illness and suffering is a form of eulogy on women's fate. The attention to detail, especially in examples such as Qingwen's sneezing or sewing, represents an endeavor—whether the fictional Baoyu's or nonfictional author's—to follow or record that suffering step by step. Baoyu could easily give the sewing job to Qingwen and immediately go to bed, but he feels beholden and emotionally bound. Although he is closest to Daiyu, he loves Qingwen and numerous other women as well. The detail of description in Qingwen's case is a sign of that same love, which is in general expressed in the narratorial tendency to linger over the qualities and vicissitudes of the beautiful ones.

Baoyu's Sexuality and His Nonsexual Intimacy

Through familiarity with the details of women's lives, the author of *Honglou meng* attempts to write on behalf of and in honor of women. In Baoyu he creates a man who is intimately familiar with women and who indirectly attempts to be one of them. Baoyu is the central figure in the garden, with "all the beauties linked through him," as the Zhiyan zhai commentary states.[65] He is the imaginary, benevolent polygamist to all the women, so benevolent that he has sex with almost no one.

Baoyu's sexuality has already been shown to be crossed and ambiguous. He is at once polygamous and heteroerotic, then homoerotic, but often undriven by sex. He is averse to base men, only liking a few feminine men like himself. He is attracted to women but suspicious of them once they marry, when he says they become infected by base male influence (ch. 77, 1101). He has sex with Xiren but later grows apart from her and is explicitly reported to have sex with no other woman until Baochai in the sequel (hints of sexual activity with other women occur, however). He has sex with his boyfriend Qin Zhong, but the description is deliberately vague, as will be seen later, and he has no further sex with Qin or other men thereafter. Baoyu also goes to the miserly-ascetic extreme of trying to reject all women. Scolded by Xiren for escaping to Daiyu's and Xiangyun's room and caught between all these women's attractions and rival attentions, he is frustrated that they can never understand him and his supposedly harmless "lust of the mind." He seeks the consolation of philosophy in the sayings of Zhuangzi, under whose influence he writes of the sources of life's complications: "nagging" (*quan*) women in the form of his maids Xiren and Sheyue, "heavenly beauty" in the form of Baochai, and "divine intelligence" in the form of Daiyu. If these distractions would disappear, he could live in equanimity. The next morning Daiyu writes satirical verses in reaction to his histrionics, while Baoyu of his own returns to his norm of floating among the women of the garden (ch. 21, 294).

His physical attraction to women is most direct in scenes such as the one in which he suddenly becomes spellbound by the snow-white arm and then beautiful face of his cousin Baochai. The narrator has just noted the sureness of Baoyu's love for Daiyu. Then Baoyu sees Baochai's arm and wishes it were on Daiyu's body, where perhaps he could caress it. He is then transfixed, even as Daiyu stands there, and she, along with Baochai, notices his loss of control (ch. 28, 401–2). Finally put out, Daiyu flicks her handkerchief at him and accidently knicks him in the eye, causing him to cry out, at which point the chapter ends.

He is more outrageous with the maid Yuanyang (Faithful), the back of whose neck so attracts him as she is sewing one day that he:

> put his face up to her neck to sniff its fragrant perfume, then reached his hand out to caress it. Its white softness wasn't a bit inferior to Xiren's. So he hovered up to her like a monkey and with a brazen grin said, "Good sister, won't you let me taste the rouge on your lips." He became stuck upon her body like toffee. (ch. 24, 329)

In this passage, the words "hovered . . . like a monkey" (lit., "monkeyed his body up to her," *hou shang shen qu*) and "brazen" (or "drooling," *xianpi*) are the same ones used in erotic romances in which a man similarly flings himself on a woman, but with the goal of having sex.[66] In this case, Yuanyang calls for Xiren to scold the young master for again indulging his bad habit; Xiren then defuses the situation by hurrying him to get ready for an outing.

As Grandmother Jia notices, Baoyu's fondness for women is not all for the sake of "that." He appears immune to sexual attraction in the genital sense, although he makes numerous advances otherwise. His interest in men, even if less developed in the novel, offers a similar pattern of initial activity without follow-up. After he discovers Qin Zhong in the act of forcing himself upon a young nun, Qin offers Baoyu any favor to make up for his transgression. Baoyu says that they can "carefully rectify accounts" later that night, at which point the narrator steps in to say that what the two actually do is not clear and has not been recorded. "This is a mystery about which we dare not make up false reports" (ch. 15, 207).

In an earlier chapter, after Baoyu's sexual initiation with Xiren, Baoyu and Qin Zhong become friends in school, where they are mirrored by another couple of handsome boyfriends. Qin asks one boy of the other couple, "Does your father mind if you have boyfriends?"—that is, *pengyou*, "friend," in this context a term for male lover.[67] One of the class bullies jeers at Qin and the boy, telling everyone in class that he saw them "kissing and feeling each other's asses" (ch. 9, 139–40).

In the above situations, Baoyu and Qin Zhong exhibit in milder form the same bisexuality as their inveterate and, according to Baoyu's theory, dirtier seniors like Jia Lian and Xue Pan, both of whom are more shameless in their lusting after men and women. Xue Pan enjoys sex with boys and young men during intervals of passing fascination, such as when he briefly joins the clan boys' school to satisfy his "taste for catamites" (*longyang zhi xing*, ch. 9, 138). As for Jia Lian, men serve his interests in case of the temporary lack of women, such as when he seeks out his boy-servants during ritual abstinence with Wang Xifeng at the time of their daughter's illness (ch. 21); he soon finds a woman instead. From what appears in other novels of the period, it is reasonable to assume that both Xue Pan and Jia Lian are penetrators. The boys in the school, however—who according to the jeer of the class bully "feel each other's asses"—are perhaps less fixed in the roles of penetrator and penetrated, and less centered upon anal intercourse itself.

Of the men Baoyu likes the most, Qin Zhong and Jiang Yuhan are like him in being bisexual. Liu Xianglian, the handsome actor of romantic roles, is a musician, swordsman, gambler, and lover, but only of women—a point he goes out of his way to make to the lecherous Xue Pan (ch. 47; perhaps he was once patronized by older or higher-ranking men, as is Jiang Yuhan, but has since grown out of such a role). With all three—Qin, Jiang, and Liu—as with his female cousins and maids, Baoyu is primarily interested in the special rapport he shares with them, not in sexual relations. In short, *Honglou meng* goes against the pattern of the erotic novels in which the hero starts with innocent youthful sex like that between Baoyu and Xiren and moves on incrementally to sex with other partners, reaching a finale in the "great glorious gathering" with all his wives in one bed. After Baoyu's first sex, *Honglou meng* provides no follow-up, whether with women or men.

What is left, then, is his nonsexual or not quite sexual intimacy, which is what makes *Honglou meng* into a novel of "mind lust." The sexual act is as if preempted and replaced by metaphorical words, actions, or objects. The nineteenth-century commentator Zhang Xinzhi responds to this suggestive absence of sexual contact when he interprets, for example, a fly-whisk to stand for the penis. A scantily clad Baoyu sleeps while Xiren, his current sexual partner, then Baochai, his future partner, sit one after the other sewing at his bedside, a fly-whisk resting nearby. *Baixi zhu* and *ying shuazi*, two words used for the whisk, recall to Zhang two euphemisms for the penis, *zhubing* and *shuazi*.[68] Other nonportrayals of sex occur when Baoyu observes Daiyu and Xiangyun sleeping or does his ablutions with them in their room. One day he wakes Daiyu from a noon nap and climbs onto her bed to chat; she carefully wipes a smudge of rouge from his left cheek. They joke for awhile, then he tickles her until she becomes breathless, after which he pleads to smell the perfume in her sleeves (ch. 19, 272–76). He freely caresses his own and other household members' maids and brazenly asks to lick their lips. When he wants to take a bath with Qingwen, she refuses, recalling the mess he once made when he and another maid took a bath for several hours, Qingwen cannot imagine doing that, even getting water on the bed (ch. 31, 434). In one scene he is outside in the garden when he needs to relieve himself. Two giggling maids give him advice as they avert their faces and say, "Squat down before undoing your underthings. Your stomach will get a chill the way you are now" (ch. 54, 755–56). Here Baoyu in effect receives training on how to urinate like a woman. The maids maintain a distance by averting their faces but probably need not do so as far as Baoyu is concerned. Like the hero of the erotic romances who deserves every woman to make love to him, Baoyu deserves every woman to play with him and every maid to attend to him while he urinates, bathes, and dresses.

Honglou meng and the erotic romances that precede and follow it all present the image of a man who is more adept than other men at making love to or understanding women and who expects or supposedly deserves women naturally to want to be around him. In Baoyu this expectation is part of an obliviousness to boundaries between himself and women he finds pleasing. In some cases he is too oblivious, as when he tries to attract the attention of the maid Caixia (Sunset), the favorite of his lackluster half-brother, Jia Huan. She resists when Baoyu takes her hand; the jealous Jia Huan then deliberately spills hot lamp oil on him (ch. 25, 346). In his attraction to supposedly pure and innocent young women, Baoyu also suffers the wiles of those women who take advantage of him in order to gain favor and advancement. The narrator uses the words "clever and scheming" (*congmin guaiqiao*) to describe one of the maids in such a case, and "entrap" (*longluo*) to refer to what she does to Baoyu (ch. 21, 291). The Zhiyan zhai commentator states that "the author suffered such deception all his life, and so did I the commentator."[69] In short, Baoyu is the childhood prepolygamist, still tumbling into his mother's lap and receiving her caresses, as he does moments before the incident with Caixia, but also still wanting all the women in the world, including other men's women, and getting caught in the rivalries between the women he already has.

The Idealization of Presexual Adolescence

Ever since *Honglou meng* became famous, readers have been known to dismiss Jia Baoyu and Lin Daiyu as aberrations impossibly unsuited for normal life. The dismissal and even indignation that the novel has generated and still generates in readers contrast remarkably with the devotion of those who have spent considerable amounts of time studying, rereading, and rewriting it, and who have managed to raise it to the level of a national classic. To raise *Honglou meng* to such a position means rejecting or forgetting the many chaste and erotic romances that were written in or about the same period, including a few that, as it happens, reached eighteenth- and nineteenth-century Europeans long before *Honglou meng* did—for example, *Haoqiu zhuan*, *Peng Shan Leng Yan*, and *Yu Jiao Li*.

In company with these other works, especially the chaste romances, *Honglou meng* stands out with its pronounced sympathy for women's suffering and its elevation of women over men. Women suffer because men and both male and female elders manipulate or abuse them and in general treat them as if they were expendable. Women are supposedly better than men because, before being infected by male influence, they are not so driven by base instincts. Given that men and elders are base, the solution proposed is for men and women to remain in a state of presexual adolescence. Men are best when they adopt feminine behavior, which amounts to an escapist rebelliousness against gender roles and other social prescriptions but also an appropriation of the feminine for the sake of self-purification. Baoyu's and other men's femininity includes bisexuality but also abeyance of driven lust. Their femininity is a solution to the problems of the overly decisive roles men and women are allowed or compelled to assume. Baoyu is allowed and expected to become a polygynist. Depending on their particular fates, women are forced to be obedient wives, concubines, or servants. Both men and women enter into marriages decided upon by their elders and are hence forced into the adversarial positions of the traditional kinship system: daughter-in-law versus mother-in-law, sister-in-law versus sister-in-law, wife versus concubine, husband and wife versus elders, husband and brothers versus wives, brothers versus brothers, husband versus wife, and so forth. Baoyu and Daiyu fleetingly escape from this system but are so disadvantaged from the start that they can only reach their hazy goal by occasional accident rather than effort, unlike the beauties and scholars of the romances. It is perhaps Baoyu's and Daiyu's inability to stand up for themselves that infuriates many readers, while the same inability captivates others.

Symmetry and the crossing of gender characteristics in *Honglou meng* and other works represent an aesthetic attempt at balance and perfection. Indulgence in sexual desire cannot belong to this system of perfection because sexuality is primarily expressed in the form of polygyny, which is hierarchical and asymmetrical. According to the chaste romances and *Honglou meng*, women cannot or should not have to survive under the rule of polygyny. In order for women to survive and for man and woman to find perfect balance in love, sex must be dismissed and man and woman must be able to cross between each other in nonsexual ways. Those ways take up the whole of the chaste romance except for the very end, when the lovers finally consummate and the woman resumes her normative role as wife and mother. *Honglou meng* invents similar ways of avoidance of sex but rarely forgets the reality of polygynous sexuality.

Traditional solutions to the problems of polygynous sexuality include complete denial in the form of monastic celibacy and partial denial in the form of Confucian moral discipline, which in general urges reverence and restraint and, in particular, does not allow a man to take a concubine except if his wife bears no son after the man attains the age of forty. *Honglou meng* still retains monastic celibacy but provides no ideal version of Confucian morality. The novel's only other escape from polygynous sexuality is adolescent "lust of the mind," which is coupled with the cohabitation of young men and women who shun as much as possible adult sexual and kinship roles.

9

THE OVERLY VIRTUOUS WIFE AND

THE WASTREL POLYGAMIST IN

LIN LAN XIANG[1]

In a heady moment, a certain happy polygamist tells one of his wives that he has all a man could desire: the best wine, the most beautiful flowers, and the most attractive women in China (*guose*). She responds by "lowering her head and saying nothing" (ch. 16, 124), then proceeds to lecture him on how he wastes time with worthless men friends ("wine and meat comrades," *jiurou pengyou*) and fails to appreciate the company of his talented wives. This scene is from the mid-Qing *Lin Lan Xiang* (The Six Wives of the Wastrel Geng), another novel like *Honglou meng* about the contrary lot of women in a society where good men are few. The didactic mission of this novel is to portray a wife who balances between two extremes: the lascivious woman who indulges her husband too much and the upright, overly virtuous woman, like the one just mentioned, who admonishes him too much. *Lin Lan Xiang* is like a narrative manual for wives of polygynists that answers the following questions: Given that women have the more difficult lot and must sacrifice themselves for the sake of their fathers, husbands, and sons, and given that a good husband is hard to find, what kind of woman makes the best—that is, most virtuous *and* well-adapted—wife of a polygynist? How far need she go in making sacrifices? How clever must she be in order to survive in such a world and finally to rear a son who is better than his father?

Lin Lan Xiang explores these questions via the story of Geng Lang and his six wives, Geng being the mildly wastrel descendant of an illustrious family (Lang puns with "dissolute"). The question of who is the best wife is answered in the person of the sixth wife, who rises from servant ranks in the latter half of the story and outdoes the other five wives, including the overly virtuous one, who sickens and dies because of what is por-trayed as an excess of self-sacrifice. Besides the example of her good character, the sixth's best offering to the family is in the upbringing of Geng's son, whom she manages to improve upon over his father. The underlying theme of the novel is that it is up to women to correct and improve men and that women can most effectively perform this role when they act inconspicuously.

In this and the next two chapters, I discuss three mid-Qing novels that, although more explicitly didactic and moralistic than *Honglou meng*, all show the same absorption with the problems of the unsettled young man in a world oriented around him and his favors. None of the three reflect the clear influence of *Honglou meng*. *Lin Lan Xiang* concentrates on the women surrounding the wastrel; *Qilu deng* and *Lüye xianzong* concentrate on the wastrel himself. In *Lin Lan Xiang*, the wife referred to in the first paragraph above is too virtuous and self-sacrificing; her co-wives, on the other hand, represent various modes of safer and less rigidly virtuous adaptation to the wastrel world.

In presenting the types of women and the gradations between them, *Lin Lan Xiang* defines six categories, each of which represents a separate mode of adaptation. After discussing the way women in the polygamous household form alliances, I will then introduce these six types of women and the evolution by which the final sixth wife emerges as the most successful. It will again be necessary to engage in more translation and storytelling than usual, mainly because some key behaviors become clear only through the example of events and recurrences of events. *Lin Lan Xiang* is unique among the novels I discuss in setting forth ways by which wives adapt to "bad" husbands. *Yesou puyan* and the erotic romances illustrate ideal mates of a benevolent polygnist; *Lin Lan Xiang* also defines ideal mates, but of a wastrel instead.

Except for a pseudonym, Suiyuan xiashi (the "Fool" or "Nobody" who "Follows Fate"), *Lin Lan Xiang*'s author remains unknown. The novel's earliest extant edition is of 1838, although it could have been written years earlier. It was again published in the late Qing and then probably not again until the 1985 Shenyang edition.[2] In terms of literary quality, critics have never had much praise for *Lin Lan Xiang*. In terms of the novel's own creative ambition, of course, it strives to match the most famous of its predecessors, especially *Jin Ping Mei*. *Lin Lan Xiang* contains sixty-four chapters of eight eight-chapter units, each of which follow patterns of development, retardation, climax, and resolution similar to the ten ten-chapter units of *Jin Ping Mei*.[3] In addition, like *Jin Ping Mei, Lin Lan Xiang* is about a polygamist with six wives, a few of whom closely parallel Ximen Qing's. Its title is also like *Jin Ping Mei's* in consisting of the names or symbols of three central female characters.

Lin Lan Xiang also resembles *Honglou meng*, although neither novel directly reflects influence of the other. Besides having thematic similarities, both are about aristocratic families with close ties to imperial founders and are centered in huge urban compounds divided into east and west sections and containing large gardens. Also like *Honglou meng, Lin Lan Xiang* has a commentary that appears in early editions of the novel (reproduced in the 1985 Shenyang edition) and that David Rolston says probably dates from the middle of the eighteenth century or slightly later.[4] As in *Honglou meng*, the commentator's point of view is similar to the author's, so much so in *Lin Lan Xiang* that some suspect the two were the same person.[5]

Lin Lan Xiang takes place in Beijing between 1425 and 1529 and narrates the domestic affairs of two generations of the Geng family, descendants of one of the founders of the Ming. Geng Lang is first betrothed to Yan Mengqing, represented by the *Lan* of the title,[6] but he cancels the marriage when her father is falsely accused of corruption. To save her father, Yan Mengqing writes a petition volunteering to suffer punishment in his place. In echo of the talented woman of the beauty-scholar romances, she makes such an impression on the authorities that they grant her father a reprieve.

Meanwhile, Geng marries Lin Yunping, the *Lin* of the title, who is of high family, and Ren Xianger, the *Xiang* of the title, who is the daughter of a rich merchant. Xianger is like Mengqing in also being sacrificed for the sake of her father, whom Geng helps to escape a predicament and who then gives Xianger to Geng in return.

Geng next marries Yan Mengqing, but as concubine rather than main wife. His fourth wife, Xuan Ainiang, is a close friend of Yan and Lin, the latter of whom arranges Xuan's inclusion in the family. Geng then adds a fifth wife, Ping Caiyun, who joins with Xianger to form an uncouth and lusty twosome, in contrast to the more proper and refined Lin, Yan, and Xuan.

Because of the jealous Xianger's plotting, a rift develops between Yan

Mengqing and Geng. Nevertheless, Yan Mengqing saves his life twice, in one case when he is ill by serving him a broth stewed with part of her finger. She dies while he is away at war but leaves him a son.

Yan Mengqing's illiterate maidservant Tian Chunwan then rises to be Geng's premier wife, supposedly superior to Yan because she is neither such a passive sufferer nor a stodgy moralist—the highly educated Yan had always tried to discipline her husband. Xianger's plotting is discovered; she declines and dies, as does Geng. His other wives help Chunwan raise Yan Mengqing's son, who achieves public glory but soon retires and then lives to the age of ninety-nine. In the end, two old women appear who had been earlier expelled from the household for having a lesbian affair (see chs. 28 and 64). They are the only nonfamily members to recall the heyday of the Geng house and the tragedy of Yan Mengqing, which they commemorate in the forms of opera and ballad.

Women's Sacrifice and Formation of Alliances

Using the family of the wastrel polygamist as setting, *Lin Lan Xiang* explores the situation of the "virtuous wife" (*xianqi*) Yan Mengqing, at the same time declaring her only an imperfect version of such a wife. The novel's commentator judges her "an ordinary, mediocre grade of superior person" (ch. 26, 205). Misunderstood by her husband, she only knows how to step back from her failed moments and proceed to other unappreciated acts of virtue, as if following a prescribed text on womanly behavior. Her mediocrity lies in a supposedly excessive dedication to form, although she is not duplicitous or hypocritical. When presented with a choice of marriage after her father's reprieve, she chooses to marry Geng because he was her original match. The value of chastity in her interpretation dictates that an original intention outweighs any subsequent accident—even if, as happened in some cases in China, that accident was the death of the betrothed (people are known to have conducted marriage ceremonies with a dead intended).[7] The formalism of social custom also dictates that because of her father's fall she is also fallen. Thus, in marrying Geng Lang, she knows that she, a woman of the upper class, must nevertheless become his concubine and not his main wife. Her dedication to high-heroic virtue is further exemplified by her observation of the time-honored act of devotion to a sick family member, the cutting off of a part of her flesh to make a medicinal broth. She cures her husband, who is ill from too much "drink and sex" (*jiuse*) with Ping Caiyun and Ren Xianger. Later, when Geng stops visiting her because of a misunderstanding, she avoids defending herself, adopting instead a posture of silent withdrawal and thus averting unseemly behavior.

Other women in the novel tend to adapt to a given situation or resort to subversion rather than conform strictly to the rules of feminine virtue. When Xuan Ainiang's father is accused of corruption and stripped of all power, Geng marries or, in effect, rescues her into his family. Her close friend and his wife, Lin Yunping, initiates the arrangements, and the mediocre Geng is happy to add the exquisite Xuan as his third wife. Xuan's wit gives her a protective shell that allows her to adapt to the situation and keeps her from being forced into further sacrificial positions. Ren Xianger is sacrificed in a more degrading way than the others. Her father, who has been unjustly jailed, gives her to Geng as a maid in return for Geng's getting him free. Unlike Yan, who is conformist, or Xuan, who is adaptive, the merchant-class Ren takes an offensive approach. Soon after entering the household as maid, she maneuvers to become Geng's favorite concubine and remains so until her death. She is the most jealous and conniving of the wives, as epitomized in her attempt to put a death curse on Chunwan, her rival for Geng's favor as premier wife. As for Ping Caiyun, she is abducted by a lecherous villain, then saved by a gallant hero, who puts her in a box and places it on Geng's property, where she is discovered and taken in as fifth wife. Although sullied by her abduction (and lucky to have made such a prestigious match), she is not resentful or jealous like Ren Xianger. Nevertheless, she becomes notorious in the household as Geng's second sexual favorite and, along with Ren Xianger, exerts an unhealthy influence on Geng. As it turns out, the two most blatantly abused women are the least disciplined and also the most sexually intimate with the man, who neither reprimands them nor sees through their manipulations of him.

The most personal and direct statements about the woman's lot appear when some of the wives form friendships before marriage and imply or actually state that it is more difficult for women than for men to make and keep friends after marriage. Lin Yunping and Xuan Ainiang exchange banter in which they imagine marrying each other: "Sister, if only you were a man," Lin begins (ch. 4, 27). They admit that either could be the man, but in the end, by an unspoken tip of the balance, Xuan Ainiang

more than Lin. After all, she has the greater wit and strength of character—her chief trait, in fact, is her ability to laugh, joke, and to tease or
banter (*nue*). They imagine themselves married and their maids becoming their chamber-wives. (*ceshi*). Later, one of the elder women notices
their closeness and remarks that they "are like a little husband and wife"
(ch. 4, 29), and that if they were married it would save the elders the
difficult task of finding decent sons-in-law (it having just been mentioned
that Geng Lang was not an ideal mate, 25). Lin Yunping's and Xuan
Ainiang's feelings for each other are described as *qianquan,* words often
used for the "intertwined" feelings of lovers (ch. 7, 49).[8] Underlying all
such references to their closeness is the fact that, once married, women
are no longer as free as men to continue seeing each other unless married
to the same man. Moreover, truly romantic and sexual involvement (if
discovered) is subject to condemnation, as in the case of the two women
expelled from the Geng house for lesbianism. In contrast to Lin and Yan,
however, the expelled women are still together at the end of the novel
when they reemerge to sing ballads about the life of Yan Mengqing.
What appears to be an actual case of lesbianism thus becomes both a
means of companionate survival for these two women and a vehicle of
eulogy for other women destroyed by their involvement with men.

A more direct statement about the vicissitudes of relations between
women appears when Yan Mengqing and Xuan Ainiang become friends.
Still unmarried, Xuan laments that she loses women friends because of
marriage, and hopes that Lin and Yan can get her joined with them in the
Geng household; otherwise she will never see them again. Yan Mengqing, who is about to marry Geng, then utters the central thematic
remark of the scene: "For men to meet a soul mate, they can go anywhere in the world. For women to meet their heart's companion, even
waiting a thousand autumns is not enough" (85).

As members of the same polygamous household, Lin, Yan, and Xuan
form a sort of female alliance of smart and capable wives, though not
always appreciated as such. Ping Caiyun and Ren Xianger form a rival
alliance which often succeeds in monopolizing Geng. But when Ren dies
and Geng wants to hold Buddhist ceremonies in honor of her soul (resembling Ximen Qing in his sorrow over Li Pinger's death), Ping finally
switches sides. In the name of *yi,* "group honor" or "righteousness," she
joins Chunwan and the others, who oppose Geng's silly extravagance in
the name of *qing,* "love" or "sentiment" (ch. 51, 395). *Yi,* a term usually

reserved for the bonds of male honor and camaraderie (as in *yiqi*), is here invoked by wives allied against their polygamist husband. The women are enforcing the rule that the man should not show excess feeling for any one of his wives, especially one other than the main wife. *Yi* and *li*, "heavenly principle," a term also invoked, represent *zheng*, "objective correctness," as opposed to *si*, "partiality" or "selfishness" (392).

Five Types of Women in the Polygamous Household

What path does a woman take given that she must participate in polygamy and that her husband is a wastrel? In *Lin Lan Xiang*, besides forming alliances and having semi–love affairs with each other, the women have individual ways of dealing with their lots. Their personal characteristics are set forth in an early conversation about marriage in which Xuan Ainiang's mother lists five types of women, each corresponding to one of Geng's first five wives (ch. 4, 25–26). The types represent five ways that a woman may deal with the situations of the polygamous household.

The first in order is Lin Yunping, who is the main wife, though only by default since Yan Mengqing was originally to be first. According to Madame Xuan's categorization, Lin is "generous and well-poised, always acting in the spirit of compromise, confident [i.e., not excessively cautious] in speech, willing to take on all tasks no matter how difficult. She is one to bring out the true color of the family" (ch. 4, 26). The novel rarely focuses on Lin, leaving her instead to represent the ideal main wife in the background. In her management of the house, she concentrates on the "general outlines," not the "individual items" and details, to which Yan Mengqing attends (ch. 31, 239).

The next in order is Xuan Ainiang. Once married to Geng, she is more of a mate to Lin Yunping and Yan Mengqing than to Geng. Her main role is to keep herself, Lin, and Yan happy despite the fact that they are married to a man like Geng. As one of the five types, "She is always laughing and joking, brisk and unrestrained. No matter how tremendous a problem, she can always dispel it. She neither cares if anyone speaks well of her, nor is she likely to cause anyone to speak poorly of her" (26). Her "philosophy of life" (*wode weiren*), as she tells Chunwan, is that "the joys of life are limited; the worries go on forever. . . . Everything—each sip, each bite—is preordained. Rather than dwell on useless worries, why not enjoy immediate happiness! . . . Above all don't be like Yan Mengqing and create your own suffering" (ch. 43, 333). In this last remark she functions as the mediator between the failed Yan Mengqing and the upcoming Chunwan. She is also the bridge between Yan Mengqing and the lowly Ren Xianger: if Yan Mengqing speaks too sparingly and Ren Xianger too rashly, Xuan Ainiang is in the middle urging them to learn from each other (ch. 19, 149). In adversity Yan Mengqing believes in "self-restraint" (*zicai ziyue*), which Xuan Ainiang opposes when she says: "Fettering yourself will only concentrate your worries more" (ch. 30, 234). Her wisdom is to "forget" (*wang*), which she vainly urges upon Yan Mengqing, whose way is to "endure" or "suffer" (*ren*, ch. 21, 164). In sex with Geng, Xuan is clever and playful without being lewd, neither too proper nor too shameless.

Yan Mengqing is known for her tendency to "remonstrate" or "admonish" (*quan*) her husband whenever she sees him doing wrong; this behavior of hers is the cause of her downfall. As the third of the five types of women, but second in the ranking of wives, she is, according to Madame Xuan, "cautious and prudent, sparing of words and laughter. She runs the home according to rule and serves her husband without fail—there musn't be too many of this type." As concerns "admonishment," each wife is different, says the narrator: "If Geng Lang is at fault in something, Lin Yunping hesitates between admonishing and not admonishing. Xuan Ainiang often admonishes him, but always injects laughter and humor, so in the end it isn't very much as if she were admonishing him. Ren Xianger and Ping Caiyun haven't the slightest idea how to admonish. Only Yan Mengqing will admonish him each and every time, which Geng Lang both loves and fears" (ch. 28, 217). Although her readiness to admonish her husband might indicate skill in speech, her speaking ability disappears when it comes to defending her own behavior. She says of herself that what looks to others like "being cautious" is actually a case of "my mouth and tongue being clumsy and stupid, so that I don't dare speak lightly" (ch. 19, 149). In short, it is easy to pinpoint her husband's actions but impossible to address her own motives and actions or apparent actions.

In labeling Yan Mengqing as a "mediocre person within the category of the nonmediocre" (ch. 26, 205), the commentator puts her just below the four purely excellent or "nonmediocre" (*buyong*) characters of the book, who are Chunwan, Xuan Ainiang, and two men who play peripheral roles as Geng Lang's superior friends (in contrast to his "wine and meat comrades"). The reason for Yan Mengqing's mediocrity is her "moralistic" or "doctrinal air" (*daoxue qi*).[9] The commentator uses a particular pair of labels to categorize each of the women; thus Yan Mengqing is overly "correct" (*duanzhuang*) and not "fluid" enough (*liuli*, in the sense of sensuous or attractive); the commentator says the same of Lin Yunping. Xuan is too "fluid" and not "correct" enough. Ping Caiyun and Ren Xianger are both "purely fluid and not in the least correct." Only Chunwan combines both qualities in the right proportion (ch. 2, 16, n. 79).[10] What the balance or not between "correct" and "fluid" means in terms of sexual behavior becomes clear when we examine Geng's sexual relations with each of his wives.

The Polygamist's Sexy Concubines

As in the erotic romances, *Lin Lan Xiang*'s sexiest women are lowest in the hierarchy of wives. Ping Caiyun, the fourth of the five types of women outlined by Madame Xuan but the fifth wife, is described as follows: "If others go east, she goes east; if west, then she goes west. Someone says yea, she says yea; someone says nay, she also says nay. She constantly changes and hasn't a single opinion of her own" (26). However, Ping Caiyun is from a scholarly family, unlike Ren, who is of the "marketplace" (*shijing*, ch. 48, 368—that is, from a merchant family). Ping thus has an element of breeding which allows her to reform in the end.

Ren Xianger is the final type: she "says both true and false and only does half of either of them. Whether she does good or evil, she does neither all the way. Low in moral capacity, she easily reaches her limit of tolerance. Her displays of talent are in vain since they only cause others to despise her" (26). She occasionally tries to improve herself, such as when she says that she ought to be like Yan Mengqing and speak with greater circumspection (ch. 19, 149), or when she attempts to learn to write poetry (ch. 20), at which Lin, Yan, and Xuan are adept (but not Chunwan, the eventual best wife). But true to her nature, Xianger fails to carry through in either of these goals.

A scene contrasting the sexuality of the five wives (before Chunwan becomes a sixth) shows Geng Lang coming home one evening to find them in various states of tipsiness:

Lin Yunping and Yan Mengqing were leaning against a large table and drinking tea. As if trying to sober up, Xuan Ainiang paced back and forth, supporting herself with the help of a maid. Geng Lang laughed, "Aunt Xuan, have you gotten drunk today?" Xuan Ainiang replied, "A ladleful is enough to get me drunk, even a spoonful. But I'm not like those two who turn into piles of wet mud with the mere smell of liquor."

When Geng Lang looked around he saw Caiyun resting with her head upon a pillow and Xianger lying sideways on the bed. Already under the influence himself, he approached and sniffed the sweet fragrances wafting from their bodies. He pressed his hand against Caiyun: she was just like rain-drenched peach blossoms, so delicate they could hardly support the weight of his hand. He touched Xianger: she was just like poplars and willows tossed in the wind, a force so strong he could hardly keep hold. Mengqing was afraid his high spirits would get the better of him and cause him to do something indecent and unsightly.

Yan Mengqing orders the servants to take the two women to their rooms and herself puts Geng Lang to bed (ch. 17, 133–34).

As the rift between Yan Mengqing and Geng Lang widens, Xianger and Ping Caiyun become more unbridled, spending days with Geng "in dissolute abandon" (*nuelang xiayou,* ch. 32, 247). As evident from the following translation, *Lin Lan Xiang's* depictions of abandon are circumspect compared to those of *Jin Ping Mei* and other erotic novels (bracketed words represent the commentator's interlineal remarks):

Geng Lang leaned on Xianger's shoulder and cradled her neck with his arm. "Good sister, how about a kiss." But Ping Caiyun was there, so Xianger gave him a good shove and said, "How dare you!" She dodged aside so quickly that he was left with nothing to lean on and fell into Ping Caiyun's arms. The two of them then tripped onto Xianger's bed, whereupon Geng Lang set to feeling and mussing her all about. This gave them all another good laugh.

When they rose, Caiyun joked with Xianger: "Sister, the thief has stolen something of yours; aren't you going to look for it?!" Xianger was about to search for whatever it was, but Geng Lang was already pulling a woman's sleep-slipper out of his sleeve. "This wasn't my doing. Little Sister just hid this in my sleeve." Xianger tried to grab it but Geng Lang held it up high. "You'll have to get it back through *her!*" Xianger looked at Caiyun and said, "You wretch; you'd better get it back for me." Caiyun replied, "That won't be difficult," as she turned to Geng Lang and said, "I'll tell you a joke and you'll give it back, all right? . . . 'Bamboo shoots of jade bound in layer upon layer, golden lotuses move step by step. Although they mostly touch the ground, they also end up facing the heavens." Geng laughed, "Wonderful! Perfect! Now let me make her face the heavens." [Commentary: As it were, to do the clouds and rain with her (327, n. 12).]

When Xianger heard this, she said, "You two are laying a trap to make a fool of me, but I'll never go along with it." Geng Lang: "Whether we kiss or not is all up to me; whether you go along or not, what say do you have? If you really mean not to go along, I'll take those phoenix-head slippers off your feet and make wine glasses of them." [Commentary: He is no different with her than with a prostitute (327, n. 13).]

Xianger, already a little drunk by this time, suddenly pushed Geng Lang into Caiyun's arms: "Let me see you two kiss now." Caiyun wasn't prepared and almost fell, but was saved just in time by Geng Lang, who managed to plant quite a few kisses upon her. (ch. 42, 322–23)

However, no intercourse follows. Xianger vomits, loses consciousness, and is carried by Geng to her bed, where Caiyun changes her into her sleep-slippers and then escapes to her own room rather than spend the night with Geng. Caiyun would not want to appear to take advantage of Geng while Xianger lay ill. The next night they drink again, but Xianger strips Caiyun naked, "not leaving her even her footbindings," ties Caiyun's incense purse and kerchief to Geng's waist, and puts Caiyun's pearl bracelet around his wrist. In her revenge, the jealous Xianger acts as if she assumes Geng was more intimate with Caiyun than with herself.

These scenes of "dissolute" behavior contrast with one of cleverness and refinement at the end of the same chapter when Geng Lang and Xuan Ainiang go to bed. He enters her room and observes her taking down her hair.

Because the maid's fingernails were too long, she couldn't undo Xuan Ainiang's hair without laborious effort. Geng Lang stood by her side and spent quite some time undoing it for her before he finally got the hair ornaments off. Then he said jokingly: "The hair oil is fragrant, the face powder is fragrant, the lipstick is fragrant, but in the end it is your flesh that is most fragrant. The fragrance of the body is called musk; the fragrance of musk is found at the navel. But I don't know for sure whether my dear's fragrance is above the navel or below it."

Xuan joked in response: "Fragrance comes from above the navel and also from below. But in the end, if there is fragrance [*xiang*], then my name is not Lin, nor Xuan, nor Shui, but Ren [*Xianger*]."

That night the two talked and laughed for awhile, then entered the mandarin duck canopy to take their perches on the phoenix pillow. (ch. 42, 326)

As in the polygamous erotic romances, brothel-like sexual play occurs between the man and his lowest concubines. The more refined Xuan Ainiang cleverly deflects Geng's attempts to be vulgar. Instead of "dissolutely abandoning themselves," Xuan and Geng "perch on the phoenix pillow."

Yan Mengqing is yet more reserved, although an exception occurs because of her attempt to mend the rift between herself and her husband. Geng visits Yan one rainy day, not having shown up in a while because of his suspicions about a fan she inscribed that somehow came into the hands of one of his male relatives. He says to her for the second time in the book that he has all a man could desire (ch. 30, 233). This time she simply encourages him to drink his wine and tells him to enjoy

"the chrysanthemums rinsing off their makeup in the rain." Geng Lang saw that she added nothing else after these words, so he drank his fill without inhibition. In a while candles were lit, the flowers became increasingly fragrant, the rain gradually heavier.

He teased Yan Mengqing: "What if I rinse off your makeup?" She smiled without answering, so he let the liquor have its way and took her as he would have taken Ping Caiyun or Ren Xianger, with lustful abandon [*nuelang xiaxie*]. Yan Mengqing submitted [*shou*] without resisting. [Commentary: Good. I've long hoped for this (238, n. 24).] (ch. 30, 234)

Unfortunately, the next morning he sees hanging to dry an article of her clothing that he once stained with his drunken vomit. He interprets this as Yan Mengqing's silent way of "scolding and admonishing" him for his former excess, although she is innocent of such intent. He leaves her room sulkily and thereafter allows their rift to become permanent. Xuan Ainiang later attempts to reconcile the two by inviting both to her room and offering Yan her bed to sleep on with Geng. But this time Yan refuses to use "lust" (*yin*) to win back his favor, afraid he will reject her again (ch. 32, 248).

Yan Mengqing takes no offensive action, as Xuan Ainiang would have through clever joking or Ren Xianger through coquetry and intrigue. She only knows self-sacrifice, the act of which consists of literally and figuratively cutting off parts of herself until she dies. She remains true to her virtue and will be commemorated for that, although superseded by a supposedly better model, Chunwan.

The Best Wife

Geng Lang regrets his split with Yan Mengqing only after she has died and the maid Chunwan begins to remind him of her.[11] Although Chunwan is superior to Yan Mengqing, as Geng Lang will feel, she is humble in her superiority in that she speaks of Yan Mengqing as an ideal impossible to surpass; in being humble, she is also self-preserving. One of the main thematic contrasts between Chunwan and Yan Mengqing is that Chunwan is illiterate, in conformity with the famous motto "It is a virtue for a woman to be uneducated" (nüzi wu cai bian shi de). Her name symbolizes simple orderliness, as in the neat arrangement of "spring rice paddies," chunwan; her hardy staple succeeds over Yan Mengqing's fragile orchid.[12] How Geng Lang is won over to Chunwan, and to Yan Mengqing through Chunwan, can be seen through a comparison of Mengqing's and Chunwan's reactions to Geng's drunkenness.

Sick from alcohol, Geng Lang vomits in Chunwan's room, having once before done so in Yan Mengqing's room and at another time having taken as reprimand Yan's hanging in plain sight a piece of cloth stained with his previous vomit. Chunwan now helps him by offering a piece of cloth that, as she tells him, Yan Mengqing left to her. To his remark upon her resemblance to Yan Mengqing,[13] she answers that she is nothing but a servant girl, causing him to exclaim, "How clever you are. Not a bit overbearing" (ch. 46, 355). Asked why she didn't learn to write poetry, she answers that if she had learned, then fans with her poetry inscribed on them might end up in the wrong person's possession, as one of Yan Mengqing's once did. Looking at her milky white hands, Geng continues, "I suppose that after Mengqing cut off her finger, she wasn't as nimble as you are now." She responds, "If there were no medicine to brew, then though her finger were whole, what use would it have been? What a waste of bracelets and nail covers just for the sake of opulence!" His conclusion: "Caiyun and Xianger are both clever with words, but they're not like you and Xuan Ainiang whose every word has foundation [*laili*]. But the past is past; there is no use speaking of it." (ch. 46, 356).

The superiority of the former servant girl lies in her knowledge of *laili*, the "foundations," "antecedents," or "references" in the history of the Geng household. She uses the past—in the form of the piece of cloth, for example—as an allusion or piece of evidence to prove her expertise in the present. All she says and does is in the service of her husband. But her service also includes clever reference to Yan Mengqing's more self-sacrificing service, as seen in Chunwan's answer to the question about Mengqing's finger: it is a matter of course that a virtuous woman amputates part of herself for the sake of her husband. After these proofs of her abilities, she wins him over and becomes premier wife, once and for all dashing any plans Xianger had to seize power (chs. 47, 48).

Li—principle, reason—wins out over *qing*—feeling, emotion. Yan Mengqing and Chunwan are the *li* wives, Caiyun and Xianger the *qing* wives. After Xianger dies, Geng Lang dreams of her one night while sleeping with Chunwan, whom he then hugs passionately. "Calling out Xianger's name, he ran his hands all over Chunwan's body" (ch. 54, 419). [Commentary: "Chunwan probably had never experienced such wildness. But I don't know if her belt came loose or not" (421, n. 37).] Chunwan bolts up and calls the maids in to light the lanterns. [Commentary: "She is afraid he will be lewd with her" (421, n. 39).] Having arrived to investigate the commotion, Xuan Ainiang subtly mocks Geng Lang for "vainly wasting his energy" on a dead person and forgetting about the "love and kindness of a living one." Geng Lang is finally "somewhat chastened and repentent" about his reaction to Xianger's death (419–20). Not long after, Caiyun dies at age 38 and Geng Lang at 40 (Xianger having died at 34), just after he and his wives receive highest honors from the emperor.

The final eight chapters of the novel center upon Chunwan and the posthumous upbringing of Geng Lang's and Yan Mengqing's son Geng Shun, whose name means "to go smoothly." During his youth, Chunwan keeps him away from unsavory friends and attractive maids and boy-servants and removes from his presence all luxurious clothing and objects (ch. 49, 376; ch. 57, 442). She catches him at the right time and guards him while "he is [still] by nature unable to control himself" (*xing bu ziding*, 376), thus preventing him from ending up like his father, who forever remained unable to control himself—the same words, *xing bu ziding*, having been used to describe Geng Lang at the beginning of the novel (ch. 1, 3).

The Hidden Influence of Virtuous Women

Once the man learns to exercise self-control, the virtuous women can prevail and the nonvirtuous women must either reform or disappear. Since the woman to begin with must reside in the inner chambers, she is at the mercy of male instability and misbehavior. As the Song dynasty Yuan Cai says in his work on precepts for family management, *Shifan* (trans. by Patricia Ebrey),

> The saying that women don't take part in outside affairs is based on the fact that worthy husbands and sons take care of everything for them, whereas unworthy ones can always find ways to hide their deeds, whatever they are, from the women. . . . For women, these are grave misfortunes [when men, especially sons, mismanage the household by gambling, etc.], but what can they do about them? If only husbands and sons could remember that their wives and mothers are helpless and suddenly repent![14]

The woman's modes of defense are self-sacrifice at the one extreme and coquetry or shrewish haranguing at the other; in between are various safer modes of adaptation.

As a report on the state of its society, *Lin Lan Xiang* delivers a message like that of *Honglou meng* and other works which declare or imply that men are in decline and that it is primarily women who retain the qualities of virtue and integrity which once belonged to men. The superior men in *Lin Lan Xiang* are peripheral and womanless characters, including a knight-errant, a poor scholar, and even a eunuch.[15] The men of high rank (most of whom are presumably polygamous) are all inferior. In lament over this state of affairs, the poem introducing chapter 16 (122) says:

> At the decline of friendship in this age, we beat our breasts in sorrow.
> Who is capable now of refined and learned discussion?
> Indeed, scholarly virtue is hardly to be found;
> The pristine beauty of the inner chamber is my only friend around.

The Way of male friendship is in decline because decent companions with whom one can refine one's poetic skills and exchange scholarly opinions no longer exist. In the beauty-scholar romances, *Honglou meng,* and *Yesou puyan,* such exchange now takes place between man and woman at home. In similar spirit, Yan Mengqing had advised Geng Lang to avoid his "wine and meat comrades" and realize the value of companionship with his talented wives.

Lin Lan Xiang also offers a practical and conservative model for running the polygamist family given the decline and unreliability of men. Yan Mengqing goes to extremes of excellence, though not in the brilliant or militant fashion of the talented beauties who manage to redefine their lots. She takes her lot to its passive extreme in high heroic manner, nobly adhering to the womanly virtue of self-sacrifice. Chunwan is a saner— that is, more self-preserving—version of the same model, a survivor who finally succeeds in the conservative task of bringing a decadent family back into order.

The conservatism of such a return to order rests on the hidden premise that women are the true movers of the family and, by extension, the whole society. The comment at the end of chapter 17 says: "If there is a virtuous wife in the home, the man will commit no transgression" (ch. 17, 134). But the provision for such success is that the "virtuous" wife should not be too well educated, like Yan Mengqing, whose educated "talent" ends up "obscuring her virtue," as one of Geng Lang's superior male friends once notes (ch. 16, 124). Again, the famous dictum states that "it is a virtue for a woman to be uneducated," to which *Lin Lan Xiang* adds that a woman must use self-sacrifice skillfully, that is, like Chunwan, not too dogmatically and without actually harming herself—uneducated, yes, but smart nevertheless.

10

THE SPOILED SON AND

THE DOTING MOTHER IN *QILU DENG*

Now that we know what ingredients make the model woman, the next question is how to arrive at the model man. The answer of the late eighteenth-century *Qilu deng* (Lantern at the Fork in the Road) is that in order for a man to become a good man, he must first experience the ordeals of the spoiled boy. If he manages to reform himself after being spoiled, then he is worth his mettle. The problem of how to raise a son is paramount in both *Lin Lan Xiang* and *Qilu deng*. In the former, the father is a failure but his son a success because of careful upbringing by a model stepmother. In *Qilu deng,* the son comes around by himself and raises his own model son. He is assisted by a woman similar to Tian Chunwan, in his case a humble concubine who knows when to interfere or not in her husband's life. Like Chunwan, she supersedes a virtuous main wife who dies because of an excess of refinement and sensitivity. A shared though unarticulated message in *Lin Lan Xiang* and *Qilu deng* is that few men can match the best of women. Something like the good mediocre man or the disciplined but also coddled man is the most that can be expected. As for the best of women, since they have few male counterparts, their existence is precarious. As for the worst of women—in *Qilu deng,* doting mothers—since they are the most culpable agents in the generation of wastrel sons, they make existence precarious for everyone, including themselves.

Qilu deng is like a fictionalized version of the genre of works about family management which already existed in China for many centuries, and to which I have previously referred. The author, Li Haiguan, himself wrote such a work, the contents of which often coincide with those of his novel.[1] What the mid-Qing *Qilu deng* adds to these sets of precepts about how the man ought to behave is a denser and lengthier narration of how it is possible for him to go astray. In an almost chapter-by-chapter progression, *Qilu deng* details the discrete moments ("forks in the road") of the young man's decline from initial innocence to utter indulgence. The denouement and ending consist of his reform into the only thing he can be after such ruination—a sober model of virtue, that is, a "mediocrely" good man. By contrast, *Yesou puyan* presents a super-model amounting to an overcompensation for all the wastrels and philanderers like *Qilu deng*'s Tan Shaowen. Tan is lucky to be able to attain the passing minimum of virtuous behavior.

Besides detailing the young man's decline, *Qilu deng* thematizes his helplessness in this process. In other words, at the same time that it blames the boy for all the harm he causes, *Qilu deng* also removes the blame by asserting that he is predisposed to act the way he does. His father and mother are at fault, the mother receiving the greater share of blame. The absence of a strict and conscientious father combined with the presence of a soft and doting mother leads to the decisive tearing of the young man's initial veil of innocence. That tear widens when he befriends other but worse wastrels, who play directly to his preexisting tendencies by addicting him to whatever pleasures they can find to stimulate him, especially gambling and sex.

In addressing the same male susceptibility to degeneration, *Yesou puyan* explicitly links the problem to carelessness in controlling sexual desire and maintaining the supply of *yang* essence. Although *Qilu deng* lacks an overt sexual paradigm, the examples of *Yesou puyan* and other works, including those of the ars erotica and medical belief, supply *Qilu deng* with a reading of the wastrel's helplessness in terms of the male predisposition to depletion. We are again pointed to the underlying assumption in these and other novels of the primacy of the male sexual cycle of energy. Tan Shaowen's innate innocence and uprightness can be read as the expurgated form of the full, erect penis—in the *Laozi* (*Tao Te Ching*), the erect penis of the baby boy (see *Laozi*, ch. 55, 116), who, moreover, "value[s] being fed by the mother" (*Laozi*, ch. 22, 77). What is the situation of absent father and doting mother if not a metaphor of the seduction and overstimulation of the young man's as yet unsettled penis? We must recall, of course, the ars erotica's and medical belief's warnings to the adolescent male about the debilitating consequences of masturbation and imprudent intercourse. The medical moralist also warns against reading about intercourse in erotic books, to which, as we will see, Tan's mother indirectly allows him access. According to this sexual logic, Tan Shaowen is already debilitated before leaving home, where, as we will also see, he sleeps in the same bed with his mother long past the normal age for doing so. He is therefore ripe for the spiraling cycles of stimulation and depletion as incited by predatory friends who lie in wait for the young wastrel.

In what follows, after briefly discussing *Qilu deng*'s textual history, its author, and its plot, I will first address the didactic contents of the novel— that is, the good and bad models it sets forth, and the truisms and bits of wisdom about women and family life that it soberly offers from the perspective of someone who has seen it all. I will then summarize the novel's description of the young man's abandon, starting from the initial moments of excitation and proceeding through the inevitable series of scenes in the life of the thorough wastrel. Throughout I will touch on Tan Shaowen's relationship with his mother and wives, who compete for his attention with his male friends, who in turn seduce him away from women and the bliss of home. As with the proverbial flatterers of the rich man discussed in the chapter on the miser, the contest among his male friends is over who is first to "lick his anus" and "cup his farts," "pull out his scrotum and carry him on their shoulders."[2] The novel's final ideal, a type most fully exemplified in what I will call the "coddled polygynist" in my later discussion of *Ernü yingxiong zhuan*, is the man who correctly internalizes the strictness of fatherly control but at the same time wins the coddling warmth of home, mother, and wives, who on their part neither overindulge him nor meddle with his affairs and make jealous demands upon him.

In contrast to novels like *Lin Lan Xiang, Lüye xianzong, Yesou puyan,* and other little-read works, *Qilu deng* has undergone a peculiar rise from and descent back into obscurity in China in recent years. Finished in 1778, it remained in manuscript form until a Loyang publisher printed a complete but uncollated edition in 1924. Feng Youlan, the well-known historian of Chinese thought, and his younger sister, Feng Shulan, produced a more scholarly edition in Beijing in 1927 but only printed the first twenty-six chapters. Several prominent scholars at the time made mention of the book, among them Guo Shaoyu and Zhu Ziqing in 1928, who both praised it, but *Qilu deng* still failed to catch on as an object of scholarly research or as popular reading matter.[3] In 1980 the Henan scholar Luan Xing finally published a collated and annotated edition in three volumes, which was soon followed by a biography of the author, Li Haiguan (*hao* Lüyuan, 1707–90), and two collections of scholarly essays on the book.[4] The 1980 edition ran to about 400,000 copies, which soon sold out, and was followed by a second edition of over 100,000, with similar results.[5] For a brief time the novel was a minor sensation, another *Honglou meng* or *Rulin waishi* in the eyes of many scholars and booksellers.[6] It was acclaimed for such things as its encyclopedic social realism, its highly unified structure (noted by Guo Shaoyu and Zhu Ziqing as well), its avoidance of eroticism and obscenity, its more colorful use of local vernacular than either *Honglou meng* or *Rulin waishi,* and its greater authenticity than *Honglou meng* in portraying the lower classes.[7] It was also criticized for its traditionalism, negative portrayal of women,[8] and dullness. In terms of literary quality, Luan Xing puts it just below *Honglou meng* and *Rulin waishi,* but above *Ernü yingxiong zhuan* and *Yesou puyan.*[9] In the end, however, after its brief stardom, *Qilu deng* has again lapsed into obscurity and remains mainly a scholar's novel; even scholarly output on it has dropped sharply.[10]

The author, Li Haiguan, was from an educated family who lived in the countryside of Henan Province. He attained the status of provincial graduate (*juren*) but never passed the metropolitan exams and had a relatively unillustrious career. According to Luan Xing, Li began the novel at about age forty-two, wrote the first eighty chapters, and then stopped for twenty years, during which he traveled around China, at one point serving as county magistrate in Guizhou Province. He returned to Henan and finished the novel in 1778 at age 71, after which *Qilu deng* circulated in his home province in manuscript form for many years until its modern printing.[11] The book is concurrent with *Honglou meng* and *Rulin waishi* and describes the same mid-Qing society but shows no sign of the influence of either; Luan Xing believes Li Haiguan was unaware of the other two.[12]

Set in the Jiajing reign period (1522–66) of the Ming dynasty, the novel takes place in the thriving former Song capital of Kaifeng, Henan. The story is about the upbringing of an only son, Tan Shaowen, born late in his father's uneventful life. The father is a literatus who, refusing government service for fear of its political dangers, instead devotes himself to matters of estate and family, especially his son's education.[13] The uneducated mother considers comfort and money more important than urging her son to study hard to serve in office.[14] After his father dies, Tan falls in with a decadent crowd of men who swindle him out of his family money until he finally awakens and regenerates himself. Tan's first wife, more cultivated and disciplined than he, fails to bear offspring and dies from despair at her husband's decline. She is succeeded by a second wife, a woman of urban merchant background who, like Tan's mother, considers money more important than books. Tan has two concubines, the first a maid who joins him before his first marriage and bears him a son, the second given to him after his reform. The second concubine is the daughter of a loyal family servant who himself plays a major role in saving Tan from disaster. The servant is like Tan's first wife in being of higher moral calibre than Tan despite being of lower status and is one of the book's main exemplars of personal virtue.

Qilu Deng on Women and Family Life

Qilu deng is about how a son arrives at being good only after he has been brought up badly. His father is stodgy and pedantic, his mother indulgent and uncultured. The young man has to ruin himself and his family before he finally reforms and raises his own good son.

In that the conjugal environment determines a child's upbringing, the book is also about problems of the relations between husband and wife. Qilu deng represents wives as harmful influences, especially when it comes to raising children and maintaining unity between male relatives. In his manual of advice to heads of families, Shifan, the Song scholar Yuan Cai addresses the pettiness and covetousness of women in situations of dividing property between brothers.[15] Though it never mentions Yuan Cai, Qilu deng might as well be considered a fictionalization of Yuan's earlier warnings. Yuan and the Qilu deng author both admit that good women exist, even ones better than men, but speak with what is for them proven conviction of the problems women create. If a wife is better than her husband, then it is mainly to his shame rather than her glory; men and especially sons are the pivot of society.

In the Confucian family, the "gentleman keeps aloof from his son," as taught in the Lunyu (book 16, no. 13). As long as he is strict and aloof, the father can rest assured that his son will stay on the right path during the stage when the son's "emotional character is not yet set and his experience not yet profound" (*Qilu deng*, ch. 21, 209). The emphasis on "not yet set" recalls Geng Lang's early inability to control himself due to his unsettled nature (*xing bu ziding*, in *Lin Lan Xiang*, ch. 1, 3). The model mother, on the other hand, should know the Confucian woman's skills of sewing and weaving (as also urged in Li Haiguan's own manual of household regulations)[16] and have knowledge of the classics on feminine behavior. As asserted in a narrator's aside in *Qilu deng*, she is a "*fu* [woman / wife] who *fu* [submits to] her husband," not a "*qi* [wife] who is *qi* [equal] and like an adversary to her husband" (ch. 85, 808).[17]

The implication of this last quote is that Tan's mother does in fact act like an equal and an adversary, and therefore dooms the well-being of both father and son. On a more concrete level, because Tan's father is away from home during the son's crucial early years, he effectively cedes control of his son to his wife. Upon return, he finds the boy reading two notorious works, *Xixiang ji* (The Romance of the Western Chamber) and *Jin Ping Mei*, both of which contain material about illicit sexual affairs. The father faints and later dies from the illness brought on by the shock of discovering his son reading these books. "Thus we see what abominable ruination women can cause," he says to himself, angry at his wife's failure to supervise the education of their son (ch. 11, 121–22).

Few men in *Qilu deng* are free of wives or concubines who "ruin things." Three men—Tan's generous gambling friend Sheng Xiqiao (chs. 69–70), a pedantic tutor (ch. 39, 362ff), and an older gentleman-literatus (ch. 67)—are all forced into embarrassing situations because of covetous or jealous women. Reverse situations also occur in which a mother is wisely protective of a child but a father is permissive (ch. 42, 390–91), or in which a widow is outstandingly virtuous (ch. 41). In the latter instance, the widow chooses suicide rather than remarriage, thus contrasting with a shrewish widow who remarries and causes her sage second husband to betray his brother (chs. 39–41). In the case of Tan's father, his pedantic nature provides the reason for both his weakness before his wife and his mortal vulnerability to the shock of discovering his son's reading material. Judged by other characters in the book, the father is too *yu*, that is, "stiff, pedantic, overly adherent to rules" (ch. 7, 67), and too "strict and inflexible" (ch. 39, 360). From the example of the shrewish widow just mentioned, however, it seems that some women exist to whom even nonpedantic and sage men are vulnerable. Again the implication is that women who "are equal and like adversaries" doom the well-being of men, who are by definition inherently weaker.

Tan's wife is a model woman with the same last name as Confucius, Kong, in other words, "a man among women." Like Yan Mengqing in *Lin Lan Xiang,* she is unable to control her husband and eventually dies of the misery caused by his misbehavior. On her death bed she warns the maid Bingmei, her husband's chamber-wife, not to upset or anger Tan: "Men are such that when they become angry they not only can't repent but they'll say you incited them. They'll always insist they are right" (ch. 47, 440). She adds that Tan is "a man without any head of his own; he's been lured by others into ruination" (ch. 47, 439). However aware of his nature she might be, as "a man among women" she is not one to take advantage of her husband's "lack of a head of his own." She can only convey the truism that women must bear the brunt of male self-frustration, and she thus warns her successor to take heed. Her warning translates into the idea that once a man is spoiled, he can take nothing but smothering love from a woman. At the same time, although *Qilu deng* does not actually say so, it seems that he cannot stand that doting love and finds any opportunity to spite or escape it, but he also then tries to rediscover it elsewhere, supposedly on his own terms—thus, for example, the case of the wastrel seeking the prostitute, as examined in the next chapter.

In summing up its conclusions about women, *Qilu deng* states that, outside of the few like Tan's first wife, most are the cause of endless troubles. A man fares well until marriage, but as soon as he marries, first there is "murmuring"—that is, female meddling—and then there are splits between fathers and sons, sons and brothers. "Therefore it is said: the first rule of running a home is not to listen to the wife" (ch. 36, 333). The "shrewish tongue" (*pojian shetou,* ch. 36, 334) and "the roar of the lioness" (*shizi hou,* ch. 39, 364) are the expressions used here as in other works to refer to women of harmful influence.

The Ruination Caused by Motherly Love

The novel traces Tan's evolution from an innocent who is afraid of gambling and prostitution to a profligate who, at his extreme, after finally interring his father's coffin in the family burial ground, turns his own home into a den of gambling and prostitution. One of *Qilu deng*'s main tasks is to describe the discrete moments and details of the spoiled son's decline—in particular, to show how and when restlessness gets the better of him. The presumption is that he is innocent and clear-headed to begin with, and that if he were to "read good books," like this novel, and "associate only with correct people," then he would be able to distinguish good from bad (ch. 61, 573). But various accidents occur that push him in the wrong direction before he attains the clarity of self-control. These accidents and his psychological changes along the way constitute the details of his downfall.

For example, back from an excursion, his father is angry to find his son outside playing, not inside studying. But the father is momentarily interrupted by something else and, when he returns, his anger has passed (ch. 1, 10). The accident of a few missed moments deprives the son of the benefit of vigorous correction. His mother does not care to begin with. Worse damage occurs when the father is away for two years on a trip to Beijing to receive special imperial honors. During the mother-indulged idleness of this period, Tan learns to experience "boredom," *men*, and acquires a taste for "fun" and "entertainment," *le* (ch. 8, 92). *Men* and *le* are two labels for new psychological developments in the young man.

The initial phase of his corruption—after he has already learned boredom and developed a need for stimulation—occurs when he forms his first bonds of male camaraderie. "Liking the wrong people" (*cuo'ai*), he swears brotherhood with gamblers and sycophants who compete to make the most money off the rich young man (ch. 15, 158; the author's manual of household regulations specifically condemns the swearing of kinship with nonrelatives[18]). At first it is a matter of minor gambling with his friend Sheng Xiqiao, an advanced hedonist but one who still upholds values of honor and righteousness (ch. 16). Sheng later helps Tan out of predicaments brought on by associations with worse male friends (ch. 27, 255).

At the beginning of his friendship with Sheng, Tan is "extremely uneasy" when Sheng wants to swear brotherhood (ch. 16, 166); his heart thumps, his face turns red. On another occasion, Tan is content to sit idly and chat, but Sheng is a type who "cannot sit leisurely" and must have "games" or "things to play with" (ch. 16, 171). Sheng gets Tan to gamble; Tan is nervous at first, but once he starts, he grows bold and soon begins to flirt with a woman hired to accompany them (172). "As people of old used to say: 'As long as that which is desirable is out of sight, the heart will not grow wild' " (ch. 17, 177; directly quoting from the *Laozi*).

Another fatal step in Tan's decline is his decision to stop telling his mother his whereabouts when he leaves home. He will not sleep in the same bed with her anymore; thus we learn that he has been sleeping with his mother until much older than normally allowed in elite households (ch. 19, 192–93).[19] While he is in his mother's care, the spoiled son cannot escape her watch for more than a few hours a day. Once he is free of her he begins to be away for days and nights in a row. On a few occasions he tries to break with his new friends and return to a steady life at home. In one such interim of repentance he spends an idyllic time with his wife and concubine until restlessness again gets the better of him (ch. 35, 328). In the end, he can always leave them and be guaranteed that they will never leave him.

In textbooklike exposition, *Qilu deng* demonstrates how each new experience exposes Tan to new excitement: going to a restaurant for the first time, to a gambling den; having his first sex with a boy actor, then a prostitute; going out at night after curfew (all in ch. 24); committing adultery with another man's wife (ch. 29); eyeing women in public places (ch. 49). He is ignorant of the fact that his friends are cheaters and sycophants whose sole livelihood is to make a profit from spoiled sons, one of the friends being such a wastrel son himself (ch. 42, 390). Their easy friendship is what first attracts Tan. As the narrator concludes, echoing the voice of male elders, in new relationships one should at first be "stiff" or "restrained" (*jushu*) and avoid immediate gregariousness (ch. 99, 926).

Tan's troubles deepen each time until he is forced into one of the direst situations of all. In order to repay gambling debts, he must sell ancestral property, including the trees around his father's grave. He is remorseful after each failure: he beats his head against the wall (ch. 25); he leaves home in desperation without telling anyone and on the road loses everything he has (ch. 44); he tries to hang himself (ch. 59). He manages to extricate himself each time, however, mainly by virtue of his high social status. Guardian angels in the form of magistrates or his father's old friends step in at the last moment to rescue him, doing so out of sympathy for a fellow of their own class.

His failures kill both his father and wife; the first dies of shock, the second of grief. His mother forgives him each time and agrees to his most deviant exploits. His second wife, a lower-class woman who likes to watch opera and play cards, never reprimands him. He has only a loyal family servant, Wang Zhong, to remind him of the proper path.[20]

The bottoming out of Tan's decline and his turn for the better occur around the time he tells his mother how much she has spoiled him. His father died too early, he says, and then, "Mother, you loved me too dearly; you spoiled me and made me turn out all wrong" (ni you jian wo taiqin, jiaoguande buxiangyang, ch. 86, 816). Although at first she does not understand—replying, "You mean loving you dearly is bad?"—she is soon brought around by her son's clear logic. Thereafter, Tan and his son study their books together until they pass the state exams.

As said near the end of the book, Tan learns to restrain himself because he has been through all the ordeals that a "wanton" (fulang) son can experience (ch. 105, 984–85). He is now a responsible official, husband, and father with an equally responsible son. Those subordinate to him need no longer fear that he will abuse his privileges as head of a family or as an official.

The Wastrel versus the Shrew

Although Qilu deng makes only passing reference to Tan's sleeping with his mother, the inclusion of this minor detail recapitulates the theme found throughout Ming and Qing fiction of the causal connection between the doting mother and the wastrel son. The implication is that a mother's doting love causes an emasculation of the young man. Comparison of Qilu deng with the chaste romances and Honglou meng is instructive at this point. The scholar is also fatherless, often raised only by his mother, and is explicitly described as having feminine features. Likewise, Jia Baoyu is raised by a strict and aloof father and is close to his grandmother and female cousins (although not particularly to his mother); he too is feminine in appearance and behavior. But a divergence occurs in the characterization of sons who have a weak fatherly and a strong motherly presence. In the perspective of works like Qilu deng and Lüye xianzong, to be examined in the next chapter, closeness with the mother causes a debilitating loss of self-control in the son, turning him into a wastrel. Works like Honglou meng and the romances, however, affirm the man's feminine qualities, engaging in the elevation and even veneration of women (though not without male-privileging effects, as I have shown in chapters above). Simply put, the difference is between condemned emasculation and affirmed feminization.

To the moralist reader, the young man's prolonged contact with his mother, other female relatives, and in-laws is nothing short of lustful and incestuous. Although *Qilu deng* avoids ascribing lust (*yin*) to Tan's relations with his mother and wives, Tan's blaming of his mother for spoiling him implies that had she not so inured him to idleness and pleasure, he would not have been predisposed to the attractions of gambling and sex. Again, comparison with *Honglou meng* is instructive. Jia Baoyu is allowed by his female elders to take a maid as sex partner. He looks like a girl; his room is like a girl's; he prefers the feminine art of poetry to the masculine one of "eight-legged" exam essays. Tan sleeps with his mother, shuns studying for the exams, and becomes so indebted because of gambling that he sells ancestral property and, in the most phallically symbolic gesture, cuts down the trees around his father's grave. In short, doting motherly love effects a castration of both self and father.

Nevertheless, the didactic project of *Qilu deng* is not only to condemn the bad influence of women but also to admit the inherent dangers of raising and depending upon a son—and to propose the need, therefore, for a kind of controlled coddling of the son and later grown man. In chapter 35, *Qilu deng* supplies a preliminary model of such controlled coddling by creating a scene of idyllic home life with the right type of women, Tan's good first wife and concubine. Although the fatherless Tan lacks an adequate sense of discipline, his interims at home with his wives constitute a salutary alternative to time spent with "wine and meat comrades." The scene of peaceful domesticity remotely foretells the situation of a late Qing story in which a young man's parents deliberately addict him to opium in order to keep him at home—and to thus protect the family savings—instead of going out to "visit prostitutes and gamble" (the notion that addiction kept men out of trouble was proverbial during the opium era).[21]

Short of either imprisoning or addicting him, how can one discipline the young man, at the same time keeping him happy at home? Based on a collective reading of *Qilu deng*, *Lüye xianzong*, *Honglou meng* and other works about wastrel sons, two answers to this question emerge. The main one implies the inevitability of wastrel behavior; the other in the meantime proposes ways by which father and mother can prevent their son from becoming a wastrel. According to the first answer, the son's predisposition can eventually work itself out, but only through the replay of the cycle of male self-containment that I have elsewhere discussed: in order to attain tempered equilibrium, the man has to experience the plunge from comfortable, innate containment into the reality of contingency.[22] He has to part from the naive, seemingly harmless anarchy of youth and enter the uncontrollable and chaotic world of the senses. He has to suffer the consequences of disobeying the rules in order to understand why the rules should be obeyed. In Tan's case, he is sandwiched between the extremes of the "dry" correctness of his father and the "wet" indulgence of his mother—behaviors which, according to the second answer, can theoretically be rectified. Once he puts such harmful influences in perspective, he begins to accept the help and advice of the only sensible people he knows, his wise family servant Wang and his maid-concubine Bingmei, who are like loyal ministers helping a reformist emperor; until the time of reform, they are exiled or ignored.[23]

Why a whole book on the wastrel son? How does he compare to the shrew, who also has whole books devoted to her? In *Shifan*, Yuan Cai says: "As a general rule, among ten or more well-behaved sons and grandsons, there will be one who is unworthy. There are cases where the dozen good ones all suffer because of the single bad one, even to the point where the family is ruined" (Ebrey, 228); also, "Having too many sons is certainly something to worry about" (213). In his work on family management, *Jiafan* (Family Forms), the famous Song historian Sima Guang (1019–1086) says, "What took a man several decades of hard work to accumulate, his sons can dissipate through extravagance in a year."[24] The problem is that of succession: how to ensure integrity in the son who inherits the wealth and power of the father. The analogy of the son to the prince or emperor is again appropriate, the problem of inheritance translating at the highest social level into the predicament of imperial succession, whether or not an author may have intended such an allegory. The emperor grows up in close company with female relatives and in-laws, harem women, and eunuchs, and is likewise subject to the dangers of spoiling emasculation. The unspoken conclusion of *Qilu deng* and other novels dealing with the wastrel son is that it is impossible to ensure healthy succession for long. It is only through the fictional, comic ending of *Qilu deng* that the son manages to reform himself and have his own good son.

As for the shrew, she is perhaps less powerfully harmful than the wastrel because she has fewer legal and customary rights. But if the man is henpecked, she can manipulate him so that in effect she has the same or greater power, even if not in name. She is a wastrel daughter, doted upon by her parents who raise her as if she were a son, like Wang Xifeng in *Honglou meng.* Although she cannot inherit the powers of the father, she does whatever she can to undermine her husband and marshal his resources. She acts desperately and outrageously, somewhat like the wastrel son. He acts out of indulgence and knowledge of his immunity, however; she out of the knowledge of her social inferiority to the man but also her hopeful mastery over him. Her livelihood can be jeopardized any time the husband wakes up from being henpecked, but he rarely does so.

From the male viewpoint, the emotional intensity of the shrew story lies in the man's frustration at his subjection to his wife, who inhibits his freedom to socialize, to manage money and property, and to seek other sexual partners. The intensity of the story about the spoiled son lies in the young man's frustration at his inability to control himself. The freedom he is given ends up by causing him to unravel. Thus, the strength of Tan's frustration in *Qilu deng* is shown when he knocks his head against the wall in remorse and cries to his mother, "I'm a failure of a person" (wo suanbude yige ren le, ch. 26, 245); or when he runs away from home, loses all he has, and discovers the raw existence of vagabonds and swindlers who nearly prevent his ever returning home; or when he tries to hang himself after yet another lapse of self-control. The shrew never attempts such self-destruction, although her path is in effect equally or even more suicidal. To keep herself going, she tries to control or destroy both the man and rival women. The spoiled son, who suffers from no shrew and thus no inhibition to his freedom, nevertheless has no sustained object. His aimlessness only leads to loss of *benqian,* "capital," both monetary and sexual, which he can recover only by returning to the normative path of learning, exam taking, and, as taught in *Lin Lan Xiang* and *Qilu deng,* listening to his loyal concubines and servants.

11

THE OTHER SCHOLAR AND BEAUTY:

THE WASTREL AND THE PROSTITUTE

IN *LÜYE XIANZONG*

Lüye xianzong (Trails of Immortals in the Green Wilds) is one of a handful of lengthy and didactically erotic novels of the Ming and Qing that present an antisexual message while explicitly describing sexual acts. The antisexual message is advanced by its ascetic hero, Leng Yubing, who early in the novel forsakes wife and worldly affairs in pursuit of Taoist immortality. The explicitly described sexual acts occur between young lovers who, despite their occupying lower levels of existence than the self-cultivating hero, are the closest to monogamous sexual lovers of any characters in Qing fiction. As will be recalled, the rule of the beauty-scholar romances was that once there was explicitly described sex, there was also polygyny. *Lüye xianzong,* however, portrays passionate sexual and emotional attachment between monogamous lovers, one pair of whom actually succeeds in marrying. All of these lovers do what the chaste beauty and scholar do not do (and what Daiyu and Baoyu by comparison only partially do): declare and act out the sexual and emotional intensity of their mutual attraction.

The hero of *Lüye xianzong* is like *Yesou puyan*'s Wen Suchen in his superhuman powers, his heroic mission to conquer human and demonic evil, and his immunity to sexual temptation. But unlike Wen, he leaves the problems of sexuality and male-female conflict entirely to the less gifted people of the world.[1] For them lust is a furious and untamable drive; their sex is noisy and rough. The author also portrays sex as a false way to immortality on the part of mainly female demons who try to sap men of their *yang* essence (as in ch. 45). Leng Yubing, whose name means "colder than ice," fights a number of these female demons, from one of whom he steals back a book containing all the secret formulas of heaven and earth (chs. 61–62). Unlike *Lin Lan Xiang* and *Qilu deng, Lüye xianzong* features neither the superiority of women nor their suffering and doom because of their relationships with inferior men. Instead, although they can be formidable partners, women yield themselves to men once they find one with supreme sexual skills. In general, as in *Qilu deng, Lüye xianzong*'s women are shortsighted and conniving. Because weak men fail to control them and themselves, women are the cause of society's myriad ills. The venality of some men even takes the form of their adoption of the seductive ways of women in order to cheat other men.[2]

The main focus of my presentation of *Lüye xianzong* will be upon the manner in which the author subsumes his portrayal of monogamous sexual love under a larger framework that declares sexual desire intractable. The same subsumption also works to hide the articulation of women's demands under the theme of the danger and inferiority of women. Three episodes of sexual encounter serve as examples in this chapter, the most important of which I have mentioned before in chapter 1: the love affair between the wastrel Wen Ruyu and the prostitute Jinzhonger, who is managed by her own parents.[3] This particular couple, the wastrel and the prostitute, represents a far opposite of the scholar and the beauty but at the same time forms an equally apt match. That is, they can be said to be made for each other just as much as the scholar and the beauty. As I said in the last chapter when comparing the shrew and the spoiled son, the latter has little to restrain him and no mission to guide him and thus aimlessly but luxuriously destroys himself. The prostitute, on the other hand, is bait her parents set out to attract the wastrel and, in effect, transfer his wealth from his family to her own. If she were a normal daughter, she would be married once and for all, bringing profit, if possible, to her natal family only once but otherwise constituting a loss. As a prostituted daughter, however, she keeps bringing profit because, as her parents know, there are always wastrels, and wastrels always fall for prostitutes. Like the wastrel's doting mother, a prostitute will cater to his pleasures in order to keep him coming back. At first, as with the scholar and the beauty, the youths' love has a liberating effect, especially in her case because she now hopes to buy herself out of prostitution, but also in his case because he feels he has now won a supposedly genuine love on his own terms and with his own resources. But as their love persists, the money that makes their liberation possible then disappears. The difference between their gendered positions emerges in the fact that her only escape is suicide, whereas he can escape by awakening in time like Tan Shaowen in *Qilu deng* or by becoming an ascetic and abandoning all family obligations, as Wen Ruyu eventually will (but hasn't yet by the end of the novel). As this and the other episodes will show, the author foregrounds the intensity and exclusivity of sexual love between two people who are like sexualized versions of the beauty and the scholar. At the same time, the author strictly frames their love within the miserly-ascetic paradigm of profit and loss and of *yang* strengthening and depletion.

The author of *Lüye xianzong* is Li Baichuan who, according to his preface, began writing the novel during his mid-thirties in 1753 in the city of Yangzhou and finished it in 1762 in Henan Province. All that we know of him derives from this autobiographical preface, which further indicates that he once suffered great loss in a commercial venture, settled in Yangzhou to nurse an illness, and during this interval began writing the novel as a cure for depression. He interrupted his writing to serve as secretary to officials and other members of the elite, gradually finishing the book during his tenures in various parts of the country. He was a lover of ghost (*gui*) stories, which he used, as other authors did, to couch political and social satire and generate flights of sometimes grotesque fantasy. Neither the novel nor any of its prefaces refer to *Rulin waishi* or *Honglou meng*. *Lüye xianzong* is thus another of several novels of major length—including *Honglou meng, Rulin waishi, Yesou puyan, Lin Lan Xiang,* and *Qilu deng*—which appeared in the mid-eighteenth century or so, all seemingly independent literary discoveries of the world of that time.

Lüye xianzong has had both one-hundred-chapter and eighty-chapter versions, the former thought to have been written first, both existing in censored and uncensored forms.[4] Few scholars in China have as yet written of this work; several major histories of literature and fiction even fail to mention it.[5] In 1927 Zheng Zhenduo praised its style and excellence of description, as have others more recently, including Tan Zhengbi and Cai Guoliang.[6] Critics consider one of the highlights of the book to be the episode about Wen Ruyu and Jinzhonger, which Zheng Zhenduo judged not only the best part of the novel but the best example of all "brothel literature" in China. As he no doubt had in mind, the prostitute plays a major role in later Qing and Republican fiction, in which she is characterized as the ruthless destroyer of men, for example, or the innocent victim hardened by fate.

The novel begins when Leng Yubing's father dies of a cold caught while viewing the moon, which perhaps signifies debilitating female influence, to which Leng is impervious because he is "colder than ice" (ch. 1, 3). His mother dies shortly after. The orphan Leng eventually passes the state examinations but is disqualified by the notorious Grand Secretary Yan Song (a real figure, 1480–1565), whom the righteous Leng boldly offends. After further encounters with the evil Yan Song, Leng leaves home to become a Taoist immortal. The narrative splits into several interconnecting plots about humans, demons, and immortals, with Yan Song and the people he harms appearing intermittently. In one episode, for example, Leng Yubing encounters a rare good female immortal battling male demons. When he asks her why she doesn't take the obvious course of refining herself into a man, she laughs: "The myriad phenomena divide into either *yin* or *yang*" (ch. 16, 115), after which they part amicably as she presents him with fruits of longevity. In more earthly contexts, Leng battles bandits, one of whose leaders is a woman who practices evil arts (ch. 26 and following), or he helps conquer Japanese pirates (ch. 78).

One of the longest episodes in the novel is about Wen Ruyu, the fatherless wastrel who in Leng's eyes nevertheless has the potential to attain immortality (chs. 36–60, with other episodes interspersed). Ruyu squanders his wealth on the prostitute Jinzhonger, who commits suicide when Ruyu fails to buy her out of prostitution. At first devastated by her death, he later meets two other women, each of whom he feels surpasses Jinzhonger. Meanwhile, Ruyu becomes Leng's disciple but by the end of the novel has not yet rid himself of sexual desire.

In another long episode, a married man named Zhou Lian has a sexual affair with his neighbor's unmarried daughter, Huiniang, who he then brings into his family as co-wife. He drives his first wife to suicide, after which a beautiful female demon captivates him and forbids him contact with Huiniang. One of Leng's disciples exorcises the demon; Zhou and Huiniang then become a good monogamous couple (chs. 79–90).

After the demise of Yan Song (chs. 91–92), Leng gathers his disciples for a test to see who is closest to enlightenment. Wen Ruyu and a female disciple, Cui Dai, still succumb to sexual temptation, thus failing the test. Leng returns them to their path of self-cultivation, swallows "a pill to break with the earth-*yin*" (ch. 98, 806), and then ascends to Taoist heaven where he is appointed to high office.

The Wastrel and the Prostitute

In its portrayals of sexual encounter, as I have said, *Lüye xianzong* is like *Yesou puyan* in taking the antisensualist stance of the main hero. It is devoid of the superior youths of either chaste or erotic romances. In *Lüye xianzong* youths have no worthy viewpoints, all worth instead deriving from years of self-cultivation and abstention. In the episodes examined below, the wives are shrewish, the husbands are henpecked. Mothers indulge their sons or try to profit from their daughters' suitors. Youths resist the control of their parents, succumb to love and sexual desire, but in the end are caught in the syndrome of "liking the new and tiring of the old," *xi xin yan jiu*.

The first episode of sexual involvement concerns the aforementioned Wen Ruyu and Jinzhonger. The prostitute is traditionally the one kind of woman who can do to the man what he usually does to her, "like the new and tire of the old," and do so loudly and brazenly. Jinzhonger takes a richer customer, Master He, while the poorer Ruyu is still living with her family. Ruyu is jealous but polite, and is even impressed by He until he overhears them having sex at night and then in the middle of the day (chs. 47, 48). At a gathering in which He is present, Ruyu and Jinzhonger sing raucous songs mocking each other, he about her inconstancy and shameless lovemaking, she about his jealousy and pretention to being her number one lover: "If you want me to be loyal to one and only one, you'll have to sew up my sex from its front to its back" (ch. 48, 388). A fight erupts in which Ruyu slaps her in front of Master He and others.

Although Jinzhonger is neither sentimentalized nor pitied, as the prostitute / singing girl often is in Chinese literature, her predicament is nevertheless spelled out from the perspective of her own thoughts. In one passage she debates with herself about merits of the poor Wen Ruyu versus the rich Master He. Although Wen has been kinder to her, she decides that He is more likely to buy her out of prostitution (ch. 49, 392). Master He suddenly departs, however, leaving Jinzhonger's parents trying to persuade Ruyu, who still commands resources, to return. Her mother and father need to make money; Jinzhonger wants to marry out of bondage (*congliang*). In character, she is "sassy, strong-headed, and as hard to deal with as a whore can be" (ch. 44, 348); she is intelligent (ch. 43, 338) and is particular about men (ch. 44, 348). She likes them to be "romantic," *fengliu,* more than she likes them to be rich, and thus ultimately she prefers the poorer but more *fengliu* Wen Ruyu to the rich Master He.

As becomes clear in the scene excerpted below, what *fengliu* means to the author of *Lüye xianzong* is Wen's ability to drive Jinzhonger into sexual ecstasy. But in contrast to the erotic romance, which tends to focus on sheer sexual performance, *Lüye xianzong* also provides the lovers with egos that battle over who surrenders first or who feels the most resentment. Although Ruyu wins, so to speak, by conquering her with his penis, he does so only after frustratedly lying in bed with her without speaking for several hours, then deciding to leave in the middle of the night, and thus sparking the outburst of anger and emotion which finally breaks their deadlock (ch. 51). Again, as I have said, they do what the scholar and the beauty and what Baoyu and Daiyu do not do: dramatize the love bond on the loudest, most vulgar and visceral levels.

A character named "Bald Miao" (Miao Tuzi) persuades Ruyu to return to Jinzhonger's home, but the lovers are initially too proud to reconcile. I have translated a lengthy part of the passage describing their reconciliation:

When Jinzhonger saw that everyone had left, she drew the pillow over and lay on the bed as before, ignoring Ruyu, who sat muttering to himself not knowing what to do. Some time passed before he noticed that she still hadn't moved. He spied some books on top of the chest and took them down, but they were only fortune-telling manuals, which he found of little interest. Meanwhile he kept stealing glances at Jinzhonger.

At about the first watch Jinzhonger got up to take the candle from Ruyu's side over to her mirror stand. She set her hair and wrapped it in a scarf, then rinsed her mouth with tea which she spat out on the floor. She went to the bed, opened out the quilt and arranged it properly, then undid the fastenings of her clothing, but stopped short of changing into her sleep slippers. She turned to him and said: "Are you going to sit there all night? Have I offended you or something?"

He replied that he would be going to sleep shortly. She took off her clothes and lay down facing the inside, while Ruyu sat immobile for the time it takes to drink two cups of tea. Then he disrobed and got under the quilt on the right side of the bed, away from Jinzhonger. There he lay face up and full of frustration.

Jinzhonger was waiting for him to plead with her and didn't want to lower herself by hugging Ruyu, who was anxious to make up but was likewise unwilling to give in. So in the end both were putting on an act and neither could get to sleep.

At about the second watch Ruyu still heard no sound of sleep from her and said to himself: "Why suffer such misery? I might as well go to the outer room and wait for dawn there. That's what I should do."

He lifted the covers to grab his clothes and started to put them on. But just as he was about to slip into his pants, Jinzhonger turned over and said, "Why are you putting your clothes on at this time of the night?"

"I'm going to fetch Master He for you."

"You still dare talk to me like that?," she replied.

"How else should I talk?"

Jinzhonger looked at him and shook her head, tears falling in streams by her pillow. Ruyu held his pants out, but couldn't get them on he was so agitated. "If you have something to tell me then why not say it clearly once and for all!"

Jinzhonger replied, "That's enough! Just slap me a few more times and that will do it!" She bolted up, took his clothes and with all her might hurled them off the bed. With anguished tears she lay down again, her face toward the inside. Ruyu dove under the covers and hugged her tightly from behind, "Are you going to keep being angry with me now!?"

Jinzhonger still wouldn't respond. Ruyu pulled her to his side, put his right leg over her body and his left arm under her neck. Then he kissed her twice on the mouth and wiped off her tears with his cheeks. Smiling he said, "Who made you love that Master He as if he were the most precious thing in the world and treat me like a pile of manure?"

"Even if I did love Master He, it was just a case of the fickle and flighty nature of a woman; there was no call to slap me!"

"You didn't have to call me degrading names in front of so many people either," replied Ruyu.

"You called me enough names to fill a shelf's-worth of books; are you going to keep tally now?! We've been together for almost a year. We've had good times and bad, and you still go so low as to slap me." She pushed him away.

He laughed, "There's no need to push me. I had no other way to get revenge. I'm going to teach you a lesson tonight and make you give in!" Without further ado, he parted her legs and blindly stabbed his penis at her *yin*-gate. Jinzhonger pleaded, "Slow down, you're hurting me."

Leaving them to their bedchambering, let us speak of Bald Miao and his Yuqinger. They finished one session and went to sleep, but he awoke and began to wonder whether Wen and Jinzhonger had made up or not. "Let me go spy on what they are up to." He threw a cloak over his shoulders and went to open the door. Yuqinger asked him where he was going. "To move my bowels," he replied.

He tiptoed out through the hall to the east-chamber window, from which he heard the most wild and furious racket. With his fingertip he hurriedly made a small opening in the paper window, then peeked inside. Ruyu had hold of her right leg; her left leg was around his waist. She wore red satin flat-soled slippers with flower designs. Her feet were short and tiny, finer than Yuqinger's by far, and made a very delightful sight. Then he looked at Ruyu's penis. It was nearly six inches long, thick and strong, and thrust in and out of Jinzhonger's *yin*-gate like a huge serpent boring into its den. In ceaseless motion, the flesh around her *yin*-gate billowed out then back in; the waters of lust gushed forth. Bald Miao said to himself, "After all these years of whoring, I've never seen it so clearly. So it's the lust waters that make that sound."

He looked again. Jinzhonger rolled her starry eyes. Her powdered face was flushed, her body was powerless to take him on, she couldn't catch her breath, she moaned and gnashed her teeth. Bald Miao was extremely entertained, but sighed, "Wen spent a simple sum of money and got what he paid for. For some reason poor old me didn't fare so well."

Then he saw Ruyu suddenly lift up both of Jinzhonger's legs and wildly thrust away, faster and faster with each stroke. Jinzhonger stared straight ahead and held on tightly to Ruyu's sides, calling out loudly, "My dearest *dada*,[7] I'm going to die this time." She shook her head furiously, then her breathing became hardly discernible, she was as if fainting, her face grew pale.

Bald Miao could take no more. He felt his penis; it was as hard as an iron spear. He rushed back to Yuqinger, only to find her out of bed, sitting on the chamber-pot taking a pee. He took no account of this, bent over and picked her up, but was too headlong and picked up the pot too. Yuqinger was frightened out of her wits.

"What are you doing!?," she yelled.

Throwing down the pot, Miao carried her to the edge of the bed, put her down, and madly drove his penis inside. But he was too excited to exercise any skillful technique, and before seven or eight thrusts, was over and done with. He took himself out, stood up, and breathed a long sigh. Then he dove under the covers and made as if to go to sleep [ignoring her raving which went on for some time; see ch. 51, 409; for censored portions, see ch. 51, 633a–634b].

Like the lovers in the erotic romance, Wen Ruyu and Jinzhonger are enviable models for inferior beings like Miao. The author portrays Wen as sexually skillful, reflecting the implicit theme of the ars erotica that men must use skill, but women need not do so and are in fact unwelcome if they do. Ruyu and two other men, who appear later in the novel, are supreme love-makers who never experience the slightest dysfunction or lack of energy, except with demon-women; it is all mortal women can do to keep up with them.

After this and one other long session of furious sex, Jinzhonger's love for Ruyu is sealed once and for all. "I have had climaxes [*diu shenzi*] ever since I began this life at sixteen, but never as strongly as now," she says (ch. 52, 415). From her perspective, passion has a liberating effect, for now she decides to try and buy herself out of prostitution and marry Wen Ruyu. In the narrator's eyes, however, her avowal of pleasure is a sign of female weakness. The last words of chapter 52 sum up Ruyu's and Jinzhonger's situation with a quotation from the so-called Classic of the Prostitute: "Nine of ten women love to make love; though you screw them to death they still want more. If indeed you can please them in that fierce battle of sex, then any flower girl in the universe will be as if in the palm of your hand" (ch. 52, 417). The commentator of the manuscript edition agrees, saying that the difference between the whore and the "good woman" lies precisely in this, that the whore will become truly loyal only if the man has superior sexual skills, regardless of his talent or wealth (ch. 52, 649a). The moral, in short, is that Jinzhonger's passion-based commitment is foolish because a wastrel will never have enough money or resolve to free her from her parents.

First, however, the power of their attraction carries Wen and Jin-zhonger through several more months, during which they make love day after day, even "during broad daylight" (ch. 55, 437), now behaving like Jinzhonger and Master He when Ruyu overheard them. The spectacle of lovemaking strikes yet another listener, in this case Jinzhonger's mother, who spies on them and discovers that the intensity of their sex produces more noise than "three or four people washing clothes" (ch. 54, 674a). She figures she has lived in vain to have missed out on such sex but still has no intention of letting her daughter marry Ruyu. Besides being a sign of female weakness, Jinzhonger's pleasure is thus also something without which a woman supposedly lives in vain. In this as in another voyeured scene shown below, *Lüye xianzong* resembles the erotic romance in foregrounding the raw ferocity of sexual passion, especially the woman's. But instead of domesticating that passion within the hierarchy of the polygynist household, *Lüye xianzong* portrays the woman pushing her monogamous determination to its disastrous extreme.

In the final stage of the love affair, Ruyu's and Jinzhonger's plan to buy her freedom fails. When her mother confronts her, Jinzhonger declares, "I am in love with him," *wo xinshang ai ta* (ch. 56, 447). Jinzhonger's father drags her down by her hair and beats her; her mother madly bites at her head and face. In a final act of defiance, Jinzhonger swallows face powder containing mercury and dies gruesomely (448).

The directness of the words "I am in love with him" is rare in Chinese fiction of the Ming and Qing, where the word *ai* or words like it meaning "love someone" rarely appear outside illicit affairs or sexual relations in the brothel.[8] *Ai* is the modern Chinese word used to translate both the noun and verb for "love" (or its European language equivalents), but in *Lüye xianzong* it denotes immoderate affection, including the excess affection of a mother for her spoiled son (Wen's mother confesses that her "loving"—*ai*—him has ultimately "killed" him, ch. 42, 326; also recall that Tan Shaowen "loves the wrong" friends, *cuo'ai*, in *Qilu deng*, ch. 15, 158). In this pejorative sense, Jinzhonger's *ai* is the sign of her being won over or driven by Wen Ruyu. Both she and he are as if addicted to each other. But although she is granted no credit, her *ai* is also an expression of a radical defiance which she acts out in the most extreme way possible by committing suicide. She is the book's negative or desublimated hero, then, whose passion is as strong an expression of self-determination as Leng Yubing's desire to stop desire, that is, to hyper-sublimate. As that desublimated hero, in using the word *ai* she says what a chaste beauty or a Lin Daiyu could or would never say, however they might feel. According to this same logic of desublimation, it could be said that instead of matched poetry, she and her lover exchange raucous songs; instead of standing face to face in cross-dress, Wen and Jinzhonger declare their love in flesh and try literally to buy liberation from her proprietor-parents. For her, *ai* is a down-to-earth counterpart of *qing* (emotion, feeling, sentiment, only occurring as a noun), the much exalted term found in both chaste and erotic contexts in the Ming and Qing referring to lofty romantic bonds. Both *ai* and *qing* (which conjoin in the modern compound *aiqing*, also used to mean "love") represent types of attachment that evade the directives of the kinship system, which deemphasizes subjective and contingent wishes in favor of hierarchical group harmony and profit. But whereas *qing* can be reaccommodated by the kinship system, as the conclusion to the late Ming play *Mudan ting* and other stories demonstrate, *ai* is too raw and direct a challenge against the miserly order of family profit.

Ai, however, undergoes a transformation of meaning when it appears in the balanced, orthodox term for affection between husband and wife, *fuqi en'ai,* "conjugal love." Here the addition of the word *en* provides the sense of "kindness" and "mutual obligation." This term is used to describe Wen Ruyu's next affair, which occurs in a dream that Leng Yubing causes Ruyu to have in which Ruyu marries a princess and becomes a high official in his father-in-law's kingdom. The Princess is "endlessly sweet and lovely," unlike Jinzhonger with her "foxish eyebrows and devilish eyes, able to overpower people with her looseness alone" (ch. 66, 525). The dream of worldly success, a common trope in Chinese narrative, carries the theme of the ephemerality of life, which by implication is itself a dream, as Leng hopes Ruyu will learn.

With Wen Ruyu and Jinzhonger, Li Baichuan portrays the rawest form of sexual love in explicit vernacular. In Ruyu's dream he goes to another extreme of description, the high erotic, by adopting the style of parallel prose and using imagery like that in the classic ars erotica. He provides only one portrayal of sex between Ruyu and his princess-wife, who are on the marriage bed for the first time:

> The one is the King's cherished Princess, a far cry from the coquettish daughter of a mere court official. The Princess's demands are far greater: she will tease, she will be headstrong, she will have her husband be humble and submissive. He must be able to fathom her innermost nature.
>
> The other[9] is an old hand of the brothels, not to be taken as an innocent in love. He is thoroughly skilled in clever talk and all manner of flirtation. He

knows how to handle every hurt, every pout. He tenderly anticipates her most delicate feelings.

The one is new to the clouds and rain; she half resists, half consents. She presses her hands to his belly to hold him back.

The other is well versed in the art of love, knows how to alternate between deep and shallow. He insists on putting the bar through the gate.

The one knits her brows and with weak voice softly pleads: "Royal son-in-law, please be considerate of me."

The other breathes hard and exerts himself; he calls out loudly: "Princess, let us do it one more time."

The one is shy and fights back pain. Her delicate tongue now extends, now retracts, but she doesn't dare raise her golden-lotus feet.

The other fixes his eyes and stares without shame. His handsome body now raises then lowers; he cares not if he rumples the flower's pistil.

In one instant the Drunken Monk vomits messily, then relinquishes life on the carnal mat, hanging his head in dejection.

Meanwhile, the Red Maid rains milky fluid, then ties up the flesh pocket, joins her palms and closes the gate.

Finished with their clouds and rain, they were both filled with heartfelt lyrics of love. Stirred again, they once more fell to. Ruyu exerted the softest and gentlest of skills in order to taste the delicate flavor of the newly broken melon. Their love this night was truly too beautiful for either words or pictures. (ch. 66, 816b–17b)

This passage contains a cross section of sometimes conflicting messages. At once the wife makes great demands and has her husband submit, but she is also headstrong and presumably vulnerable to the husband's psychological superiority, that is, his "clever talk." Like Jin-zhonger, she can be formidable but also vulnerable before a capable and experienced male opponent. She is at once in pain, something not found in the ars erotica, but then ecstatic and ready to commence lovemaking again, illustrating a typical transition in Ming and Qing erotic fiction. The husband is at once gentle and rough, considerate and careless. He is well versed in the art of love, but his penis is compared to a Drunken Monk who ejaculates and hangs his head in dejection. The ars erotica, of course, urges *shenghuan,* "withdrawal while still erect," and does not admit the state of sadness after coitus. Only in *Yesou puyan* do we also find the idea, much more elaborated than here, that once the act is over the pleasure is all gone. It is possible that the author lifted his words from one or more sources of erotic love poetry, of which plenty existed in the Qing, in order to create what to him was a standard-sounding high erotic scene. However, as formulaic as the language in this passage or the use of the dream trope might be, the author nevertheless hints at a scene of sexually gratified monogamy that he will hint at again in the next episode of sexual encounter, which ends in a hard-won and real, not oneiric, monogamy between two self-determined lovers.

The Addiction to Sexual Desire

Like *Jin Ping Mei* and *Rou putuan*, *Lüye xianzong* portrays sexual involvement on a course of increasing indulgence and addiction. In the logic of *Lüye xianzong*, men become addicted because of lack of self-control and poor upbringing, which generally means overindulgent parents, especially the mother, or else lack of one or both parents, especially the father. Women become addicted to sex, as I have already said, once they meet a skilled lover, whom they will then do anything to keep. The end to indulgence in either case comes only after death or ordeal.

In the novel's third episode of sexual love, Li Baichuan depicts the situation of adultery. A happily married man, Zhou Lian, has an affair with his neighbor's unmarried daughter, Qi Huiniang, whom he meets one day when she peeks at him studying. He ascertains her daily schedule of going to the toilet, climbs over their neighboring wall at the right time, and has sex with her. As with the Princess in Ruyu's dream, it is Huiniang's first sex, but the author describes her pain in prose and thus more graphically. Zhou Lian's ejaculation is stronger than usual by "three or four times," causing him to faint (ch. 81, 1025b). Being new to this experience, Huiniang thinks he has died. In later sessions, however, she begins to taste her first pleasure and thinks it no wonder that "women do such bad things; they can't help themselves!" (1030a). She reckons no one else but Zhou has such skill and wants to marry him even if she becomes his second wife.

Li Baichuan defies the rule of other (especially late Ming) Chinese fiction about adultery by having the lovers happily marry in the end. After the suicide of his first wife and his near death at the hands of a female sex demon, Zhou Lian survives to redeem himself in a final monogamy. On the way to that ending, Li Baichuan provides several lengthy descriptions of ecstatic sex, one of which has Huiniang's mother overhearing the youths from the other side of the toilet door:

> Suddenly she heard the sound of a man and woman having intercourse [*nannü jiaogou zhi sheng*]. Taken aback, she hurriedly blew out the lamp and listened carefully: indeed it was her daughter and some man, making coarse noises and uttering wanton words that were beyond description. The sound of thrusting reverberated through the door. Mme. Pang felt herself go limp; overcome, she slumped to the floor. She was about to charge in, but hesitated because, whatever resulted, she would end up losing face. There was nothing to do but sit on the steps and await the outcome. She wondered who it could be doing such things with her daughter.
>
> By the time daylight came, the sounds of breathing and thrusting echoed in harmony. Her daughter's voice became louder and louder, still completely undigestible to the proper ear. The man's words were wanton and unbridled, but whose voice it was she still couldn't tell.
>
> The old woman sat there growing more upset, then angry, then outraged. The sounds reached such a pitch of wildness and ferocity that she began to claw desperately at her chest. Then the two youths ended their wantonness, and their lustful calls turned to murmuring conversation. Soon the man said, "It's time—I must be going." In another moment Huiniang emerged, only to see her mother sitting on the steps by the door. (ch. 83, 1054b–1055b)

This is the second time in the novel that a mother overhears the loud sex between her daughter and lover. The prostitute Jinzhonger's mother regrets that she missed such good sex in her lifetime but otherwise feels no shock. Huiniang's mother is shocked by her virgin daughter's sex but then delighted to discover that the man is their rich neighbor Zhou. In fact, he and Huiniang succeed in marrying because of the support of all the parents involved: his, hers, and his first wife's. Zhou gains his parents' approval by playing the spoiled boy and refusing to eat until they acquiesce. Huiniang's mother agrees because she covets the Zhou family wealth. Like Jinzhonger's mother, she is thus another woman who profits from her own daughter's sexual liaisons. Huiniang's father, an antimercenary pedant who opposes the marriage, is driven out of the house by Huiniang's mother, who has the marriage conducted in his absence (ch. 84). The mother later placates the father by giving him good food, then undressing and "raping" him (ch. 85, 1085b). The pedant is thus another man who cannot control himself or his wife, who is so dangerous that she "rapes" him into submission. Lastly, the father of Zhou's first wife is bribed into signing a contract allowing the marriage as long as the two wives are equal in status (ch. 84). Here money again provides the motivation, while contractual agreement legitimizes the demotion of a legally primary wife.

However, no one consults the first wife, who in jealous defiance chooses confrontation over compromise and isolates herself by refusing to surrender to the addition of a new wife. She remains defiant when Zhou brandishes his penis at her and asserts that her jealousy is all for the sake of that organ. He threatens that he will cease having sex with her if she fails to cooperate. The commentator of the manuscript edition states: "To a woman this thing is her living treasure; Zhou Lian is by no means exaggerating" (ch. 81, 1033b). She uses black magic to win back her husband, but fails and commits suicide.

In a manner typical of the *Lüye xianzong* author, he turns to the fantastic as a shorthand and allegorical way of presenting his didactic message. A strange wind suddenly carries Zhou to the abode of a female demon who forces him to become her consort. Although he notes the ominous coldness of her vagina, she completely wins him over (ch. 87, 717; ch. 88, 722). Since Zhou misses his family, however, the demon consents to accompany him back home but forbids him to visit Huiniang. His mother and his father-in-law attempt to outwit her but fail ridiculously, after which one of Leng Yubing's disciples finally exorcises her.

In the story of Zhou Lian and Huiniang, the author again detours from his main purpose of charting male enlightenment through ascetic self-cultivation. He has all along avoided making successful marriage into a centerpiece of his novel, instead focusing on the intractability of earthly desire. Greed leads to thoroughgoing abuse of core human values. Lust is a matter of conquering one opponent after another until one is finally conquered oneself. But with Zhou and Huiniang, the author maps a route to monogamous harmony that appears in no other novel studied in this book, including the chaste romances. Along this route, Zhou Lian first plunges into the thrills and tempests of promiscuity and polygyny, encounters the same disasters of jealous rivalry and physical depletion as other intemperate polygynists in Chinese fiction, but, unlike the others, finally emerges into happy monogamy. In short, the ordeal of polygyny leads to the peace of monogamy—however tangentially or inadvertently that conclusion is drawn.

Women's Demands and the Danger of Women

Yesou puyan and *Lüye xianzong* are similar in the fury and roughness of the sex they portray but differ in the way they frame that portrayal. *Yesou puyan* affirms intimacy up to but not including genital contact and orgasm, beyond which sex becomes grotesquely abnormal. *Lüye xianzong* portrays no excusable sexual or romantic acts but nevertheless describes genital pleasure in as full-blown a way as erotic works that openly affirm such pleasure. Li Baichuan depicts lust as the main link between the sexes. The author is interested neither in the kind of love (*qing*) found in *Mudan ting, Honglou meng,* or other fiction about deep sentimental attachment, nor in the type of rational friendship that characterizes Wen Suchen's polygamous marriage in *Yesou puyan. Lüye xianzong*'s characters profess love (*ai*) for each other but base their love on a sexual fulfillment that is unstable and at times comical as they go through what are depicted as the antics of intercourse. Jinzhonger's and Wen Ruyu's sex is noisier than "three or four people washing clothes"; Bald Miao takes Yuqinger while she is on the chamber pot; Zhou Lian and Huiniang have their trysts in the outhouse as her mother listens, clawing at herself, outside. In the temptation of Cui Dai, a female disciple of Leng Yubing, her Taoist lover has a penis too large to fit into any woman (see ch. 97, 1235a–1238a). In general, as I have said, sex in *Lüye xianzong* is a contest in which one partner, male or female, wins over the other. Jinzhonger arrives at her love for Wen Ruyu because of his superior sexual skills; she commits suicide for him. Huiniang's love is likewise sealed because of the pleasure she experiences with Zhou Lian; she is even willing to become his second wife. Her mother "rapes" her pedant father to obtain his agreement to their daughter's marriage. The demoness seduces Zhou Lian, then robs him of *yang* energy and forbids him contact with Huiniang.

The examples of Jinzhonger and Huiniang demonstrate that good sexual skill is an elementary way to capture a woman, as also affirmed in the "Classic of the Prostitute" quoted in the novel. Likewise, the male *ars erotica* teaches learnable techniques of intercourse and thereby implies that it is easy to please a woman in sex and thereby win her allegiance.

Nevertheless, female conquerors are never far away. Some are no more than mirror images of sexually conquering men, although such women are always condemned as more horrendous. However, like the shrew story, *Lüye xianzong* also allows for the existence of female demands that cannot be met simply sexually, and which in the broadest sense take the form of the woman's refusal to be treated as expendable. *Lüye xianzong* portrays that refusal in the guise of Jinzhonger's and Zhou's first wife's suicides, for example, and in the demoness's requirement that Zhou no longer see Huiniang and that no one try to exorcise her. But put into such hysterical or demonic form, the woman's demands—including Jinzhonger's *ai*—dissolve into the masculine themes of the danger of women and the intractability of sexual desire. These themes culminate in enlightenment, which though available to some women is mainly the man's final ability to look coldly at sex and at women. In the end, making sexual techniques easy to learn and looking coldly at women amount to the same thing, the estrangement of men from women, and thus self-containment (or the illusion of it) as the man's surest means of survival.

12

THE BENEVOLENT POLYGAMIST AND

THE DOMESTICATION OF SEXUAL PLEASURE

IN *SHENLOU ZHI*

In previous discussion, the term benevolent polygamist has referred to the hero of erotic romances who is a potent collector and rescuer of women, all of whom he satisfies sexually and treats civilly, and none of whom are jealous or shrewish. The image of the benevolent polygamist, like the idea of the benevolent emperor, has both its constructed façade— that is, its normative hierarchies and ideal forms—and its correspondence to some real situation, for example, relatively few acts of violent anger or arbitrary punishment on the man's part, and little laxity in his performance of responsibilities. The notion of the good or benevolent polygynist is like that of the benevolent dictator or slaveowner, for example, each oxymoronic but nevertheless sustained in its own specific way.

This chapter and the next are about such polygamists in two post-mid-Qing novels, *Shenlou zhi* (The Mirage of Love) and *Ernü yingxiong zhuan* (Tales of Boy and Girl Heroes), which I will use to examine retrospectively the other works I have covered so far. Published perhaps as early as 1804, *Shenlou zhi* is a twenty-four-chapter erotic romance which revises the image of the benevolent polygynist by placing him in a somewhat more recalcitrant world than usual and by having him compromise and surrender some of his wastrel privileges.[1] It performs its modification of this character without naming any specific work upon which it improves or elaborates. In contrast, like many other nineteenth-century novels, *Ernü yingxiong zhuan* openly articulates what it is revising: *Honglou meng* and, by implication, the scholar-beauty romance as well. It posthumously resolves the failed triangular relationship of Baoyu, Daiyu, and Baochai, and ends with a more fully realized fantasy of the coddled polygynist than the one I briefly mentioned in the chapter on *Qilu deng*. *Shenlou zhi* portrays the self-gratified polygynist who has a slight conscience, someone who almost admits that someday he could in fact lose all he has. In contrast, *Ernü yingxiong zhuan* starts with an emasculated prepolygynist like Jia Baoyu, but then redeems him both via his acquirement of inner strength and through external assistance in the form of a female savior, in his case a martial version of the "man among women."

Shenlou zhi and *Ernü yingxiong zhuan* appear at a time of major decline in Qing China, when a substantial and increasing portion of the male population was addicted to opium. By the time of *Ernü yingxiong zhuan's* writing in the third quarter of the nineteenth century, the drain of silver from China due to the opium trade had already exerted devastating consequences on the Chinese economy. *Shenlou zhi* mentions the lucrative trade with Westerners in Canton but does not refer to opium, and is of course too early to register the Opium War of 1839–42. *Ernü yingxiong zhuan* refers to opium, but neither mentions the Opium War nor foregrounds the situation of widespread addiction. These two novels—although others could be chosen in their place—open up two lines for future investigation: one the fictional representation of opium addiction and contact with the West, the other the phenomenon of the revision of *Honglou meng* in the form of either direct sequels or novels like *Ernü yingxiong zhuan* that use different characters and settings but still openly revise or improve upon the earlier novel. Contact with the West and addiction to opium are like emblems of irretrievable loss of the prosperity of the early to mid-Qing period, which ends around the late Qianlong era in the 1790s, when anecdotal evidence indicates that opium addiction had already become very deep-rooted. The revision of *Honglou meng*, which began a few years after the novel's appearance in 1791, likewise constitutes an attempt to reverse loss. That is, authors save Baoyu, Daiyu, and others from a tragic ending—whether by making a virtuous beauty and an upright scholar out of Baoyu and Daiyu, for example, or by transforming Baoyu into a benevolent polygynist who marries Daiyu, Baochai, and other women of the garden. "Loss" mainly gains meaning retrospectively through the lenses of the fictional and collective imagination, which to a certain extent always harks back to the "good old days." *Shenlou zhi* and *Ernü yingxiong zhuan* extend those old days of prosperity by providing what in comparison to the earlier *Honglou meng*, *Qilu deng*, and *Lüye xianzong* are easy solutions to the problem of the wastrel. *Ernü yingxiong zhuan*'s failure to foreground opium addiction or the Opium War is a particularly strong example of fantasy and denial. Other nineteenth-century novels, however, which I will not make space for in this study, portray the wastrel entering the new phase I have just mentioned. That is, with the addition of opium, a quantum leap now occurs in the wastrel's opportunity to seek pleasure and repletion while at the same time, in the fictional allegory, debilitating himself, his family, and ultimately the whole imperial system and its mode of production. *Yaguan lou* (Tower of Elegant View, circa 1820), for example, tells the story of a young wastrel— son of a miser—who becomes addicted to opium through contact with prostitutes, suffers a severe case of venereal disease (rare in early to mid-Qing erotic fiction), but finally recovers and conquers his addiction. The late Qing Peng Yang'ou's *Heiji yuanhun* (Wronged Ghosts of Black Addiction, 1909) traces opium addiction through several generations in a family starting with the great-great-grandfather, who is the progenitor of addiction in both his descendants and in all of China starting at the end of the Qianlong period.

In order to clarify the retrospective role I assign to *Shenlou zhi,* this chapter will first briefly discuss the revisionary aspects of *Shenlou zhi* in light of previous fiction, then report on its setting in Guangdong Province and its representation of trade there with Westerners. Afterwards, I will give a detailed view of *Shenlou zhi* in relation to *Yesou puyan, Honglou meng, Jin Ping Mei,* and the chaste and erotic romances by discussing two topics: the hero's evolution from sexual initiate to experienced polygynist, and the portrayal of male sexual bosses, of whom the hero is a relatively harmless example by comparison with others in the novel.

The Mirage of Love

Growing from age fourteen to sixteen in the story, the hero Su Xiaoguan is neither a Confucian sexual superman like Wen Suchen nor a bad-tempered and promiscuous wastrel like Ximen Qing, nor is he a sexually ambivalent loather of men like Jia Baoyu. He is a hedonist who enjoys good sex with his five wives and tends to shun adultery and visits to brothels. He sympathizes with women, rescues them, provides them a good home, and in the end has no more ambition than to enjoy a domestic life at play with his "sisters" (*jiemeimen*), as he calls his wife and four concubines (ch. 17, 23a). He rejects both officialdom (Xiaoguan, his childhood name, means to "laugh at officials") and commercial enterprise, especially the risky form of trade in which his father engages with "foreign devils" (*yangguizi,* ch. 1, 11a) at the Canton harbor. His is the ethic of a wealthy, benevolent, polygamist landlord in deep southern China, shut off from the politics of the nation to the north and the commerce of the outer world to the south.

Like other erotic novels of comparable length (e.g., *Rou putuan, Xiuping yuan, Taohua ying, Hudie mei,* and *Xinghua tian*), *Shenlou zhi* portrays one sexual encounter after another and has the same self-determining lovers who enjoy artful lovemaking and other civilized activities such as drinking wine and composing poetry. *Shenlou zhi,* however, has a broader but more uniquely local social compass. Besides the usual domestic scene, it includes descriptions of governmental corruption and popular unrest, and locates these subjects in a setting that is unusual to Chinese fiction up to its time, Guangdong Province. It is also more attentive to everyday detail. Cynical about education, government service, and government-supervised trade, devoid of scholar-beauty manifestos and patterns of legitimizing symmetry, *Shenlou zhi* exhibits a frank and relatively nonmoralistic hedonism found in few other surviving works of fiction outside of Li Yu's of the early Qing. It encloses itself in a comfortable interior while at the same time recognizing external trouble and vaguely predicting grand-scale disaster in the near future.

Of the few scholars who have written on *Shenlou zhi,* most have shown a reserved admiration for it. Dai Bufan claims that it is the best piece of fiction written between the late eighteenth and the late nineteenth centuries, grading it at the level of "upper middle" or even "lower high." Zheng Zhenduo was excited to discover the book in the Bibliothèque Nationale in 1927 and praised it for its realism and fluid style. Wang Xiaolian wonders why it has been neglected for so long when it contains such valuable material on the Guangdong of its times. Cai Guoliang considers it one of the better "second or third rate" novels below the two best novels of the period, *Rulin waishi* and *Honglou meng.* Lin Chen, however, criticizes the novel's imitativeness and idealization of polygamy, although he notes its "realism," especially in describing the machinations of trade with foreigners in Canton.[2] For Cai Guoliang and Dai Bufan, the novel's portrayal of social unrest in Guangdong Province is a harbinger of the greater disorder of the Taiping Rebellion, which launched its hybrid Christian (and antiopium) movement from the same region a few decades after the novel was written (Cai, 30; Dai, 278).

Shenlou zhi is about a young man, Su Xiaoguan (formal *ming* name Jishi), whose father works as a government-licensed merchant in one of the Cantonese houses of foreign trade (i.e., *yanghang;* trade with foreigners was restricted to Canton from 1757; the "cohong," a term not used in the novel, were set up in 1760 as the only channels through which trade could be pursued).

A corrupt official extorts money from Xiaoguan's father and his associates, jailing them until Xiaoguan uses influence to secure their release. Meanwhile, Xiaoguan has an affair with Suxiang, the elder sister of his fiancée, Huiruo. But Suxiang quits Xiaoguan for another youth, Wu Daiyun, because of Wu's large penis.

Xiaoguan next has an affair with Wu's sister, Xiaoqiao, who is forced to leave home, however, when her father presents her as concubine to the corrupt official; Xiaoguan vows loyalty but can do nothing to rescue her. After being given a third woman, Xiaoxia, he meets a Tibetan monk who gives him a powerful aphrodisiac, which enables him and Xiaoxia to become great lovers.

The same monk later kidnaps four of the corrupt official's women, then gathers forces to set up rule in eastern Guangdong Province. The corrupt official divorces Wu's daughter, Xiaoqiao, because she never smiles. Xiaoguan is happy to take her in and soon adds two more concubines for a total of four plus his wife, Huiruo.

In the final chapters, the corrupt official falls from power, while rebels and good government forces join to defeat the Tibetan monk. In the end, as Xiaoguan's friends prepare for exams or receive appointment as officials, he refuses all rewards and instead settles down on his estate. As his mentor says, Xiaoguan of everyone has best managed to avoid overdoing the Four Vices of "Drink, Lust, Greed, and Wrath."

Guangdong and the Contact with Foreigners

Shenlou zhi reproduces many character types found in previous vernacular fiction: the corrupt and lecherous official and his sycophants; the lone Tibetan monk with his potent aphrodisiacs and retractable penis; the lascivious woman; the sexy concubine and the more prudent wife (after her initial seduction by trickery, Huiruo refuses intimacy with Xiaoguan until marriage); righteous rebels, here led by a stalwart from Shandong (home of the *Shuihu zhuan* bandits); and a wise strategist who leads the rebels. *Shenlou zhi* shuttles between several worlds, all well-known to readers of Chinese fiction: the public domain of officials and wealthy merchants, the underworld of rebels and monks, and the domestic and erotic world of polygamists and the women they marry or "steal." Of these worlds, the erotic receives the most but by no means only emphasis.

The novel is unique because of its location in Guangdong Province and its reference to commerce there between Chinese and foreigners (most Ming and Qing vernacular fiction takes place in the cultural and political centers of Jiangnan and Beijing and areas between like Shandong).[3] The commerce appears only at the beginning of *Shenlou zhi*, and no foreigners themselves play a role. Western objects, of course, occur in vernacular fiction starting in the early seventeenth century—for example, spectacles, tobacco, telescopes, watches, clocks, toys, and art—and are items of either curiosity or common use.[4] However, *Shenlou zhi* is perhaps the first novel to contain a description of the trade and its role in the lives of Chinese. Xiaoguan's father's wealth includes numerous Western objects, beginning with the fancy watch he dangles before one of the corrupt official's underlings as a bribe (ch. 1, 6ab). Later, the official is cashiered and forced to surrender his property, which includes: "28 self-chiming clocks," "182 large and small foreign watches," "120 foreign glass lamps," and "1000 bolts of Dutch camlet in all colors" (ch. 18, 9ab).

Not all objects said to be "foreign" (*yang*) are necessarily European. The Tibetan monk owns "a cloud bed" (*yunchuang*) and "a rain bed" (*yuchuang*), both "made by foreigners" (*yangren suozao*, ch. 19, 9ab). The beds have "controls" and "levers" (*guanlie* and *jiguan*) that in the cloud bed fasten down virgins whom the monk rapes, and in the rain bed move the woman's body to and fro as the monk lies on top. The provenance of these beds is a mystery, although they can possibly be associated with the "virgin cart" (*tongnü che*) found in stories about Emperor Yang of the Sui dynasty. The "virgin cart" is likewise a bed fitted with a "control" or "mechanism" (*jichu*) which locks virgins in place for the emperor to rape.[5] Whatever the case may be, the intricate and the diabolical often converge, regardless of geographical origin. At the same time, Tibet and other non-Han peripheries were commonly stereotyped as places in which people engaged in evil and barbaric sexual practices, as exemplified in *Yesou puyan*. Moreover, cleverness and intricacy of movement and design are features that Chinese commonly associated with Western objects, both artistic and utilitarian.[6] Westerners thus easily fit into the same stereotype of the sexually sadistic and diabolical.

The Good Polygamist, Nonwastrel, Nonmiser

Xiaoguan is another example of a reformed Ximen Qing. He is a good son, good manager of his estate after his father dies, and a good local public servant. In direct contrast to the miser-landlord, he allows poor peasants in debt to him to pay according to their means and burns all the debt receipts. He forgives old unpaid rents and discounts new ones (ch. 9). At the height of his benevolence, during a drought, he sells his stored rice at more than the regular price but still substantially less than the inflated rate (ch. 20).

Yet he is the same successful lover of women who appears in erotic romances like *Xiuping yuan, Taohua ying,* or *Hudie mei*. Women automatically like him and typically present themselves or are presented to him as paramours or concubines. As in *Xinghua tian* and other works, such heroes benefit women by taking them on as concubines and thereby rescuing them from undesirable situations: widowhood (*Taohua ying, Xinghua tian*), nunhood (*Taohua ying*), poverty and indebtedness (*Shenlou zhi*), a jealous main wife (*Hudie mei*), a homosexual husband (*Taohua ying*), prostitution (*Xinghua tian*), or simply the uncertain future of marrying bad husbands (*Shenlou zhi, Hudie mei, Xinghua tian*). Some of the women are in the end too lustful and die from lack of constant attention (*Taohua ying, Hudie mei*), or are too promiscuous and have to be given to lesser men (*Shenlou zhi*).

Shenlou zhi follows Xiaoguan's progress from an initiate to an experienced lover, from his first secret affair with the sister of his future wife to the legitimate sex he has with his wife and concubines. As in the erotic romance, he acquires sexual skills from outside the conjugal realm, in his case from the Tibetan monk who teaches him the use of aphrodisiacs and from an extramarital lover who teaches him tricks such as fellatio and unusual positions for intercourse. Back in the security of home, he and his wives thus enjoy the benefits of diversions learned from the sexual underground.

His sexual experience starts with the playful daring of adolescent lovers. He approaches the napping Suxiang, who has been flirting with him for some time; they are not yet fifteen years old. She yawns and stretches; her hand touches his face. She thinks it's her sister but discovers, to her feigned shock, that it is Xiaoguan. He sips tea from her cup and, like Baoyu, enjoys the taste of her lip rouge on the rim (ch. 2, 4b–5b). They have a flirtatious discussion: she has "heard" that he is already betrothed (i.e., to her sister). He declares that he only wants Suxiang and sidles up to her "making a monkey face," *houzhe lian* (6a). She acts scandalized and threatens to hit him. He offers her any place to hit. Then

> he reached his hand into Suxiang's right sleeve. Now in this summer weather she was only wearing a broad-sleeved linen blouse, so he had but to slip his hand inside to feel a soft and smooth, tight and firm little breast. Suxiang recoiled: "Little boy, you're getting naughtier and naughtier."
>
> He withdrew his hand and put it around her shoulder, "Nice sister, let's go over there and play."
>
> "Don't be silly, someone will be coming."
>
> Xiaoguan put his face up to her cheek and was just about to start kissing her when the maid came in with their tea. (ch. 2, 6ab)

When they finally succeed in finding a secluded place to have intercourse, he is too hasty, and she can only "draw her moth-eyebrows together and tremblingly endure it":

> On this Xiaoguan's first entry into the beauteous realm, he couldn't avoid selling off his goods in excess haste. Not a few seconds had gone by and the jade mountain had already collapsed. They wiped clean the virgin blood and cuddled each other closely.
>
> Xiaoguan asked, "My dear Sister, why aren't you saying anything? Am I just dreaming?"
>
> "What do you expect me to say?"
>
> "Was it good just now?"
>
> "It hurt so much how could it be 'good'?"
>
> Xiaoguan felt her below and said, "Putting this thing in such a little place is naturally going to hurt. It will be better next time."
>
> Suxiang grasped his hand tightly and told him, "Be still. Let's rest for a while before we go." (ch. 4, 8b–9a)

As I have said, little or no commentary accompanies descriptions such as these in *Shenlou zhi*. The progression from "entry into the beauteous realm" (an old cliché of erotic fiction), to "jade mountain . . . col-laps[ing]," and then to Suxiang's complete lack of pleasure nevertheless serves the author's purpose of injecting sardonic and negating, but at the same time nontrenchant, notes into his descriptions of sexual play. *Yesou puyan* and *Lüye xianzong*, in contrast, would focus on the ephemerality or intractability of sexual pleasure, denying the possibility of the harmony and expertise that Su Xiaoguan will eventually achieve.

It is not unusual in the erotic romance for the young hero's first affair in some way to discontinue. His first partner is a lascivious or fallen woman, for example, or an older woman whose daughter it is more appropriate for him to marry. Unexceptionally, then, Suxiang soon begins an affair with a more attractive and powerful friend of his. Xiaoguan is mystified and hurt by her sudden coldness, but when he discovers the largeness of the other boy's "thing" (*dongxi*), reckons it is no wonder that she left him and decides to be content with his more virtuous Huiruo (ch. 6, 5b–6a). Xiaoguan's gentlemanly failure to be stirred by jealousy appears on a later occasion as well (ch. 20, 12a).

In a more advanced stage of his sexual life, Xiaoguan makes love to his sexiest concubine, Xiaoxia, who is a few months pregnant:

> Jishi embraced Xiaoxia from the rear and soon reached the flower's heart. Xiaoxia turned her head and looked at him lovingly; she lifted her thigh to meet his approach and let him penetrate to the root. Jishi felt utmost pleasure and kept on until dawn when he ejaculated in one great torrent [*yixie ru zhu*]. (ch. 14, 12b)

Intercourse until dawn is a common hyperbole, as is the cliché, *yixie ru zhu*. In *Jin Ping Mei*, which seems to provide the underlying foil to this scene, Ximen Qing also has sex with the pregnant Li Pinger, to whom he causes discomfort (ch. 27). Pan Jinlian is jealous of Li Pinger both for the whiteness of her skin, which strongly attracts Ximen Qing, and for being pregnant with Ximen's child. Xiaoguan, in contrast, never harms his wives, who are moreover never jealous.

As his sexiest concubine, Xiaoxia is still less lustful than the women he meets outside the home. Madame Ru teaches him the art of fellatio, for instance. The wife of a man who uses her to seduce and blackmail Xiaoguan, Mme. Ru instead likes Xiaoguan and protects him from the plot. After a few cups of wine during one of their trysts, "her starry eyes began to roll with lust, and wanton feelings to surge like waves," the image of rolling or side-looking eyes, *xieshi,* being formulaic for abandon (ch. 19, 4b–5a). "Desiring to captivate him and become his favorite," she has him try the new position of sitting on the bed while she places herself on his lap. On another occasion, he enjoys "the new variation of left three thrusts and right four" with Mme. Ru and another woman, Yerong, whom the Tibetan monk had earlier kidnapped and whom Xiaoguan later gives away to a man she had been secretly meeting. The wise polygynist Xiaoguan sees Suxiang and these women in a different light from his wives, who would never abandon him for another man, and would never use sex to manipulate him and elevate themselves.

Xiaoguan has a younger brother-in-law who is still naive about what men and women do together. Chuncai (meaning "spring talent" but punning with "fool material") makes ingenuous observations about politics, money, and sex. His first reaction to the notion of friends visiting prostitutes is to ask why someone would want to play with "strangers" (*mosheng ren,* ch. 5, 2b). Later, he is the innocent asking the experienced about the facts of life:

> "I have a question to ask you. You're my classmate and my brother-in-law, so you should be able to give me some advice. . . . My mother says they're going to get me a wife next year. But I think: 'What fun is there in a stranger?', and I don't want to go through with it. But they've already set it up. Now what is it that you are supposed to do on the first day?"
>
> "There isn't much to it. You just go to sleep with her, that's all," Xiaoguan replied.
>
> "If you don't want to discuss it then just say so. Why tell me such nonsense? I see people giving birth to sons and daughters; now how do they do it?"
>
> "When you go to sleep with her, she'll be the one to tell you. You don't need others to teach you."
>
> "Oh, so you mean a wife is also a professor? But my sister Suxiang has been married for more than two months now and still hasn't given birth. Does that mean she doesn't know how to profess?"
>
> Xiaoguan laughed, "Even I don't know the answer to that." (ch. 8, 4ab)

In this passage the innocent "Fool Material" is nervous because soon expected to be vigorous "Spring Talent." In his foolish mouth, however, the fear of women and marriage appears easy to tame. Only foolish sons doted upon by their mothers are afraid of prostitutes and getting married. Chuncai is like a gross caricature of Jia Baoyu, while Su Xiaoguan is the example of an experienced and self-confident polygynist who recalls, however, a not distant time when he too felt apprehension, in his case with Chuncai's own sister. Nevertheless, he is now the expert. First prostitutes, maids, or female peers, if possible, then multiple wives: such is the sexual curriculum of all important men like him.

Male Sexual Bosses

As promiscuous as Xiaoguan may be, he is not as aggressive as the male bosses who hurt and enslave their sexual partners. A scene of male homosexuality at the beginning of *Shenlou zhi* provides the first example of the male sexual boss. A corrupt official (the one referred to above) lusts for a servant boy bringing in tea; the doors are closed; the boy massages the official's legs; then the official has the boy undress and present his buttocks. Knowing what is expected of him and eager to please, the boy submits as he grits his teeth and yelps with pain. When it is over, he leans against a table for a while to recover. As he walks past other servants in the outer room, they "make faces at him" and tease him (ch. 1, 10ab). The novel makes no further reference to homoerotic sex except for a passing mention that Xiaoguan "only likes women" (*zhuan hao nüse,* ch. 15, 6a).

Having no son, the corrupt official later hires the Tibetan monk, who is said to have the power to cause sons to be born. After observing the monk do somersaults, which expose the fact that the monk has no penis (ch. 9, 12a), the official allows him to mingle freely in his harem. The monk is in fact master of a method called "retracting the dragon," *na long zhi fa* (14b–15a), by which he can retract and extend his penis at will.[7] At first the monk makes the women glad he is around but later kidnaps some of them and becomes the most abusive man in the novel (ch. 19).

Another of Xiaoguan's sexual foils is his friend Wu Daiyun, whose large penis lures Suxiang away from Xiaoguan. Wu soon tires of her and in one scene has her strip naked, whips her, and demands that she cut hair from her head for him to compare with the pubic hair of his new favorite (ch. 14, 14b).[8] Suxiang's story exemplifies the polygynist law that men can go from one vagina to the next, gaining greater stature as they go, but that women who climb the social ladder of penises, if they are not clever enough, instead subject themselves to degradation and expulsion. Suxiang is *Shenlou zhi*'s fallen woman, one who has her mind on sex too early and too eagerly. In the end she renounces marriage to become a nun.

In another scene, Wu Daiyun, Xiaoguan, and others are listening to two singing girls, twelve and thirteen in age. The drunkwn Wu flirts with one of them, "hugging her and crooning, 'I'll provide for you and no one else.'" She tells him to "be more respectful," but he continues to "paw her up and down," making it impossible for her to pry loose (ch. 14, 8a). Xiaoguan, in contrast, is a model of decency, just like Baoyu in the company of Xue Pan and others at Feng Ziying's party (*Honglou meng*, ch. 28).

Xiaoguan himself cannot be completely exempted from this list of womanizers, however. While confined to his study by his strict father, he takes advantage of his maids for any opportunity to "slake his thirst." At his request, his mother provides him with chambermaids who wait on him at night. When he asks one of them to sleep with him, she replies:

> "I don't presume to be so fortunate. I do not have the custom of sleeping with men. Let me get Wuyun to accompany you." Thus she got free of him, laughing as she went over to lay out her bedding. But Xiaoguan jumped naked from the bed, grabbed her, stripped her of all her clothes, and took her into his bed.
>
> "How old are you this year?"
>
> "Fourteen."
>
> "Foolish maid; fourteen and you still don't understand these things. Give it a try. I'm no virgin. For the time being, we can pretend that you are Wuyun."
>
> The maid couldn't but grit her teeth and submit. The next day [the other maid] fell under the same knife—all we can do is chalk it up to Xiaoguan's youthful miscreancy. (ch. 6, 15a)

Like other prepolygamists, including Jia Baoyu, Xiaoguan has the privilege of being pampered by maids, who are usually assumed to be sexually available and even privileged if invited to have sex with him. Also like Baoyu, Xiaoguan prefers young maids because he "dislikes the dirtier old ones" (13b). In *Shenlou zhi*, however, the maids are like extensions of doting motherly care. In allowing Xiaoguan access to them, his mother cushions him from the strictness imposed by his father. Baoyu's mother, in contrast, allows him a chambermaid as sexual partner but at the same time uses the maid to keep moral watch on him and thus, in effect, extend the reach of fatherly control.

The author of *Shenlou zhi* portrays even the cruelest of male characters with a minimum of moralizing. In one instance he channels criticism of men through the anger of a female character. The corrupt official complains because his new concubine, Wu Xiaoxia, Xiaoguan's former lover and Wu Daiyun's sister, never smiles or laughs. Her father urges her to comply, saying that he used to scold her for laughing too much. If she will smile, he says, the official will give him a promotion: "If only for the sake of filiality, can't you smile a little?" She responds, "Why don't you have a few more smiling daughters and give them all to the Superintendant of the Censorate! Then you can get yourself promoted to Prefect or even Governor!" (ch. 9, 18a).

The insolence of a daughter to her father is the closest *Shenlou zhi* comes to portraying the uncooperative woman. But while *Shenlou zhi* dramatizes the helplessness of women and satirizes and exposes lecherous and venal men, it does not go as far as works like *Honglou meng* or *Lin Lan Xiang* in eulogizing women who are sacrificed and exploited. Such is the extent of its self-imposed limit of decency.

Xiaoguan, Suchen, and Baoyu

Coming from a part of China far from the capital and the Jiangnan region, *Shenlou zhi* is unlike Qing erotic romances, which narrowly focus on a hero's sexual adventures. Some of the differences from erotic romances are minor. *Shenlou zhi* still retains the man who has easy access to young women, including ones of his own class whom he eventually marries. But the lustful Suxiang overstimulates herself by reading pornographic novels and abandons the hero for a man with a larger penis. Women do not abandon the hero in the erotic scholar-beauty romance, and men in other works in general do not fail to be jealous if women cheat on them. The virgin's pain during her first intercourse and the boy's pain from anal rape also set *Shenlou zhi* apart. In other erotic romances, the virgin's pain and the catamite's moans are formulaic signs of bliss rather than references to actual discomfort or harm.[9]

Shenlou zhi is most distinct in that it places the hero's sexual success in a more diversified context than other romances. As in *Jin Ping Mei*, Xiaoguan's sexual adventures are dispersed among and in some cases overwhelmed by surrounding events, such as the plunder of his home by bandits just as he and his newly wed Huiruo are naked in bed (ch. 8). He turns from being a sexual hero into the traditional victim of bandit attack: in his case, the son of an ostentatious, excessively rich landlord who, as such, inevitably attracts plunder in an area and period of social unrest. He and his wife live through the attack, but his father dies of fright. Sick of the weight of wealth and power, Xiaoguan decides to ease the financial burdens of the poor tenants of his estate. At the same time, he becomes more confirmed in his disdain of work and in his dedication to domestic pleasure. He is a man who has everything given to him but is willing to give some of it up. Having too much invites destruction by forces he is powerless to defeat: peasant bandits from below and corrupt officials from above.

Shenlou zhi represents a new though minor development in Chinese eroticism. Its combination of "local color" (*bendi fengguang*), the "trivial details" (*suosui*) of the lives of men and women (words from the novel's preface), and the hedonist ethic of Su Xiaoguan have little or no follow-up in literary history, having as predecessor only the rational hedonism of Li Yu of the early Qing. Set among larger works which treat the question of the formation of the young man, *Shenlou zhi* skirts serious issues like the intractability of desire and the degeneration of the wastrel. Like the heroes of the erotic romances, Xiaoguan has an innately balanced sense of his capacities. He is an easy solution to the problem that Jia Baoyu and Wen Suchen represent in their opposing poles of under- and overvaluation of masculinity. Baoyu undervalues men in his disgust with male baseness and his esteem for women; Suchen overvalues men in his supreme confidence as healer and keeper of women. Xiaoguan is neither as sensitive and apologetic as Baoyu, nor as messianic of *yang* virtue as Suchen. He takes Baoyu's "lust of the mind" and puts it back into flesh, unlike the orthodox Suchen who will have nothing to do with lust, whether of the mind or the body. He takes Suchen's chaste supermasculinity and brings it back to earth, unlike Baoyu who lacks the will to take up a man's role in the real world. Xiaoguan shares Baoyu's desire to live among women and have as little as possible to do with the world outside the home. But he also shares Suchen's immunity to the weakening powers of love and Suchen's ability to perform competently as male head of house.

13

ERNÜ YINGXIONG ZHUAN AS ANTIDOTE

TO *HONGLOU MENG*

Ernü yingxiong zhuan (Tales of Boy and Girl Heroes), in forty chapters, is by a Manchu bannerman named Wen Kang, who probably wrote his work between the early 1850s and the late 1870s.[1] One of numerous nineteenth-century novels written with *Honglou meng* in mind, it features the same configuration of gender issues that *Honglou meng* shares with the chaste romances: the softness and powerlessness of men, the superiority of women, and the resolution of this imbalance into either monogamy or polygamy. Moreover, in *Ernü yingxiong zhuan* as in other works, female superiority functions as a device for the correction of male weakness, a correction which in contrast to *Honglou meng*, however, reaches a complete and unambiguous resolution. The novel ends with the woman's return to her normative kinship roles of wife and mother, and—in extreme contrast to *Honglou meng*—with the man resuming the role of benevolent, polygynous head of family.

    Ernü yingxiong zhuan parallels *Shenlou zhi* in creating what in retrospect looks like the last optimistic vision of how the polygamous man and his women should be. The two works contrast in the same way as the chaste and erotic romances, with *Ernü yingxiong zhuan* continuing the chaste tradition and *Shenlou zhi* the erotic. But fiction has undergone many changes since the early Qing—in particular, the transformations resulting from the appearance of *Honglou meng*. That event colors the chaste and erotic solutions offered by these two novels and puts them farther from the early Qing romances than they might otherwise have been. Although *Shenlou zhi*'s inheritance from *Honglou meng* is debatable, such things as the portrayal of male sexual bosses and of a daughter's insolence to her father make its eroticism less utopian than in erotic romances like *Xiuping yuan, Hudie mei,* or *Taohua ying*.[2] *Ernü yingxiong zhuan*'s inheritance from and reaction to *Honglou meng*, as I have said in the last chapter, is announced in the book itself. As I will view it, *Ernü yingxiong zhuan* is a lengthier than usual chaste romance written to correct and improve upon *Honglou meng*. It has the basic defining features of the beauty-scholar novel but gives these features new significance through deliberate reference to *Honglou meng*. As posed by virtue of the novel's juxtaposition with *Honglou meng*, the central question is how to get one man married to two women—that is, "three people happy in one bed," *yichuang san hao*[3]—plus have the man take a loyal maid as concubine, all in a fashion seemly and agreeable to everyone involved. In *Honglou meng*, Jia Baoyu fails to marry the two women, although he was not in fact trying. But from the perspective of *Ernü yingxiong zhuan*, Baoyu should have succeeded, and in the present case his replacement does (recalling some of the sequels to *Honglou meng* which have him succeed in marrying Baochai, Daiyu, Xiren, and others as well).

Besides the antidotal revision of *Honglou meng*, the other topic of this chapter will be the coddled polygynist, about whom I have briefly spoken before and whose portrayal represents a fusion of the themes of female superiority and benevolent polygyny. Although I have said that *Ernü yingxiong zhuan* continues the tradition of the chaste romance, it also in fact crosses into the erotic romance—echoing earlier stories of two-wife polygyny—by portraying a hero who, though chaste, effeminate, and inferior to women, is also a polygynist. The novel accomplishes this combination by means of two methods borrowed from previous works but recombined in this one: (1) the recuperative function of the superior woman, already prominent but not as decisive in *Honglou meng, Lin Lan Xiang,* and *Qilu deng;* and (2) the sublimation of male-female sexual incompatibility by means of a nonsexual and infantile eroticism. The result is a coddled polygynist hero whose self-confidence and potency in effect reside not in himself—as would be the case in *Yesou puyan, Shenlou zhi,* and other erotic romances—but in his superior wives.

The essential message of the first method, the recuperative function of the superior woman, is that the man needs a number of women to take care of him. Everyone must believe that he is happy that way and will be less apt to misbehave. In other words, women are there to protect the man from his weak self; they keep him from destroying himself and others along with him. On his part, he ought to be careful not to overstep the rules of being coddled; otherwise women turn into shrews, battle among each other, and sap the man of the little strength he has left in his coddled state. In short, as *Lin Lan Xiang* and other sources state, polygyny has its laws of collectivity and does not entirely serve the whim of the wastrel.

The second method by which *Ernü yingxiong zhuan* fuses female superiority and benevolent polygyny involves the staging of scenes of infantile innocence and health, the purpose of which is to preempt the pollution caused by sexual lust. Male-female incompatibility is premised in the ars erotica and demonstrated in novels such as *Jin Ping Mei, Honglou meng, Lin Lan Xiang,* and *Lüye xianzong. Ernü yingxiong zhuan* defines that incompatibility in terms of lust and pollution, which it repairs through its explicit critique and revision of *Honglou meng* and its own improved version of intimacy that is erotic but not sexual. The novel stages its erotic displacement by means of the replacement of sexual fluids by urine, which in a series of recurring scenes metaphorically floats the polygynist and his two wives together without their having any sexual intent. *Ernü yingxiong zhuan* thus picks up on the adolescent utopia of *Honglou meng* but pushes it on to full resolution in the form of adult polygyny, which nevertheless retains its infantile aspect and is only made possible because of the reparative efforts of the superior woman.

In what follows, I will explore the above points by first continuing the retrospective comparison with earlier fiction begun in the last chapter. After discussing in this light the character types of the warrior woman and the soft male hero, I will then turn to *Ernü yingxiong zhuan*'s portrayal of innocence and health through both its arrangement of sexual intimacy via ablution and Wen Kang's critique of *Honglou meng.*

As defined in the novel's prefatory chapter, the "Boy and Girl" (*ernü*) of the book's title indicates the idea of "warm and soft" (*wenrou*) "innate disposition" (*tianxing*). "Hero" or "heroes" (*yingxiong*) refers to the "brave and valiant" (*xialie*) response to the vicissitudes of "human affairs" or "human situations" (*renqing*).[4] In other words, in their "boy-girl" aspect, men and women interact according to tender and innate "childlike" disposition. But in their "heroic" aspect, men and women respond to exigencies in brave, martial fashion; women in particular do not necessarily follow the prescribed rules of feminine behavior. The ideal person combines both aspects (*yishen jianbeide*, prologue, 5) and is never civil and gentle to the exclusion of being martial and unflinching, and vice versa.

As with *Honglou meng* and many other Ming and Qing works, critics have proposed correspondences between the contents of *Ernü yingxiong zhuan* and the author's own life or political figures of his times.[5] In spite of such allusions, however, the novel is oblivious to the issues of the Opium War and the growing foreign incursions into China. Outside of a few references to opium—but several descriptions of the tobacco-smoking habits of the central characters, including one of the young wives—*Ernü yingxiong zhuan* registers little evidence of Western influence or disturbance.[6] Wen Kang not only repairs *Honglou meng* but, like the author of *Yesou puyan,* constructs a harmonious Confucian China beset with only temporary, completely solvable problems. In short, by not being foregrounded, the West is rendered entirely extraneous.

The most widely known part of the book is the episode in the first half in which the heroine, "Thirteenth Sister," Shisan Mei, saves both her future husband, An Ji, and her co-wife-to-be, Zhang Jinfeng, from the cannibalistic monks of Nengren Temple. Thirteenth Sister's character and deeds have inspired drama, oral storytelling, and fiction, including Zhang Henshui's famous novel of the 1920s *Ti xiao yinyuan* (Fate in Tears and Laughter).[7] The second half of the book reads like an extremely long denouement, although it occasionally provides vivid descriptions of places and characters.[8] The author creates in fictional form, especially in the uneventful latter half, the ideal household he was supposedly unable to have in his own life, in which he suffered the decline of his formerly prominent family and the failure of his sons.[9]

Ernü yingxiong zhuan resembles *Yesou puyan* and *Qilu deng* in its dedicated promotion of Confucian ideology. The hero is both an obedient servant of the empire and a diligently filial son. When summoned by his father from another room, for example, he spits out his food on the table so as not to appear while chewing, as he recalls is dictated by the *Li ji* or Book of Rites (*Ernü yingxiong zhuan,* ch. 33, 580). But in contrast to *Yesou puyan* and *Qilu deng, Ernü yingxiong zhuan* has received more recognition from both the public and scholars, the latter of whom have especially praised its use of language. In his 1925 article, for example, Hu Shih remarks that although Wen Kang affirms precisely the kind of characters which *Rulin waishi* satirizes for their dedication to examination success,

Ernü yingxiong zhuan uses a more lively and earthy vernacular than either *Rulin waishi* or *Honglou meng.*[10]

The story of *Ernü yingxiong zhuan* begins with the hero's father, An Xuehai, who succeeds late in life both in having a son and attaining the *jinshi* degree. But soon after assuming office, he is unjustly cashiered and arrested, at which time his sheltered son must leave home for the first time, travel a great distance with a large sum of money, and bribe the authorities into releasing his father.

The son, An Ji, is waylaid by his own servants, nearly eaten by cannibalistic monks, and then rescued by a young woman, He Yufeng, alias Shisan Mei, "Thirteenth Sister," who is engaged in the life mission of avenging her father's death. In addition, she rescues a young woman, Zhang Jinfeng, and Zhang's mother and father, entrapped by the same evil monks, and immediately sets about having An and Miss Zhang betrothed. Soon after, Thirteenth Sister meets An Ji's parents, who agree to An's marriage to Miss Zhang but want Thirteenth Sister to marry him as well. Mr. An then informs Thirteenth Sister that her enemy (who caused her father's death) has been executed for his crimes.

The rest of the novel (chs. 19 to 40) relates how the An's persuade Thirteenth Sister to become a proper woman again and marry young An, how An prepares for and succeeds in the state exams, and how in the end he takes a loyal family maid as concubine. Thirteenth Sister's heroic behavior resurfaces only once in the second half of the book, when she foils thieves trying to rob the An home (ch. 31).

The Warrior Woman Thirteenth Sister

The martial nature and adventures of He Yufeng in *Ernü yingxiong zhuan* are characteristic of what has since become known as the *wuxia xiaoshuo* ("martial hero" novel, or martial or military romance), a very popular genre in the Qing and after. He Yufeng is an example of the female warrior (*nüxia*) who appears in numerous works like *Shuihu zhuan* (Water Margin), *Yangjiafu yanyi* (The Yang Family Saga), *Shuo Tang sanzhuan* (Three Histories of the Tang), and *Nüxian waishi* (History of the Female Immortal).[11] Some of these women are either "barbarians" or daughters of bandit chiefs; some fight for dynastic forces. Some are attracted to or marry male counterparts; and some, like Thirteenth Sister, eschew involvement with men.[12] Thirteenth Sister is also like male warriors and rebels (especially those in *Shuihu zhuan*) in having a warrior alias, keeping her original identity secret from all but a select few, and residing on a remote mountain which she leaves only for brief excursions, which include the robbing of bad rich people (ch. 8). In her case, her mission of vengeance requires her to maintain secrecy in order to be able to surprise and kill her enemy when the right time comes.

The typical novel in which warrior women appear is about battles for dynastic power, bandit rebellion, or personal vendetta and struggle for justice. *Ernü yingxiong zhuan* begins as a story about justice and revenge; however, after the first half, it turns into a story about marriage and social success. Although *Ernü yingxiong zhuan* is thus cross-generic, for present purposes I will examine the warrior woman in light of the *Honglou meng* beauty-scholar story rather than the martial romance. Nevertheless, the former must be seen as growing out of the latter, as I will reflect in the discussion below.

The generic resemblances between *Ernü yingxiong zhuan* and the chaste romances consist mainly of the exchange of gender characteristics, the theme of the woman's superiority, and the set of simple equivalences or symmetries in the relations between the marriage partners. For example, An Ji is an only son with no siblings; Zhang and He are only daughters with no siblings (He Yufeng is an orphan). Zhang and He look alike (ch. 13, 182) and share the character "Phoenix," *Feng,* in their names. Most importantly, An Ji is girlish, while He Yufeng is boyish. The characteristics of the beauty-scholar novels take on special meaning in light of *Ernü yingxiong zhuan*'s reaction to *Honglou meng*. For An to take two wives and a concubine is proper to chaste beauty-scholar novels like *Yu Jiao Li*—and *Ernü yingxiong zhuan* is scrupulously chaste. However, since it is consciously written to correct the errors of *Honglou meng,* the novel makes sure that its version of Daiyu, that is, He Yufeng / Thirteenth Sister, is not spurned or abandoned, that the two wives are not jealous, as Daiyu and Baochai supposedly are, and that the loyal maid Changjie—who corresponds to Xiren in *Honglou meng*—is premaritally chaste and is married to the hero, not someone else, as Xiren is.

The superior woman in *Ernü yingxiong zhuan* differs from her female counterparts in both the beauty-scholar romance and *Honglou meng*. Like the chaste beauty, Thirteenth Sister practices masculine behavior but without disguising as a man. The superior women of *Honglou meng* also remain as women (that is, do not disguise as men), but are not martial and mobile outside the home like Thirteenth Sister. Combining elements from (1) the tradition of the warrior woman (*xianü*) and (2) the bold and capable beauty of the beauty-scholar romances, she is a super-corrective model for unsuccessful members of both sexes, especially those depicted in *Honglou meng*. She is called a "valiant hero of the powder-and-rouge brigade" (ch. 5, 70), an expression similar to the more common "man among women," *nüzhong zhangfu*. In contrast, the man An Ji is girlish and weaker than He Yufeng; he needs prodding in order to get things done; otherwise he enjoys staying home and having an easy life.

The heroine He Yufeng passes through two phases in the book: In the first half she is Thirteenth Sister, avenging her father's death and living out her childhood aptitude for heroic deeds. In the second half she resumes her original identity, that of He Yufeng, and reverts to her "innate" (*tianxingde*) way of being a woman, although she is still less traditionally feminine than her co-wife, Zhang Jinfeng. When she is Thirteenth Sister, she has no pretentions of acting in a feminine way—that is, staying at home, being delicate and modest, and expressing tender emotion. But when she returns to being He Yufeng, she is said to become increasingly possessed of *ernü rouchang*, literally, the "soft feelings of boy-and-girl" (ch. 20, 321). By the time she marries An Ji, her "chivalrous spirit has completely disappeared" (*xiaqi quanxiao*, ch. 27, 448), and she has learned how to be "sweet and charming" as a young woman should (or "delicate and bashful," *jiaochi*, ch. 27, 463). Nevertheless, when thieves enter the family compound one night, although she keeps herself concealed, she manages to trap one and shoot another with a poisoned arrow (ch. 31).

In portraying He Yufeng's recovery of "innate" nature, the author first foregrounds the origin of her martial identity, which begins to dissolve after she learns that her enemy is dead. As An Ji's father An Xuehai relates, she is the daughter of his (Xuehai's) sworn brother, who was killed by a man who tried to force He Yufeng into marriage. With her father's death, she swore vengeance and declared that she would never marry. An's father also relates other details about her youth: she played like a boy when she was a child; during the ritual in which the one-year-old baby is allowed to choose between masculine and feminine objects, she grabbed toy weapons, in obvious mirror opposition to *Honglou meng*'s Jia Baoyu, who reached for bracelets, rouge, and the like (*Ernü yingxiong zhuan*, ch. 19, 305). Since her father had no son, he treated her like a boy (ch. 19, 306; also ch. 8, 114). When scolded for playing like a boy and not learning how to sew, she responded: "You don't mean that all girls are good for is to be hired by mothers-in-law to do their household labor, do you!?" (ch. 14, 199). Against such brashness, An Ji's father and mother make it their goal to teach her the sense of shame (*xiu*) proper to a woman.

When she commences her mission of avenging her father, her boyish predisposition comes to full bloom. Unlike the women of beauty-scholar novels, who match or outdo men in poetry and examination learning, she challenges men on the brute level of strength and martial arts. She encounters a group of men staging a duel, the loser of which must put on woman's makeup and wear flowers in his hair. She asks them why makeup and flowers are incompatible with being a "hero" (*yingxiong*) and then overpowers the chief ruffian (ch. 15, 233). As she later announces to them, her lifelong mission is to punish all "obstinate and unruly men" (ch. 16, 236). In assigning superhuman qualities to Thirteenth Sister, Wen Kang has her performing such feats as tackling men much bigger than she and nonchalantly lifting huge stones—even though she has had bound feet since age seven (ch. 14, 199). The superwoman, like *Yesou puyan*'s superman, is a super-correction of "obstinate and unruly men" and other bad male characters. She is a woman reprimanding men by using the same methods as men but with greater ease and righteousness.

In spite of her ability to outdo men, however, she never disguises as one. Like other female warriors, she observes the etiquette of maintaining proper physical distance from men, as when she helps the weak and frightened An Ji stand up by extending him her bow instead of her hand (ch. 6, 82).[13] Although she swears never to marry, she is gradually won over to marriage by An's parents and the other young wife-to-be, Zhang Jinfeng, who tells her that in everything she and He are "valiant heroes" (*yingxiong haojie*) and bend to no one's will. But when it comes to marriage, "hero no longer means anything and we can only follow heaven; we can only tumble into our mother's arms and do whatever she tells us" (ch. 26, 446), which is to get married. He Yufeng then kneels in front of An Ji's mother, hugs her, and cries out, "My dearest own mother" (447). The second half of the novel is largely taken up with episodes such as this in which He Yufeng, the Ans, and the Zhangs return to the normal path of running a family and having the young husband succeed in public life.

The Soft Male Hero

The hero An Ji is another "scholar-talent," *caizi*, or another Jia Baoyu, but is more pathetic in his girlish weakness and timidity than the heroes of the beauty-scholar romances and less sensitive to women than Baoyu. His "girlishness" (*nühai'er side, nühai'er yiban*)[14] is most vivid in his first encounter with Thirteenth Sister, whose mastery over the situation in Nengren Temple towers over his whimpering ineptness. In order to illustrate this contrast, it is necessary to describe that first scene.

On his mission to rescue his father, An Ji stays at a dirty, common inn full of unsavory people who pass through selling their services. A young woman rides up on a donkey, startling An Ji since he is unused to unfamiliar women. She is extremely beautiful, has very small bound feet, and a cold, steely look. Announcing that she is waiting for someone, she takes up a position at the door to her room and stares across at An Ji, who has been peeking at her from behind the curtain of his door and now finds that he can't stand to be looked at (ch. 4, 56–57). Afraid that she is another of the unsavory types who frequent the inn, he asks that a stone roller (*liuzhou*) be moved in to prop shut his door. She obliges by carrying in the huge stone—in a process described at length (60–61)—and then asks him where he wants it put and what he plans to do with it. He is shy like a girl but manages to pull himself together, "suppress his embarrassment," and tell her his story (ch. 5, 63–64). He then breaks down crying; she sympathizes and promises to help.

The scholar of the chaste romance is also like a woman, but mainly in his nonhirsute looks and his gentle disposition; he is rarely so timid and emotional.[15] In *Ernü yingxiong zhuan,* Thirteenth Sister acts "like a boy" to further herself; An Ji's acting "like a girl" is a sign of weakness. In general, as I have said previously, the scholar of the romances never crosses over as much as the beauty, who disguises as a man and succeeds like the most successful of men. In the scene at the inn, however, An Ji exhibits a complete switch of gender roles as he shyly occupies a feminine position behind the curtain while Thirteenth Sister stares at him like a man.

Nevertheless, he is no different from the scholar of the romances when it comes to assuming the role of polygamist, especially in his initial refusal to marry more than one woman. In discussing with Zhang Jinfeng the issue of taking another wife, he claims that family rules allow him to do so only after age fifty if he has had no son, adding that the inclusion of another woman would "dilute our love for each other" (using the word *en'ai*, ch. 23, 385). He finally accepts the proposal to marry both Zhang and He only when it is clear that Zhang, his mother, and father all want He to join the family.

As the hero of the latest novel discussed in this study, An Ji represents one of Qing fiction's final reductions and codifications of male character along a line going back to the beauty-scholar novels of the early Qing. The model is of a girlish boy who at home is a tame polygamist-father and abroad is an obedient servant of the state. In other words, he fathers children, passes exams, serves in office, and is good for nothing else. He has capable wives who manage the home and succeed in revitalizing a long neglected, unprofitable estate, which An Ji's father had years before let go. He Yufeng foils robbers one night while her husband sleeps with his other wife; he emerges with sword drawn only after He Yufeng has eliminated all danger. The author steadfastly refuses to allow An Ji the least bit of brilliance or valiance, portraying nothing beyond a mild man who studies diligently and listens to his father, mother, and wives.

Sexual Intimacy via Ablution

Like almost every novelist treated in this study, Wen Kang takes it upon himself to deal with the situation of intimacy between the sexes. Although he avoids description of sexual acts and has man and woman maintaining proper ritual distance, he manages to convey erotic atmospheres nevertheless, just like other authors who portray cross-gendered characters. The best examples of intimacy are in the scenes in which Thirteenth Sister rescues An Ji from the cannibalistic monks, an episode which must be described at length in order to clarify adequately the effect of erotic sublimation. As in *Yesou puyan*, a series of close but innocent physical contacts between him, her, and Zhang Jinfeng seal them into their eventual polygamous marriage. The result is the victory of innocence and health over the pollution of sexual lust, which registers itself only by its absence.

Thirteenth Sister finds An Ji tied up and ready to be eaten, his clothing torn and in disarray. She easily undoes the ropes tying his upper body, but when it comes to "the ropes around his lower half . . . , she feels awkward about undoing them" (ch. 6, 81). She then cuts the ropes with her knife and lets them unravel by themselves. In a scene not long after, she urges him to come out from behind a partition to meet the Zhangs, but he will not emerge because, as he says, his clothing is ripped: "My chest is exposed and I am naked" (ch. 8, 108). Annoyed at his prudishness, she urges him again, but to no avail. He finally confesses that he has "peed" in his pants from fright (109). She wonders why: "All I've done is take a knife and kill some worthless monks." At her further insistence, he finally thinks of a solution: he wrings out his pants, wipes off his hands, then steps out.

A second instance of intimacy by way of urination occurs later when Thirteenth Sister notices a troubled look on Zhang Jinfeng's face. Suddenly she understands: "Is it that you need to take a pee?" Zhang wants a regular chamber pot. Thirteenth Sister says: "You're an adult, aren't you? When you have to pee, why can't you just say so? What's all the holding back? Now you say you have to have a chamber pot and nothing else will do. I beg your pardon, but where are you ever going to find such a thing in a monk's temple? Hurry, follow me!" (ch. 9, 127).

All she can find is a wash basin, which she empties out. Then Zhang Jinfeng "hastily drew her hands inside her sleeves to undo her skirt and let down her undergarment. She covered the rim of the basin with her long outer robe, then squatted down and proceeded to pee without making the slightest bit of noise" (*yaque wushengde,* 127).

After Zhang finishes, Thirteenth Sister relieves herself as well, but more noisily and with greater alacrity since she wears fewer layers of clothing. "She looked at the basin and saw that Miss Zhang's pee had practically filled it up." She poured it out in the courtyard then brought it back inside.

> Now Thirteenth Sister's method of relieving herself differed greatly from Miss Zhang's. To begin with, all she wore was a waist-length jacket and a pair of pants. She never wore a skirt, much less a long outer robe. She let down her underwear and began to pee before she had even finished squatting: "*Hua la la, keng lang lang,*" she burst forth in a loud torrent. From the side Zhang Jinfeng remarked to herself, "What a handsome pair of thighs, snow-white and powdery soft just like mine. You'd never believe she was so skilled in fighting or had such strength!" (127–28)

The scene ends with Thirteenth Sister returning the unemptied basin to its stand. A narratorial aside excuses her lack of restraint by saying that her nature prevents her from being shy and affected like a modest girl (*zhezhe yanyan, niuniu nienie,* 128). Further, two women together need not be discreet, and anyway she had been holding back for a long time. A comparable scene in earlier chaste romances would have a male-impersonating woman sleeping in the same bed with her future co-wife, in some stories fondling her and perhaps discovering how appealing a woman's body is (e.g., *Qingmeng tuo*), in others not touching her at all (e.g., *Fenghuang chi,* in which the maid does the touching).

Up to this point we have seen the author arrange intimate encounters between An Ji and Thirteenth Sister, then between Thirteenth Sister and Zhang Jinfeng. He presents in highly muted form two extremes of the female erotic as stereotyped in Chinese fiction: the warm and soft, and the loud and assertive. All this is by way of preparing for step three of the establishment of intimacy via urination between An Ji and the two women. As the Qing commentator notes at this point, truth rests in the lowliest matter.[16]

In a third incident involving urination, An Ji is about to pick up a chicken they have cooked in order to separate its parts. But Thirteenth Sister suddenly remembers that his hands are dirty from wringing out his urine-soaked pants. She tells him, "Forget about it with those two hands of yours." He runs off and begins to wash in the unemptied basin into which Zhang and Thirteenth Sister had just urinated. "Thirteenth Sister yelled, 'You needn't go to such trouble. You don't want to use that basin to wash your hands!' He answered: 'Don't worry; the water is not cold. I just now used it to wipe my face; it's still warm.' " It is too late to stop him; Zhang is embarrassed; Thirteenth Sister acts as if nothing has happened. Meanwhile Zhang's mother has already taken the chicken apart (ch. 9, 132).

Much later, the above intimacies gain final significance when An's father and Zhang Jinfeng try to persuade Thirteenth Sister, now referred to as He Yufeng, to marry An Ji. He Yufeng refuses, citing that the issue of her marriage was the cause of her father's death to begin with (ch. 25, 410). An's father lists a number of famous and valiant women in history, none of whom ever resisted marriage (414–15). Still refusing to give in, He Yufeng explains how at the Nengren Temple she could have followed "the hackneyed formula of the scholar and the beauty and arranged her own marriage, without anyone being able to prevent her" (417). But she had not given into that temptation because she had her own separate will (*zhi*) then as now. However, she begins to weaken after more arguments and even a supernatural indication of the rightness of the threesome's marriage. The final turning point comes when Zhang reminds her of the intimacies at the temple. Zhang notes that when He Yufeng saw An Ji with his torn clothes and went to untie him, "their breaths had [already] joined" and "their flesh had [already] touched." When he washed his hands in the makeshift urine basin, as Zhang continues, "in the end he might as well have been washing his hands in your chamber pot!" (ch. 26, 446).[17] At a previous time, He Yufeng would have laughed off such words, the narrator notes, but now she hears them as if they were thunder. She realizes that she is in effect already married to An Ji by virtue of these contacts.

Keeping the Hero Correct After Marriage

The martial half of *Ernü yingxiong zhuan* is over at about the twentieth chapter, more or less corresponding to the length of the typical beauty-scholar romance. He Yufeng has reached her turning point and can be relied upon from now on. Young men, however, always potential wastrels, are a different case. The true test of their stability comes during times of routine comfort, when it is easy for them to grow restless and bored (*men*), and, like Tan Shaowen in *Qilu deng,* to develop a taste for entertainment (*le*). The recuperative function of the superior woman must therefore continue beyond her premarital acts of heroism in order to prevent the postmarital anticlimax from leading into decadence.

The problems of the postmarital half of the novel thus center on keeping An Ji correct and making him a success. A dangerous lapse occurs when he takes to hedonistic leisure after his marriage to the two beauties. Chapter 30 begins with his wearing fancier clothes than usual and contentedly watering chrysanthemums. He proposes a drinking party with his wives, who are alarmed at his failure to be serious about his studies. They refuse to allow him personally to pour drinks for them and will only have the maids pour. Still, like Geng Lang in *Lin Lan Xiang,* he finds drinking with two beautiful wives to be a supreme joy. When Zhang and He try to steer him out of his hedonistic mood, he almost creates a scene but then controls himself just in time. He reasons that if he ignores their admonishments, he may end up with two lions roaring at him for the rest of his life (ch. 30, 518–19, 528). In short, he forswears the excesses of hedonism, thereby avoiding the pitfalls of the henpecked husband, whose indulgences, both open and secret, are the cause of endless anger in his shrewish wife or wives.

Maintaining polygamous correctness figures once again in a less critical but nevertheless carefully engineered situation, the arrangement of the maid Changjie's concubinage to An Ji. At this point, the novel's most pronounced critique of *Honglou meng* also takes shape as the author brings to completion his repair of the earlier novel's failed three-wife marriage. Changjie suddenly begins to play a noticeable role in chapter 34, which contains a long passage comparing *Ernü yingxiong zhuan* to *Honglou meng*. The chaste Changjie compares favorably to Xiren, Jia Baoyu's unchaste personal maid. Changjie's concern for An's welfare is recorded numerous times throughout the rest of the novel. When he returns home from taking the examinations, she is ready with his tea, fixed exactly to his taste and held out for him with two hands raised high—as taught by his mother so that no hands touch when the cup is transferred.[18] Like Yuanyang in *Honglou meng*, Changjie swears to serve the An family forever and never to marry (ch. 40). However, when An is assigned to a post that is too distant for him to be accompanied by his now pregnant wives, the family feels that he must have a companion to attend to his personal needs. It becomes apparent to all that he should have Changjie as concubine. Later his assignment is suddenly changed to a closer location, making her concubinage unnecessary. But they have already conducted a formal ceremony, which included sleeping together; and besides, neither Zhang nor He are jealous of Changjie. As in the beauty-scholar romances, a great deal of storytelling effort goes into making such polygamous arrangements seem necessary and proper.[19]

Wen Kang's Criticism of Honglou meng

Ernü yingxiong zhuan's references to *Honglou meng* appear mainly in the chapter 34 passage, which lists the reasons that An Ji, his wives, and other characters are superior to Jia Baoyu, Daiyu, Baochai, and others.[20] Although Jia Baoyu is more talented than An Ji, the narrator says, only An Ji succeeds in public service. The difference lies in parentage: in raising Baoyu, Jia Zheng "is cultured but not really cultured, correct but not really correct" (ch. 34, 611–12).[21] Wen Kang further implies that the chief cause of woe in *Honglou meng* is the jealousy between Baochai and Daiyu. Baochai "keeps a lock on her match of gold and jade and secretly hatches treacherous plots. Daiyu is jealous of Baochai's match of gold and jade and never ceases giving vent to bitterness and sarcasm" (ch. 34, 612). In contrast, He Yufeng and Zhang Jinfeng are harmonious and happy to marry the same man.

Finally, Wen Kang claims to be writing his story in a healthy spirit. He is not possessed of what he calls the "forever unstemmable and poisoned resentment" of the author of *Honglou meng* (ch. 34, 613). To Wen Kang, *Honglou meng* is a decadent book that has poisoned the air with its portrayals of bored, unconstructive youth, of lascivious relations between juvenile master and maids, and of misguided love matches—criticisms echoed by many others in post–*Honglou meng* China. Like the characters of *Yesou puyan*, no one in *Ernü yingxiong zhuan* experiences the ennui of Jia Baoyu; all are interested in life and brimming with energy and dedication; no one is prone to sarcasm.

Health and Pollution

Ernü yingxiong zhuan corrects *Honglou meng* by creating two new versions of Jia Baoyu—one male, An Ji, and one female, Thirteenth Sister. At first An Ji is almost another Jia Baoyu, timid and girlish. He succumbs to the pleasures of staying at home and enjoying the company of his wives. But he proves himself first by summoning the courage to rescue his father and later by accepting the advice of his wives to study for the exams. Thirteenth Sister is a female mirror-opposite to Baoyu. As a baby she reaches for male toys; as an adult she surpasses men in strength and courage. An Ji is better than Jia Baoyu, but Thirteenth Sister is even better. Still, in the end, she finds enough softness in herself to overcome her excess of heroism and assume the role of wife and mother.

The healthy spirit of *Ernü yingxiong zhuan* is its main weapon against— or antidote to—*Honglou meng*. If it weren't for such health, how could An Ji wash so blithely in his wives' urine? That cleansing contains a secret lesson: An Ji succeeds where Jia Baoyu fails because he goes beyond

Baoyu by washing in his wives' urine. Jia Baoyu cannot compare because he only likes women's lip rouge and their used face-washing water (in which he washes his face while visiting Shi Xiangyun's and Daiyu's room early one morning). Unfortunately for Baoyu, as the example of *Ernü yingxiong zhuan* might teach us, his washing in women's waste is too lustful and deliberate. Furthermore, the water he uses isn't dirty enough to justify his marriage to two women.

It is not that An Ji likes pollution, however. He is oblivious and enthusiastic about washing in what he doesn't discover is urine, which evidently smells good to him. He compares with another well-known hero who wins his wife through immersion in her waste, the oil peddler of the late Ming story from *Xingshi hengyan* (Enduring Tales to Arouse the World), "The Oil Peddler Wins the Flower Fairy."[22] He pays a huge sum in order to spend one night with a beautiful courtesan, only to find her too drunk to do anything but be sick. He is content to lie by her side and, when she vomits, to catch the mess into his robe. The next morning he shrugs off the sacrifice by saying, "This is only your humble servant's robe, fortunate to have been stained with some of the young lady's left-over wine."[23] She is touched; and eventually they marry, a high-class courtesan and a humble but sensitive peddler of cooking oil.

The significance of female waste must be considered in light of the taboo against female pollution as defined in traditional folk and medical belief. The focus of such belief is on women at menstruation and childbirth, which are supposedly dire sources of pollution and ill health (and the effects of which, along with exposure of parts of the female body, function in various forms as weapons in military romances featuring women warriors, and reportedly in real battle situations in eighteenth- and nineteenth-century China).[24] One of the greatest dangers to the newborn is the residually noxious effect of the birthing woman. The closest *Ernü yingxiong zhuan* comes to portraying the birthing woman has a mother with large and richly flowing breasts feeding two healthy newborns (ch. 39, 743–44). An Ji's father accidentally walks in on her, sees two full breasts feeding the two babies at once, and starts to scurry away. "Don't be so squeamish," he is told; in the countryside no one "shuns" the sight of nursing mothers. Nursing breasts are like urine and vomit in being positive transformations of harmful and lascivious female effluvia. Like the innocent urine, breast milk belongs to *Ernü yingxiong zhuan*'s portrait of health—the father of the newborns, after all, is himself a vigorous man over ninety years old (ch. 39, 741). The belief in female pollution is thus evident only through its sublimation. Wen Kang invents no miser who learns to love the smell of night soil as a shield against his wife's shrewish "scattering." No man struggles to keep up with a more sexually powerful woman; no woman suffers as Wang Xifeng does from chronic gynecological ailments; no warrior woman exposes her body as a weapon against male enemies. *Ernü yingxiong zhuan* confines the woman's discharge to positively flowing urine and milk and in so doing either disavows pollution or assumes that it—and jealousy—can be healthily overcome.

The ideals of the chaste romance still prevail in *Ernü yingxiong zhuan*: heroes and heroines treat each other with respect, behave properly, and achieve marital happiness. Although the heroine does not disguise as a man, she still acts like one in order to achieve her goals. By virtue of the gender-crossing philosophy of "boy-girl heroism," she is allowed a constructive, masculine heroism as long as she is on her mission of vengeance. In being constructively masculine, she avoids being malevolent like the shrew, who tries to destroy men and rival women and bellows her opposition to polygamy and men's privileges in general. As for polygamy, although it is in the man's favor, the hero in *Ernü yingxiong zhuan* is only half a man anyway and is further justified in his taking of two wives by the irrevocable accident of mutual exposure, which takes the form of innocent urine-water that floats the threesome together.

Innocence and health, in fact, are recurring emblems of repair and justification in *Ernü yingxiong zhuan*. In the context of late Qing China, signs of health include, for instance, the fact that *Ernü yingxiong zhuan*'s characters smoke only tobacco, as exemplified by the young wife Zhang Jinfeng (probably illustrating the custom among women of Manchuria and north China in those times). Like the warrior-woman who punishes "obstinate and unruly men," the robust, tobacco-smoking beauty in effect outshines inferior, opium-smoking wastrels, although it is of course improbable that Wen Kang had any such theme in mind (but Zhang does contrast with the pedant and his filthy pipe-smoking habit, ch. 37, 684–85). In retrospect, we readers might say that a woman should oppose polygamy, just as China should have opposed foreigner-imposed opium. But the novelist, if able to use our current vocabulary, might reply that superwomen accepting a modest form of polygamy—or smoking a modest form of opium—embody healthy, renewed versions of the cultural superego, of which men seem to have temporarily lost sight. In short, the recuperative function of the superior woman effects a rescue of the weak man and then returns him to the role of patriarch and polygamist.

Summing up the positive and reparative features of this novel, then, we may say that—in face of a decadent society and its obscene fiction and by way of avoidance, transformation, or antidotal correction, whatever the case may be—*Ernü yingxiong zhuan* portrays tobacco instead of opium; urine and milk instead of blood and sexual fluids; premarital intimacy by accident rather than intention; chaste bigamy (plus concubine) instead of erotic polygamy; capable and fertile women instead of jealous, lascivious, and barren shrews or women who cry and waste away; and a coddled but obedient husband instead of wastrels, philanderers, misers, or celibates. *Ernü yingxiong zhuan* directs itself against Western incursions and accompanying social disintegration after all by staging its correction of *Honglou meng* at a time when no one could have missed the impact of the Opium Wars, the Taiping uprising, and numerous other signs of anarchy and dysfunction.

14

PROMISCUOUS POLYGYNY AND

MALE SELF-CRITIQUE

The preceding chapters have addressed the belief in both the power and the expendability of women and the ways in which this belief informs the sexuality of characters in eighteenth-century fiction. In this chapter I will revert to the generalizing mode of chapter 1 in which I drew a composite of archetypal male and female behavior in eighteenth-century novels. The following is then an overview of the society in which the hierarchies engendered by polygyny constitute the norms around which everyone revolves.

The contrast between chaste and erotic romances provides the most clear-cut account of how sexuality is defined in the fictional society: where there is absence of sex, there is monogamy or at most two-wife polygamy; where there is sex, there is polygamy, which includes concubinage, prostitution, and adultery. In general, when women are sexualized, their expendability is assumed. They are sequestered inside the home and discouraged from having relationships with other women; a woman's finger isn't considered important unless cut off and served to the man. The penis becomes a treasure over which women vie in situations of polygamous rivalry—as said in *Lüye xianzong*, "To a woman this thing is her living treasure" (ch. 81, 1033b). The most respectable way for the woman to survive her fate of expendability is to become a model of chastity, whereby she becomes superior to even men, especially in the so-called latter days of history when the "luminous virtue" of the cosmos "only takes hold in women," no longer in men. In the alternate world of chaste female superiority, male self-deprecation and desexualization complement female chastity. Two final novels, one from the early Qing, the other from the later mid-Qing, reillustrate this complementarity and show how it points to a less obvious theme: the weakening of the rigid alienation of the sexes which defines man and woman as either pro-creative or libidinous sexual beings. Instead man and woman assume the alternatingly masculine / feminine or nurturing / infantile body of the cross-aligned self.

Chaste and Unchaste Heroines in

Jin Yun Qiao and *Jinghua Yuan*

Jin Yun Qiao, a seventeenth-century novel which was later borrowed and rewritten as Vietnam's national epic, is about a woman who never con-summates with her husband; instead, the husband also marries her sister and has sex only with her.[1] At the beginning of the story, the heroine Cui Qiao admires a famous prostitute before whose grave she offers devo-tion. She then falls in love with a man, her eventual husband, but is unable to marry him because her father suffers calamity that Cui Qiao can only undo by selling herself. For the next fifteen years she becomes the sexual partner of "everyone" but her future husband: first she is sold into prostitution, then becomes the concubine of a man whose jealous wife contrives to enslave her, then again falls into prostitution, is re-deemed by a bandit chief, and finally reunites with her original husband-to-be, who has meanwhile married her sister. Back in the beginning, before they were separated, Cui Qiao and her husband-to-be had met secretly and nestled in each other's arms. When he wished to have sex, she refused, telling him that in order to have a successful end they must have a proper beginning. Fifteen years later, after they are finally re-united, she again refuses to have sex, now saying that she does not wish to do with him what she suffered as humiliation from other men. The husband suddenly realizes that "she is in fact a sage and hero, not just a woman."[2]

In *Jin Yun Qiao,* the man's bigamy is with two sisters, who can be likened to one woman divided into two aspects. Cui Qiao's sister is the normal woman-wife with whom the man begets sons. Cui Qiao is the woman he loves romantically and sexually—that is, through secret and illicit meetings or via prostitution and concubinage. The division is between the proper wife about whom there is no story to tell, and the sacrificed woman who is the raison d'être of whole novels. In *Jin Yun Qiao,* the devaluation of the male takes the form of the absence of heroic men and the smallness of men's roles in general, including the husband's. To the man, a woman is either a procreative partner or an unchaste-turned-chaste sage whom he elevates above everyone else. Although Cui Qiao loses her chastity and suffers degradation at the hands of countless men, in the end she reconstructs her chastity or its near equivalent and thereby surpasses all men and other women.

Read in light of *Jin Yun Qiao,* the roles of Baochai and Daiyu in *Honglou meng* resemble the Cui sisters' in terms of the situation of two-wife polygamy that is recurrent in Qing fiction. In short, Baochai is a version of the woman who becomes the hero's procreative wife; Daiyu is a version of the woman who is sacrificed through illicit love and ends by being elevated into celibacy and sagehood, although Daiyu dies a literal death instead of the symbolic one of sagehood.

Jinghua yuan, written in the early nineteenth century by Li Ruzhen (1763?–1830?), plays with the same theme of female superiority found throughout the Qing, even quoting the famous words of Xie Ximeng about the "luminous virtue" of the cosmos only "taking hold in" women, no longer in men (ch. 42, 307).[3] The women in *Jinghua yuan* are talented in all the important aspects of knowledge and sometimes also in martial arts; they are cheerful and untragic. They are loyal to men to the point of being unquestioningly willing to commit suicide if their husbands die in battle. But they are not sexy or sentimental. Romantic and sexual love are almost nonexistent in *Jinghua yuan,* which comes closest to explicit eroticism in only a few scenes of minor graphic description. One of the male protagonists, Lin Zhiyang, is kidnapped by the female "King" of the Country of Women (who is dressed as a man), and is forced to dress as a woman in order to serve as imperial concubine. The attendants wash his private parts in preparation for intercourse with the "King," which almost but does not quite take place (ch. 33). Later in the novel, a joke is told about two maggots looking up at the anus of a constipated girl sitting on the toilet (ch. 75). Scenes such as these recall Wen Kang's descriptions of intimacy via urination or Xia Jingqu's portrayal of Suchen's diarrhea or his great urination. The point in common is that when novelists avoid explicit erotic depiction, they replace the lascivious sexual body with the innocent and infantile body of ablution, urination, and defecation.

In downplaying the role of sex, *Jinghua yuan* takes a radical stance against bound feet, which the polygamous romances treat with erotic interest. The novel describes in detail the pain and deformity that were forced upon women in former times (chs. 12, 32, 34). Although the novel never explicitly promotes the elimination of bound feet, the extent of detail in these descriptions in itself bears a polemic intensity. Moreover, this etching of women's suffering coincides with the portrayal of male heroes who pale next to the female stars of the book. Lin Zhiyang and his male companions are repeatedly outdone by the young talented women they meet.[4] As part of this turning of tables, the author has Lin actually cross-dress and experience the agony of having his feet bound.

Despite the radical treatment of this one subject, however, *Jinghua yuan* generally promotes Confucian values, as evidenced in its prominent endorsement of the traditional precepts of female virtue at the beginning of its first chapter (ch. 1, 1). The rescue of maidens in exile is mainly to repair damage done at the beginning of the story because of a fight between rivalrous heavenly goddesses. This havoc results on earth in the advance of the female emperor, Wu Zetian, who whimsically orders all flowers to bloom at once in midwinter. That act, like her empresshood itself, is against natural order. Her willfullness is an alternate version of the shrew's sexual insatiability and indomitable rage; Empress Wu is, of course, notorious in Ming and Qing fiction, including *Jinghua yuan* itself, for having numerous male lovers. The novel ends with the reinstatement of good women (the maidens) over bad (the empress), and with the return to power of the legitimate male ruler, whose advancement, like Wen Suchen's in *Yesou puyan*, represents the reestablishment of virtuous male energy and the abolition of sensual vices.

Alienation and Alliance between Men and Women

The examples of *Jin Yun Qiao* and *Jinghua yuan* allow us to make some final generalizations about the carving of relations between men and women in Qing fiction. As portrayed in numerous works, the situations of male-female relations reduce to either (1) division into separate and alienated worlds, whether conjugally oriented or not, or (2) a cooperation by which men and women form alliances of hard-won monogamy or temperate polygamy. In the situation of separate worlds, shrews overwhelm abject husbands; misers isolate themselves from wives and sons; promiscuous polygynists alienate rivalrous or spurned wives; celibates and other enlightened men escape petty and insatiable women; or chaste women and matriarchal sages tower over wastrels or otherwise inferior or devaluated men. In the society of cooperation, the beauty and scholar join in happy monogamy; or virtuous co-wives ally to serve and coddle their mild-mannered husband, who receives their admonishments agreeably and never exceeds the proper limits of passion with any of his wives.

As I have drawn it, the alienation between the shrew and the miser is a caricature of the normalist mode of male-female relations; the society of cooperation, on the other hand, represents an aspired to ideal. The so-called normalist situation could be described as follows: Men and women occupy two mutually exclusive camps that are as if primordially defined. Men govern the outside world but have their choice of access to or control over the inside; women govern the inside but have little access to or control over the outside. Men are polygamous and sexually nomadic, unless poverty or other unfortunate or unusual circumstances force them into monogamy or bachelorhood. Sometimes so-called enlightenment brings men into a more dedicated than usual form of bachelorhood, monastic celibacy. Women are normally forced into marriage no matter what; they are restricted to one sexual partner, unless they become prostitutes, in which case they are "everyone's wife," as described in *Jin Yun Qiao* (ch. 1, 259). Men create detailed lore about the sexual capacities and attributes of women, and view their own bodies as on a continuum from regulated containment to dissipation. Whether miser, monk, stalwart hero, or polygynist, a man views himself as safest and purest when he dismisses women from his consciousness. Some women meet this dismissal with heroic self-sacrifice and unlimited, thankless giving; others accommodate through creation of clever modes of defense; and still others pound at the door of male containment and do whatever they can to subvert or sabotage male freedom.

By way of either exceeding or overturning the norm, as portrayed in *Jin Yun Qiao, Jinghua yuan,* and other works, women become extreme exceptions and tend to fit two types. At one end—that of exceeding the norm—is the female hero or sage, who is chaste or only modestly sexual; at the other end—that of overturning the norm—is the female tyrant or boss, in other words, the shrew, who is sexually insatiable. The female hero and sage are superior to the man and put him to shame; they are correctives of inferior or mediocre men. At the same time, they are viewed as ultimately provisional models, that is, "men among women," or "sages, not just women." As for the female tyrant, she is like a mirror image of the male tyrant, except that she is considered more grotesque— just as the chaste beauty is more virtuous than the most virtuous man. The empress Wu Zetian, for example, is as notorious with her male lovers as bad emperors are with their harems, but she is considered more of an abomination than he. Like the chaste heroine, the female tyrant is also a temporary figure, soon replaced by the vindicated or remolded man. As the man sees it, when women get the upper hand, they merely switch the tables on the men, as if all along the relationship between men and women is a battle which only one side or the other can win, whether the stakes are moral virtue or political power.

The male complements of these female extremes are (1) the man as temperate polygamist, monogamist, or self-deprecator, and (2) the man as henpecked husband, miser, or ascetic. The first type, the counterpart to the chaste or sage woman, is sorry for women's suffering and opposed to male baseness and decadence. He makes up for women's hard lot and men's baseness by elevating women above men and eschewing or limit- ing his polygynous sexual freedom. The male apologist separates himself from the lascivious other man who suffers from karmic retribution or sexual enervation. Other men may be base or impotent, but he himself is effeminate and sensitive to women (e.g., Jia Baoyu, the monogamous scholar), and in some cases also sexually potent (e.g., Suchen, Xiaoguan). He allies himself with superior women such as beauties or widow sages. At its extreme, male self-devaluation manifests itself in attempts to trans- pose male and female roles and thereby jar the traditional exclusiveness of gender categories, implying unprecedented modes of interaction.

The second type of man represents the impotent counterpart to shrewish force. Confronted with the shrew, the man shrinks and trem- bles, replaces desire for women with desire for money, or achieves enlight- enment and dismisses women from his consciousness. Although male privilege is a bastion in both real and fictional societies, it is nevertheless diluted by preoccupation with male impotence and its' cures. The fear of impotence has at its core the man's perceived inability to hold back his ejaculation during intercourse; it is as if so much as a leaf falling on his back will make him lose control.[5] In this view, women are naturally capa- ble and strong in sex; men must learn methods of self-control; women are, men observe and perform. Many variations of these perceptions of male-female imbalance exist: for example, "The woman's superiority over the man is like that of water's ability to put out fire," or "A woman's desire does not cease until she is buried beneath the earth." Whether the man is sexual boss, the nicer promiscuous polygynist, or the yet nicer temperate polygynist, he must govern his house well. Otherwise his women and other underlings will destroy him and each other in their attempts to monopolize his *yang*-potency.

To rephrase and expand the above: the typical man proceeds on his own or in league with other men, in either case mostly or completely oblivious of women. If he allows himself to regress too much from the normal male mode, he becomes too aware of women and suffers the depletion of *yang* energy. Sometimes others cause him to regress, such as when he is brought up as the coddled but mild-mannered son doted upon by mother or grandmother. By way of opposing and outflanking woman and mother, he may regress even further by becoming grotesque woman-mother himself, as does the coquettish mother-of-waste miser and keeper of the outhouse, or by retreating into the misogynistic consolation of philosophy, as Baoyu does briefly in his imitation of Zhuangzi (ch. 21). Another form of departure—in effect, escape—from the normal mode of male behavior is that of self-critique and remolding. Such departure leads to some form of desexualization and typically involves the dialectical transposition of gender roles, where man and woman become like parallel couplets. In actual form, however, crossing of gender is less perfectly balanced than literary parallelism, tending to deflate the man and inflate the woman, making her into a superior version of a man. Crossing of gender thus appears to be another form of escapist regression, like the miser's, a self-centered, makeshift, and infantile attempt to preempt sexual division. In other words, all such regression is infantile and make-believe, an indication of the man's refusal or inability to give up the authority he has or thinks he has. The miser's make-believe is to replace the woman and become both man and woman in himself. The self-deprecator erases himself and lets there only be woman. He rejects the traditional father, does not replace him, but pretends the woman is a better version of himself, his father, and all other men. The self-deprecating man removes sex from the scene—to him, all sex is contaminating—and, as enacted in the predenouement sections of *Honglou meng*, suspends man and woman in an adolescent state suggestive of androgyny, with him at the center.

The transcendence of sex is a predictable strategy for opposing the society of polygamous lust. The motto of that strategy is that sex is base and ephemeral, that is, always a matter of "liking the new and tiring of the old." In its version of transcendence, *Yesou puyan* declares genital pleasure to be superfluous but affirms kissing, caressing, and naked embrace. The author portrays man and woman taking care of each other's naked bodies in states of energetic imbalance—such as fever and diarrhea, accidental ingestion of aphrodisiac, and infertility. Each nurtures the other through a bestowal of curative *yin* or *yang* energy. Evil takes the form of cannibalistic appropriation of another's essence and of grotesque manipulation and abuse of the genitals. *Ernü yingxiong zhuan* displays the urinating bodies of An Ji, He Yufeng, and Zhang Jinfeng, and assigns them identities by the way they urinate; it allows the sight of nursing breasts, which are portrayed as richly flowing. *Honglou meng* and the beauty-scholar romances portray young men and women communing through the exchange of matched poetry. Heroes and heroines look alike or easily pass as members of the opposite sex. Even works that contain explicit descriptions of sex portray man and woman engaging in the artful and civilized love of the ars erotica; lovers avoid acting in a lascivious or appropriating way. Although it takes polygyny for granted, the high erotic reduces as much as it can the appearance of the sacrifice and appropriation of women that is more obvious in "lower" contexts.

Desexualization and the focus upon the woman at the expense of the man continue into twentieth-century literature. In the so-called Mandarin Ducks and Butterfly fiction of the early decades of this century, Rey Chow observes love stories in which the man participates "only by being weak, sick, dead, [or] far away."[6] The main part of the drama leaves the woman to struggle alone. Going to a greater extreme than the beauties and scholars of the early Qing, the lovers in these stories need not even marry, much less touch each other (Chow, 69–70). The woman's struggle becomes the stage for playing out the failure of modern China, just as the failures of the polygamous family were played out through the sufferings of Daiyu and other female characters in *Honglou meng* and other works of Qing fiction. The "masochistic" man, as Rey Chow describes, idealizes the woman into a being pure and untouched by sexuality, and therein he finds refuge. He looks to the woman in such a helplessly expectant way, however, that nothing is left for man or woman but a state of frozen, impotent weeping. Chow finds the core of this crisis to lie in the man's inability to fuse "sensuality" and "affection" into his apprehension of the woman. In the vocabulary of Qing fiction, in other words, the man conceives of either the sexy concubine and lascivious shrew or the widow sage and chaste beauty. The man's split of the woman is also a split of himself; he is either the promiscuous polygynist / sexual boss or the coddled husband on the way to being the self-contained miser or ascetic.

The goal of the hero in the erotic romance *Xiuping yuan* is "to read all the number one extraordinary books," thereby to gain the knowledge "to pass all the number one difficult exams," and then to "marry all the number one beautiful women" (ch. 1, 4b). The key to upward mobility for him and all others is to find the right formula or book and thereby prevail over as many competitors and persecutors as possible, perhaps even to become "number one." There are numerous formulas, books, and strategies for attaining this goal: a "Book of Heavenly Wisdom" (*Tianshu*) for the would-be imperial unifier, a book of test questions and answers for the would-be official, a war manual for the general, a sex manual for the polygynist, a manual of cosmic secrets for the would-be immortal, a manual of alchemy for the seeker of gold, and so forth—all primarily for the man's use. Women may steal these books from men, as do Xiwangmu or the female demons in *Lüye xianzong,* or they may compose their own sets of formulas, as do prostitutes in *Jin Yun Qiao* and *Xiuping yuan* (and as did prostitutes in real China), having lists of techniques for captivating customers and soaking them of their wealth, including tricks for subduing men in sexual intercourse.[7]

Those who oppose the society of the "number one" polygamist have few formulas of their own. They try to escape by elevating women and reviling men, or by promoting androgyny and the imaginary world of perpetual adolescence. Monogamy and romantic love are other alternatives. Monkhood and nunhood are time-honored fallbacks if all else fails. In recent history, the selfless asexuality of Communist morality from the thirties to the seventies and after in many ways recreates the fictional world of perpetual adolescence (though with dedicated political engagement rather than elitest withdrawal), and supersedes the mores of a society ruled by polygyny, concubinage, and prostitution.

In spite of the fact that only 10 percent or less of Chinese men could afford to be polygamists, or that polygamy is now outlawed and exists only clandestinely, real or fictional polygamy allows us to observe the aspirations of the "number one" male writ large. His central tenets include the expendability of women and other men, the preciousness of semen and *yang* strength in general, and the importance of containing men and women within set roles and types of activity. The miser-ascetic and the number one man are alike in equating attachment to women with loss of essence. These men act as if they are self-directed, as if they can escape the necessary interaction with and determination by women. However much they succeed or fail to quantify themselves and women into discrete, manageable segments, they still believe that "brothers are like hands and feet; a wife is like a piece of clothing" (*xiongdi ru shouzu, qizi ru yifu*).

NOTES

1 Potent Polygamists and Chaste Monogamists

1. Numerous Chinese sources relate the general features and history of polygamy and concubinage, e.g., Chen Dongyuan, 1926; Chen Guyuan, 1936; and Chen Peng, 1990. In English, see Jaschok, 1988, and Watson and Ebrey, 1991; and on women, marriage, and concubinage in the Song, see Ebrey, 1993, *The Inner Quarters,* which provides useful background to this study. Ebrey notes an important shift in the Song dynasty, the "growth in the market for women as maids, concubines, courtesans, and prostitutes" (265). She states that the "great growth in the money economy in the Sung and the development of commercialized cities" coincided with a growing tendency among men to go from merely visiting pleasure quarters to actually purchasing women to bring home as concubines (217–18).

2. See Fang, 1986. Instead of *renqing,* the term *yan qing,* "telling of feelings," is sometimes used.

3. Naquin and Rawski, 1987: x–xi.

4. As summarized by Naquin and Rawski, 1987: 106.

5. See Naquin and Rawski, 1987: 74. For an early example in fiction of opium addiction, see *Yaguan lou,* circa 1820.

6. In my application of these terms and methods, I am inspired by the psychoanalytic theories of Freud, Jacques Lacan, and recent feminist critics such as Jane Gallop, Naomi Schor, and Kaja Silverman.

7. On this distinction, see Coward and Ellis, 1977: chs. 5, 6; Easthope, 1991: 130–32; and Silverman, 1992: 29–35.

8. In Freudian and Lacanian psychoanalysis, the symbolic order is primarily structured by the Oedipus complex (instead of Oedipus, however, I will substitute patriarchal polygamist). Lacanian theory also speaks of the Name-of-the-Father and the symbolic role of the phallus. The word "symbolic" is significant in distinguishing

penis as actual organ from the phallus, which symbolizes unmediated fullness, unimpaired self-presence, something said to be lacking in all subjects but nevertheless claimed by conventional masculinity and denied to the woman. See Gallop, 1982: 95; and Silverman, 1992: 15–16, 41–42.

9. See Silverman, 1992: 48–49.

10. She uses these words in speaking of the "dominant fiction" (1992: 30).

11. Silverman, 1992: 161–62, quoting LaPlanche and Pontalis, 1973: 318. The "mise-en-scène" is one "in which what is *prohibited* (l'interdit) is always present in the actual formation of the wish" (their emphasis).

12. That is, "permutations of roles and attributes are possible" (LaPlanche and Pontalis, 1973: 318).

13. A theorization of this term in the context of this book would first have to take into account the term's postindustrial and postcolonial historicity.

14. See, for example, Ropp, 1981, on the portrayal of female excellence; Wu, 1988, on shrews and jealousy; Hinsch, 1990, on male homosexuality; Edwards, 1990a, 1990b, on male veneration of women, and 1993, on women and social power; Lu, 1991, on sublimated and perverse aspects of sexuality; and Zeitlin, 1993, on gender dislocation.

15. See, e.g., Furth, 1986, 1987, 1988, on gender in traditional medicine; Carlitz, 1991, on prescriptive works about female behavior; Handlin, 1975, Ko, 1992, and Widmer, 1989, 1992, on women's education and literary and artistic activity; Chang, 1991, on late Ming images of women; Waltner, 1981, Mann, 1987, and Leung, 1993, on widow chastity; and Rowe, 1992, on women and the family in social thought. See also the essays in Watson and Ebrey, 1986, on marriage and inequality.

16. See *Zui chunfeng,* ch. 4, 10b–11a. For fuller bibliographical references, see chapters below and bibliography.

17. See ch. 2, 4a; that is, maintaining chastity is too dull, but being unchaste is still "not completely satisfying."

18. On the so-called "uterine" family, see Wolf, 1972: 37; and Wolf and Huang, 1980: 64.

19. "Natal" refers to the family into which she was born; "uterine" refers to herself and her children.

20. *Laozi jiaoshi,* 239, my translation; see also D. C. Lau's translation, 1976: 120.

21. *Haoqiu zhuan,* taken to England in 1719, has 1761, 1829, and 1842 translations. *Yu Jiao Li,* which Hegel mentions in his *Philosophy of History,* has 1826 and 1842 translations. On the introduction of these works to Europe, see Lu Xun, 1973: 245–46; Su, 1985: 12–13; Wang, 1988; and Hessney, 1979: 25, 326–45.

22. See, however, *Jinghua yuan,* ch. 34, for a description of footbinding, in this case forced on a man.

23. On pregnancy, abortion, and infanticide, see McMahon, 1988a: 102. On venereal disease, see *Qilu deng,* ch. 64, 607–8; *Yaguan lou,* chs. 14–15; and *Jin Shi yuan quanzhuan,* ch. 24.

24. For all these, see *Nao huacong*, ch. 6, 39b, and elsewhere.

25. See the discussion of female pollution in ch. 13 of this volume.

26. See *Yesou puyan*, ch. 64, 4a; *Chan Zhen yishi*, ch. 21; and McMahon, 1988a: 114, 120. Naked women are part of stratagems in military romances, e.g., *Yangjiafu yanyi*, 159 (in the episode called "Mu Guiying qin Liulang"), and reportedly figured in real battle situations of this period (see Naquin, 1981: 101).

27. See *Zui chunfeng*, ch. 4; and Furth, 1987: 22. In *Yangjiafu yanyi*, the fluids of a woman giving birth in the midst of battle cause the defeat of the barbarian enemy (164); see also Chen, 1992: 101.

28. See also *Chan Zhen yishi*, chs. 5–7; McMahon, 1988a: 112; and *Lin Lan Xiang*, ch. 10, 76, in which two maids discuss menstrual irregularity.

29. See *Taohua yanshi*, ch. 3, 13ab.

30. See *Langshi qiguan*, ch. 25.

31. See, for example, *Zui chunfeng*, ch. 7; *Wusheng xi*, by Li Yu, story 5.

32. See van Gulik, 1974, and Hinsch, 1990: 173–78. *Lin Lan Xiang* contains a possible example of exclusive lesbianism (chs. 28 and 64). Men in fiction actually state their preference for sex with men, e.g., *Nao huacong*, ch. 6, 36b; but, although women engage in sex with each other, they do not articulate their preference; see ch. 6 of this volume.

33. "Mean," *jian*, refers to the fact that such commoners—distinguished from *liang-min*, i.e., "good" or "respectable commoners"—were not eligible to sit for government exams.

34. See Naquin and Rawski, 1987: 126.

35. See the opera *Yanzi jian*, by Ruan Dacheng, and its crudely transformed novel version of the same name, which includes scenes of ribaldry and sexual allusion.

36. See Naquin and Rawski, 1987: 61–63, who refer to Colin Mackerras's discussion of the so-called clapper operas (Mackerras, 1975: 29–31).

37. See Xu, 1984: 1997 (precise period not indicated). On adoption, see Waltner, 1990.

38. See Wolf and Huang, 1980: 334.

39. See Pasternak, 1985: 324; and Wolf and Huang, 1980: 222, 227.

40. The novel portrays five uxorilocal husbands, three of whom are covert bigamists. See chs. 10, 11; 19, 20; 23, 24; 25, 26; and 28.

41. The only example I know of *tongyang xi* is in the second story of Li Yu's *Wusheng xi* (Miss He; thanks to David Rolston for this reference).

42. See Naquin and Rawski, 1987: 38 and 108.

43. See Xu Ke, 1984: 1997 (precise period not indicated).

44. See Xu Ke, 1984: 2044 and 2114.

45. Cited in Feng and Chang, 1990: 214–15.

46. See Mann, 1987: 37–56; T'ien, 1988: 126–48.

47. See, e.g., Xu Ke, 1984: 2042–43.

48. See Xu Ke, 1984: 2001–2.

49. See *Taohua ying,* ch. 10, 8b.

50. Baker, 1979: 20.

51. Naquin and Rawski, 1987: 38, 110.

52. See Wolf and Huang, 1980: 68; Naquin and Rawski, 1987: 34.

53. Also of the mean class were police, jailers, gatekeepers, and yamen runners. Some of these managed to sit for exams anyway. The Yongzheng emperor tried to allow for change of status, and the Qianlong emperor enacted a law in 1771 that allowed third-generation members of this class to take exams. See Naquin and Rawski, 1987: 117–18.

54. See Elman, 1991: 17.

55. See Feng and Chang, 1990: 222–23. Naquin and Rawski say seventeen or eighteen for women and twenty-one for men (1987: 108).

56. See examples in fiction below and in Xu Ke, 1984: 2095 and 3507; and Feng and Chang, 1990: 216–17.

57. Naquin and Rawski, 1987: 111.

58. The legal complexity of this transition can be traced in terms of legislation against the various forms of bigamy, polygamy, and adultery; see Meijer, 1971. A brief account in Chinese of this influence and transition can be found in Jiang, 1991: 296–300.

59. See McMahon, 1988a: 10, 41–43, 140–41 on the miser, and 42, 115, and elsewhere on the shrew.

2   Polygamy According to Fiction and Prescriptive Models

1. On marriage laws and customs, see Chiu, 1966: 32, and Chen Guyuan, 1987: 48–49. An exception occurred, for example, in the situation called *jiantiao,* in which, besides his own wife, a man married a wife (or wives) to carry on the line of a childless uncle (or uncles; Chiu: 33–38). Note that it was a worse crime for a woman to be a bigamist than a man (Chen: 54).

2. On "acquiring concubines" in the Song, see Ebrey, 1993: 219–22.

3. Jie of the Xia spent huge sums on his favorite Moxi and then rejected her for two other favorites; see Karlgren, 1946: 326–27. Zhou's favorite was Daji; You's favorite was Baosi, who wanted to eliminate the Empress. For Zhou's story, see *Shi ji* (Han dynasty), 1972: ch. 3, 105–8, in the Yin Annals. For the account of You, see *Shi ji,* ch. 4, 147, in the Zhou Annals.

4. *Zuo zhuan,* Duke of Zhao, year 28. See Legge, 1871: 726–27, which I have modified considerably.

5. *Zuo zhuan,* Duke of Zhao, year 1. Legge, 1871: 580–81, which I have modified.

6. The earliest ars erotica texts are dateable to at least 168 B.C. On multiple intercourse with many women, see the Mawangdui text *Yang sheng fang* under the two

entries entitled *zhi* as found in *Mawangdui Hanmu boshu*, 1985, 101, no. 31; 102, no. 34; 114, no. 170—and in Zhou and Diao, 1988: 264–65 and 300. See also Harper, 1987: 539–93. My quote is from a Tang era text in *Ishimpō bōnai* (in Chinese, *Yixin fang*), by Tamba Yasuyori, 1976: 23, citing the *Sunü jing*. Translations will be mine unless otherwise noted. For reference to English translations of *Ishimpō*, see below.

7. *Ishimpō*, 26, from the *Shenxian jing,* one of several texts collected in the *Ishimpō*.

8. From the *Fangji,* Legge, 1967, vol. 2: 299.

9. From the *Quli,* Legge, 1967, vol. 1: 77–78.

10. From the *Neize,* Legge, 1967, vol. 1: 454–55. I have removed Legge's parentheses in this and in the following quotations.

11. From the *Quli,* slightly modifying Legge, 1967: 77.

12. From the *Quli,* Legge, 1967: 61–62.

13. See Chiu, 1966: 49.

14. Translated by Ebrey, 1984: 286–87.

15. See McMahon, 1988a: ch. 1.

16. Health is defined in numerous ways, but this one is common: "Vital substances are sealed within the body and heteropathy sealed out." See Sivin, 1987: 97.

17. On medical images of the female condition, see Furth, 1986: 43–66, especially 48–51; and on concepts of pregnancy, childbirth, and infancy, see Furth, 1987: 7–35, especially 13.

18. Furth, 1986: 63.

19. Furth, 1987: 9, 12–16.

20. Furth, 1987: 29.

21. Furth, 1986: 9.

22. That is, *Mencius,* fourth century B.C., translated by Lau, 1970: 161 (*Mengzi yizhu,* 255). This famous quote belongs to Gaozi, whom Mencius is in the process of refuting.

23. From the *Liyun,* Legge, 1967, vol. 1: 380, changing "men" to "humans."

24. See the *Qiu zi* (Seeking progeny) section in *Ishimpō,* 257.

25. See Harper, 1987, and Li and McMahon, 1992. Douglas Wile's *Art of the Bedchamber,* 1992, provides discussion and translation of texts from the Mawangdui to the Ming and Qing, including ars erotica works for women. Other general discussions of the ars erotica can be found in van Gulik, 1974, and Ruan Fang Fu, 1991.

26. Translated in Wile, 1992: 122–33.

27. Translated in Wile, 1992: 136–46.

28. On this point, see Li and McMahon, 1992. The historical context of the early ars erotica is still insufficiently understood, as is the early history of polygyny. Important changes did occur in pre-Han times and later, as Melvin Thatcher points out, for example, in marriage practices after the establishment of the Qin empire (1991: 47–48). How such changes relate to the ars erotica is urgently in need of study.

29. See section twenty-eight, *Bōnai (Fangnei,* In the Bedchamber), in van Gulik, 1974: 125–54 (a partial and rearranged translation, with some sections in Latin); Levy

and Ishihara, 1989; and Wile, 1992: 85–94, 100–113 (also a partial and rearranged translation).

30. This is the *Sunü jing* as found in fragmented form in the *Ishimpō*; see 23. Other texts cited below that are broken up and quoted throughout the *Ishimpō* are *Yufang mijue*, *Yufang zhiyao*, and *Dongxuanzi*, among others.

31. See the *Weizhi* section in *Baopuzi*, by Ge Hong, 1985: 129. The title *Sunü jing*, incidentally, appears in the *Xialan* section of the *Baopuzi* and in the *Hanshu* bibliography.

32. From a general medical work *Yifang leiju* cited in Zhou Yimou, 1989: 73–74. The same idea is found in the *Xiu zhen yanyi* (Ming?) as translated by Wile, 1992: 138.

33. Both quotes from *Sunü jing*, in *Ishimpō*, 32; the quote about fire and water also occurs, for example, in the Ming novel *Dengcao heshang*, ch. 1, 1b.

34. *Sunü jing*, *Ishimpō*, 39.

35. *Yufang mijue*, in *Ishimpō*, 296. These are a few of the numerous taboos.

36. *Dongxuanzi*, in *Ishimpō*, 89 and 103.

37. *Sunü jing*, in *Ishimpō*, 39; and *Yufang zhiyao*, 98.

38. *Dongxuanzi*, in *Ishimpō*, 103.

39. *Sunü jing*, in *Ishimpō*, 39.

40. *Dongxuanzi*, in *Ishimpō*, 103. See also the *Shixie* section of the *Ishimpō*, 228ff. The *Dongxuanzi* advises emitting two or three times out of ten, 236.

41. The late Ming *Langshi qiguan* portrays the man both succeeding and failing in ejaculation control (chs. 13, 21, and 23); *Wushan yanshi* contains a lengthy description of a man engaging in ejaculation control (ch. 8).

42. See Li and McMahon, 1992: 161. I have modified the translation of the parts of this passage which appeared in Li and McMahon, 1992, 161. For *zhongshen you kong*, based on readings in the Mawangdui arts of the bedchamber, *kong*, "empty," should be read as *kong*, "hole" or "opening"; *zhongshen*, lit. "middle of the body," is a term for penis.

43. See *Yufang mijue*, in *Ishimpō*, 114. See also Wile, 1992: 87.

44. *Yufang mijue*, in *Ishimpō*, 93.

45. *Sunü jing*, in *Ishimpō*, 32.

46. See Wile, 1992: 193–94.

47. Like the "male" ars erotica, the "female" arts could have been available to any number of people by virtue of oral or written transmission. See *Yufang mijue*, in *Ishimpō*, 75, on "nourishing the *yin*"; for the above quote, see Wile, 1992: 195 (from the *Xiwangmu nüxiu zhengtu shize*), and 214 for a similar quote.

48. Two other women, Xuannü and Cainü, also appear. Van Gulik translates *su* as "plain," Wile as "immaculate."

49. As she tells him in the *Ishimpō*, 123 and 127, under "Ten Movements" (*shidong*) and "Five Signs of Desire" (*wuyu*). These two lists also appear in the Mawangdui text *He yinyang* with some variation; see *Mawangdui Hanmu boshu*, 1985, vol. 4: 155.

50. *Yufang mijue*, in *Ishimpō*, 290ff.

51. See Yao Lingxi's *Si wu xie xiaoji* on auspicious and inauspicious qualities of male and female pubic hair and facial features (1941: 45).
52. *Yufang mijue*, in *Ishimpō*, 290–91.
53. *Yufang mijue*, in *Ishimpō*, 296.
54. See *Dongxuanzi*, in *Ishimpō*, 164, 171, and 175; van Gulik, 1974: 128–30; and *Sunü miaolun*, 122.
55. See *Ishimpō*, 151–52, and van Gulik, 1974: 128. The novel *Xiuping yuan* has examples of the first, third, and fourth positions, ch. 18, 4b.
56. See the *Sunü miaolun*, 125–26, which gives the most detailed description of the application of "nine shallow and one deep."
57. See *Sunü miaolun*, 121ff.
58. The *Ishimpō* and *Sunü miaolun* use numerous terms for thrusting: *ci*, "to pierce," one of the most frequent; *cha*, "to insert" (e.g., *Sunü miaolun*, 139); and *chou*, which does not occur together with *song*, however (e.g., *Dongxuanzi*, in *Ishimpō*, 103).
59. *Dongxuanzi*, in *Ishimpō*, 103, 89. This text is written in a particularly high literary style.
60. See end of ch. 13, where he suggests that he and Pan Jinlian imitate the pictures of an erotic album he has borrowed.
61. See, for example, *Xingshi yinyuan zhuan*, 1981, ch. 2, 24, in which, as in *Jin Ping Mei*, the book is an illustrated manual of sexual positions.
62. See *Jin Lan fa*, ch. 4, 8b, in which the *fangzhong zhi shu* consists of an aphrodisiac. Also see, e.g., *Xinghua tian*, ch. 2, 33, in which the *fangshu* consists of aphrodisiacs and *qigong* exercises both to "solidify the semen" (*gu jing*, i.e., suppress ejaculation) and strengthen the penis (see ch. 6 of this volume); and *Taohua ying*, ch. 5, 17b, in which a monk lectures briefly against drawing too much essence from women during sex. For descriptions of men actually practicing ejaculation control, see *Langshi qiguan*, chs. 13, 21, 23, and *Wushan yanshi*, ch. 8, 2b–3a.
63. *Rou putuan*, van Gulik collection, ch. 1, 1a, 2a. See the translations of this novel by Richard Martin, 1963, and Patrick Hanan, 1990.
64. See McMahon, 1988a: 86–87.
65. *Nao huacong*, ch. 3, 17ab.
66. See the *Laozi xianger zhu jiao jian* (edited by Rao Zongyi, 1956: 12); and also the earlier *Shiwen*, section 7, which has: "Close off the *qi* in order to replenish the brain," that is, withhold ejaculation in order to redirect energy upwards (the *Shiwen* can be found in *Mawangdui Hanmu boshu*, 1985, vol. 4: 149, no. 63, and Li and McMahon, 1992: 180).
67. See *Zui chunfeng*, ch. 4, 19b, and *Langshi qiguan*, ch. 20, 18b–19a.
68. See *Nao huacong*, ch. 6, 36b, which uses "nine shallow and one deep."
69. See translations by Egerton, 1939; Waley, 1940; and Roy, 1993.
70. *Yufang mijue*, in *Ishimpō*, 19.
71. *Jin Ping Mei cihua*, 1963, ch. 29, 6a.

72. See, for example, *Xinghua tian*, ch. 2.

73. Recall one of the ancient words for penis, "jade whip," *yuce* (the *yu* of which, of course, differs from *yu*, to "drive"). See *Mawangdui Hanmu boshu*, 1985: 145 and 156 (from *Shiwen*, section 2, and *He yinyang*, section 6, respectively).

74. See McMahon, 1988a: 84–85, and chs. 72–73 of *Jin Ping Mei*.

75. *Erke pai'an jingqi*, by Ling Mengchu, 1981, story 34, 494; see also McMahon, 1988a: 27.

76. Pu Songling's *Liaozhai zhiyi* also contains stories featuring male loyalty to one woman, e.g., "Hu Siniang," "Cui Yun," and "A Bao."

77. The edition I cite is called *Dongyou ji*, by Fang Ruhao, 1988, ch. 21, 167.

3 Shrews and Jealousy in Seventeenth- and Eighteenth-Century Vernacular Fiction

1. Note also, however, that one of the words for a dissolute man is *langzi*, literally, "wave-man," which likewise carries the water radical.

2. See the discussion of military romances, warrior women, and female pollution in ch. 13 of this volume.

3. See *Lunyu*, book 9, no. 18.

4. See *Lunyu*, book 16, no. 7 and no. 13: "A gentleman keeps aloof from his son" (translated by Lau, 1979: 142).

5. See, for example, Pu Songling's story "Shanhu" in *Liaozhai zhiyi*, 1978, 1409–16.

6. *Du* means to be jealous or envious, but the presence of the female radical builds in a gendered meaning.

7. *Yiwen leiju*, 1985, 613–16, quote from 613.

8. See Wu, 1988: 363–82. Wu's article appeared after the earlier version of this chapter, which appears in a 1987 conference volume *The Power of Culture* (1993), minus the section on the ars erotica. The chapter now benefits from Wu's article, as I will note in all cases. She covers a much wider range of material, though she does not include *Liaodu yuan* or the *Erke* 10 story. On the shrew in Pu Songling's fiction, see Zeitlin, 1993: 127–31. On jealousy in the Song, see Ebrey, 1993: 165–71.

9. *Xihu erji*, 1981, story 11, 196.

10. *Xingshi yinyuan zhuan*, 1981, prologue, 5.

11. Wu, 1988: 366–67, notes that the Ming essayist Lü Kun voiced the same opinion.

12. In Wang Tingna's *Shi hou ji*, the wife arranges four ugly or deformed women as concubines for her husband (Wu, 1988: 377).

13. For more discussion of this play, see Wu, 1988: 371.

14. For *zhimu*, see *Yiwen leiju*, 613; for *canggeng*, see *Xihu erji*, 196. Both say they quote from the *Shanhai jing*, for which see *Shanhai jing jiaozhu*, 1980, 147, on *zhimu*. According to Wu, the soup is one of the stock motifs in the shrew story (1988: 371, n. 25); see *Cu hulu*, ch. 4.

15. The edition used is *Cu hulu*, microfilm of original in Naikaku bunko. Further discussion follows. The idea of the superior man sleeping in a separate bed is also found in Sun Simiao's *Qianjin yifang* (Tang; in Wile, 1992: 19); and *Yang xing yan ming lu*, ch. 6, "Yu nü sunyi" (Song?; in Wile, 1992: 113–14), in *Zhengtong daozang*, 1962, vol. 572, 8.

16. *Xihu erji*, 206, and *Zui chunfeng*, ch. 2, 6a.

17. *Lunyu*, book 17, no. 25; translated by Lau, 1979: 148.

18. See *Xingshi yinyuan zhuan*, prologue, 5–6.

19. See Tan, 1980: 237, for this anecdote, a source for story 2 in Feng Menglong's *Jingshi tongyan*.

20. Wu notes Ming and Qing writers, including Feng Menglong, who link female jealousy with insatiability (1988: 377–78).

21. See *Yufang mijue*, in *Ishimpō*, 291: "Avoid intercourse with jealous women . . . and those whose vaginal waters are overabundant"; and *Yufang mijue*, 62: "Those who nourish their *yang* must not let women discover [lit., secretly peek at] these arts."

22. See *Yufang mijue*, in *Ishimpō*, 75–76.

23. See *Yufang mijue*, in *Ishimpō*, 67, 69.

24. The edition used is *Liaodu yuan*, the Yannan tang edition, microfilm of original in Naikaku Bunko.

25. The preface writer is the pseudonymous Jingtian zhuren, "Master of Tranquility."

26. See Tan and Tan, 1984: 342. See *Jin Shi yuan quanzhuan*.

27. Lasciviousness (*yin*) and haughtiness coincide in one of the main characters of *Qingmeng tuo*, an erotic novel probably of the early Qing discussed in ch. 6 of this volume.

28. Free women in ancient Rome may have had the same idea; they could space out pregnancies by sharing sexual activities with the husband among several women. See Rouselle, 1989: 303.

29. *Erke pai'an jingqi*, 1981, story 6, 96. On uxorilocal marriage, see Wolf and Huang, 1980: ch. 16; in the Song, see Ebrey, 1993: 236–40. Such marriages may function in a "preservative" sense, i.e., to continue the descent line in a family with no sons; and they may function to add to the labor force of the wife's family (216). See also Pasternak, 1985: 309–34.

30. Pasternak finds cases of uxorilocal marriage indicating the practice to be more stable and fertile in certain communities than in others. In general, the husbands tended to be older than usual for marriage, indicating that such marriage was a last resort (1985: 325–26); they also tended to be poor and not to be living with relatives at the time of marriage (319). Wolf and Huang corroborate this (1980: 218), also noting that the more older brothers there are, the less likely a family is to be willing or able to support younger brothers in more costly "major"—i.e., virilocal—marriages (220).

31. Wu cites some of these lists and others (1988: 378–80 and nn. 47, 52, and 57).

32. For this part of the quote, see *Xihu erji*, story 11, in the Naikaku bunko edition, 9ab.

33. See *Xihu erji*, 1981, story 11, 201–2. In the textual variation after *yehu*, I have chosen the Naikaku bunko version (9b) because it parallels the passage in Ling Mengchu's story below. On the *yehu*, see the following note.

34. Since *po gua*, "break the melon," and *po shen*, "break the body," mean to have the first intercourse, I assume that the expression in this passage, *po ti*, "break the body," means the same thing. Sun Xun of Shanghai Normal University helped me to interpret this line.

35. The urinary receptacle, with its spout for inserting the penis, is an object of the woman's hate in *Xihu erji*, *Erke pai'an jingqi*, and *Cu hulu* (ch. 1, 6b), all of which date from the late Ming or early Qing. These objects, also called "night pots," *yehu* and *huzi*, took numerous shapes, one of which was a four-legged animal with a spout for its mouth. They appear in archaeological remains from as early as the Han. Liu Tingji describes them in his *Zaiyuan zazhi* (circa 1715), reporting that some were shaped like horses upon which one could sit (1985, vol. 2, 1310).

36. These rules are translated more fully in McMahon, 1988a: 115. See also Wu, 1988: 379–80.

37. See *Chan Zhen yishi*, by Fang Ruhao, 1975, ch. 21, 15b–18b; also in the 1986 edition, 323–25.

38. Wu notes that shrews are often ugly or repulsive (1988: 377).

39. On the male use of the female voice and the idea of "male ventriloquism," see Widmer, 1992: 124, and Bruneau, 1992.

40. See Ebrey, 1993: 37–43, for a brief tracing of the first adoption of footbinding.

41. These examples are discussed in Ropp, 1981: 120–51.

42. Women in *Honglou meng* are similarly agile, but the narrative is not specific about whether or not they have bound feet. For the debate on this question, see Liu Mengxi's *Hongxue* (1990: 272–74). Warrior women in military romances, e.g., *Lümudan*, do have bound feet.

43. *Xihu erji*, 206.

44. *Xingshi yinyuan zhuan*, 1981, ch. 100, 1426. For a partial translation under the title of *Marriage as Retribution*, see Wang, 1982: 41–94.

45. See ch. 81, for example, on Tong Nainai, and chs. 55–56 on Tiao Geng. Also see ch. 32, 468, and ch. 81, 1151, on how women excel men. However, Tong Nainai later comments on how men's knowledge and insight are better than women's (ch. 84, 1200).

46. See Manfred Porkert's summary of the polar aspects of *yin* and *yang*, especially his use of "active" and "structive" to characterize the complementary aspects of the two (1982: 14–22).

47. See the 1976 Taibei edition of the *Xingshi yinyuan zhuan*, ch. 39, 326 (passage deleted in the 1981 Shanghai edition); a monk in ch. 93 has the same problem.

48. See the 1976 edition, ch. 79, 654. Jijie is the reincarnation of Di Xichen's wife from his former reincarnation as Chao Yuan, whose affair with a prostitute drove his wife to suicide.

49. This connotation of "collapsed grape arbor" goes back at least to the Yuan dynasty. See the collection of jokes by Feng Menglong, *Guangxiao fu*, 1987, 27. The expression occurs as early as the Yuan in a *sanqu* by Guan Hanqing (Li, 1991: 5).

50. The edition used is a microfilm of the original in Naikaku bunko. The author pseudonym is Fu ci jiao zhu, "Master of the Doctrine of Subduing Women." Sun Kaidi suggests that because of the similar printing format, this book and two late Ming collections of male homoerotic stories, *Bian er chai* and *Yichun xiangzhi*, might be by the same author and / or from the same publishing house (1981: 112). As for dating the work, since it refers both to Wu Bing's (died ca. 1647) play *Liaodu geng* (ch. 10, 10a) and Fang Ruhao's two novels of circa the 1620s (see below), at the earliest it is from the late Ming, early Qing.

51. Besides using the common term *shinü*, *Cu hulu* also refers to her as a "female eunuch," *citaijian* (ch. 6, 7a). The description of her vagina is on 14ab.

52. The wife in Wang Tingna's *Shi hou ji* also journeys to hell. See also Wu, 1988: 374 and n. 37.

53. See beginning of ch. 10. The mention of the wife of Yang Wei is a rare case of allusion since, like *Cu hulu*, *Chan Zhen yishi* and its sequel, *Chan Zhen houshi* (also quoted in *Cu hulu*, ch. 13, 1ab), are not well-known works. Aside from Chu Renhuo's (ca. 1630 to ca. 1675) possible use of *Chan Zhen yishi* as a source for *Sui Tang yanyi*, I know of no other allusions in fiction to the two Fang novels. See Hegel, 1977: 127, 153.

54. Yenna Wu confirms this in, e.g., her reference to Xie Zhaozhe's (1567–1624) listing and categorization of jealous women in legend and history (1988: 366).

55. See *Cu hulu*, ch. 9, 6a, about the shrew vis-à-vis the emperor, and ch. 16, 5a and following vis-à-vis the gods.

4 The Self-Containing Man: The Miser and the Ascetic

1. See the discussion of Lü Dongbin in McMahon, 1988a: 37–39.

2. *Xingshi hengyan*, by Feng Menglong, story 17, 2b–3a.

3. *Ai se jingqi*, see *Houhan shu*, 1965, 2750, biography of Gan Shi et al. The second quote is from Wang Jia, *Guang zi xu* and is cited in van Gulik, 1974: 286, "to treasure one's spirit and to save one's semen."

4. *Taiping guangji*, 1986, vol. 4, 1207–11 (juan 165).

5. *Gujin xiaoshi*, 1985, 303–16 (juan 13).

6. In one joke, a servant who steals meat from his master is forced to eat flies in order to vomit up the meat; see "Luanrou" in *Gujin xiaoshi*, 312.

7. The edition used is *Changyan dao*, in *Gudai zhongpian xiaoshuo*, 1986; its preface bears the date 1804. See Cai, 1985: 54–64. It is also found in an edition called *Fuweng zhuan* located in the Beijing University library.

8. A character with the same name, whose son is likewise a wastrel, appears in *Yaguan lou*.

9. The story is in *Zhaoshi bei*, 1985 (also published in 1956), 69–104, and is translated by Rainier Lanselle as "Les latrines de la fortune" (1987: 153–219); see also McMahon, 1988a: 141.

10. See the Bu yue zhuren edition in Beijing University library, ch. 7, 13a.

11. *Xingshi yinyuan zhuan*, 1981, ch. 1, 4.

12. From *Wufeng yin*, in Beijing University library, ch. 11, 2b. A colloquial description of stinginess has a person "sucking the finger he uses to pick his asshole," *kou piyan, cuo zhitou*. A colloquialism referring to fawning behavior to an important person is "to slurp his crack and lick his asshole," *liu gouzi, tian piyan*.

13. *Yesou puyan*, 1975, ch. 14, 104–5.

14. *Shi wu pi*, 1985, ch. 1, 472–73.

15. Another is a brief reference in *Shi wu pi*, ch. 14, 607.

16. *Chijue* literally means to line up in rank, but *chi* perhaps puns with *shi*, "shit," and *jue* with *jue* or *jiao*, "chew." *Chijue* also perhaps puns with *shijue'er*, literally "shit peg," a colloquial expression for a solid piece of feces (as opposed to loose diarrhea).

17. See Graham, citing the *Huainanzi*, 1989: 54–57.

18. On Legalism, see Graham, 1989: 267 and following. Translations are mine (in order to keep wording consistent in certain cases), unless otherwise indicated. See "Yangquan," in *Hanfeizi*, 1973, 32. Also see Liao, 1959: 56–57.

19. On *wuwei* in *Laozi*, see Graham, 1989: 232–34, in Legalism, see Graham: 288–92.

20. See "Jie Lao," in *Hanfeizi*, 101; Liao, 1959: 181. Also see Lau, 1976: 120 (ch. 59); and *Laozi jiaoshi*, 239.

21. *Hanfeizi*, 107; Liao, 1959: 189–90.

22. See "Yu Lao," in *Hanfeizi*, 122; Liao, 1959: 221.

23. *Hanfeizi*, 122; Liao, 1959: 221. Also see Lau, 1976: 108 (ch. 47); and *Laozi jiaoshi*, 189.

24. Molière's miser is always afraid someone will discover where his money is or how much he has. He locks the doors whenever he goes, "keeps a key ever so securely dangling from his side" (quote from *Xingshi hengyan*, story 17, 2b–3a), and trusts no one, not even himself.

25. Lau, 1976: 105 (ch. 44); *Laozi jiaoshi*, 180.

26. Lau, 1976: 107 (ch. 46); *Laozi jiaoshi*, 186; *Hanfeizi*, 107; Liao, 1959: 191.

27. Lau, 1976: 120 (ch. 59); *Laozi jiaoshi*, 241–42.

28. Translated by Lau, 1976: 91 (ch. 32); *Laozi jiaoshi*, 132.

29. Translated by Lau, 1976: 66 (ch. 10), and 85 (ch. 28); *Laozi jiaoshi*, 40, 112.

30. See *Shenlou zhi* in ch. 12 of this volume and Zeitlin, 1993: 109–16.

31. See *Qingsuo gaoyi*, by Liu Fu, 1983, 79.

32. For a Ming version (1569) of the Ji Dian story, see Lu Gong, 1986: 235–89, in which he both protects his temple (264–65) and brings it alms (259–60, 270–71).

33. See a Qing version of the Ji Dian story in *Xihu jiahua*, 1981, 175. The same episode is found in Lu Gong, 1986: 260, in which Ji Dian exposes himself three other times (246, 254, and 267).

34. See Lu Gong, 1986: 245–46. Li Kui, a nonmonastic, brutish, *xia* type in *Shuihu zhuan*, perhaps distantly echoes this move in his fondness for fighting naked.

35. Lu Gong, 1986: 253.

36. See the version of Ji Dian's story by Tianhuacang zhuren, called *Ji Dian dashi zuiputi quanzhuan*, Baoren tang edition in the Beijing University library, ch. 7, 1b–2b. The modern *Xihu jiahua* edition has him placing the shoe on her "stomach," 171.

37. *Lüye xianzong*, ch. 44, 347–48. The Taoist immortal Lü Dongbin also refuses sex with a prostitute and instead tries to convince her of the benefits of "internal intercourse," *neijiao*. See *Lüxian feijian ji*, by Deng Zhimou, microfilm of original in Naikaku bunko, ch. 11, 23b–24a.

38. *Shi wu pi*, ch. 1, 471, perhaps echoing Song Jiang in *Shuihu quanzhuan*, 1976, ch. 21, 306.

39. See Furth, 1986: 61: "Women did not have the option of strength through abstinence. . . . Sexual activity was imperative if a woman was to remain normal, but at long-range cost."

5 The Chaste "Beauty-Scholar" Romance and the Superiority of the Talented Woman

1. This chapter also appears in Tani Barlow and Angela Zito, eds., *Body, Subject and Power in China* (1994), and benefits from the suggestions of Barlow, Zito, and anonymous reviewers. The present version makes minor adjustments, adds the section on *Fenghuang chi*, and the concluding discussion of masochism.

2. Ropp, 1981: 128–30; Mann, 1987: 50; Ko, 1992.

3. See Ropp, 1981: 129–30, on Li Zhi. Another sixteenth-century thinker, Lü Kun, also wrote about the talent and independence of the woman. See Handlin, 1975: 13–38, and 1983: ch. 6.

4. The allusion is to a statement of a Song poet Xie Ximeng, who refers to the "luminous virtue" of the cosmos no longer "taking hold in" men but only in women. See Aiyama, 1983: 84–109, and Liao, 1986: 210–13; this allusion is discussed more fully in the chapter on *Honglou meng* later in this volume.

5. Ropp, 1981: 130–31. See also Zeitlin, 1993.

6. Hanan, 1988: 103–4 and 151.

7. See my later discussion of *Honglou meng*. On Wu Jingzi, see Ropp, 1981: 132–40 and 140–51; and Lin, 1935: 127–50 (cited by Ropp).

8. See Chang, 1991: chs. 1–3.

9. See Ko, 1992; Widmer, 1989 and 1992; and Robertson, 1992.

10. Mann, 1987: 43, 49. Recall my discussion in ch. 3 of *Xingshi yinyuan zhuan* and the Widow Chao.

11. The ideas in this and numerous paragraphs below were stimulated by the generous comments of Tani Barlow.

12. The first work was translated by John Francis David, London, 1829, and the second two were translated by Stanislas Julien, Paris, 1826 and 1842, respectively.

13. The reaction against "decadence" already begins in the 1640s in story collections such as *Zui xing shi* and *Qingye zhong* (Hanan, 1985: 189–213). See the preface to *Hua tu yuan*, for example, which criticizes illicit love and calls for love based on true *yuan* or destiny. See McMahon, 1988a: ch. 5, on *Haoqiu zhuan* and the reaction against late Ming decadence.

14. It is possible to view the chaste woman as a model of purity in the eyes of the Ming loyalist who opposes the inferior and barbarous Manchus. Support for this view lies in the known association between Ming loyalists and talented women writers and painters in the mid–seventeenth century, as discussed by Kang-i Sun Chang (1991) and Ellen Widmer (1992).

15. On female playwrights, see Hua Wei, 1993, "The Lament of Frustrated Talents: An Analysis of Three Women's Plays in Late Imperial China." The chantefable, called *tanci*, was composed and sung by and for women. In one of them, *Zai sheng yuan*, the woman Meng Lijun becomes *zhuangyuan* (first in the imperial examinations), then prime minister, and even when discovered to be a woman, she refuses to give up her prime ministership.

16. Many scholars have written about authorship. See, for example, Lin Chen, 1988: 85–115, and Hessney, 1979.

17. See Lin, 1988: 57, for an echo of this point.

18. This is also found in Li Yu's works (Hanan, 1988: 95).

19. According to Christina Yao, the terms *caizi* and *jiaren* have been linked together since the Tang to refer to three types of love stories: those involving a relationship between a gifted man and a courtesan, between a man and a ghost or spirit, and between elite young men and women involved in premarital affairs (Yao 1983).

20. See Cheng, 1984: 34, and Lin, 1988: 61–65. Lin notes that the formulaic plot of the beauty-scholar romance can be found in early Ming literary tales (63). Ming operas such as Xu Wei's *Nüzhuangyuan* and Wu Bing's *Lümudan* supply the *caizi jiaren* story with the themes of the remarkable woman and the replacement of passion with wit (Hessney, 1979: 94–95, 107–9).

21. See, e.g., *Yanzi jian*, a romance barely transformed into fictional form from the famous opera of Ruan Dacheng.

22. Lu, 1973: 245–55, which discusses *Yu Jiao Li*, *Ping Shan Leng Yan*, and *Haoqiu zhuan*. The fullest treatment in English of these romances is Hessney, 1979, which discusses *Yu Jiao Li*, *Haoqiu zhuan*, *Ping Shan Leng Yan*, *Hua tu yuan*, and others. See also Zhou, 1990.

23. Lin, 1988: 55–84; Lu, 1973; Li, 1984: 59; and Cao, 1984: 45; to cite a few.

24. Guo, 1934: 194–215 and 303–23; see Lin on Guo, 1988: 54.

25. See Lin, 1988: 214–18. *Bian er chai* is a collection of romances with all male *caizi-jiaren*-like characters (McMahon, 1988a: 73–78).

26. The term appears, for instance, in the infamous late Ming pornographic novel *Langshi qiguan*, ch. 13, 4b, in which it is applied to adulterous lovers just before they begin oral-genital intercourse. The term can also be found, for example, in *Wan Ru Yue*, 23, 56, and 145, the last occurrence in the title of the final chapter: "The beauties and the scholar unite in grand union"; in *Yanzi jian*, ch. 1, 1b; *Fenghuang chi*, ch. 2, 8b–9a; in the prefaces to *Feihua yong* and *Tiehua xianshi*; and in *Xing fengliu* (ch. 1, 1). When the term has a negative connotation, it may be because such stories are considered cliché, or because they are considered to lead to immorality. For other occurrences, see Li, 1984: 60.

27. See Lin, 1988: 56–57, and *Zaiyuan zazhi*, by Liu Tingji, 1985, 1284. Liu puts the mildly erotic romance *Qingmeng tuo* in a list with *Ping Shan Leng Yan, Fengliu pei, Chun liu ying,* and *Yu Jiao Li,* which he finds inferior but still not to the point of "greatly corrupting public morals" like *Rou putuan, Bian er chai, Langshi qiguan* and others.

28. Liu Tingji also has *jiaren caizi.* Many scholars discuss *Honglou meng*'s references to *caizi jiaren* fiction; see Lin, 1988: 65–74, Li, 1984: 79–80, and Miao, 1984: 214–31. *Rulin waishi* does not mention scholar-beauty books, but makes similar satirical use of the term scholar-beauty (*Rulin waishi,* 1984, ch. 8, 156; ch. 28, 382; and ch. 34, 469).

29. See *Zhuchun yuan xiaoshi,* "Kaizong mingyi," 1–2.

30. Lin, 1988: 81–84, 247.

31. Widmer also notes the association between Ming loyalists and female literati in the seventeenth century. Such loyalism had subdued itself by the eighteenth century but perhaps still endured in vestigial form through the continued existence of groups of women writers and artists (Widmer, 1989: 8; 1992: 138, 142).

32. She also appears in drama of the preceding period, e.g., Xu Wei's *Nüzhuangyuan,* in which the male-impersonating heroine becomes a *zhuangyuan.* Ellen Widmer suggests that the story of Xiaoqing, the "female talent" (*nücaizi*) of late Ming fame, had a strong influence on the theme of talented women in seventeenth-century fiction (1992: 120).

33. Dressing as a man occurs in many earlier stories, those of Mulan and of the failed lovers Liang Shanbo and Zhu Yingtai being two of the most famous, both of the Six Dynasties. For a more thorough discussion of female cross-dressing, see Zeitlin, 1993: 116ff.

34. See *Yuzhi ji, Yu Jiao Li, Dingqing ren, Sai hong si, Lin er bao, Wan Ru Yue, Fenghuang chi.*

35. Hessney, 1979: 166–69, also discusses the complementarity of their match.

36. Stories with an only son and / or only daughter are, for example, *Zhuchun yuan, Yuzhi ji, Dingqing ren, Fenghuang chi, Xing fengliu, Feihua yong.*

37. See Hessney, 1979, and 1985: 214–50, especially 223–24.

38. In Ling Mengchu's *Pai'an jingqi,* story 34, the man infiltrates a harem; in *Xingshi*

hengyan, story 8, the man seduces a young woman. In the Qing, see *Yu Lou Chun* and *Nao huacong.*

39. See Li Yu's *Wusheng xi,* story 6; *Bian er chai,* stories 3 and 4; and the Qing novel *Pin hua baojian.*

40. Charlotte Furth notes that physically androgynous men in the Ming and Qing were seen as having "erotic motivation and moral complicity" (1988: 18). For a lengthier discussion of "dislocation in gender," see Zeitlin, 1993: 98–131.

41. Lin Chen notes the women's punctiliousness in demonstrating mutual respect in, e.g., *Yu Jiao Li, Chun liu ying, Yuzhi ji, Lin er bao, Dingqing ren* (1988: 80). See *Wan Ru Yue,* ch. 10, for a lengthy working out of ranking.

42. Most of the published editions are from the Chunfeng wenyi Press in Shenyang. Rare editions include those I have read at the Beijing University library and those available on microfilm or microfiche, which I have read at Princeton University Gest Library.

43. *Baigui zhi,* 1985; the earliest edition is from 1805. See Lin, 1988: 401–5.

44. *Fenghuang chi,* edition in Beijing University library. It is pre–1754 because it appears in the *Hakusai shomoku* (Lin, 1988: 194–97).

45. Shen Fu, 1980, 12; translated into English by Pratt and Chiang, 1983: 44–45. In 1641 Liu Shi, the scholar-poet courtesan of late Ming fame, evidently disguised herself as a man in order to travel alone to visit Qian Qianyi, whom she married in the same year (Chang, 1991: 15; Chen, 1980: 343).

46. In *Qingmeng tuo,* she wraps material around her normal shoes, then puts on socks and men's shoes (ch. 12, 4a). See Fengyin lou edition of *Wufeng yin* in Beijing University library. In Pu Songling's *Liaozhai zhiyi* story "Yan Shi," the male-impersonating woman also stuffs her shoes. Stuffing material into their shoes was also a technique bound-footed women used in the early twentieth century.

47. *Feihua yong,* 1983; see Lin, 1988: 85–98, 261–63.

48. *Yu Jiao Li,* 1981. Scholars from Lu Xun (1973: 246–48) on have written about this "classic." See Lin, 1988: 139–43 and 242–44; Zhong, 1984: 159–73; Chen, 1984: 174–89; and Hessney, 1979. Two-wife polygyny is found in *Liaozhai zhiyi,* by Pu Songling, e.g., "Liancheng," and "Xiao Xie."

49. In *Fenghuang chi,* her talent is "ten times better than a man's," ch. 4, 8b.

50. See, e.g., *Baigui zhi,* ch. 3. The motif is an old one, occurring in the story of Liang Shanbo and Zhu Yingtai of the Western Jin.

51. *Lin er bao,* 1983; see Lin, 1988: 267–70.

52. *Wan Ru Yue,* 1987. Lin Chen and Xiao Xiangkai say that this novel was written after *Yu Jiao Li* and *Ping Shan Leng Yan* (Lin, 1988: 184–90; Xiao, 1987: 166–75).

53. *Zhuchun yuan xiaoshi,* 1985; see Lin, 1988: 234–39. The prologue also mentions the erotic *Qingmeng tuo* and *Xiuping yuan,* both of which it criticizes as inferior works.

54. Lin notes that despite the unclear dating of this book, this kind of indirect communication between sensitive women could not have been found in the early Qing (1988: 238).

55. *Dingqing ren,* 1983; Lin, 1988: 271–75; Zhang, 1985: 124–37.

56. Other novels feature such foil characters as well, often as here for the comic relief of portraying a wife prevailing in a conjugal quarrel. See *Wan Ru Yue,* ch. 14 and following; *Wufeng yin,* chs. 5, 7; and *Baigui zhi,* ch. 12.

57. Recall that the character *jian,* composed of three *nü* (i.e., woman) radicals, means "evil"; the *Shi ji* records a statement to the effect that having three women is excessive (1972: 140).

58. Hanan, 1988: 58–62.

59. See the third and especially fourth stories of *Bian er chai,* discussed in McMahon, 1988a: 76–78.

60. See *Haoqiu zhuan,* ch. 8, 101; *Yu Jiao Li,* ch. 5, 62; *Xing fengliu,* ch. 8, 65; *Dingqing ren,* ch. 6, 49. Hessney also discusses "expediency" (1979: 194–96).

61. As in *Feihua yong,* ch. 16, 155.

62. See Gilles Deleuze, 1967; Bogue, 1989; Chow, 1991; and Silverman, 1992. For a treatment of eroticism and perversion in *Jin Ping Mei* and *Les Liaisons Dangereuses,* see Lu, 1991.

63. See Deleuze, 1967: 53–54, 60. In the works of Sacher-Masoch, the nineteenth-century Frenchman who posthumously lent his name to the concept of masochism, the man educates and trains the woman for her role as superior figure, in effect handing her weapons for the destruction of the father or father figure. In training the woman for her dominant role, the man channels through her the harsh words and behavior that he then has her direct to himself. It is important to note, of course, that neither miser nor shrew, scholar nor beauty, are as self-consciously manipulative of their "victims" as are their French counterparts, who, for example, write each other letters detailing their love conquests (see Lu Tonglin, 1991: 19–20). None of the Chinese types is as coldly obsessive in his or her desire to dominate others. The extreme self-consciousness of the subjects in the Western context (whether the characters of *Les Liaisons Dangereuses,* of Freudian analysis, or of Deleuze's Sade and Masoch) in fact constitutes one of the greatest differences from the pre-twentieth-century (pre–industrial revolution, precolonial) subjects of Chinese fiction.

64. On the "sexless man," see Deleuze, 1967: 46; the man thus becomes "purged of the inner father" (Bogue, 1989: 49). See also Deleuze, 1967: 28–29, 60.

65. Masoch's works are likewise devoid of obscene and specific description (Deleuze, 1967: 31–32).

6 The Erotic Scholar-Beauty Romance

1. See Hessney, 1985: 246–47, on mild ribaldry in *Haoqiu zhuan.* Other comparably chaste romances are *Sai hong si, Yu zhi ji,* and *Xing fengliu.*

2. *Jin Shi yuan*'s preface says that *Qingmeng tuo, Yu Lou Chun, Yu Jiao Li,* and *Ping Shan Leng Yan* "have been very popular for a long time."

NOTES

3. I have not been able to gain access to *Chundeng nao;* see summaries in An and Zhang, 1990: 540–43, for the first two, and in Lin, 1988: 339–43, for the third.

4. See the Heying lou edition in Beijing University library, ch. 7, 13b, using only the words "do the clouds and rain."

5. *Jinxiang ting,* 1984, ch. 3, 28; explicit passage is censored in this edition. For a brief discussion of the book, see postface of this edition by Ding Lingwei, 171–73. An uncensored edition can be found in the Beijing University library. The concubine reappears briefly in ch. 12.

6. See Wolf and Huang, 1980: 94–95, who note that a man might settle on a marriage deal in which his wife marries into his family but he agrees to provide support to her aging parents. In other words, a major marriage still could include some uxorilocal-type service. Many varieties of arrangement existed.

7. The edition used is from the Beijing University library, with "Bu yue zhuren ding" on the title page. See *Zaiyuan zazhi* (1284) and Lin Chen, who feels it is pre-1681 (1988: 350–53). The 1749 mention is in the preface to *Jin Shi yuan.*

8. A third woman, maid of the first, disguises as a man to escape a forced marriage; in the end the hero refuses to take her for himself, despite her desire to marry him, and instead marries her to the former husband of the lascivious woman.

9. The scholar also becomes a servant in the beauty's home in *Xing fengliu, Xiuping yuan,* and *Zhuchun yuan;* in *Ying Yun meng* he becomes a secretary. All these instances recall the famous story of Tang Yin (Tang Bohu) of the Ming dynasty, who disguised himself as a commoner in order to get a job in the same household as a maid he loved. The story is found in many forms, e.g., *Jingshi tongyan,* story 26, by Feng Menglong, as "Tang Jieyuan yixiao yinyuan," and in Ming and Qing plays such as *Sanxiao yinyuan.*

10. In this and other novels (e.g., *Haoqiu zhuan, Xing fengliu,* and *Dingqing ren*), a maid is called upon to replace the beauty in a forced marriage. In *Jinxiang ting* the maid commits suicide for the sake of the beauty's freedom, ch. 8.

11. Tan Zhengbi says he once had an early Qing edition but gives no evidence of date; see Tan and Tan, 1984: 414–15. The novel must be pre-1754 since it appears in the Japanese *Hakusai shomoku,* a list of books imported to Japan from China between the late 1600s and 1754. The text I use is the Siyou tang cangban found in the Beijing University library, also with "Bu yue zhuren ding" on its title page.

12. Not discussed by Lin Chen or Tan Zhengbi, but found in Sun Kaidi, 1982: 164. The edition used is from the van Gulik collection and is not paginated.

13. The hero in *Jinxiang ting* makes similar statements, ch. 1, 3–4.

14. Such female helpers usually marry the hero, but in *Ying Yun meng,* when the helper discovers he is loyal to another woman, she and he swear brother-and-sisterhood rather than become lovers; see the 1986 edition, ch. 2, 258. The wives are of different social ranks, and some are helpers as well in *Jinxiang ting.*

15. West and Idema believe this phrase (in the reverse order of *daofeng dianluan*) refers to mutual oral intercourse, but I find no evidence to support this definition (1991: 152).

16. The term *jianmin* does not appear in the story. Naquin and Rawski indicate that being a jailer was not necessarily an unenviable job; thus, the "mean" jailer is perhaps not so low after all (1987: 117).

17. See also the late Ming story collection *Yipian qing*, story 13, and the following discussions of *Taohua ying* in this chapter and *Lin Lan Xiang* in ch. 9 of this volume.

18. This work has both 12- and 24-chapter editions; citations here will be from the 12-chapter edition (I did not gain access to the other) published by Xiaohua zhai and located in the Beijing University library.

19. See such cases in *Yesou puyan, Chan Zhen yishi, Ernü yingxiong zhuan, Shenlou zhi,* and *Fengliu heshang.*

20. Anal intercourse is described two times, in several dozen characters, 67a and 71a. The difference between penetrator and penetrated was also of vital importance in male homoerotic relations in ancient Rome; see Richlin, 1993.

21. The edition used is in the van Gulik Collection; see Sun Kaidi, 1982: 183. It appears on Ding Richang's 1868 list of censored books.

22. When he then goes back to Heroine One, he himself takes and gives her an aphrodisiac called "through-the-night pill," *tongxiao wan*, which enlargens their genitals (ch. 7, 2b–3a). In another illustration of expertise, he uses the techniques of first "nine shallow and one deep," then "half shallow and half deep" (3a).

23. Lin Chen posits that the same group of "pornographers" produced *Taohua ying* and two other erotic novels, *Sai hua ling* and *Chundeng nao* (1988: 113–15; see also 337–39). The edition used is missing its first pages, but is supposedly the Wanxiang zhai version and is found in the Beijing University library; the pseudonymous author is given as Yanshui shanren, as found at the very end of the last chapter.

24. Since I have been able to see two Qing editions of *Xinghua tian*, I will give two page references for it, the first from the 1979 Nagoya photoreprint, the second from the edition found in the van Gulik Collection. It is listed in Sun, 1982: 179, and is on Ding Richang's 1868 list. Hou Zhongyi attributes it to the Qianlong period in An and Zhang, 1990: 541–42.

25. In this case "the method of driving women" is mainly based on an aphrodisiac made according to "the art of *gui* x x" (unreadable to me; "x" looks like the character *bi* meaning spoon or ladle). *Gui*, "turtle," appears in simplified form and is a vulgar word for penis; *bi* is a homonym for the vulgar word for vagina. I have not seen this expression anywhere else. The drug is made according to alchemical methods in a stove for forty-nine days (ch. 5, 17a).

26. He is perhaps referring to the teaching found in the ars erotica that if the man penetrates too deeply, although he may benefit himself, he brings harm to the woman. See the Ming *Sunü miaolun*, 125–26. *Zhiyin*, "deepest *yin*," might also be read as *zhi yin*, "make the *yin* arrive" (to oneself), that is, to absorb the woman's *yin*.

27. See *mu nan*, ch. 6, 23ab, *pi'ai*, 19b, and *jinshi*, 20a. For a discussion of male homosexuality in Ming and Qing fiction and other sources, see Hinsch, 1990: 118–61.

28. A similar scene, in some parts the same word for word, appears in *Nao huacong,*

in which the hero continues with both the penetrator and his wife; see the Benya cangban edition in Beijing University library, ch. 6, 38b.

29. *Taohua ying, Nao huacong, Chundeng nao,* and *Wushan yanshi* all tell of a man who sleeps with the hero and then lets the hero sleep with the man's wife.

30. For the evil monk, see *Fengliu heshang* or *Shenlou zhi.* For the homosexual who dies or fades from the narrative, see *Xinghua tian* or *Yu Lou Chun.*

31. A possible reference to *Rou putuan* is in the monk who gives the hero aphrodisiacs and sits on a *putuan,* "round straw mat" (ch. 2, 20, 5b).

32. Meaning unclear; *bi* means "compare" or "rival," among other things (and is conceivably a homonym for *bi,* "cunt"), while *jia* carries the sense of "armour," ch. 2, 30, 5b–6a.

33. Of two women who fondle each other before sex with the hero in *Wushan yanshi,* one is the wife of a homosexual, the other is the homosexual's younger sister.

34. The bedding includes "Western cotton," *xiyang mianbu* (ch. 13, 171, 6a), which might indicate that the novel is post-mid-1700s, since trade in such items did not really get under way until then. The fact that *Xinghua tian* refers to the hero's twelve wives by the term used in *Honglou meng,* "the twelve hairclasps," *shi'er chai* (see title of ch. 13 of *Xinghua tian*), suggests that the work is post–*Honglou meng,* which puts it anywhere from the 1790s to 1868, when it appeared on Ding Richang's list of censored books.

35. Ch. 14, 188, 10a. Li Yu notes the lascivious nature of the apricot, *xing,* a traditional emblem of the beautiful and sexy woman; see Hanan, 1988: 233, n. 35.

36. See also *Jin Shi yuan,* chs. 7, 8, 17, 18, and 24; *Wufeng yin,* chs. 5, 11; *Yu Lou Chun,* ch. 2; and *Taohua yanshi,* chs. 1–6.

37. In Gilles Deleuze's terms, the story of the miser and the shrew can be retold as a version of the story of the sadist and the masochist (or the latter two as versions of the former). When the Sadean fantasy is reduced to the characters of the Oedipal family, the father and daughter are said to unite to torture and destroy the mother. In so doing, like the miser, the sadist demonstrates his hatred of motherly love, procreativity, and the aspects of passion and unlimited giving in the woman-mother. As Deleuze adds, the sadist wishes to deny all sentiment and enthusiasm and to attain a state of timeless, pure negation. In the fantasy of Masoch, the son and mother ally to deride and destroy the father, who represents the supreme and impersonal law of the superego (Deleuze, 1967: 111–12). Like the shrew, the cold Masochean woman mocks the rigid and impecunious laws of the father and denies him his symbolic superiority (see Deleuze, 1967: 42–50).

7 A Case for Confucian Sexuality: Chaste Polygamy in *Yesou Puyan*

1. This chapter is a revised version of an article that appeared in 1988 in *Late Imperial China* 9 (2): 32–55. At that time I benefited greatly from the comments of an anony-

mous reader and the scholarly and editorial guidance of Charlotte Furth. The present version has added many details, made some corrections, and in general fit the article into the context of the book.

2. See n. 7 on editions used.

3. According to Hou Jian, the book is over one million characters long (1974: 11).

4. C. T. Hsia has dismissed the author: "Despite his Confucian orthodoxy, Hsia Ching-ch'ü . . . has a licentious imagination and places his hero Wen Pai *tzu* Su-ch'en, a supreme genius in all civil and military arts, in every kind of improbable adventure" (1977: 270). Using Freudian terms, Hou Jian writes of the novel's "abnormal psychology" and refers to the hero's "neurosis," "Oedipus complex," and "mother fixation" (Hou, 1974: 17, 18).

5. Hsia states that the " 'scholar-novelists' utilize the form of a long narrative not merely to tell a story but to satisfy their needs for all other kinds of intellectual and literary self-expression" (1977: 269).

6. Lu Xun, 1973: 317.

7. I use two editions: the 154-chapter Shijie shuju version (Taibei, 1975), which deletes sexually explicit passages, and the 1881 152-chapter Piling huizhen lou edition, which includes the erotic passages but has lacunae elsewhere, and which has been reprinted by Tianyi chubanshe in Taibei in 1985. Page numbers refer to the Shijie shuju edition except when it is necessary to use the Piling huizhen lou edition, which is indicated by numbers such as 1a, 1ab, etc. Chapter numbers given without page references refer to the Shijie shuju edition unless otherwise noted. The 1881 edition lacks numerous passages that the Shijie shuju edition fills in. The lacunae occur in both erotic and nonerotic portions and so are not a part of a censorship. The Shijie shuju edition is most heavily abridged in the erotic passages of chapters 68–71, which correspond to chapters 65–69 in the 1881 edition. The 1881 edition has an excellent commentary taken from an earlier version of the book, but this commentary is occasionally missing, especially in the highly erotic passages. I have not seen the 1882 edition, which Sun Kaidi, Lu Xun, and Zhao Jingshen consider unreliable because probably finished by another author (see their articles in n. 9).

8. In his preface to the Taibei Shijie shuju edition (originally 1935?), which censors the obscene passages, Zhao Tiaokuang says that earlier abridged editions deleted the learned discourses and kept the eroticism (p. 3).

9. Qian, 1979: 162–67; Jiang, 1984: 239; Lu Xun, 1973: 317–21; Sun, 1985: 238–47; Tan, 1978: 411–15; Zhao, 1980: 433–47; also see, *Zhongguo xiaoshuo shi,* 1978: 305–6, and other literary histories.

10. This information was related to me by Mary Mazur, who has done a biographical study of Wu Han.

11. See Zheng Yimei's *Yilin sanye,* a collection of notes and anecdotes about scholars, writers, and artists of the Republican period (1982: 180). Chen Yupi of the Academy of Social Sciences in Beijing has helped me identify Wu and Zhou.

12. See Hsia, 1977: 270, n. 7. This information has also been related to me by scholars in China.

13. See ch. 143, 527–30, for the list of Wen's family members.

14. See Zhao, 1980: 441. Lu Xun (1973: 320) also refers to this relationship and reports that Yang was a student of Li Guangdi (1642–1718). My information on Xia's life is mainly from Zhao.

15. Wen later has two illnesses in which he temporarily loses his mind due to demonic influences—the first time for more than three years, the second for about six years.

16. See Zhao, 1980: 444; and Hummel, 1943: 412–13, for a biography of Gao.

17. Zhao, 1980: 445.

18. Zhao, 1980: 446–47.

19. Zhao, 1980: 445, quoting from an earlier document by someone who apparently knew much about Xia.

20. See the Yangzhu chapter in *Liezi jishi* (1979: 237); Qian, 1979: 162, and Hou, 1974: 15–16.

21. See Hou, 1974: 13, who notes the book's meticulous recording of the passage of time. The author takes liberties with some historical events, such as the beginnings and endings of Ming reign periods. Many historical and personal references are given in Qian (1979) and Sun (1985).

22. The establishment of Confucianism in Europe is not narrated at length; Europe is recognized for its exquisite inventions and realistic art works. One foreign woman is an object of curiosity: does her body function in the same way as Chinese people's? On the inventions, see ch. 147, 564; on the artwork, see ch. 149, 575. The curiosity about body functions (pulse) is clear in ch. 148, 566–67. On the West in *Yesou puyan* and other works, see Idema, 1990.

23. Ming-Qing medical treatises on begetting identify the woman's fertile period with the first one or two days after the end of the menses; they also imply that male potency increases with continence (information provided by Charlotte Furth).

24. In one illustration of this principle, the author provides an instance of a long kiss without intercourse between two lovers who begin at the end of one chapter and are still kissing at the beginning of the next (chs. 51–52 in the uncensored (Piling huizhen lou) edition; omitted at the end of ch. 53 of the Shijie shuju edition).

25. From the *Yang bing yongyan*, by Shen Jiashu, as quoted by Zhou Yimou, 1989: 99–100.

26. See 1881, ch. 5, 11b–12a. The three situations occur in chs. 3, 4; 6, 7, 8; and 16, 17. Another brief scene of nude proximity occurs in ch. 15.

27. Literally, afraid of the mere sound of the snap of the bowstring.

28. See ch. 8, 57, in *Yesou puyan*, 1975, and ch. 16, 122, in *Lin Lan Xiang*.

29. See Nivison, 1966: 265–66; Ropp, 1981: 127ff; Chang, 1991; and Ko, 1992.

30. See ch. 78, 8–9; ch. 79, 20; and for the emperor's harem, ch. 108, 237–38.

31. See ch. 96, 150, in the Shijie shuju edition, with omissions. Suchen's cure for the emperor, who suffers from too much intercourse with women, is first to have him lie down with one young boy hugging him from the rear, then with another hugging him from the front, in so doing reinvigorating himself with *yang* energy (ch. 87, 81).

32. By Tianhuacang zhuren; see the Baoren tang edition in the Beijing University library. See also ch. 3 of this volume. For the episode of sitting back-to-back with a possessed young woman, see Lu Gong, 1986: 276.

33. See ch. 4 of this volume.

34. Fingers or hands are shown entering or touching female genitals four times in chs. 27 and 29 of the 1881 edition. Once it is to examine the body of a woman who has died from an overdose of aphrodisiac (ch. 27, 2b). Shortly after, this touching occurs when a woman who committed suicide after being discovered having sex with a monk is cleaned by her father of the messy evidence below before she is prepared for burial (ch. 27, 13a). A third time it is one woman testing to see whether another sleeping woman is a virgin (ch. 29, 1b); shortly after it is the masturbation of the woman who touched the sleeping woman (ch. 29, 1b).

35. A glancing mention of the ars erotica in the form of an album of erotic pictures (*chungong ce*) occurs in ch. 29, 3a.

36. Suchen argues against Buddhist and Taoist interlocutors on several occasions, during one of which he argues that Buddhism has long died out in India and has been replaced by Islam. He then asks why China should still have a religion which is extinct elsewhere (1975: ch. 2, 14; see also ch. 10).

37. The master is the second and more extreme of two such harem masters; the first is in chs. 26–32.

38. A common euphemism for the vagina, probably referring to the area around or just inside the entry.

39. This term usually refers to the clitoris.

40. See 1881: ch. 94, 13b (ch. 96 of the Shijie shuju edition).

41. See Dudbridge, 1970: 114–18, for a discussion of sources. For copulation between a woman and a dog, for example, see the *Liaozhai zhiyi* story called "Quan jian," and between man and donkey, see the note in Yao Lingxi's *Si wuxie xiaoji*, 1941: 57.

42. *Mengzi*, 4a, no. 17; Lau, 1970: 124.

43. *Mengzi*, 3b, no. 3; Lau, 1970: 108.

44. Roddy, 1990: 259–60.

45. Such detail is found in descriptions of the country woman Liu Laolao, for example, who farts and has loose bowels. Another example is the maid Xiren's discovery of a sticky fluid on Baoyu's thigh when she helps him change clothes, thus discovering that he ejaculated in his dream.

46. Kangxi is recorded as having had fifty-six children by thirty consorts. Eighteen of his thirty-six sons also had sons, making 123 grandsons altogether. He had twenty daughters, of whom eight lived to maturity and married. See Spence, 1974: 122.

47. As described by Benjamin Elman, for example (1984). The New Text view took Confucius "as a messianic sage in his own right, an 'uncrowned king' (*suwang*)" (23), like the "unappointed minister" Wen Suchen.

8 Polygyny, Crossing of Gender, and the Superiority of Women in *Honglou Meng*

1. Aroma and Skybright are the names given them in the widely read translation, *The Story of the Stone,* by David Hawkes (1973 and after). See also Yang and Yang, 1978–80. For easier cross-referencing, I will supply the names Hawkes gives to these and others; note that he gives English names to lower-class characters only.

2. See *Honglou huanmeng,* 1990, for example.

3. Edwards, 1990a: 411.

4. In Chang's studies, the talented woman takes the form of the courtesan (1988, 1991). Chang also discusses the man's use of the woman's voice in love poetry conveying sentiments of Ming loyalism (1988). Widmer shows that the "gentlemanly patronage of creative women" was an important part of this loyalism (1992: 119, 122–23, 138–39).

5. See Huang, 1991, and his 1993 conference talk. Epstein, 1994, also discusses the fluidity of gender configurations as an important feature of Ming and Qing literature, including *Honglou meng.*

6. Some scholars even dispute that he is the author. See Liu Mengxi's *Hongxue,* 1990: 294–300 on Dai Bufan's opinions, and 304–5 on Pan Zhonggui's. For general information on authorship and early manuscripts, see also Hsia, 1968: 249–53, and Rolston, 1990: 456–81.

7. A 120-chapter version possibly existed before Gao E's work. See Guo Yushi's study of "Red Studies," *Honglou yanjiu xiaoshi gao,* 1980: 45–46. Guo also wrote a sequel to this volume, *Honglou yanjiu xiaoshi xugao,* 1981. I will cite both in much of what follows.

8. The first to note the separate authorship of the last forty chapters was supposedly Yu Rui (1771–1838), who denounced the sequel (see Guo, 1980: 61). But the subject of separate authorship was not a major issue until Hu Shih revived it in 1921.

9. Of course, there are textual differences between the various editions of the "original" eighty chapters as well, but they are of a less distinct nature than those between the Cao and Gao versions. The 1982 edition will be the one used for this discussion. Yu Pingbo edited a 120-chapter version, with the first eighty chapters based on Cao texts coming out in 1958, and the final forty chapters appearing in 1963, but these editions were never mass-produced to the extent of the others and have not been reprinted; they are called *Honglou meng bashihui jiaoben* and *Honglou meng houbu sishihui.*

10. There is difference of opinion on the Cao family status: e.g., Zhou Ruchang at

one extreme says that the Caos were Manchu bannermen or naturalized Manchus; others at the opposite extreme say that they were Chinese bannermen of the lowest rank, i.e., bondsmen who were servants of the Manchu royalty. See Liu, 1990: 326–28.

11. See Wu Shih-ch'ang's *On the Red Chamber Dream*, 1961: 273.

12. See Ying Bicheng's *Lun Shitou ji gengchenben*, 1983: 53–56. Some say there was also a third edition in 1792 which was never as common (even a fourth has been said to exist; see Xu and Xu, 1982: 383). See Han Jinlian's *Hongxue shi gao*, 1981: 95–96.

13. For more examples, see Wu, 1961: 259–60, and Ying, 1983: 29–31.

14. See Wu, 1961: 255–58 and 246–50.

15. See Wu, 1961: 236–37.

16. Wu, 1961: 355. Cao's original home (*jiguan*) is said by some to be in Manchuria as well (see Liu, 1990: 323–26). A stereotype still transmitted today is that "the Northeast has three great oddities" (*dongbei you san daguai*), one of which is married and typically older women who smoke.

17. See Guo, 1980: prologue, 2, and Wu, 1961: 4.

18. See Guo, 1980, 1981; Han, 1981; Liu, 1990. In her article on Wang Xifeng, Louise Edwards also examines the novel in light of nineteenth- and twentieth-century readings (1993).

19. See Guo, 1980: 147–54.

20. Guo, 1980: 158, referring to Zheng Kuangyan in 1919.

21. See Guo, 1981: 162, referring to Jing Meijiu in 1934.

22. Guo, 1980: 18.

23. Guo, 1980: 141–42, citing Wang Mengyuan of 1916.

24. Guo, 1980: 69, n. 8, referring to two separate commentators, one in 1812, the other in 1821.

25. Guo, 1981: 198.

26. Guo, 1981: 265.

27. Liu, 1990: 6.

28. See Liu, 1990: 272–74.

29. He notes that the "stubborn stone" out of which Baoyu was transformed could grow and shrink from its huge size to the size of a fan pendant; Ximen Qing's jade was a "root" of disaster, Baoyu's a "root" of life. See Guo, 1981: 126–36, and Kan's book, called *Honglou meng jue wei*, 1925: 18a–20a.

30. On Hu Shih, see Hsia, 1968: 3; for the others, see Guo, 1981: 183, 256, and Liu, 1990: 312. Liu Ts'un-yan observes that *Honglou meng* was not elevated to the status of literary "giant" until the May Fourth era (Liu, 1982: 2, 40). C. T. Hsia also compares *Honglou meng* with the best of Western fiction but criticizes the novel's adherence to the "episodic convention" of Chinese fiction (1968: 1, 15, 17).

31. See Guo, 1982: 67, 87, 96. On Mao Dun's dismissal of *Honglou meng*, see Hsia, 1968: 5.

32. See, e.g., Plaks, 1976; Edwards, 1990a, 1990b, 1993; Lu, 1991; Wang, 1992; Lee, 1993.

33. Hawkes, 1973: ch. 2, 83. All translations are mine unless, as here, otherwise indicated.

34. For a variation of this quotation, see ch. 49, 673, which uses the word *lingxiu* to refer to the excellence of women.

35. See Liao, 1986: 210–13; and Aiyama, 1983: 84–109 (thanks to Chen Yupi for these references). Louise Edwards also cites Liao and provides an interesting and more detailed discussion of the theme of feminine purity in light of the binary of pure vs. polluted or goddess vs. whore (1990a).

36. See Liao, 1986: 210. The four Lus are Lu Xun and Lu Kang, two generals of the Eastern Wu; and Lu Ji and Lu Yun, literati of the Western Jin.

37. See *Rulin waishi*, 1984, ch. 11, 167. None of these references mention Xie's name.

38. According to Eugene Cooper and Meng Zhang, Chinese families considering cousin marriage preferred the man's marriage to his mother's sister's daughter over marriage to his father's sister's daughter; thus *Honglou meng* in fact reflects a real customary preference (1993).

39. Andrew Plaks has discussed another complementarity: in terms of the Five Phases (*wuxing*), Baochai represents "metal," Daiyu "wood" (1976: ch. 4).

40. Hawkes, 1973: ch. 21, 421; in Chinese, ch. 21, 293.

41. This whole passage is deleted in Gao E's version; see Ying, 1983: 39.

42. This scene is modeled on one from the *Xixiangji*, in which the maid similarly prays for her mistress Cui Yingying, in this case so that Cui will soon find a husband (see act 3 in West and Idema, 1991: 205). Baoyu is thus feminized through analogy to Cui Yingying.

43. As in the descriptions of Baochai in ch. 5, 89, and ch. 28, 402.

44. See Chen Qinghao, ed., 1979: ch. 26, 432, single-column interlineal comment from the Jiaxu (1754) and Gengchen (1760) editions (on terms for and placement of comments, see Rolston, 1990: 53–57).

45. See Chen, 1979: ch. 43, 526, from a double-column interlineal comment in the Gengchen edition; and Wu, 1961: 58.

46. Guo, 1981: 265.

47. Guo, 1981: 290, n. 9, and Wu, 1961: 55–61. The confusion is likely to last since it is not always clear whether the commentator is Zhiyan zhai; others also participated in this many-layered and often recopied commentary.

48. See Wang Yao's "Wenren yu yao," 1986: 141–44.

49. For the connection between male beauty and homosexuality in the Six Dynasties, see Hinsch, 1990: 64–76.

50. This passage is also deleted in the Gao E version; see Ying, 1983: 16.

51. She uses the word *cao*, "fuck," ch. 16, 214. For more examples and further discussion of Wang's masculinity, see Edwards, 1993: 38–39 and 44.

52. Much has been written on *yiyin*; see, for example, Feng, 1981: 159–80, Su, 1983: 39–58.

53. C. T. Hsia cites the passage in ch. 79 in which it is said that Baoyu "indulged in all sorts of sports with his maids" (ch. 79, 1146–47; Hsia, 1968: 286). Although Hsia believes it unlikely that the author implied "sexual orgies," the passage is ambiguous enough to allow for some sort of sexual play.

54. On detail and the feminine, see Schor, 1987, which has inspired my discussion here and elsewhere.

55. In echo of such scenes, one of the *Honglou meng* commentators, Zhang Xinzhi (fl. 1850), uses the words *yiyin* to describe the episode in which Baoyu helps Pinger with her cosmetics. See *Honglou meng sanjia pingben*, 1988, ch. 44, 703, 707.

56. 1990b: 77.

57. See Chen, 1985: 266–67.

58. Hawkes, 1977: ch. 49, 479; in Chinese, ch. 49, 679–80.

59. Furth, 1986: 48–49.

60. Furth, 1986: 50–51, 59.

61. See Furth, 1986: 63, and *Honglou meng,* chs. 21 and 77.

62. See, for example, ch. 55, 769, and ch. 72, 1019. For further discussion of Wang Xifeng's illnesses, see Edwards, 1993: 39–42.

63. See ch. 65, 936. Also see the Six Dynasties poetry collection, *Yutai xinyong.*

64. See Zhang Tianyi, quoted in Guo, 1981: 226, and Guo's comment: "In all she does, Baochai keeps everyone in mind; Daiyu has only one person in mind, Jia Baoyu."

65. See Chen, 1979: ch. 17, 254, from a prechapter comment in the Gengchen and Jimao (1759) copies; and Wu, 1961: 155–58.

66. See *Wufeng yin,* ch. 2, 9b (*xianzhe lian*), where the hero flirts with and forces himself on the heroine's maid; and *Shenlou zhi,* ch. 2, 6a (*houzhe lian*), where the hero flirts with and seduces the heroine's sister.

67. For this use of *pengyou,* see also *Rulin waishi,* 1984, ch. 30, 409.

68. See *Honglou meng sanjia pingben*, 1988, ch. 36, 567–68. *Zhubing* occurs as *chenbing* in some Qing texts, perhaps due to lexicographical confusion; see also *yuchen* in *Rou putuan,* ch. 3, 20a.

69. See Chen, 1979: ch. 21, 352, from a double-column interlineal comment in the Gengchen edition.

9 The Overly Virtuous Wife and the Wastrel Polygamist in *Lin Lan Xiang*

1. This chapter was first delivered at a panel for the Midwest Conference of Asian Affairs in 1989 at East Lansing; I have benefited from the comments and talks given by copanelists David Roy and David Rolston.

2. This is the edition used here. A Taibei photoreprint of a Qing edition also exists,

Lin Lan Xiang, 1985. It is worth considering the possibility that the author was a woman, but no solid evidence to this effect has shown up so far.

3. See Rolston, 1987: 113–23, and 1989.

4. See Rolston, 1989.

5. On *Lin Lan Xiang,* see Lin, 1988: 412–16; Qi, 1990: 376–80; Rolston, 1987; Wang, 1988: 147–62; Yu, 1985: 498–516; Zhang, 1987: 63–84; Zheng, 1988: 28–33.

6. That is, the orchid that is overshadowed by the "forest," *lin,* i.e., Lin Yunping, and out-"fragranced" by the invidious *xiang,* i.e., Ren Xianger.

7. See Chen, 1986: 159.

8. See also this word used between Chunwan and Xuan, ch. 60, 463.

9. The words *toujin qi,* similar in meaning, are used in the same commentary note to describe Lin Yunping; see ch. 5, 39, n. 61, and Rolston, 1987: 120.

10. *Liuli* is cousin to *huopo,* "lively," which Ping says Yan is not (ch. 22, 172).

11. See ch. 29, 228, for an early reference to the resemblance.

12. See Rolston, 1989.

13. For another occasion on which she reminds him of Mengqing, see ch. 42, 324.

14. Translated by Ebrey, 1984: 220; I have modified the English of the last sentence.

15. For the knight-errant, see ch. 12, 93; the poor scholar, ch. 16, 122–23; and the eunuch, see Yu, 1985: 507.

10   The Spoiled Son and the Doting Mother in *Qilu Deng*

1. See his *Jiaxun zhunyan,* found in Luan, 1982b: 141–52.

2. See *Xingshi yinyuan zhuan,* 1981: ch. 1, 4, and *Wufeng yin,* ch. 11, 2b.

3. See Guo, 1982: 1–8, and Zhu, 1982: 9–17.

4. The edition used is *Qilu deng,* by Li Haiguan, 1980. The biography is in Luan Xing, 1982a: 1–65. The essay collections are *Qilu deng luncong* 1, 1982, and *Qilu deng luncong* 2, 1984.

5. See Liu, 1982: 49. These figures may be inflated since contemporary publishers in China are known to exaggerate the number of copies printed.

6. See Liu, 1982: 50.

7. Zhang, 1982: 148.

8. Hu, 1982: 134.

9. See Luan's preface in *Qilu deng,* 1980: 10.

10. See Allan Barr on educational issues in *Qilu deng* (in Elman, forthcoming), and on Tan Shaowen's weakness of character (1993 A.A.S. conference paper).

11. On the circulation of the novel, see Luan, 1982b: 186.

12. See Luan's preface in *Qilu deng,* 1980: 20.

13. On his excuses for not serving, see Wu and Chen, 1982: 116–17.

14. See Wu and Chen, 1982: 123.

15. Translated by Ebrey, 1984: 206–7 and 225.

16. Luan, 1982b: 150.

17. The pun on *fu* recalls one in the Han dynasty *Bohu tong* (Discussions in the White Tiger Hall, an imperially sponsored work on cosmos and ritual, 79 A.D.), which uses a different *fu*, however, meaning "to obey." See Tjan, 1949–52: 562.

18. Luan, 1982b: 144. See also *Qilu deng*, ch. 99, 930.

19. She says, "Now you even refuse to sleep on the big bed"; he has changed to sleeping on a makeshift "rattan bed," *tengchuang* (ch. 19, 193).

20. See the article on the loyal servant by Shang, 1982: 105–13.

21. See Wu Jianren's story "Heiji yuanhun," in 1986: 444 (not the same as Peng Yang'ou's novel *Heiji yuanhun*).

22. See also McMahon, 1988a.

23. The concubine finally speaks up and gives him wise advice in ch. 76; the servant, kicked out twice (chs. 32, 53) and shunned other times, is finally allowed to return in ch. 83.

24. Translated by Ebrey, 1984: 40.

11 The Other Scholar and Beauty: The Wastrel and the Prostitute in *Lüye Xianzong*

1. At only one point is there reference to his sexual activity; after a long departure, he returns home and "plays" (*wanshua*) daily with his wife (ch. 4, 27; see n. 4 for editions used). Later, after he returns from a much longer absence, he indicates that he will join her in the bedroom in a few days, but she indignantly refuses.

2. Wen Ruyu is swindled by a friend who is said to become less manly and more effeminate the lower he sinks (ch. 40, 312). One of ten bad traits a man should avoid is to "imitate the woman's way of using her eyes to win someone over" (ch. 64, 509).

3. On Ruyu, see ch. 36, 279, and ch. 42, 326. Often mother and father in such cases mean the adoptive parents who buy the daughter from her destitute real parents, for example. But in *Lüye xianzong* it is clearly stated that she is their real daughter, i.e., *qinsheng nü'er*, ch. 43, 336.

4. A photo-reprint of the complete illustrated and hand-copied edition was published in traditional binding by Beijing University Press in 1985. It has prefaces said to be by two of the author's friends and comes with a commentary. A censored version in one hundred chapters was published by the same press in 1986, without commentary. Pagination will refer to the complete edition when the page number plus "a" or "b" appears; otherwise I will refer to the more easily obtained censored edition.

5. E.g., *Lüye xianzong* is mentioned in none of the following texts: Liu Dajie's *Zhongguo wenxue fazhan shi*, Zheng Zhenduo's *Chatu Zhongguo wenxue shi*, the Chinese

Academy of Social Science's *Zhongguo wenxue shi* (1979), Lu Xun's *Brief History of Chinese Fiction* (although Lu Xun does mention the work in *Xiaoshu jiu wen chao—zashuo*), or the Chinese Department of Beijing University's *Zhongguo xiaoshuo shi gao* (1960).

6. See Zheng, 1986: 1396; Tan, 1935: 419–21; and Cai, 1985: 65–82.

7. A woman's term of endearment commonly found in erotic works such as *Jin Ping Mei*.

8. An example of *ai* as in "I love only you" occurs between unmarried sexual lovers in the late Ming erotic romance *Langshi qiguan*, a forbearer of the Qing polygamous erotic romance (ch. 30, 21a). As Lu Tonglin relates, *ai* in *Jin Ping Mei* is used to denote Ximen Qing's fondness for parts of his lover's body; in *Honglou meng* and other works, it often denotes fond care for objects, not people (Lu, 1991: 11, 161–62, 165). In compound expressions such as *bo'ai* ("universal love for fellow beings"), and *en'ai* (as in "conjugal love," see below), *ai* in contrast refers to an idealized harmonious love, not an obsessive or possessive one.

9. The formula of switching from "the one" to "the other" is common in vernacular fiction, e.g., *Xiyou ji*, in which it is applied to battling heroes and demons, and *Jin Ping Mei*, in which it is applied to battling lovers.

12 The Benevolent Polygamist and the Domestication of Sexual Pleasure in *Shenlou Zhi*

1. See Liu, 1967: 7, 336. I use an undated, 24-*juan* edition from the Beijing University library, published by Yushan Wei Juntian (appearing on the last page), and differing in pagination from the one of 1804 (the earliest extant edition). A warning against copyright infringement appears on its title page. Numerous editions exist: one of 1807 (Sun, 1982: 145), 1858 (Dai, 1980: 277), an undated one with a different title (Tan and Tan, 1984: 375–76), an uncensored Taibei edition of 1983, and at least two censored mainland versions, one of 1987, the other 1988.

2. Dai, 1980: 277–80; Zheng, 1957: 1293–94; Wang, 1983: 303–39; Cai, 1985: 23–32; Lin, 1988: 405–9. For more information on the book, see also An and Zhang, 1990: 533–35, and the two recent mainland editions.

3. A mild Guangdong chauvinism is apparent in remarks about the beauty of the area (e.g., ch. 19 on Chaozhou), and in a comparison of the simple and honest people of Guangdong with the crafty people of Jiangsu and Zhejiang (ch. 7, 19a).

4. See Idema, 1990.

5. See Shen, 1957: 5. A *yunchuang* with a *jiguan* can also be found in *Yesou puyan*, ch. 94, 13b.

6. See *Yesou puyan*, chs. 147–49.

7. The somersault recalls the stories about Ji Dian, whose penis does show. In *Pai'an*

jingqi, 34, the method of retracting the penis is called *suo yang zhi shu*, "the technique of shrinking the yang" (1966: 725), and is practiced by a man in nun's disguise who, like the Tibetan, is associated with the White Lotus Sect. Tan Zhengbi cites as source for this story a Ming account of a man with a retractable penis who disguises himself as a nun (1980: 734). Judith Zeitlin discusses the use of this account in *Liaozhai zhiyi* and other sources (1993: 109–16).

8. Bringing someone's head down to one's (or someone else's) genitals or feet is a type of degradation, insult, or curse that takes numerous forms. Li Guijie has Ximen Qing cut a lock of Pan Jinlian's hair so Li can put it in her shoe (ch. 12, 15a–16a). The taunt of having someone drink one's foot-washing water carries the same implication (see the saying in *Jin Ping Mei*, ch. 13, 12b, and ch. 91, 2a). Jia Zheng tells a joke about a henpecked husband who returns home late, his wife's punishment for which is to make him lick her feet, which she is in the midst of washing (*Honglou meng*, ch. 75, 1076–77).

9. See, for example, the scene of anal intercourse in *Taohua ying*, ch. 9, 20a; for virginal pain, see the passage, translated in the last chapter, of the lovemaking between Wen Ruyu and the Princess.

13 *Ernü Yingxiong Zhuan* as Antidote to *Honglou Meng*

1. The earliest published edition is of 1878, before which the novel circulated in manuscript form. The edition used here goes by an alternate title, *Xianü qiyuan*, 1980, from a 1935 Shanghai edition. According to Song Yi's postface to the 1983 edition, Wen Kang was born around the end of the Qianlong and beginning of the Jiaqing reign periods (circa the 1790s) and died before 1865. In his postface to the 1990 edition, however, Er Gong places Wen's birth around 1798 and death between 1866 and 1877. The novel supposedly had fifty-three chapters, but the last thirteen have been lost; ch. 40 is longer than usual and ends in medias res. The 1990 edition reproduces the nineteenth-century commentary by Dong Xun (1807–1892). Recent discussions of this novel that came to my attention too late to be incorporated into this chapter are Epstein, 1992, 1994. She also understands the novel as a response to *Honglou meng*.

2. On the possible references to *Honglou meng* in *Shenlou zhi*, see Wang, 1983, Dai, 1980, and Cai, 1985. The main possible examples are these: a woman who lures a man into a nighttime tryst but then has waste water thrown down on him (*Shenlou zhi*, ch. 14); Xiaoguan's fondness for the company of his *jiemeimen*, "sisters"; his dislike of "dirty" older women servants; and his fondness for the taste of lip rouge on the edge of Suxiang's tea cup.

3. See *Ernü*, ch. 23, 368; the threesome marriage is also compared to "the three legs of a tripod," 369.

4. See the prefatory poem on p. 1 and the discussion on p. 4.

5. Some have also said that Wen Kang, a Manchu, whose characters occasionally speak Manchu, consciously wrote his book in opposition to what he saw as the anti-Manchu *Honglou meng*. See the 1935 preface by Zhao Tiaokuang in the 1980 edition of *Xianü qiyuan*, 5–7.

6. For references to opium, see ch. 15, 219, and ch. 38, 721; for tobacco smoking among women, see ch. 30, 520, and ch. 37, 676, 678 (and elsewhere), and by a man, ch. 37, 684ff.

7. For an earlier form of Thirteenth Sister, see *Pai'an jingqi*, 4 (Sun, 1985: 256–57). The famous episode is referred to by either the words for the inn in which Thirteenth Sister first meets An Longmei, "Yuelai dian," or by the name of the temple, "Nengren si." On the influence of *Ernü* on *Ti xiao*, see Chang Hen-shui, Sally Borthwick, trans., 1982: 257 and 281, n. 29.

8. For example, see the description of the cramped and dirty city spaces of Beijing in ch. 32, the scene at the examination quarters in ch. 34, and the filth and strange manners of the old pedant in ch. 37. These same passages are singled out by Zhang Juling in her discussion of the novel (1990: ch. 15).

9. See biographical accounts in Sun, 1985, Hu, 1980, and postface to 1990 edition.

10. Hu, 1980: 468–78. He sees *Ernü yingxiong zhuan* as an "unself-conscious [*buzijuede*] *Rulin waishi*" (472).

11. On female warriors, see Chen, 1992.

12. See Chen, 1992: 99.

13. Thus observing the rule of *nannü shoushou buqin*, words quoted in the book; see also her observation of *nannü butongzuo*, ch. 16, 237.

14. See ch. 3, 38, 40, and ch. 5, 63.

15. Other men who, like An Ji, cry out of emotionality rather than bravery or sublime sentiment can be found, for example, in the romance *Yiwai yuan*, ch. 6, in *Yaguan lou*, ch. 6 (in which a young wastrel cries), and in the case of Jia Baoyu.

16. See 1880 commentary edition published by the Juzhen tang, ch. 9, 4a, or the 1990 Qilu shushe edition, 168: "Through the obscene he brings out the true character of the two women. This is what is called, 'The dao is found in filth.'" This is the only commentary edition. The commentator is Dong Xun (1807–92), as identified by Sun, 1985: 258–61. The same publisher printed the first edition of the novel in 1878 without commentary (Sun, 1985: 248–49).

17. *Guanfangpen'er* is a receptacle women use for urination. The expression for "wash the hands" is *shanle zhuale* in the 1880 commentary edition. The 1980 Guangxi edition (*Xianü qiyuan*), from a 1935 edition, has *xile shou'erle*.

18. Ch. 35, 629–30; Zhang Juling cites this passage as an illustration of Manchu household manners (1990: 266–67).

19. See, e.g., *Wan Ru Yue, Zhuchun yuan, Lin er bao, Yu Jiao Li*, and *Dingqing ren*.

20. See other references to *Honglou meng* in ch. 23, 368, and ch. 26, 436.

21. See also Ying, 1979: 113, on the implication that Zheng is a wife-fearer.

22. That is, "Mai you lang duzhan huakuei," story 3.
23. *Xingshi hengyan*, 1959, story 3, 35a; also see McMahon, 1988a: 56–58.
24. See Chen, 1992: 101. A woman gives birth in the midst of battle and causes the defeat of the barbarian enemy by fazing him with the birth "pollutant" (*Yangjiafu yanyi,* 164). See Naquin, 1981: 101, 198–99, n. 69, on records of the use of female "pollutants" and women exposing themselves in millenarian revolts in the eighteenth and nineteenth centuries.

14   Promiscuous Polygyny and Male Self-Critique

1. See Thong, 1973.
2. The edition used is the annotated one edited by Liu Lianli, 1985: 255–462; for this quote, see ch. 20, 457–58. A nonannotated Shenyang 1983 edition also exists.
3. Li Ruzhen, *Jinghua yuan*, 1990. See also ch. 36, 256. Also see the translation by Lin Tai-yi, *Flowers in the Mirror.*
4. See Hsia, 1977: 294–95.
5. See *Langshi qiguan,* ch. 13, 3b.
6. Chow, 1991: 51.
7. See *Jin Yun Qiao,* ch. 7, and *Xiuping yuan,* ch. 4.

BIBLIOGRAPHY

Primary Sources

If the work lacks an identifiable author, I omit the pseudonym, giving the title, the publishing house when possible, and the library or collection in which the book may be found (rare works only). For consistency, I also list authored novels and all other pre-twentieth-century sources by their titles, except if the work is a translation, in which case I list it according to the translator under Secondary Sources. The list of novels only includes works to which I have had access and have actually cited and read for this study.

Baigui zhi. 1985. Shenyang: Chunfeng wenyi chubanshe.

Baopuzi neipian jiaoshi. 1985. Ge Hong. Wang Ming, ed. Beijing: Zhonghua shuju.

Bian er chai. Microfilm of Ming edition in Palace Museum, Taibei, Taiwan.

Chan Zhen yishi. 1975. Fang Ruhao. Taibei: Tianyi chubanshe.

——. 1986. Harbin: Heilongjiang renmin chubanshe.

Changyan dao. 1986. In *Gudai zhongpian xiaoshuo,* 113–215. Hangzhou: Zhejiang guji chubanshe.

Chundeng mishi. Hand-copied edition. Van Gulik Collection.

Chunqiu zuozhuan zhu. 1981. Yang Bojun, ed. Beijing: Zhonghua shuju.

Cu hulu. Microfilm of original in Naikaku bunko.

Dengcao heshang. 1985. Taibei: Tianyi chubanshe.

Dingqing ren. 1983. Shenyang: Chunfeng wenyi chubanshe.

Dongdu ji. Fang Ruhao. Beijing University library.

Dongyou ji (same as *Dongdu ji*). 1988. Fang Ruhao. Hangzhou: Zhejiang guji chubanshe.

Erke pai'an jingqi. 1981. Ling Mengchu. Taibei: Zhengzhong shuju.

Ernü yingxiong zhuan. [1880] n.d. Wen Kang. Dong Xun, commentator. Republican period reprint of Beijing, Juzhen tang edition. Shanghai Shida library.

———. 1983. Wen Kang. Beijing: Renmin wenxue chubanshe.

———. 1990. Wen Kang. Dong Xun, commentator (1880). Jinan: Qilu shushe.

Feihua yong. 1983. Shenyang: Chunfeng wenyi chubanshe.

Fenghuang chi. Beijing University library.

Fengliu heshang. Hand-copied edition. Beijing University library.

Fusheng liuji. 1980. Shen Fu. Beijing: Renmin wenxue.

Guangxiao fu. 1987. Feng Menglong. Hubei: Jingchu shushe.

Guang zi xu. [1936] 1982. Wang Jia. In *Meihua wenxue mingzhu congkan,* ed. Zhu
    Jianmang. Shanghai: Shanghai shudian.

Gujin xiaoshi. 1985. Feng Menglong. Shijiazhuang: Huashan wenyi chubanshe.

Hanfeizi jijie. 1973. Wang Xianshen, ed. Taibei: Shijie shuju.

Haoqiu zhuan. 1981. Zhengzhou: Zhongzhou shuhuashe.

Heiji yuanhun. 1982. Peng Yang'ou. In *Wan Qing wenxue congchao: xiaoshuo sanjuan,* ed.
    A Ying, 107–212. Beijing: Zhonghua shuju.

"Heiji yuanhun" (not the same as above). 1986. Wu Jianren. In *Wu Jianren xiaoshuo
    xuan,* ed. Zhong Xianpei, 439–50. Xuchang, Henan: Zhongzhou guji chubanshe.

Honglou huanmeng. 1990. Beijing: Beijing daxue chubanshe.

Honglou meng. 1982. Cao Xueqin. Beijing: Renmin wenxue chubanshe.

Honglou meng bashihui jiaoben. 1958. Yu Pingbo, ed. Beijing: Renmin wenxue chu-
    banshe.

Honglou meng houbu sishihui. 1963. Yu Pingbo, ed. Beijing: Renmin wenxue chu-
    banshe.

Honglou meng sanjia pingben. 1988. Shanghai: Guji chubanshe.

Houhan shu. 1965. Beijing: Zhonghua shuju.

Hua tu yuan. 1983. Shenyang: Chunfeng wenyi chubanshe.

Hudie mei. Siyou tang cangban. Beijing University library.

Ishimpō bōnai [Yixin fang]. 1976. Tamba Yasuyori. Tōkyo: Edo bungakusen, vol. 6.

Ji Dian dashi zuiputi quanzhuan. Baoren tang. Beijing University library.

Jin Lan fa. Beijing University library.

Jin Ping Mei cihua. 1963. Hong Kong: Wenhai chubanshe.

Jin Shi yuan quanzhuan. Wencui tang. Beijing University library.

Jin Yun Qiao. 1983. Shenyang: Chunfeng wenyi chubanshe.

———. 1985. In *Ming Qing zhongpian xiaoshuo xuan,* ed. Liu Lianli, 255–462. Hangzhou:
    Zhejiang wenyi chubanshe.

Jinghua yuan. 1990. Li Ruzhen. Beijing: Renmin wenxue chubanshe.

Jinxiang ting. 1984. Shenyang: Chunfeng wenyi chubanshe.

Langshi qiguan. n.d. Fengyuexuan Ruxuanzi. In *Zhongguo guyan xipin congkan,* no. 5.
    Hong Kong: Huawen.

Laozi jiaoshi. 1984. Zhu Qianzhi, ed. Beijing: Zhonghua shuju.

Li ji Zhengzhu. 1985. Taibei: Taiwan Zhonghua shuju.

Liaodu yuan. Yannan tang. Microfilm of original in Naikaku bunko.

Liaozhai zhiyi. 1978. Pu Songling. Zhang Youhe, ed. Shanghai: Guji chubanshe.

Liezi jishi. 1979. Beijing: Zhonghua shuju.

Lin er bao. 1983. Shenyang: Chunfeng wenyi chubanshe.

Lin Lan Xiang. 1985. Shenyang: Chunfeng wenyi chubanshe.

——. 1985. Taibei: Tianyi chubanshe.

Lümudan quanzhuan. 1986. Shanghai: Guji chubanshe.

Lunyu yizhu. 1980. Yang Bojun, ed. Beijing: Zhonghua shuju.

Lüye xianzong. 1985. Li Baichuan. Beijing: Beijing daxue chubanshe (complete edition).

——. 1986. Beijing: Beijing daxue chubanshe (censored edition).

Lüxian feijian ji. Deng Zhimo. Microfilm of original in Naikaku bunko.

Mengzi yizhu. [1960] 1984. Yang Bojun, ed. Beijing: Zhonghua shuju.

Nao huacong. Benya cangban. Beijing University library.

Pai'an jingqi. 1966. Ling Mengchu. Li Tien-yi, ed. Hong Kong: Zhengzhong.

Ping Shan Leng Yan. 1983. Shenyang: Chunfeng wenyi chubanshe.

Qilu deng. 1980. Li Haiguan. Zhengzhou: Zhongzhou shuhuashe.

Qingbai leichao. (see Xu Ke).

Qingmeng tuo. Beijing University library.

Qingsuo gaoyi. 1983. Liu Fu. Shanghai: Guji chubanshe.

Rou putuan. Fengshan lou. Van Gulik Collection.

Rulin waishi. 1984. Wu Jingzi. Shanghai: Guji chubanshe.

Sai hong si. 1983. Shenyang: Chunfeng wenyi chubanshe.

Shanhai jing jiaozhu. 1980. Yuan Ke, ed. Shanghai: Shanghai guji chubanshe.

Shenlou zhi. Yushan Wei Juntian. Beijing University library.

——. 1983. Taibei: Guangya.

——. 1987. Beijing: Baihua wenyi chubanshe.

——. 1988. Jinan: Qilu shushe.

Shi ji. 1972. Sima Qian. Beijing: Renmin chubanshe.

Shi wu pi. 1985. In *Ming Qing zhongpian xiaoshuo xuan,* ed. Liu Lianli, 463–640. Hangzhou: Zhejiang wenyi chubanshe.

Shifan (see *Yuanshi shifan*).

Shuihu quanzhuan. 1976. Hong Kong: Zhonghua shuju.

Sunü miaolun. 1951. In van Gulik, *Erotic Colour Prints of the Ming Period,* part 2.

Taiping guangji. 1986. Beijing: Zhonghua shuju.

Taohua yanshi. Heying lou. Beijing University library.

Taohua ying. Wanxiang zhai. Beijing University library.

Wan Ru Yue. 1987. Shenyang: Chunfeng wenyi chubanshe.

Wufeng yin. Fengyin lou. Beijing University library.

Wushan yanshi. Xiaohua xuan. Beijing University library.

Wusheng xi. 1970. Li Yu. In *Li Yu quanji,* ed. Helmut Martin. Taibei: Chengwen.

Xianü qiyuan. [1935] 1980. Wen Kang. Nanning: Guangxi renmin chubanshe.

Xihu erji. 1981. Zhou Qingyuan. Hangzhou: Zhejiang renmin chubanshe.

———. Microfilm of original in Naikaku bunko.

Xihu jiahua. 1981. Zhao Dacheng, ed. Hangzhou: Zhejiang renmin chubanshe.

Xing fengliu. 1981. Shenyang: Chunfeng wenyi chubanshe.

Xinghua tian. Van Gulik Collection.

———. 1979. Nagoya: Publisher unknown (collection called Yan wenxue congshu).

Xingshi hengyan. 1959. Feng Menglong. Taibei: Shijie shuju.

Xingshi yinyuan zhuan. 1976. Taibei: Shijie shuju.

———. 1981. Shanghai: Shanghai guji chubanshe.

Xiuping yuan. Van Gulik Collection.

Yaguan lou. Hand-copied edition. Beijing University library.

Yangjiafu yanyi. 1980. Shanghai: Guji chubanshe.

Yanzi jian. Beijing University library.

Yesou puyan. 1881. Xia Jingqu. Piling huizhen lou. Beijing University library. (Reprinted in 1985. Taibei: Tianyi chubanshe)

———. 1975. Taibei: Shijie shuju.

Ying Yun meng. 1986. In *Gudai zhongpian xiaoshuo,* 217–464. Hangzhou: Zhejiang guji chubanshe.

Yiwai yuan. Beijing University library.

Yiwen leiju. 1985. Ouyang Xun. Shanghai: Guji chubanshe.

Yixin fang (see *Ishimpō*).

Yu Jiao Li. 1981. Shenyang: Chunfeng wenyi chubanshe.

Yu Lou Chun. Xiaohua zhai. Beijing University library.

Yu zhi ji. 1983. Shenyang: Chunfeng wenyi chubanshe.

Yuanshi shifan. 1975. In *Siku quanshu zhenben.* Taibei: Shangwu.

Zaiyuan zazhi. 1985. Liu Tingji. In *Liaohai congshu,* vol. 2. Shenyang: Liaoshen shushe.

Zhaoshi bei. [1956] 1985. Shanghai: Guji chubanshe.

Zhengtong daozang. 1962. Taibei: Yiwen yinshuguan.

Zhuchun yuan xiaoshi. 1985. Shenyang, Chunfeng wenyi chubanshe.

———. Van Gulik Collection.

Zui chunfeng. Xiaohua xuan. Beijing University library.

Secondary Sources

Aiyama Kiwamu. 1983. "*Kōrō mu* ni okeru nyonin sūhai shisō to sono genryū." *Chūgoku bungaku ronshū* 12:84–109.

An Pingqiu and Zhang Peiheng, eds. 1990. *Zhongguo jinshu daguan.* Shanghai: Shanghai wenhua.

Baker, Hugh D. R. 1979. *Chinese Family and Kinship.* New York: Columbia University Press.

Barlow, Tani, and Angela Zito, eds. 1994. *Body, Subject, and Power in China*. Chicago: University of Chicago Press.

Barr, Allan. 1993. "Folly and Prodigality in *Qi lu deng*: the Case of Tan Shaowen." Paper given at the conference for the Association of Asian Studies, Los Angeles.

———. Forthcoming. "Four Schoolmasters: Educational Issues in Li Haikuan's *Lamp at the Crossroads*." In *Education and Society in Late Imperial China*, ed. Benjamin Elman and Alexander Woodside. Berkeley: University of California Press.

Bogue, Ronald. 1989. *Deleuze and Guattari*. London and New York: Routledge.

Borthwick, Sally. "Translator's Preface to *Fate in Tears and Laughter*." *Renditions* 17–18:255–61.

Bruneau, Marie Florine. 1992. "Learned and Literary Women in Late Imperial China and Early Modern Europe." *Late Imperial China* 13 (1): 156–72.

Cai Guoliang. 1985. *Ming Qing xiaoshuo tanyou*. Hangzhou: Zhejiang wenyi chubanshe.

Caizi jiaren xiaoshuo shulin. 1985. *Ming Qing xiaoshuo luncong* 2. Shenyang: Chunfeng wenyi chubanshe.

Cao Bisong. 1984. "Caizi jiaren xiaoshuode jinbu yiyi he xiaoji yiyi." In *Ming Qing xiaoshuo luncong* 1:43–48. Shenyang: Chunfeng wenyi chubanshe.

Cao Xueqin. See David Hawkes or Yang and Yang.

Carlitz, Katherine. 1991. "The Social Uses of Female Virtue in Late Ming Editions of *Lienü zhuan*." *Late Imperial China* 12 (2): 117–48.

Chang Hen-shui. See Sally Borthwick.

Chang, Kang-i Sun. 1988. "The Idea of the Mask in Wu Wei-yeh (1609–1671)." *HJAS* 48 (2): 289–320.

———. 1991. *The Late Ming Poet Ch'en Tzu-lung: Crises of Love and Loyalism*. New Haven: Yale University Press.

Chen Dongyuan. [1926] 1986. *Zhongguo funü shenghuo shi*. Taibei: Shangwu.

Chen, Fan Pen. 1992. "Female Warriors, Magic and the Supernatural in Traditional Chinese Novels." In *The Annual Review of Women in World Religions*, vol. 2, ed. Arvind Sharma and Katherine K. Young, 91–109. Albany: State University of New York Press.

Chen Guyuan. [1936] 1987. *Zhongguo hunyin shi*. Taibei: Shangwu.

Chen Peng. 1990. *Zhongguo hunyin shigao*. Beijing: Zhonghua shuju.

Chen Qinghao. 1979. *Xinbian Shitou ji Zhiyan zhai pingyu jijiao*. Taibei: Lianjing chubanshe.

Chen Tiebin. 1984. "Lun *Yu Jiao Li*." In *Ming Qing xiaoshuo luncong* 1:174–89. Shenyang: Chunfeng wenyi chubanshe.

Chen Yinke. 1980. *Liu Rushi biezhuan*. Shanghai: Guji chubanshe.

Chen Zhao. 1985. *Honglou meng xiaokao*. Shanghai: Guji chubanshe.

Cheng Yizhong. 1984. "Lue tan caizi jiaren xiaoshuode lishi fazhan." In *Ming Qing xiaoshuo luncong* 1:34–42. Shenyang: Chunfeng wenyi chubanshe.

Chiu, Vermier Y. 1966. *Marriage Laws and Customs of China*. Hong Kong: Publisher unknown.

Chow, Rey. 1991. *Women and Chinese Modernity*. Minneapolis: University of Minnesota Press.

Cooper, Eugene, and Meng Zhang. 1993. "Patterns of Cousin Marriage in Rural Zhejiang and in *Dream of the Red Chamber*." *Journal of Asian Studies* 52 (1): 90–106.

Coward, Rosalind, and John Ellis. 1977. *Language and Materialism: Developments in Semiology and the Theory of the Subject*. London: Routledge and Kegan Paul.

Dai Bufan. 1980. *Xiaoshuo jianwen lu*. Hangzhou: Zhejiang renmin chubanshe.

Deleuze, Gilles. 1967. *Presentation de Sacher-Masoch*. Paris: Les Editions de Minuit.

Dudbridge, Glen. 1970. *The Hsi-yu chi: A Study of Antecedents to the Sixteenth-Century Chinese Novel*. Cambridge: Cambridge University Press.

Easthope, Antony. 1991. *Literary into Cultural Studies*. London and New York: Routledge.

Ebrey, Patricia. 1984. *Family and Property in Sung China: Yuan Ts'ai's Precepts for Social Life*. Princeton: Princeton University Press.

———. 1993. *The Inner Quarters: Marriage and the Lives of Chinese Women in the Sung Period*. Berkeley: University of California Press.

Edwards, Louise. 1990a. "Women in *Honglou meng*: Prescriptions of Purity in the Femininity of Qing Dynasty China." *Modern China* 16 (4): 407–29.

———. 1990b. "Gender Imperatives in *Honglou meng*: Baoyu's Bisexuality." *Chinese Literature, Essays, Articles, and Reviews* 12:69–81.

———. 1993. "Representations of Women and Social Power in Eighteenth Century China: the Case of Wang Xifeng." *Late Imperial China* 14 (1): 34–59.

Egerton, Clement, trans. 1939. *The Golden Lotus*. London: G. Routledge and Sons.

Elman, Benjamin. 1984. *From Philosophy to Philology*. Cambridge: Harvard University Press.

———. 1991. "Political, Social, and Cultural Reproduction via Civil Service Examinations in Late Imperial China." *Journal of Asian Studies* 50 (1): 7–28.

Epstein, Maram. 1992. "Beauty is the Beast: The Dual Face of Woman in Four Ch'ing Novels." Ph.D. dissertation, Princeton University.

———. 1994. "Playing with Gender: Performance of Authenticity in the Late-Qing Novel *Ernü yingxiong zhuan*." Preliminary draft of a paper.

Fang Zhengyao. 1986. *Ming Qing renqing xiaoshuo yanjiu*. Shanghai: Huadong shifan daxue chubanshe.

Feng Erkang and Chang Jianhua. 1990. *Qingren shehui shenghuo*. Tianjin: Renmin chubanshe.

Feng Yu. 1981. "Lun taixu huanjing yu Jingxuan Xiangu." *Honglou meng yanjiu jikan* 6:159–80.

Furth, Charlotte. 1986. "Blood, Body, and Gender." *Chinese Science* 7:43–66.

———. 1987. "Concepts of Pregnancy, Childbirth, and Infancy in Ch'ing Dynasty China." *Journal of Asian Studies* 46 (1): 7–35.

——. 1988. "Androgynous Males and Deficient Females: Biology and Gender Boundaries in Sixteenth- and Seventeenth-Century China." *Late Imperial China* 9 (2): 1–31.

Gallop, Jane. 1982. *The Daughter's Seduction: Feminism and Psychoanalysis.* Ithaca: Cornell University Press.

——. 1985. *Reading Lacan.* Ithaca: Cornell University Press.

Graham, A. C. 1989. *Disputers of the Tao.* Lasalle, Illinois: Open Court.

Guo Changhe. 1934. "Jiaren caizi xiaoshuo yanjiu." *Wenxue jikan* 1 (1–2): 194–215 and 303–23.

Guo Shaoyu. 1982. "Jieshao *Qilu deng.*" In *Qilu deng luncong* 1:1–8. Henan Province: Zhongzhou shuhuashe.

Guo Yushi. 1980. *Honglou meng xiaoshi gao.* Shanghai: Shanghai wenyi.

——. 1981. *Honglou meng xiaoshi xugao.* Shanghai: Wenyi chubanshe.

Han Jinlian. 1981. *Hongxue shi gao.* Shijia zhuang: Hebei renmin.

Hanan, Patrick. 1985. "The Fiction of Moral Duty: the Vernacular Story in the 1640s." In *Expressions of Self in Chinese Literature*, ed. R. Hegel and R. Hessney, 189–213. New York: Columbia University Press.

——. 1988. *The Invention of Li Yu.* Cambridge: Harvard University Press.

——, trans. 1990. Li Yu. *Carnal Prayer Mat.* New York: Ballantine.

Handlin, Joanna. 1975. "Lü K'un's New Audience: The Influence of Women's Literacy on Seventeenth-Century Thought." In *Women in Chinese Society*, ed. Margery Wolf and Roxanne Witke, 13–38. Palo Alto: University of Stanford Press.

——. 1983. *Action in Late Ming Thought: the Reorientation of Lü K'un and Other Scholar-Officials.* Berkeley: University of California Press.

Hanley, Susan B., and Arthur P. Wolf, eds. 1985. *Family and Population in East Asian History.* Palo Alto: Stanford University Press.

Harper, Donald. 1987. "The Sexual Arts of Ancient China as Described in a Manuscript of the Second Century B.C." *HJAS* 47(2):39–93.

Hawkes, David, trans. 1973 and 1977. Cao Xueqin. *The Story of the Stone.* Harmondsworth: Penguin.

Hegel, Robert. 1977. "*Sui T'ang yen-i* and the Aesthetics of the Seventeenth-Century Suchou Elite." In *Chinese Narrative*, ed. Andrew Plaks, 124–59. Princeton: Princeton University Press.

Hegel, Robert, and R. Hessney, eds. 1985. *Expressions of Self in Chinese Literature.* New York: Columbia University Press.

Hessney, Richard. 1979. "Beautiful, Talented, and Brave: Seventeenth-century Scholar-Beauty Romances." Ph.D. dissertation, Columbia University.

——. 1985. "Beyond Beauty and Talent: The Moral and Chivalric Self in *The Fortunate Union.*" In *Expressions of Self in Chinese Literature*, ed. Hegel and Hessney, 214–50. New York: Columbia University Press.

Hinsch, Bret. 1990. *Passions of the Cut Sleeve: The Male Homosexual Tradition in China.* Berkeley: University of California Press.

Hou Jian. 1974. "*Yesou puyan* de biantai xinli." *Chung-wai Literary Monthly* 2 (10): 8–23.

Hsia, C. T. 1968. *The Classic Chinese Novel: A Critical Introduction.* New York: Columbia University Press.

——. 1977. "The Scholar-novelist and Chinese Culture: A Reappraisal of *Ching-hua yuan.*" In *Chinese Narrative,* ed. Andrew Plaks, 266–305. Princeton: Princeton University Press.

Hsiao-hsiao-sheng. See Clement Egerton, David T. Roy, or Arthur Waley.

Hsiung, S. I., trans. 1968. *The Romance of the Western Chamber,* by Wang Shih-fu. New York: Columbia University Press.

Hu Shih. 1980. "*Ernü yingxiong zhuan* kaozheng." In *Zhongguo xiaoshuo kaozheng,* 457–80. Shanghai: Shanghai shudian.

Hu Shihou. 1982. "Shi lun *Qilu deng* de sixiang qingxiang." In *Qilu deng luncong* 1:129–36. Henan: Zhongzhou shuhuashe.

Huang, C. S. 1980. *Marriage and Adoption in China, 1845–1945.* Palo Alto: Stanford University Press.

Huang, Martin. 1991. "The Dilemma of Chinese Lyricism in the Qing Literati Novel." Ph.D. dissertation, Washington University.

——. 1993. "Male Literati Anxiety and the Problem of Gender in *Honglou meng.*" Paper given at the conference of the Association for Asian Studies, Los Angeles.

Hummel, Arthur. 1943. *Emminent Chinese of the Ch'ing Period.* Washington, D.C.: U.S. Government Printing Office.

Idema, Wilt L. 1990. "Cannon, Clocks and Clever Monkeys: Europeana, Europeans and Europe in Some Eighteenth Century Chinese Novels." In *White and Black: Imagination and Cultural Confrontation,* ed. Minieke Schipper et al, 55–82. Amsterdam: Royal Tropical Institute.

Jiang Ruicao. [1915] 1984. *Xiaoshuo kaozheng.* Shanghai: Guji chubanshe.

Jiang Wobin. 1991. *Zhongguo qiqie.* Shijiazhuang: Hebei renmin chubanshe.

Kan Duo. 1925. *Honglou meng jue wei.* Tianjin: Tianjin Dagong Bao guan.

Karlgren, Bernard. 1946. "Legends and Cults in Ancient China." *Bulletin of the Museum of Far Eastern Antiquities* 18:199–365.

——, trans. 1950. *Shujing. The Bulletin of the Museum of Far Eastern Antiquities* 22:1–81.

Ko, Dorothy. 1992. "Pursuing Talent and Virtue: Education and Women's Culture in Seventeenth- and Eighteenth-Century China." *Late Imperial China* 13 (1): 9–39.

Lacan, Jacques. 1977. *Écrits: A Selection.* Trans. Alan Sheridan. New York and London: Norton.

——. 1981. *The Four Fundamental Concepts of Psycho-analysis.* Trans. Alan Sheridan. New York and London: Norton.

——. 1985. *Feminine Sexuality.* Ed. Juliet Mitchell and Jacqueline Rose. Trans. Jacqueline Rose. New York and London: Norton.

Lanselle, Rainier, trans. 1987. *Le Cheval de Jade; Quatre Contes Chinois du XVIIe Siecle* [Translation of *Zhaoshi bei*]. Paris: Editions Picquier.

LaPlanche, Jean, and J.-B. Pontalis. [1967] 1973. *The Language of Psychoanalysis.* Trans. Donald Nicholson-Smith. New York: Norton.

Lau, D. C., trans. 1970. *Mencius.* Harmondsworth: Penguin.

———. 1976. *Lao Tzu.* Harmondsworth: Penguin.

———. 1979. *Analects.* Harmondsworth: Penguin.

Lee Wai-yee. 1993. *Enchantment and Disenchantment: Love and Illusion in Chinese Literature.* Princeton: Princeton University Press.

Legge, James, trans. 1871. *The Ch'un Ts'ew, with the Tso Chuen.* Hong Kong: Lane, Crawford, and Co.

———. 1967. *The Book of Rites.* New Hyde Park, N.Y.: University Books.

Leung, Angela Ki Che. 1993. "To Chasten Society: The Development of Widow Homes in the Qing, 1773–1911." *Late Imperial China* 14 (2): 1–32.

Levy, Howard, and Akira Ishihara, trans. 1989. *The Tao of Sex.* Lower Lake, Calif.: Integral Publishing.

Li Jinghua. 1991. "Guanyu 'daole putaojia.'" *Wenxue yichan* 2:5.

Li Ling and Keith McMahon. 1992. "The Contents and Terminology of the Mawangdui Texts on the Arts of the Bedchamber." *Early China* 17:145–85.

Li Ruzhen. See Lin Tai-yi.

Li Sai. 1984. "Shi lun caizi jiaren pai xiaoshuo." In *Ming Qing xiaoshuo luncong* 1:49–83. Shenyang: Chunfeng wenyi chubanshe.

Li Yu. See Patrick Hanan or Richard Martin.

Liao, W. K., trans. 1959. *The Complete Works of Han Fei Tzu.* London: Arthur Probsthain.

Liao Zhongan. 1986. "*Honglou meng* sixiang yuanyuan yili." In *Fanchu ji*, 210–13. Beijing: Beijing Shifan xueyuan.

Lin Chen. 1988. *Mingmo Qingchu xiaoshuo shulu.* Shenyang: Chunfeng wenyi chubanshe.

Lin Tai-yi, trans. 1965. Li Ruzhen. *Flowers in the Mirror.* London: Peter Owen.

Lin Yutang. 1935. "Feminist Thought in Ancient China." *T'ien Hsia Monthly* 1 (2): 127–50.

Liu Mengxi. 1990. *Hongxue.* Beijing: Wenhua yishu chubanshe.

Liu Tingji. *Zaiyuan zazhi.* In *Liaohai congshu*, vol. 2. Shenyang: Liaoshen shushe, 1985.

Liu Ts'un-yan. 1967. *Chinese Popular Fiction in Two London Libraries.* Hong Kong: Longmen Bookstore.

———. 1982. "Introduction: 'Middlebrow' in Perspective." *Renditions* 17 & 18: 1–40.

Liu Yanzhao. 1982. "Yibu bubei wangquede shu." In *Qilu deng luncong* 1:49–58. Henan: Zhongzhou shuhuashe.

Lu Gong, ed. 1986. *Ming Qing pinghua xiaoshuo xuan.* Shanghai: Guji chubanshe.

Lu Tonglin. 1991. *Rose and Lotus: Narrative and Desire in France and China.* Albany: SUNY Press.

Lu Xun. [1930] 1973. *A Brief History of Chinese Fiction.* Trans. Yang Hsien-yi and Gladys Yang. Westport, Conn.: Hyperion Press.

Luan Xing. 1982a. *Qilu deng yanjiu ziliao.* Zhengzhou: Zhongzhou shuhuashe.

———. 1982b. "*Qilu deng* ji qi liuchuan." In *Qilu deng luncong* 1:183–91. Henan Province: Zhongzhou shuhuashe.

Mackerras, Colin. 1975. *The Chinese Theatre in Modern Times.* London: Thames and Hudson.

McMahon, Keith. 1988a. *Causality and Containment in Seventeenth-century Chinese Fiction.* Leiden: Brill.

———. 1988b "A Case for Confucian Sexuality: The Eighteenth-Century Novel *Yesou puyan.*" *Late Imperial China* 9 (2): 32–55.

Mann, Susan. 1987. "Widows in the Kinship, Class, and Community Structures of Qing Dynasty China." *Journal of Asian Studies* 46 (1): 37–56.

Martin, Richard, trans. of Franz Kuhn's German. 1963. *Prayer Mat of Flesh,* by Li Yu. New York: Grove Press.

Mawangdui Hanmu boshu. 1985. Beijing: Wenwu chubanshe.

Meijer, M. J. 1971. *Marriage Law and Policy in the Chinese People's Republic.* Hong Kong: Hong Kong University Press.

Miao Zhuang. 1984. "*Honglou meng* yu caizi jiaren xiaoshuo." In *Ming Qing xiaoshuo luncong* 1:214–31. Shenyang: Chunfeng.

Naquin, Susan. 1981. *Shantung Rebellion: the Wang Lun Uprising of 1774.* New Haven: Yale University Press.

Naquin, Susan, and Evelyn Rawski. 1987. *Chinese Society in the Eighteenth Century.* New Haven: Yale University Press.

Nivison, David. 1966. *The Life and Thought of Chang Hsueh-ch'eng (1738–1801).* Stanford: Stanford University Press.

Ōtsuka Hidetaka. 1987. *Zōho Chūgoku tsūzoku shosetsu shomoku.* Tōkyo: Kyuko shoin.

Pasternak, Burton. 1985. "On the Causes and Demographic Consequences of Uxorilocal Marriage in China." In *Family and Population in East Asian History,* ed. Hanley and Wolf, 309–34.

Peterson, Willard J., Andrew Plaks, and Ying-shih Yu, eds. 1993. *The Power of Culture: Studies in Chinese Cultural History.* Hong Kong: Chinese University Press.

Plaks, Andrew. 1976. *Archetype and Allegory in the Dream of the Red Chamber.* Princeton: Princeton University Press.

———, ed. 1977. *Chinese Narrative.* Princeton: Princeton University Press.

Porkert, Manfred. 1982. *The Theoretical Foundations of Chinese Medicine.* Cambridge: MIT Press.

Pratt, Leonard, and Chiang Su-hui, trans. 1983. *Six Episodes of a Floating Life,* by Shen Fu. Harmondsworth: Penguin.

Qi Yukun et al. 1990. *Zhongguo gudai xiaoshuo yanbian shi.* Lanzhou: Dunhuang wenyi.

Qian Jingfang. [1912] 1979. *Xiaoshuo congkao.* Taibei: Changan chubanshe.

Qilu deng luncong 1. 1982. Henan Province: Zhongzhou shuhuashe.

Qilu deng luncong 2. 1984. Henan Province: Zhongzhou guji.

Rao Zongyi, ed. 1956. *Laozi xianger zhu jiao jian.* Hong Kong: Tongnam Publishers.

Richlin, Amy. 1993. "Not Before Homosexuality: The Materiality of the Cinaedus and the Roman Law against Love between Men." *Journal of the History of Sexuality* 2 (4): 523–73.

Robertson, Maureen. 1992. "Voicing the Feminine: Constructions of the Gendered Subject in Lyric Poetry by Women of Medieval and Late Imperial China." *Late Imperial China* 13 (1): 63–110.

Roddy, Stephen. 1990. "*Rulin waishi* and the Representation of Literati in Qing Fiction." Ph.D. dissertation, Princeton University.

Rolston, David. 1987. "*Lin Lan Xiang yu Jin Ping Mei*." *Wenxue yichan* 5:113–23.

——. 1989. "A Missing Link between the *Jin Ping Mei* and the *Honglou meng*?" Paper given at the Midwest Conference of Asian Affairs, East Lansing.

——, ed. 1990. *How to Read the Chinese Novel*. Princeton: Princeton University Press.

Ropp, Paul. 1981. *Dissent in Early Modern China*. Ann Arbor: University of Michigan Press.

Rouselle, Aline. 1989. "Personal Status and Sexual Practice in the Roman Empire." In *Fragments of a History of the Human Body*, ed. Michel Feher, vol. 3: 301–33. New York, NY: Zone; Cambridge, Mass: distributed by MIT Press.

Rowe, William T. 1992. "Women and the Family in Mid-Qing Social Thought: The Case of Chen Hongmou." *Late Imperial China* 13 (2): 1–41.

Roy, David T., trans. 1993. *The Plum in the Golden Vase*, by Hsiao-hsiao-sheng. Princeton: Princeton University Press.

Ruan Fang Fu. 1991. *Sex in China*. New York: Plenum.

Schor, Naomi. 1985. *Breaking the Chain: Women, Theory, and French Realist Fiction*. New York: Columbia University Press.

——. 1987. *Reading in Detail: Aesthetics and the Feminine*. New York and London: Methuen.

Shang Daxiang. 1982. "Lue lun yipu Wang Zhong." In *Qilu deng luncong* 1: 105–13. Henan Province: Zhongzhou shuhuashe.

Shen Fu. See Leonard Pratt and Su-hui Chiang.

Shen Yinbing. [1927] 1957. "Zhongguo wenxuenei de xingyu miaoxie." In *Zhongguo wenxue yanjiu*, ed. Zheng Zhenduo. Beijing: Zuojia.

Silverman, Kaja. 1992. *Male Subjectivity at the Margins*. New York and London: Routledge.

Sivin, Nathan. 1987. *Traditional Medicine in Contemporary China*. Ann Arbor: Center for Chinese Studies.

Spence, Jonathan D. 1974. *Emperor of China*. New York: Knopf.

Su Hongchang. 1983. "Lun Cao Xueqin zai *Honglou meng* chuangzuozhongde dazhi tan qing." *Honglou meng yanjiu jikan* 11:39–58.

Su Xing. 1985. "Tianhua cang zhuren ji qi caizi jiaren xiaoshuo." In *Caizi jiaren xiaoshuo shulin*, 9–26.

Sun Kaidi. [1930] 1985. "Guanyu *Ernü yingxiong zhuan*." In *Cangzhou houji*, 248–61. Beijing: Zhonghua shuju.

——. 1981. *Riben Dongjing suojian xiaoshuo shumu*. Beijing: Renmin wenxue chu-banshe.

——. 1982. *Zhongguo tongsu xiaoshuo shumu*. Beijing: Renmin wenxue chubanshe.

Tan Zhengbi. [1935] 1978. *Zhongguo xiaoshuo fada shi*. Taibei: Qiye shuju.

——. 1980. *Sanyan Liangpai ziliao*. Shanghai: Shanghai guji.

Tan Zhengbi and Tan Xun. 1984. *Guben xijian xiaoshuo huikao*. Hangzhou: Zhejiang wenyi.

Thatcher, Melvin P. 1991. "Marriages of the Ruling Elite in the Spring and Autumn Period." In *Marriage and Inequality in Chinese Society*, ed. Rubie S. Watson and Patricia Ebrey, 25–57. Berkeley: University of California Press.

Thong, Huynh Sanh, trans. 1973. *The Tale of Kieu*. New York: Random House.

T'ien Ju-k'ang. 1988. Male Anxiety and Female Chastity. Leiden: Brill.

Tjan, Tjoe Som, trans. 1949–52. *Po Hu T'ung, the Comprehensive Discussions in the White Tiger Hall,* by Ban Gu. Leiden: Brill.

Van Gulik, Robert. 1951. *Erotic Colour Prints of the Ming Period*. Tokyo: Privately published.

——. 1974. *Sexual Life in Ancient China*. Leiden: Brill.

Waley, Arthur, trans. 1940. *Chin Ping Mei*. New York: Putnam.

Waltner, Ann. 1990. *Getting an Heir*. Honolulu: University of Hawaii Press.

Wang, Chi-chen, trans. 1982. *Marriage as Retribution,* by P'u Sung-ling (ascribed). *Renditions* 17 and 18: 41–94.

Wang, Jing. 1992. *The Story of Stone*. Durham: Duke University Press.

Wang Lina. 1988. *Zhongguo gudian xiaoshuo xiqu mingzhu zai guowai*. Beijing: Xuelin.

Wang Shifu. See S. I. Hsiung, or Stephen H. West and Wilt Idema.

Wang Xiaolian. 1983. "*Shenlou zhi*—yibu chengxian qihou de qianze xiaoshuo." In *Shenlou zhi,* 1983. Taibei: Guangya.

Wang Yao. 1986. "Wenren yu yao." In *Zhongguo wenxue shi lun,* 129–75. Beijing: Beijing daxue chubanshe.

Wang Yongjian. 1988. "*Lin Lan Xiang, Jin Ping Mei, Honglou meng.*" *Honglou meng xuekan* 3:147–62.

Watson, Rubie S., and Patricia Ebrey, eds. 1991. *Marriage and Inequality in Chinese Society*. Berkeley: University of California Press.

Wei, Hua. 1993. "The Lament of Frustrated Talents: An Analysis of Three Women's Plays in Late Imperial China." Paper given at the conference of the Association for Asian Studies, Los Angeles.

West, Stephen H., and Wilt Idema, trans. 1991. *The Moon and the Zither: the Story of the Western Wing,* by Wang Shih-fu. Berkeley: University of California Press.

Widmer, Ellen. 1989. "The Epistolary World of Female Talent in Seventeenth-Century China." *Late Imperial China* 10 (2): 1–43.

——. 1992. "Xiaoqing's Literary Legacy and the Place of the Woman Writer in Late Imperial China." *Late Imperial China* 13 (1): 111–55.

Wile, Douglas. 1992. *Art of the Bedchamber.* Albany: SUNY Press.

Wolf, Arthur, and C. S. Huang, eds. 1980. *Marriage and Adoption in China, 1845–1945.* Stanford: Stanford University Press.

Wolf, Margery. 1972. *Women and the Family in Rural Taiwan.* Stanford: Stanford University Press.

Wolf, Margery, and Roxanne Witke, eds. 1975. *Women in Chinese Society.* Stanford: Stanford University Press.

Wu, Shih-ch'ang. 1961. *On the Red Chamber Dream.* Oxford: Oxford University Press.

Wu, Yenna. 1988. "The Inversion of Marital Hierarchy: Shrewish Wives and Henpecked Husbands in Seventeenth-Century Chinese Literature." *HJAS* 48 (2): 363–82.

Wu Zhida and Chen Wenxin. 1982. "Fengjian moshi tongzhi jiejide zhengtongpai renwu—lun Tan Xiaoyi jianyu Jia Zheng bijiao." In *Qilu deng luncong* 1: 114–28. Henan Province: Zhongzhou shuhuashe.

Xiao Xiangkai. 1987. "Bie kaile yige shengmiande yibu caizi jiaren xiaoshuo—*Wan Ru Yue.*" Postface to *Wan Ru Yue*, 166–75. Shenyang: Chunfeng wenyi chubanshe.

Xu Cunren and Xu Youwei. 1982. *Chengkeben Honglou meng xinkao.* Taibei: Guoli bianyiguan.

Xu Ke. 1984. *Qingbai leichao.* Beijing: Zhonghua shuju.

Yang Xianyi and Gladys Yang, trans. 1978–80. *A Dream of Red Mansions*, by Cao Xueqin. Beijing: Foreign Languages Press.

Yao, Christina Shu-hwa. 1983. "*Cai-zi jia-ren:* Love Drama during the Yuan, Ming, and Qing Periods." Ph.D. dissertation, Stanford University.

Yao Lingxi. 1941. *Si wuxie xiaoji.* Tianjin: Tianjin yinshua gongsi.

Ying Bicheng. 1979. "*Honglou meng* yu *Ernü yingxiong zhuan.*" *Honglou meng yanjiu jikan* 1:107–28.

———. 1983. *Lun Shitou ji gengchenben.* Shanghai: Guji chubanshe.

Yu Zhiyuan. 1985. "*Lin Lan Xiang* lun." In *Lin Lan Xiang*, 498–516. Shenyang: Chunfeng wenyi chubanshe.

Zeitlin, Judith. 1993. *Historian of the Strange: Pu Songling and the Chinese Classical Tale.* Stanford: Stanford University Press.

Zhang Guoguang. 1982. "Woguo gudaide 'jiaoyu shi' yu shehui fengsu hua." In *Qilu deng luncong* 1: 137–73. Henan Province: Zhongzhou shuhuashe.

Zhang Juling. 1990. *Qingdai Manzu zuojia wenxue gailun.* Beijing: Zhongyang minzu xueyuan chubanshe.

Zhang Jun. 1985. "Man shuo *Dingqing renzhongde qing.*" In *Caizi jiaren xiaoshuo shulin*, 124–37. Shenyang: Chunfeng wenyi chubanshe.

———. 1987. "Lun *Lin Lan Xiang* yu *Honglou meng:* Jian tan lianjie *Jin Ping Mei* yu *Honglou meng*de lianhuan." In *Ming Qing xiaoshuo luncong* 5:63–84.

Zhao Jingshen. [1937] 1980. *Xiaoshuo congkao.* Jinan: Qilu shushe.

Zheng Jijia. 1988. "Lun *Jin Ping Mei, Lin Lan Xiang, Honglou meng* ticai, zhuti de jicheng he fazhan." *Yancheng jiaoyu xueyuan xuekan* 3–4: 28–33.

Zheng Yimei. 1982. *Yilin sanye*. Beijing: Zhonghua shuju.

Zheng Zhenduo. [1927] 1957. *Zhongguo wenxue yanjiu*. Beijing: Zuojia.

——. [1927] 1986. "Shiba shijide Zhongguo wenxue." In *Wenxue dagang*, 1359–1418. Shanghai: Shanghai shudian.

Zhong Ying. 1984. "Ping *Yu Jiao Li*." In *Ming Qing xiaoshuo luncong* 1:159–73. Shenyang: Chunfeng.

Zhongguo tongsu xiaoshuo zongmu tiyao. 1990. Jiangsu sheng shehui kexue yuan. Beijing: Zhongguo wenlian chuban gongsi.

Zhongguo xiaoshuo shi. 1978. Beijing: Renmin chubanshe.

Zhou Jianyu. 1990. "Caizi jiaren xiaoshuo yanjiu." Ph.D. dissertation, Social Sciences Academy of China (Beijing).

Zhou Yimou. 1989. *Zhongguo gudai fangshi yang sheng xue*. Shenyang: Zhongwai wenhua chuban gongsi.

Zhou Yimou and Diao Zuotao, eds. 1988. *Mawangdui yishu kaozhu*. Tianjin: Tianjin kexue jishu chubanshe.

Zhu Yixuan. 1985. *Honglou meng ziliao huibian*. Tianjin: Nankai daxue chubanshe.

Zhu Ziqing. 1982. "*Qilu deng*." In *Qilu deng luncong* 1: 9–17. Henan Province: Zhongzhou shuhuashe.

GLOSSARY OF CHINESE CHARACTERS

The following list includes all underscored terms, expressions, and quotations, names of fictional works, their authors, and (if premodern) their publishers, major characters in these works, and Ming and Qing political and literary personages. Not included, with minor exceptions, are characters for such things as the names of modern scholars and their works, minor characters of novels, and most names of pre-Ming and Qing works and personages.

ai　愛

ai hongde maobing　愛紅的毛病

ai se jingqi　愛嗇精氣

Aiyama Kiwamu　合山究

An Ji　安驥

An Xuehai　安學海

bai　敗

Baigui zhi　白圭志

baixi zhu　白犀塵

bao　暴

bao shen　寶神

Baopuzi　抱樸子

Baoren tang　寶仁堂

bendi fengguang　本地風光

benqian　本錢

Benya cangban　本衙藏板

bi   屄

Bian er chai   弁而釵

bijia gongfu   比甲工夫

Bu yue zhuren   步月主人

bushou guimen   不守閨門

butan nüse   不貪女色

buyong   不庸

buzijuede   不自覺的

cai   財

caibu zhiyin   採補至陰

Cainü   采女

cainü   才女

caizhan   採戰

caizhu   財主

caizi jiaren   才子佳人

canggeng   倉庚

cao   肏

Cao Xueqin   曹雪芹

ceshi   側室

cha   插

chai   柴

Chan Zhen houshi   禪真後史

Chan Zhen yishi   禪真逸史

Chang Jie   長姐

Changyan dao   常言道

chanmian   纏綿

Chao Yuan   晁源

chenbing   塵柄

Cheng Weiyuan   程偉元

Chijue tang   齒爵堂

chouchang   惆悵

chousong   抽送

chu bing　除病

chuan　傳

Chun liu ying　春柳影

Chuncai　春才

Chundeng mishi　春燈迷史

Chundeng nao　春燈鬧

chungong cezi　春宮冊子

chuntai　春態

chunyi pu　春意譜

ci　刺

Ciji shi　雌雞市

citaijian　雌太監

ciwu　此物

congliang　從良

congmin guaiqiao　聰敏乖巧

Cu hulu　醋葫蘆

cubing　醋病

Cui Qiao　翠翹

cuo'ai　錯愛

da jiba dada　大毣髫達達

da luanfu　大卵脬

dada　達達

Dai Zhen　戴震

danran　淡然

danxue　丹穴

dao jiao la　倒澆蜡

daole putaojia　倒了葡萄架

daoxue qi　道學氣

daoyin　導淫

de　德

Dengcao heshang　燈草和尚

Di Xichen　狄希陳

dianluan daofeng　顛鸞倒鳳

dijia　敵家

Ding Richang　丁日昌

Dingqing ren　定情人

dingshu　定數

diu shenzi　丟身子

Dong Xun　董恂

Dongbei you san da guai　東北有三大怪

Dongdu ji　東度記

dongxi　東西

Dongxuanzi　洞玄子

du　妒

Du Shaoqing　杜少卿

duan　端

duanzhuang　端莊

duo yu shao nü　多御少女

dushi　妒石

dushu junzi　讀書君子

enü　惡女

Erke pai'an jingqi　二刻拍案驚奇

erliu renwu　二流人物

ernü rouchang　兒女柔腸

Ernü yingxiong zhuan　兒女英雄傳

Erpai　二拍

Fang Ruhao　方汝浩

fangshu　房術

fangzhong shu　房中術

fanli　凡例

Feihua yong　飛花咏

Feng Menglong　馮夢龍

Fenghuang chi　鳳凰池

fengliu　風流

Fengliu heshang   風流和尚

Fengliu pei   風流配

Fengyin lou   鳳吟樓

fengyue   風月

Fengyue xuan Ruxuanzi   風月軒入玄子

fu (obey)   服

fu (submit)   伏

fu (wife)   婦

Fu ci jiaozhu   伏雌教主

fulang zidi   浮浪子弟

fuqi en'ai   夫妻恩愛

furen jianshi   婦人見識

furen yunian ru tu fang xiu   婦人慫念入土方休

Fusheng liuji   浮生六記

fushi   副室

Fuweng zhuan   富翁傳

Gao Bin   高斌

Gao E   高鶚

ge shan qu huo   隔山取火

geng   羹

Geng Lang   耿郎

Gengchen   庚辰

gu jing   固精

Guan Hanqing   關漢卿

guanfangpener   關防盆兒

Guangxiao fu   廣笑府

guanlie   關捩

gui (ghost, demon)   鬼

gui (turtle)   龜

gui x x zhi shu   龜匕匕之術

Gujin xiaoshi   古今笑史

guose   國色

Hakusai shomoku　舶載書目

hanfu　悍婦

hanza　含咂

haojie　豪傑

Haoqiu zhuan　好逑傳

haoxia　豪俠

He yinyang　合陰陽

He Yufeng　何玉鳳

hehuan chuang　合歡床

hehuan shenghui　合歡勝會

Heiji yuanhun　黑籍冤魂

　　(same as "Heiji yuanhun")

Heying lou　合影樓

hongchen　紅塵

Hongdou　紅豆

Honglou huanmeng　紅樓幻夢

Honglou meng　紅樓夢

Hongxue　紅學

hou shang shen qu　猴上身去

houting　後庭

houzhe lian　猴著臉

hua heshang　花和尚

Hua tu yuan　畫圖緣

huan jing bu nao　還精補腦

huangdi xing　黃帝性

Huanxi yuanjia　歡喜冤家

Hudie mei　蝴蝶媒

hui jin ru tu　揮金如土

hui jing　回精

huixie　穢褻

huopo　活潑

huzi　壺子

Ishimpō bōnai 醫心方房內

Ji Dian (Ji Gong) 濟顛 (濟公)

Ji Dian dashi zuiputi quanzhuan 濟顛大師醉菩提全傳

Ji Yun 紀昀

Jia Baoyu 賈寶玉

Jia Lian 賈璉

Jia Zheng 賈政

jiafa 家法

Jiafan 家範

jiahua 佳話

jian 姦

Jiangnan 江南

Jiangyin 江陰

jianmin 賤民

jiantiao 兼祧

jianyin 姦淫

jiao 嚼

jiaochi 嬌癡

jiaogou hui 交媾會

jiaohe 交合

jiaren caizi deng shu 佳人才子等書

Jiaxu 甲戌

jichu 機處

jie 節

jie du 節度

jiemeimen 姐妹們

jiguan 機關

Jijie 寄姐

jiliu yongtui 急流勇退

Jimau 己卯

Jin Lan fa 金蘭筏

Jin Ping Mei 金瓶梅

Jin Shi yuan　金石緣

Jin Yun Qiao　金雲翹

Jin Zhonger　金鍾兒

jinbude　進步的

jing　精

jinggong zhi niao　驚弓之鳥

Jinghua yuan　鏡花園

Jingshi tongyan　警世通言

Jingtian zhuren　靜恬主人

jinshi　今世

Jinxiang ting　錦香亭

jinyu　金玉

jiuqian yishen　九淺一深

jiurou pengyou　酒肉朋友

jiuse　酒色

ju nei　懼內

jue　嚼

jushu　拘束

Juzhen tang　聚珍堂

kong (empty)　空

kong (hole)　孔

kou piyan, cuo zhitou　扣屁眼，嗾指頭

kuaiyi　快意

laili　來歷

Langshi qiguan　浪史奇觀

langzi　浪子

Laozi xianger zhu jiao jian　老子想爾注校箋

le　樂

Leng Yubing　冷于冰

lengxiao　冷笑

leshi　樂事

li (principle)　理

li (ritual)　禮

Li Baichuan　李百川

Li Guangdi　李光地

Li Haiguan　李海觀

Li Kui　李逵

Li Pinger　李瓶兒

Li Ruzhen　李汝珍

Li Yu　李漁

Li Zhi　李贄

Liang Shanbo　梁山伯

liangmin　良民

Liaodu geng　療妒羹

Liaodu yuan　療妒緣

Liaozhai zhiyi　聊齋誌異

Lin Daiyu　林黛玉

Lin er bao　麟兒報

Lin Lan Xiang　林蘭香

Lin Ruhai　林如海

Lin Yunping　林雲屏

Lin Zhiyang　林之洋

Ling Mengchu　凌濛初

lingqiao　靈竅

linse gui　吝嗇鬼

Liu Fu　劉斧

liu gouzi, tian piyan　溜溝子, 舔屁眼

liu kehen　六可恨

Liu Shi (Rushi)　柳是 (如是)

Liu Tingji　劉廷璣

liuli　流麗

liuzhou　碌磚

"Liwa zhuan"　李娃傳

lixi　利息

lohan　羅漢

long　攏

longluo　籠絡

longyang hui　龍陽會

longyang zhi xing　龍陽之興

lu　爐

Lü Dongbin　呂洞賓

Lü Kun　呂坤

Lu Xun, Kang, Ji, Yun　陸遜, 抗, 機, 雲

"Luanrou"　臠肉

Lümudan　綠牡丹

lushui fuqi　露水夫妻

Lüxian feijian ji　呂仙飛劍記

Lüye xianzong　綠野仙蹤

ma jie　罵街

"Mai you lang duzhan huakuei"　賣油郎獨占花魁

maobing　毛病

Mawangdui Hanmu boshu　馬王堆漢墓帛書

men　悶

Meng Lijun　孟麗君

Meng Yulou　孟玉樓

Miao Tuzi　苗禿子

min　抿

ming　命

mo shu xie jing　莫數寫精

mosheng ren　陌生人

mu nan　慕男

Mudan ting　牡丹亭

Mulan　木蘭

muqian　母錢

na long zhi fa　納龍之法

nahua　那話

Naner 難兒

nanfeng 男風

nanfeng 南風

nannü butongzuo 男女不同坐

nannü jiaogou zhi sheng 男女交媾之聲

nannü shoushou buqin 男女授受不親

nao 鬧

Nao huacong 鬧花叢

neijiao 內交

Nengren si 能仁寺

ni you jian wo taiqin, jiaoguande buxiangyang
你又見我太親，嬌慣的不像樣

niaoqi 溺器

nihuan 泥洹

nücaizi 女才子

nue 謔

nuelang xiaxie 謔浪狎邪

nuelang xiayou 謔浪狎游

nühai'er side 女孩兒似的

nühai'er yiban 女孩兒一般

Nüxian waishi 女仙外史

nüxinghua 女性化

nüzhong daru 女中大儒

nüzhong nanzi 女中男子

nüzhong zhangfu 女中丈夫

Nüzhuangyuan 女狀元

nüzi wu cai bian shi de 女子無才便是德

Ouluobazhou 歐羅巴洲

Pa po jing 怕婆經

Pan Jinlian 潘金蓮

Peng Yang'ou 彭養鷗

pengyou 朋友

pi'ai 僻愛

pianfang 偏房

Piling huizhen lou 毗陵彙珍樓

pilu 皮盧

Pin hua baojian 品花寶鑑

Piner 顰兒

Ping Caiyun 平彩雲

Ping Shan Leng Yan 平山冷燕

Pipa ji 琵琶記

po gua 破瓜

po shen 破身

po ti 破體

pofu 潑婦

pojian shetou 潑賤舌頭

Pu Songling 浦松齡

qi 氣

qi (ride) 騎

qi/qi 妻/齊

Qi Huiniang 齊蕙娘

qian 淺

Qian Qianyi 錢謙益

Qian Shiming 錢士命

Qian Yu 錢愚

Qianjin yifang 千金醫方

qianmiande wushi 前面的物事

qianquan 繾綣

qiao 竅

qiecuo 切磋

qigong 氣功

Qilu deng 歧路燈

Qin Zhong 秦鐘

qing 情

Qing bai lei chao　清稗類鈔

qingbo　輕簿

Qingmeng tuo　情夢柝

qingshuang　清爽

Qingsuo gaoyi　青瑣高議

Qingwen　晴雯

Qingye zhong　清夜鐘

qinsheng nü'er　親生女兒

qiu po　求婆

qiu zi　求子

qu　趣

quan (admonish)　勸

quan (expediency)　權

"Quan jian"　犬姦

quanjie　勸戒

que se　郤色

ren　忍

Ren Xianger　任香兒

ren yi li xin zhi　仁義禮信智

renjian zhibao　人間至寶

renqing xiaoshuo　人情小説

Rou putuan　肉蒲團

ru zhui　入贅

rufuren　如夫人

Rulin waishi　儒林外史

ruo bujing feng　弱不經風

Ruyi jun zhuan　如意君傳

Sai hong si　賽紅絲

Sai hua ling　賽花鈴

San Yan　三言

sanhen　三恨

se (sensuality)　色

se (frugal)　嗇

seliang　色量

seyu　色慾

"Shanhu"　珊瑚

shanle zhua'erle　汕了爪兒了

Shen Fu　沈復

Shen Jiashu　沈嘉樹

Shen Qiongzhi　沈瓊枝

Sheng Xiqiao　盛希僑

shengchan zhi ku　生產之苦

shenghuan　生還

shenghui　勝會

Shenlou zhi　蜃樓志

shi　屎

shi 'ge yanse　使個眼色

Shi hou ji　獅吼記

shi se xing ye　食色性也

Shi wu pi　世無匹

shi wu you po　實無有婆

Shi Xiangyun　史湘雲

shidong　十動

shi'er chai　十二釵

Shifan　世範

shijing　市井

shijue'er　屎概兒

shinü　石女

Shisan mei　十三妹

Shiwen　十問

shixie　施寫

shizi hou　獅子吼

shou　受

shu (skill)　術

shu (comb)　梳

shuai　衰

shuazi　刷子

shubi　梳篦

Shui Furen　水夫人

Shuihu zhuan　水滸傳

shun shui tui zhou　順水推舟

Shuo Tang sanzhuan　説唐三傳

shutong　書童

si　私

Si wuxie xiaoji　思無邪小記

sihaizi　私孩子

sihui gaomu　死灰槁目

siqing　私情

Siyou tang　四友堂

Song Jiang　宋江

Su Xiaoguan (Jishi)　蘇笑官 (吉士)

Su'e　素娥

Suiyuan xiashi　隨緣下士

Sugu　素谷

Sui Tang yanyi　隋唐演義

Sujie　素姐

Sun Jiagan　孫嘉淦

Sun Simiao　孫思邈

Sunü jing　素女經

Sunü miaolun　素女妙論

suo yang zhi shu　縮陽之術

suosui　瑣碎

suwang　素王

taijiquan　太極拳

Tamba Yasuyori　丹波康賴

Tan Shaowen　譚紹聞

tanci　彈詞

Tang　湯

Taohua yanshi　桃花艷史

Taohua ying　桃花影

tengchuang　藤床

Ti xiao yinyuan　啼笑因緣

Tian Chunwan　田春畹

Tian Shi　田氏

tiandijian lingshu zhi qi zhi zhongyu nüzi　天地間靈淑之氣只鍾於女子

Tianhuacang zhuren　天花藏主人

Tianshu　天書

tianxing　天性

Tiao Geng　調羹

Tiehua xianshi　鐵花仙史

timu　題目

ting renjia bangsheng　聽人家捹聲

tong fang　同房

tong fu yangtai　同赴陽臺

Tong Nainai　童奶奶

tongfang　通房

tongnü che　童女車

tongxiao wan　通宵丸

tongyangxi　童養媳

tou qing　偷情

toujin qi　頭巾氣

tu shengren　土聖人

Wan Ru Yue　宛如約

wang　忘

Wang Tingna　汪廷訥

Wang Xifeng　王熙鳳

wang xing　忘形

wanshua　玩耍

356

Wanxiang zhai　畹香齋

washi　瓦石

Wen Kang　文康

Wen Ruyu　溫如玉

Wen Suchen　文素臣

Wencui tang　文粹堂

wenrou　溫柔

wenruo shusheng　文弱書生

wo suanbude yige renle　我算不的一個人了

wo xinshang ai ta　我心上愛他

wode weiren　我的為人

Wu Bing　吳炳

Wu Han　吳晗

Wu Jianren　吳趼人

Wu Jingzi　吳敬梓

Wu Jinzhuang　武進莊

Wu Zetian　武則天

wuchang　五常

Wufeng yin　五鳳吟

wumei　嫵媚

Wushan yanshi　巫山艷史

wushi er zhan　五世而斬

wuwei　無為

wuxia xiaoshuo　武俠小說

wuxing　五行

wuyu　五欲

xi fen ru jin　惜糞如金

Xi Shi peng xin er pin mei　西施捧心而顰眉

xi xin yan jiu　喜新厭舊

xia　俠

Xia Jingqu　夏敬渠

xialie　俠烈

xiang　香

Xiangling　湘靈

xianpi　涎皮

xianqi　賢妻

xianü　俠女

Xianü qiyuan　俠女奇緣

xianzhe lian　涎著臉

xianzi　仙姿

xiao guan　小官

xiao jiao　小腳

xiao laogong　小老公

xiao laopo　小老婆

xiao qie　小妾

xiao sheng　小生

Xiaohua xuan　嘯花軒

Xiaohua zhai　嘯花齋

Xiaoqing　小青

Xiaoren guo　小人國

xiaqi quan xiao　俠氣全消

Xie Ximeng　謝希孟

Xie Zhaozhe　謝肇淛

xienue　諧謔

xieshi　斜視

Xihu erji　西湖二集

xile shou'erle　洗了手兒了

Ximen Qing　西門慶

xing　性

xing buziding　性不自定

Xing fengliu　醒風流

xing li　性理

Xinghua tian　杏花天

xingqu　興趣

Xingshi hengyan 醒世恒言

Xingshi yinyuan zhuan 醒世姻緣傳

xipa 喜帕

xiongdi ru shouzu, qizi ru yifu 兄弟如手足, 妻子如衣服

Xiren 襲人

xiu (shame) 羞

xiu (night) 宿

Xiu zhen yanyi 修真演義

Xiuping yuan 繡屏緣

Xiwangmu nüxiu zhengtu shize 西王母女修正途十則

Xixiang ji 西廂記

xiyang mianbu 西洋棉布

Xiyi 希夷

Xiyou ji 西遊記

Xu Ke 徐珂

Xu Wei 徐渭

Xuan Ainiang 宣愛娘

xuanchan fu 玄蟬附

Xuangu 璇姑

Xuannü 玄女

Xue Baochai 薛寶釵

Xue Pan 薛蟠

Yaguan lou 雅觀樓

yan 嚴

yan gai song 偃蓋松

Yan Mengqing 燕夢卿

yan qing 言情

Yan Song 嚴嵩

yang 陽

Yang bing yongyan 養病庸言

Yang Mingshi 楊名時

yang sheng 養生

Yang sheng fang　養生方

Yang Wei zhi fu　羊委之婦

Yang xing yan ming lu　養性延命錄

yangguizi　洋鬼子

yanghang　洋行

Yangjiafu yanyi　楊家府演義

yangren suozao　洋人所造

yangwei　陽萎

Yannan tang　延南堂

Yanshui shanren　煙水山人

Yanzi jian　燕子箋

yaque wushengde　鴉雀無聲的

yatou　丫頭

yehu　夜壺

yeren xian pu　野人獻曝

Yesou puyan　野叟曝言

yi　義

yibei　異被

yichuang　異床

yichuang sanhao　一床三好

Yichun xiangzhi　宜春香質

Yifang leiju　醫方類聚

yifu duoqi　一夫多妻

yifu erqi　一夫二妻

yifu yiqi　一夫一妻

Yilin sanye　藝林散葉

yin (of yin / yang)　陰

yin (lascivious)　淫

yinfu　淫婦

ying shuazi　蠅刷子

Ying Yun meng　英雲夢

yingling zhi qi buzhongyu shi zhi nanzi, er zhongyu furen
英靈之氣不鍾於世之男子, 而鍾於婦人

yinguo baoying　因果報應

yingxiong　英雄

"Yingying zhuan"　鶯鶯傳

yiniang　姨娘

yinqi (yin "gas")　陰氣

yinqi (sex tools)　淫器

yinshu　淫書

yinyang jiaogou　陰陽交媾

yinyang peihe　陰陽配合

yinyang xiangzi　陰陽相資

Yipian qing　一片情

yiqi　義氣

yiqi sanqie　一妻三妾

yishen jianbei　一身兼備

yitaitai　姨太太

Yiwai yuan　意外緣

Yiwen leiju　藝文類聚

yixie ru zhu　一洩如注

Yixin fang (see *Ishimpō*)　醫心方

yiyin　意淫

you nü'er zhi tai　有女兒之態

yougu　幽谷

youwu　尤物

yu (drive)　御

yu (pedantic)　迂

Yu Jiao Li　玉嬌梨

Yu Lou Chun　玉樓春

Yu nü sunyi　御女損益

yu qiang　踰牆

Yu Zhengxie　俞正燮

Yu zhi ji　玉支璣

Yuan Cai　袁采

Yuan Mei　袁枚

Yuan shi shi fan　袁氏世範

yuanjia　冤家

yuce　玉策

yuchen　玉塵

yuchuang　雨床

Yuelai dian　悦來店

Yufang mijue　玉房秘決

Yufang zhiyao yuhu　玉房指要

yuhu　玉户

yujing　玉莖

yumen　玉門

yunchuang　雲床

yunyu　雲雨

Yuqing　玉卿

Yuqinger　玉磬兒

yuren　玉人

Yushan Wei Juntian　虞山衛峻天

zai hang　在行

Zai sheng yuan　再生緣

Zaiyuan zazhi　在園雜志

zaokang zhi qi　糟糠之妻

ze ding　擇鼎

zhan xie dibu　占些地步

Zhang Jinfeng　張金鳳

Zhang Xinzhi　張新之

Zhang Xuecheng　章學誠

Zhaoshi bei　照世盃

Zhaoyang qushi　昭陽趣史

zhen (battle formations)　陳

zhen (true)　真

zheng (main)　正

zheng (steam)　蒸

Zheng Yimei　鄭逸梅

zhengjing shi　正經事

zhengse　正色

Zhengtong daozang　正統道藏

zhezhe yanyan, niuniu nienie　遮遮掩掩, 扭扭捏捏

zhi (make arrive)　至

zhi (term in Mawangdui)　治

zhi (will)　志

zhiji　知己

zhimu　指目

Zhiyan zhai　脂硯齋

zhong　中

zhongshen you kong　中身有空

Zhou Lian　周璉

Zhou Xinfang　周信芳

Zhou Yueran　周越然

zhu　朱

Zhu Yingtai　祝英台

zhuan hao nüse　專好女色

zhubing　麈柄

Zhuchun yuan xiaoshi　駐春園小史

zhuochou biren　濁臭逼人

zi jia zile　自嫁自了

zicai ziyue　自裁自約

zidong　自動

ziqian　子錢

zongfa　宗法

zongjiao　總角

zuan xue yu qiang   鑽穴踰牆

Zui chunfeng   醉春風

Zui xing shi   醉醒石

zuowei   坐位

INDEX

Bound feet (*cont.*)
ings, 215; *Honglou meng*'s lack of reference to, 182, 302 n. 42; *Jinghua yuan*
against, 286, 294 n. 22; sleep-slipper,
214–15, 239, 241; squeezing of, 127, 133

Caizi jiaren: use of as term, 105–6, 134,
306 n. 19, 307 n. 26, 307 n. 28
Cao Xueqin, 20, 179–83, 188, 316 n. 6
Catamite. *See* Male homosexuality: catamite
Celibate. *See* Ascetic
Censorship, 20–21, 38, 48
Changyan dao, 85–87, 88, 92; edition, 303
n. 7
Chan Zhen houshi, 51, 303 n. 50, 303 n. 53
Chan Zhen yishi, 51, 70, 80, 303 n. 50, 303
n. 53
Character types, 4, 10; composite description of, 12–17, 287–92
Chaste beauty, 10, 12, 169, 178, 193–94,
207, 220, 234, 243, 270–71, 287–88, 291;
as female hero or sage, 285, 287–88;
as model for Ming loyalist, 102, 179,
182, 306 n. 14, 316 n. 4
Chaste-erotic polarity, 53, 100, 151, 283–
84; *Ernü yingxiong zhuan* and *Shenlou
zhi*, 265; in terms of shrew and miser,
148–49; *Yesou puyan* and *Honglou
meng*, 149, 176–77
Chaste intimacy, 95, 151, 158–64, 167,
191, 198–203, 274–77
Chaste romance, 11, 17, 29, 53, 98, 159–
60, 169, 220, 230, 290, 306 n. 20;
against decadence, 101–2, 131, 147, 306
n. 13; asymmetry camouflaged, 118;
and crossing of gender characteristics, 108, 124, 270–74; defined, 103–6,
148–49; detail sparse in, 104, 111, 125,
131, 148; distinguished from erotic romances, 100, 104, 111, 122, 124–25, 129,
131–32, 148–49; editions, 308 n. 42;
and expediency, 122, 166; and *Honglou
meng*, 106, 177–78, 184–86, 189, 193,
202–3; and idealization of woman,

113, 123–25, 185; language polite and
refined in, 104, 125; in light of *Ernü
yingxiong zhuan* and *Honglou meng*,
266, 270–71, 276, 281; light eroticism
in, 111, 116; and *Lüye xianzong*, 234;
and neutralization of sexual differences, 103, 123; rational optimism of,
122–23; and remarkable woman, 99–
101, 105, 107, 193–94; standards of,
127–29, 131, 177, 234. *See also* Cross-
dressing; Scholar-beauty romance;
Superiority of women; Symmetry
Chastity: of anus, 140; female, 23; and
female excellence, 101; recon-
structed, 285; value of, 140, 208; of
widow, 23, 73, 90, 101, 151, 226, 291
Cheng Weiyuan, 180
Childbirth, 52, 67; pollution of, 36, 280,
295 n. 27, 325 n. 24
Children: upbringing of, 24, 205–6, 218,
221
Chundeng mishi, 140–42, 146–47
Coddled man, 73, 177, 221, 231, 289
Coddled polygamist (polygynist), 16,
223, 251–52, 266–67, 282, 287, 291; defined, 266–67
Companionship between man and
woman, 53, 99, 101, 159–60, 170–71,
219–20; in marriage, 53, 159–60, 219–
20. See also *Zhiji*
Concubine(s), 132, 221, 293 n. 1; average
number of, 22; benefits of having, 67;
control of, 35, 59, 178, 189; as helpers,
134–35; learned discussion with, 155,
159; and main wife, 43, 67, 127, 133,
136, 137, 143–44, 189, 208, 256; rules
for taking, 31, 204, 273–74; sexiness
of, 12, 127, 143–44, 213–17, 256, 259,
291; terms for, 30–31
Confucius, 56, 60, 127, 156, 225, 227, 316
n. 47; in Europe, 314 n. 22
Courtesan: companionship with literatus, 101, 159–60. *See also* Prostitute
Cross-dressing, 7–8, 168, 307 n. 33; of
the beauty, 10, 99, 107, 109–12, 114–18,

INDEX

138, 186, 193, 276, 307 n. 32; and bound
feet, 111; in *Honglou meng*, 186, 189,
193–94; in *Jinghua yuan*, 285–86; vestige of, 131–32, 135, 193. *See also* Female impersonation
Crossing of gender characteristics, 16,
99, 108, 112, 121, 203, 288–90; in *Ernü
yingxiong zhuan*, 270–74, 281; in
Honglou meng, 177, 182, 186–89
Cu hulu, 15, 60, 75–80, 303 n. 51, 303 n. 53;
edition, 303 n. 50; henpecked hus-
band in, 75–76

Deleuze, Gilles, 8, 309 n. 63, 312 n. 37
Dengcao heshang, 298 n. 33
Desexualization, 11, 16, 124–25, 148–49,
177, 185, 283, 289–91, 309 n. 64. *See
also* Feminization of men
Desire (sexual): and Confucian canon,
36; as cure, 162; greater than the capacity to fulfill it, 50–51; insatiable,
170; intractable, 235, 248, 250; mise-
en-scène of desire, 7–8, 294 n. 11; regulation of, 31, 173; replaced by desire
for money, 81, 92, 288; same in man
and woman, 51, 107
Detail: adumbrative, 133, 167; contrast
between chaste and erotic romance,
104, 111, 124–25, 128, 130–31, 148–49;
contrast between *Honglou meng* and
Yesou puyan, 149, 173, 191; and controlling vision, 174–75, 191; explicit,
104, 167, 173; impoverishment of, 148;
intricate, 152, 191; particularistic, 19,
125, 149; sexual, 3, 130; in *Shenlou zhi*,
254, 264; sparse, 104, 309 n. 65; unchaste, 130; and women's lives, 191–
98. *See also* Sex: explicit portrayal of
Dingqing ren, 119–20, 127
Ding Richang, 21, 311 n. 21, 311 n. 24, 312
n. 34
Dongdu ji, 51
Dongxuanzi, 298 n. 40, 299 n. 59
Dong Xun, 323 n. 1, 324 n. 16
Doting mother, 10, 13, 260, 262, 289; and

emasculation, 230–32; and wastrel
son, 150, 221–32, 235, 243

Economic mode of production, 5–7;
and the miser, 5–6, 84, 86
Effeminate scholar (or man). *See* Feminization of men
Ejaculation: control of, 298 n. 41, 299 n.
62; difficulty of control, 136, 288;
fainting after, 246; formulaic term
for, 41, 259; frequency of, 298 n. 40;
and impotence, 288; Jia Baoyu's, 173,
315 n. 45; retention of, 33, 39, 41, 63; Su
Xiaoguan's 259; Wen Suchen's, 162,
164, 173
Emperor, 6, 143, 218, 232, 256; benevolent, 251; and chaste beauty, 109,
122, 156, 160; cure of, 315 n. 31; and
miser, 86; and shrew, 81, 303 n. 55;
and wastrel, 232. *See also* Kangxi
emperor
Erke pai'an jingqi, 70. *See also Er pai*;
Ling Mengchu
Ernü yingxiong zhuan, 3, 16, 29, 223, 224,
251–52, 265–82, 290; An Ji, 268–80,
290, 324 n. 7; An Ji and Baoyu, 273,
278–80; An Xuehai, 269, 271, 276;
Changjie, 270, 278; Changjie and
Xiren, 270, 278; chaste intimacy, 274–
77; as chaste romance, 265–66, 270–
71, 273, 277, 281; coddled polygynist,
266–67; He Yufeng (see *Ernü ying-
324 n. 16*; cross-generic, 270; detail,
324 n. 6; parallels with *Shenlou zhi*,
251–52, 265; polygamy, 266–67, 273–
274–77, 324 n. 7; as erotic romance,
266; exchange of gender characteristics, 270–74, 281; fusion of female superiority and benevolent polygyny,
266–67; He Yufeng (see *Ernü yingxiong zhuan:* Thirteenth Sister); infantile eroticism, 266–67; nursing
breasts, 280, 290; opium, 252–53, 268,
324 n. 6; parallels with *Shenlou zhi*,
251–52, 265; polygamy, 266–67, 273–

Superiority of women (*cont.*)
277–78, 282, 288; Jia Baoyu's theory
of, 184–85, 203; and male baseness,
124–25, 177–78; as recurrent theme,
10–11; in sex, 39, 41, 62–65, 288–89;
theme of, 11–12, 54. *See also* Inferiority of men
Sutra of Wife-fearing, 15, 60, 61, 81
Symbolic order, 4–9, 293 n. 8; of miser,
shrew, and polygamist, 27, 150–51
Symmetry, 99–100, 110, 123, 131, 169; and
asymmetry, 99, 108, 118; cross-
gendered, 14; defined, 103, 107, 112–
13, 118, 186; in *Ernü yingxiong
zhuan*, 270; of experience, 112; in
Honglou meng, 176–77, 185–90, 203;
and male self-deprecation, 124; and
poetry, 113; in two-wife polygyny,
113–15, 116. *See also* Chaste romance

Taiping guangji, 85
Talented beauty (or woman). *See*
Chaste beauty; Superiority of
women
Tang Yin (Bohu), 310 n. 9
Taohua yanshi, 104, 128
Taohua ying, 142–44, 145, 257, 299 n. 62,
323 n. 9; edition, 311 n. 23
Temperate polygamist, 16, 56–57, 82–
83, 173, 288, 289; defined, 83
Tibetan monk, 16, 94, 255–57, 261. *See
also* Ascetic; Sex adept
Tobacco, 4, 181, 195 (snuff), 268, 281–82,
317 n. 16, 324 n. 6
Two-wife polygyny, 16, 53, 68, 99, 113–
20, 125, 283, 308 n. 48; in *Ernü yingxiong zhuan*, 266; in *Honglou meng*,
186–87, 285; interpretation of, 120–
22; in *Jin Yun Qiao*, 284–85; term for,
30

Urination: and identity, 290; intimacy
by way of, 274–77, 279–80, 285; observed, 139, 162 (Wen Suchen), 301
(Jia Baoyu), 275 (Thirteenth Sister);

and perversion, 50; receptacles for,
70, 241, 275–77, 302 n. 35, 324 n. 17; replacement of sexual fluids by, 267,
280–82
Uterine family, 15, 294 n. 19
Uxorilocal marriage, 2, 21–22, 67–68,
295 n. 40, 301 n. 29, 301 n. 30, 310 n. 6;
and polygyny, 129, 132, 139, 141

Vagina, 157, 160, 161, 163, 241; coldness
of, 44, 248; euphemisms for, 45, 127,
136, 160, 163, 241, 315 n. 38, 315 n. 39;
examined, 161, 163, 315 n. 34; fluids of,
41, 45–46, 136, 241, 245, 301 n. 21; impenetrable, 59, 303 n. 51; inferiority to
anus, 145; of main wife, 135–36; making music, 163–64; and pubic hair,
143, 161, 299 n. 51
Vinegar. *See* Jealousy: and vinegar
Virgin's blood, 19, 23, 133, 258
Virgin's pain, 23, 245, 246, 258, 262, 263,
323 n. 9; sympathy for, 23, 133
Vital essence, 1; appropriation of, 290;
conservation of, 59; stealing of, 42,
47, 84. See also *Yang* essence

Wan Ru Yue, 116–18, 125, 307 n. 26, 308 n.
41, 308 n. 52
Warrior woman, 8, 12, 96, 168, 267,
269–72; and bound feet, 302 n. 42;
and pollution, 280–81
Wastrel, 1, 2, 8, 10, 13, 46, 54, 74, 206,
222–23, 226–33, 287; as alter ego of
potent polygamist, 1; and doting
mother, 150, 221–32; emperor, 232; Jia
Baoyu as, 177; nonwastrel, 257; and
opium, 231, 253; predisposition of,
222–23, 231–32; and prostitute, 13–14,
227, 235–36, 238–44; solutions to
problem of, 150, 167, 231–32, 252; son
of miser, 88, 253; and superior
woman, 8; as term, 27; versus shrew,
232–33, 235; wives' adaptation to,
205 6, 211 10
Wen Kang, 265, 323 n. 1, 324 n. 5

Keith McMahon is Associate Professor of Chinese
Language and Literature at the University of Kansas,
and author of *Causality and Containment in
Seventeenth-Century Chinese Fiction*.

Library of Congress Cataloging-in-Publication Data

McMahon, Keith.
Misers, shrews, and polygamists : sexuality and male-female relations
in eighteenth-century Chinese fiction / by Keith McMahon.
p.   cm.
Includes bibliographical references (p.   ) and index.
ISBN 0-8223-1555-6 (cloth). — ISBN 0-8223-1566-1 (pbk.)
1. Sex customs—China. 2. Man-woman relationships—China.
3. Sex in literature. I. Title.
HQ18.C6M36 1995
306.7'0951—dc20   94-33072CIP